D1591044

PHILIPPE DE COMMYNES

Memory, Betrayal, Text

IRIT RUTH KLEIMAN

Philippe de Commynes

Memory, Betrayal, Text

UNIVERSITY OF TORONTO PRESS
Toronto Buffalo London

ISBN 978-1-4426-4562-2

Printed on acid-free, 100% post-consumer recycled paper with vegetable-based inks.

Library and Archives Canada Cataloguing in Publication

Kleiman, Irit Ruth, 1973–
Philippe de Commynes : memory, betrayal, text / Irit Ruth Kleiman.

Includes bibliographical references and index.
ISBN 978-1-4426-4562-2

1. Commynes, Philippe de, ca. 1447–1511.   2. Commynes, Philippe de,
ca. 1447–1511. Mémoires.   3. Louis XI, King of France, 1423–1483 – Influence.
4. France – History – Louis XI, 1461–1483.   5. Betrayal – France – History –
15th century.   6. Historians – France – Biography.   7. Diplomats – France –
Biography.   I. Title.

DC106.9.C8K54 2013   944'.027092   C2012-905712-6

This book has received the Weiss/Brown Publication Subvention Award from the
Newberry Library. The award supports the publication of outstanding works of
scholarship that cover European civilization before 1700 in the areas of music,
theater, French or Italian literature, or cultural studies. It is made to commemorate
the career of Howard Mayer Brown.

University of Toronto Press acknowledges the financial assistance to its publishing
program of the Canada Council for the Arts and the Ontario Arts Council.

University of Toronto Press acknowledges the financial support of the Government
of Canada through the Canada Book Fund for its publishing activities.

Contents

Acknowledgments

I have run up many debts in writing this book, and I am glad of this chance to acknowledge them, even if my words are a poor payment for years of good counsel.

Paul Archambault, Joël Blanchard, and Jean Dufournet lived in *continuelle residence* with Commynes long before I first opened the *Mémoires*'s pages. I have learned much from each of them, so that I pay hommage as well as offering thanks.

The Boston University Center for the Humanities, the Boston University College of Arts and Sciences, and the Department of Romance Studies, all provided financial support so that this book could become a book.

Tom Conley, Dominique de Courcelles, Elisabeth C. Goldsmith, T. Jefferson Kline, Bob Levine, Christopher Maurer, Jeffrey Mehlman, Nancy Regalado, and Joshua Rifkin, all read chapter drafts and more. Their advice has made this a much, much better book. The 2008–9 Fellows' Seminar of the Boston University Center for the Humanities forever changed my understanding of the craft of writing. I give special thanks to James Winn, whose encouragement has been decisive.

Canaan Boyer gave research assistance, and let no blizzard stop her. My thanks go to Hélène Becquet, Cédric Giraud, Amy C. Graves-Monroe, Jenny Knust, Louisa Shea, Markus Stock, and J. Keith Vincent for years' worth of nourishing conversations about Commynes, literature and history, and the meaning of life. Pierre Mifsud and Philippe Vuarand accepted my family into their home, and set a place for us at their table. I don't know where I'd be in a pinch without Susan Munro, who has a way with words and authors.

Virginie Greene has been there every step of the way. I am humbled by her example, and grateful for her teaching and her friendship. Alan Greene has had to endure shop talk, blueberry season, and worse. He has my thanks for that, and for other things besides.

Roberto Rey Agudo kept me going through it all with kindness and bottomless mugs of coffee. Gracias.

PHILIPPE DE COMMYNES

Memory, Betrayal, Text

Introduction

Ung prince ou aultre homme qui ne fut jamais trompé ne sçauroit estre que une beste, ne avoir congnoissance du bien et du mal, ne quelle differance il y a.

– Commynes, *Mémoires*

The *Mémoires* of fifteenth-century diplomat Philippe de Commynes bear witness to a watershed moment for modern conceptions of both historiography and the individual subject. Commynes, a diplomat specializing in clandestine operations, served the French king Louis XI (1461–83) during his campaign to undermine aristocratic resistance and consolidate the sovereignty of the French throne. Since Commynes had himself abandoned Louis's rival, Burgundian duke Charles the Bold (1467–77) in order to join the king, he has frequently been seen as a spoil of this war, and as a traitor to his feudal lord. The *Mémoires* put forward an account of Louis XI's reign; their narrative traces the shape of royal power, studies and critiques that power, and renders an account of the narrator's own defining experience of it. The experience of royal authority is inseparable from the authority of experience which Commynes claims for himself. This book examines the symbiosis between writing and betrayal in Commynes's representation of Louis's reign, in the relationship between author and king, and in the emergence of the memoir as an autobiographical genre. My arguments centre on the roles that textuality and narrative play in the difficult negotiation between royal subjection and individual subjectivity.[1] Drawing on diplomatic letters and court transcripts as well as the *Mémoires* themselves, I lay bare a disruptive, autobiographical remembrance within the *Mémoires*' account of Louis's campaign for royal domination. I suggest that the specificity of Commynes's *Mémoires* – their nascent modernity and their affective saturation – lies in their author's narrative of self-through-subjection.

Philippe de Commynes

Commynes was born around 1445, and orphaned shortly thereafter.[2] A cousin raised him and saw to his education. Debts were Commynes's primary inheritance, however, and his education was not a lavish one.[3] Commynes professed himself unskilled in Latin, for example. Considering the importance of Latin to both the diplomatic and the historiographic traditions through which we approach Commynes, this lack of Latin learning stands out as an immediately pertinent consequence of orphanhood. Commynes's handwriting, illegible by his own admission, hints that this skill remained awkward throughout his life.

At the end of his teenage years, or, in his own words, "au saillir de mon enfance, et en l'eage de pouvoir monter a cheval" (when I left childhood, and was old enough to ride a horse),[4] Commynes entered service at the Burgundian court, where several generations of his family had also made their careers.[5] Philip the Good was duke (1419–67), and the future Charles the Bold was still Count of Charolais. Charles was far more resolute in his opposition to the French king than was Duke Philip, and the two were at odds. The Croÿ family had just convinced the duke to sell the Somme River towns back to Louis XI, "dont ledict conte son filz fut fort troublé" (about which his son the count was very stirred up [9]). It was into Charles's service that Commynes entered in November 1464, on the eve of the aristocratic uprising known as the Guerre du Bien Public, the War of the Public Weal.

When Charles marched into battle against Louis XI a few months later, the greater part of France's aristocracy behind him, Commynes was beside him, dazzled by what he believed to be the irresistible force of the count whose favourite he had already become. Over the next years, Commynes proved his mettle. The *Mémoires* portray him again at Charles's side as he traversed the Low Countries subduing rebellious towns. Then, in October 1468, he was at Péronne, during that hotly disputed summit between Louis XI and Charles. At Péronne, Commynes came face to face for the first time with the man who was to exert such unrivalled fascination over him, Louis XI, the Spider King.[6]

We do not know exactly what transpired between Commynes and the king during their meeting at Péronne, nor much about what happened between them during the years that followed. After Péronne, Commynes continued to form part of Charles's innermost circle. Then, in August 1472, Commynes disappeared in the middle of the night. He reappeared three weeks later, alongside Louis XI. The archives leave only the barest clues as to "what happened." Of this life-altering decision Commynes writes in his *Mémoires*, as if in passing, "envyron ce temps, je vins au service du Roy (et fut l'an mil ccccLxxii)" (around this time, I came into the king's service (and it was the year 1472) [226]). Considering that the *Mémoires* have been called the "confessions of a traitor," this is a strange and troubling silence.[7] This silence lies at the heart of the *Mémoires*.

Immediately, Commynes became the king's favourite, a powerful advisor with unrivalled knowledge of Louis's enemy. Lands, pensions, titles, and a wife: Louis gave them all to Commynes. He gave Commynes a new name, as well. The seigneur de Renescure had stayed close by Charles; now the seigneur d'Argenton slept in the king's room.

So long as Charles the Bold lived, Commynes's position at the royal court remained untouchable. The view clouds after Charles's death on the battlefield outside Nancy in January 1477. In the aftermath, there seems to have been friction between memorialist and king over the accession of Charles's lands, the same places where Commynes had grown up and spent his first adult years, and where his family still lived. Whatever the dynamics between Louis XI and Commynes after this point, Italy, not Flanders or Burgundy, became the primary arena for Commynes's talents. Already Commynes was Louis's favoured interlocutor with the Milanese ambassadors at the French court. In April 1478, after the Pazzi conspiracy, Commynes descended in haste to Florence as the king's ambassador. Thereafter, Commynes's personal fortunes became increasingly entangled with the (mis)fortunes of the Medici family and their bank.

On the final day of August 1483, roughly eleven years after Commynes first came to the royal court, Louis XI passed away. His son, Charles VIII (1483–98), remained a few months shy of majority. For all intents and purposes, Anne de Beaujeu, backed by her husband Pierre, held the regency for her younger brother. In this role, she demonstrated the intuitive, ruthless feel for power that so made her "her father's daughter." The disgruntled rallied around the flighty Louis d'Orléans, the future Louis XII. In the succeeding months, a kind of "Mad War" (as Paolo Emilio called it), *une guerre folle* or *insana militia*, began to take shape. The group's audacity proceeded in lockstep with its lack of discipline, and their discontents grew more fractious with each setback. Commynes was one of the masterminds behind the operation. Eventually, he ended up in jail, lucky enough not to be on trial for treason.

Commynes's knowlege of Italy provided the leverage he needed to return to the ambit of public life during the early 1490s, but he never again knew the same influence as under Louis XI. As one of the Crown's ambassadors to Venice during the First Italian War, Commynes did what he could for Charles VIII, but his efforts had little chance of success against the League of Venice. Commynes's opposition to the invasion was, in any case, well known at court. When Louis XII (1498–1515) finally ascended to the throne, he seems to have done little to bring Commynes along with him back into power. Commynes's final years were lived out in a kind of involuntary semi-retirement from public life, darkened by acrimony and unceasing lawsuits. We know the elderly Commynes not from his *Mémoires* but rather from the paper trail he left in court. He died at his estates at Argenton in October 1511. No testament, inventory of his library, or original manuscript of the *Mémoires* has ever been found.[8]

The Birth of a Genre

Commynes began to write his *Mémoires* during the years that followed his disgrace, during a time of house arrest, in exile from a court that wanted little to do with him, and in grave financial straits.[9] They open with a sort of epistolary prologue that implies Commynes began them, at least, as notes in response to the request of an Italian archbishop named Angelo Cato, known as a physician, astronomer, and humanist, "pour satisfaire a la requeste qu'il vous a pleu me faire de vous escripre et mectre par memoire ce que j'ay sceu et congneu des faictz du roy Loys unzeiesme" (to satisfy the request you made that I write and put down from memory what I knew and experienced of the deeds of King Louis XI [1]). In this prologue, Commynes announces he will proceed chronologically, beginning with his earliest knowledge of the king and proceeding up to Louis's death. In the exact words Commynes's uses, his statement of purpose is so rich that it is fair to see the whole of my book as preparing us to fully apprehend all that his discourse promises (and hence, we will return to this prologue in my final chapter). At a more mundane level, some pragmatic view of the *Mémoires*' shape is likely to benefit readers less familiar with the details of Louis XI's reign. The following schema presents the contents and structure of the *Mémoires*, and nods to key dates.

Prologue   Addresses Angelo Cato; presents the *Mémoires* as a chronological account of the time from Commynes's entry into court service until the king's death.

Book I   Commynes enters Charles's service at the Burgundian court (autumn 1464). Stages of the Guerre du Bien Public (1465).

Book II   Follows the struggles between Louis XI and Charles the Bold, concluding with the meeting between the king and duke at Péronne (October 1468).

Book III   Analyses the motives of Louis XI's principal opponents and the conflicts between them. Critiques Charles's military campaigns in the Low Countries. Commynes joins the king's court. First episodes in *connétable* Saint-Pol's difficulties (early 1470s).

Book IV   Charles's military ambitions near the German border. The misadventures of Saint-Pol. Louis XI negotiates peace with Edward IV. Charles hands Saint-Pol over to the king and thus sets in motion his own undoing (1474–6).

Book V   Charles the Bold's defeat and death (1476–7). Louis XI manoeuvres for control of Burgundy. Important considerations on governance and consent.

Book VI   Post-1477 Franco-Burgundian politics and the marriage of Mary of Burgundy. Commynes sent to Florence (April 1478). Illness and death of Louis XI (early 1480s–83). Reflections on a generation of rulers (1453–83).

Michael Jones's popular 1972 Penguin classics translation of the *Mémoires* goes further than this, and distils the contents of Commynes's work to a six-line list of progressively more violent, less successful Burgundian military campaigns. A similarly knowing synopsis might replace this list of floundering campaigns with details about the men and territories that Louis XI brought under his "obedience," a word Commynes uses with continually accelerating frequency. In fact, Commynes takes no such bird's-eye view, nor could he have, given his own place within so many still-unfolding events. His narrative weaves in and out of the sequence first promised, often looping back to provide a missing piece of background information, or pontificating on some theme which has ignited his tendencies to digression and didacticism. Commynes also frequently expects his reader to be already in-the-know, and if his style could be summarized in two adjectives, my choices would be granular and confidential.

It is no simple matter to assess the relations between Commynes's individual talent and the traditions on which the *Mémoires* draw. To do so requires that we be equally precise about the many points of continuity and rupture between Commynes and his potential influences. Neither endeavour can be satisfactorily realized. Rather than fail in an attempt to reckon Commynes's similarities with or debts towards Joinville's *Vie de Saint Louis*, Burgundy's thriving court culture of translated Roman historiography and contemporary chroniclers, Italian *ricordanze*, parahistorical genres such as the *miroir des princes*, or the burgeoning forms of early modern autobiography, it seems wiser to limit ourselves to speaking about Commynes's narrative of Louis XI.[10] To approach this question of tradition and innovation, I suggest that we instead consider the possibilities Commynes infuses into the word *Mémoires*, destined for a long and rich descendance. It is through this word that we may best appreciate Commynes's contributions to both autobiographical and historical genres.

When Commynes refers to the narrative he writes as his "mémoires" he steps away from the safety of precedent. In so doing he initiates a new literary genre, one defined by its first-person vision of history. The birth of this genre lies in the distinction between Commynes's narrative and prior acceptations of the word, whose potential meanings included a dossier of legal proofs or arguments; the mental faculty of possessing good sense and a sound mind; the receptacle within the brain where memories were stored; the subject of remembrance or the object remembered; and the act of remembering, or especially of memorization, as per the importance of mnemonics and other memory devices to medieval rhetoric and culture.[11] At a certain point in the process of writing, Commynes began to refer to his text as "ces mémoires" (154, 344, 352, 380, 425, et alia), and to speculate about "ceulx qui verront ces *Memoyres* pour le temps advenir" (those who will see these *Mémoires* in times to come [427]). Despite these allusions, we do not know much about how Commynes actually composed the *Mémoires*. From the "Séjour de deuil pour la mort de Philippe de Commines," a prosimetrical complaint poem written for Commynes's widow, Hélène de Chambes, we know that the *Mémoires* circulated within a small circle during their author's lifetime, but we do not have an autograph or contemporary manuscript.[12] Most important, we do not know how the *Mémoires* came first to be published by Galliot du Pré in the spring of 1524, some twelve and one half years after their author's death.

When the *Mémoires* were first published, they bore the title *Cronique & hystoire … du roy Loys XIe*.[13] The title *Mémoires* was only restored to Commynes's text some twenty-eight years later, in 1552, by royal historiographer Denis Sauvage, who referred to Commynes as the father and godfather of the genre, meaning that he both gave birth to it and named it.

> J'estime tant de la vivacité de voz sains jugemens, debonnaires Lecteurs, que je me tien tout asseuré que ne trouverez aucunement estrange qu'ayons changé l'ancien tiltre de ce present volume, incontinent qu'aurez entendu, pour noz raisons, que le pere mesme en a esté le parrain (comme l'on dit communément) le nommant Memoires, ainsi que nous, en plusieurs & divers passages, que trouverez en lisant.

> [I so respect the vivacity of your healthy opinions, charming Readers, that I am entirely confident that you will not find it the least bit strange that we have changed the former title of this present volume, just as soon as you hear, as our reasons, that the father himself was the godfather of it (as it is commonly said) calling it *Mémoires*, like we do, in several and various passages, which you will discover in reading.][14]

The restoration of this title points to a shift in appreciation of the *Mémoires'* deeper content. The displacement of the word "chronicle" by the word "memoir" marks a fundamental reorientation from an external world of deeds towards an internal and subjective one built from a patchwork of critical reflections. It is also important, therefore, that this title, *Mémoires*, suggests the potential for identification between reader and text. The title *Mémoires* signals a turn towards the interior voice of the historical narrator as a witness to history. The legacy of the word *mémoire* in both its legal and literary uses hints that future generations of *Mémoires*-writing authors recognized the outlines of a totalizing, internalized relation to royal authority in their ancestor Commynes, and that this recognition was like recognizing the fuzzy outlines of one's own face in a grandfather's portrait.

The contradictions of a world lurching towards a myriad of revolutions criss-cross Commynes's text. The events and ideas cast for his readers reveal Commynes on the verge of what Mario Sbriccoli, in his study of treason, called one of the epochs of European political thought's greatest flowering ("uno dei momenti di massima fioritura del pensiero politico europeo").[15] During the few decades between the moment when Commynes began to write and when Denis Sauvage restored the title *Mémoires* to his text, France – indeed all of Europe – broke with the authority and security of its past models. Crown, church, individual, text and Text, history and History – all were fractured or shattered, then put slowly back together again. The slow canonization of Commynes's narrative under the title *Mémoires* goes hand in hand with the birth of a form that would come to dominate early modern letters. The rise of the memoir as a literary and historical genre closely follows the construction of a French absolutist state and the careers of its greatest statesmen.[16] The *Mémoires* are neither the reflection of this pivotal moment in European history nor a simple product of its crises. The *Mémoires* participate in the intellectual, spiritual, and material revolutions through which Modernity was first conceived.[17]

Memory, Betrayal, Textuality

Memory, betrayal, textuality. These three interdependent terms are central to our understanding of the *Mémoires*.

Collective Memory and Private Remembrance

Two facets of memory dominate Commynes's narrative. One is the highly personal memory that our own age associates with identity and interiority; this is the aspect of memory with which this book will be principally concerned. The other is collective memory, the presence of the past in the associations that help a "we" to cohere. (Somewhat surprisingly, there has yet to be a study of memory as either a theme or a structuring element in Commynes's text.)[18] Commynes uses the expressions "mon temps," or "son temps," as a synonym for the way that a lifespan presents each individual with a generationally determined perspective on the world. The word *mémoire* is bound together with the notion of belonging to a time and place, and of the community forged through the shared experience of history.[19] The conjunction between individual, private memories and the use of generational memory to demarcate a historical moment both realizes and reflects a fusion between collective and individual identity, one that challenges us to think carefully about Commynes's writing of history.[20] The title *Mémoires* demands that we consider what it means to be a historical subject.

Born roughly a decade after the 1435 Treaty of Arras, and shortly before Normandy returned to the French Crown in 1449, Commynes had no lived memories of the Burgundian-Armagnac civil war. This is not to say, however, that he had no memory for this event. The scars that it left in collective memory can be seen in his narration at key moments. "Tous maulx sont commencés par rapports et puys par divisions, desquelles se sont sourses les guerres, de laquelle viennent la mortalité et famyne: et tous ces maulx procedent de faulte de foy" (All evils are begun in malicious words and in discord, out of which come the source of wars, from which come death and famine: and all these evils proceed from lack of faith [424–5; cf. 123]). This fear is so powerful, and the terms Commynes uses to talk about it so stark, that one feels behind his words the spiritual and material terror depicted by his contemporary, Albrecht Dürer, in his *Four Horsemen of the Apocalypse*. "Est il nulle plaie ne persecution si grande que guerre entre les amys et ceulx qui se congnoissent, ne nulle hayne si mortelle?" (Is there any suffering or torment so great as war between friends and those who know each other, or any hatred so deadly? [418]) Fear that assassinations like those of 1407 and 1419 could again occur – that France could return to a state of civil war – percolates through his text.[21] These are events that Commynes's grandparents would have experienced. Their presence in his text opens a window on the inheritance of memory and its relationship to national identity.

The tropes of memory also come to the surface when Commynes evokes the relics that survive to remind us of human destruction – the precious gems looted after Charles's military defeats, or the gravestones that alone prove the "French" once held Sicily, "ce royaulme de Napples et … l'isle de Cecille et aultres provinces que les François ont possedé par longues annees; et pour toutes enseignes n'y est memoyre d'eulx que par les sepultures de leurs predecesseurs" (the kingdom of Naples … and the island of Sicily and other provinces which the French possessed for many years; for every sign of it, there is nothing to remember them by but the graves of their ancestors [441]). Books, especially history books, can also be such relics: "tous les livres en sont faictz qui ne serviroient de riens, si n'estoit pour ramener a memoyre les choses passees" (all the books which have been made would be of little use, if it weren't to recall to memory things past [122]). The title *Mémoires* conjures what has been lost, and what remains. Memory and writing are intertwined for Commynes, as they have been since Plato, whose model of memory was that of an image imprinted into wax through which the absent is made present.[22] In this book, the aspect of memory that will most often concern us is that of recollection, the vividly seen images which the body summons from the past and places before the eyes. What absent, ghostly body does Commynes summon when he narrates "ces mémoires"? At times that of Charles the Bold, at times the narrator's own, and always, I would suggest, that of the king, Louis XI.

On the Subject of Betrayal

Betrayal, the second of these terms, is both the hoariest and the hairiest – that is, both the most ancient and the most difficult of the three. Betrayal occupies us in ways biographical, historical, and textual, and must do so from the beginning of our endeavour. Ideas about the "betrayal" in Commynes's biography have exerted tremendous influence over both scholarly and popular readings of the *Mémoires*. People have been fighting over how to interpret Commynes's migration from Burgundy to royal lands for nearly as long as his text has been in print. (We will see more of these debates in chapter 1.) A literary reading of the *Mémoires* has the capacity to bring us beyond past impasses of a more disciplinarily historical nature. Attention to the textures of betrayal within the *Mémoires* as a whole enables us to characterize Commynes's defection in more historically just terms, while acknowledging its importance within a narrative economy.

Commynes's posthumous reputation as a traitor forms part of an essentializing construction that surrounds his persona as an implied author. We would do well to follow the example of historians like Joan Scott, and to question the tendency, endemic to writings about Commynes, to think about terms which are historically constructed – traitor, betrayal – as historically fixed entities. The expansion of royal authority exerted a normative pressure on those who lived through Louis's reign, but this pressure was not a smoothly monolithic entity, but rather a current or an unpredictable tension. The words "traitor" and "loyal subject" possess a reciprocally constitutive force for one another; each describes a highly fluid position of transgression, resistance, or complicity. Commynes himself struggles in and through his narrative with what betrayal, treachery, and loyalty are, and with their consequences. Writing about a historical context entirely distinct from Commynes's own, Scott nonetheless issues a welcome caveat:

It is not individuals who have experience, but subjects who are constituted through experience. Experience in this definition then becomes not the origin of our explanation, not the authoritative (because seen or felt) evidence that grounds what is known, but rather that which we seek to explain, that about which knowledge is produced. To think about experience in this way is to historicize it as well as to historicize the identities it produces.[23]

Long after the civil wars between Burgundians and Armagnacs came to an end, the legacy of betrayal and its aftermaths lingered in the ways "French" people thought about themselves, each other, and the bonds between them. In a striking study of treason prosecutions during the years that followed the Treaty of Arras, Yvonne Lahners has shown how, for those who lived from day to day or year to year in a context of major political and social instability, the categories of betrayal and allegience could be, at best, problematic.[24] The geographies of Commynes's Franco-Burgundian identity straddled multiple, often conflicting loyalties, at a time when the boundaries of loyalty and disloyalty were themselves being redrawn. Rather than declare the *Mémoires* an anthology of betrayals, or debate whether Commynes did or did not betray Charles the Bold, it is helpful to think of his narrative as constantly engaged in a critical reflection on the qualities of loyalty and betrayal. The *Mémoires* paint the nuances of human suffering and obstinacy with exquisite sensitivity. Men of all places and all times experience the same passions; their actions are vain strivings to satisfy a craving for power; jealousy and suspicion gnaw at the human heart.

There is every reason to believe that sinuous affective bonds to the duke gripped Commynes before his departure, and that these remained so even when severed, well beyond Charles's death. As regards Louis XI, Commynes's relationship with his king was the single most significant human relationship in his life. This relationship was indeed a human one, as much as an internalized relation to the crown Louis XI wore. There is one point of concord among those who have responded to the *Mémoires* in writing. Couched in the expressive vocabulary of each critic's time, five hundred years of readers have agreed that the relationship between Commynes and his king was, in the discourse of our own time, intense, and even fusional.

Finally, might we not consider that juridical and sociological approaches to Commynes's betrayal remain ultimately beside the point? Charles saw Commynes as a traitor and treated him as one. This made him one for all intents and purposes, regardless of how the duke's assessment might fit into a more abstracted view of legal history. Numerous courtiers of Commynes's epoch served successively at two or more courts.[25] Ultimately, however, I would submit that it matters little how many others moved between Burgundy or Brittany and royal France. Charles never forgave Commynes for abandoning him, and so long as Charles was alive, Commynes could not go home again. There are tantalizing indications that Commynes would have liked to return to the Low Countries during the years after Charles's death. This return was never realized. Commynes died far from the homeland of his childhood and youth. He died in exile. Whether or not Commynes "betrayed," he lived the life of a traitor.

A TALE OF TWO BETRAYALS

There are, in fact, two betrayals to consider surrounding Commynes's biography and the origins of the *Mémoires*. Both pose difficulties for reasons juridical, historical, narrative, and affective. One has been a subject of critical commentary for more than 450 years. The other has been largely ignored. In the mythology of the first, Commynes "betrays" Charles the Bold for Louis XI. This betrayal has generated no end of polemics. It is less widely known that on his deathbed, Louis XI "betrayed" Commynes. We will place this second betrayal under the microscope in chapter 4, but even before we begin, we need to know that one of Louis's dying acts was to repudiate his counsellor and chamberlain in a way that left Commynes bereft of the king whom he mourned, and also of home, fortune, and reputation. This betrayal has rarely been acknowledged. This second, "underread" betrayal has the capacity to catalyse a fundamental realignment in our understanding of the *Mémoires*.[26] Unlike the *Mémoires* he would write five to ten years later about Charles VIII's Italian War, Commynes's *Mémoires* of Louis's reign are a work of retrospective memory, written long after the king's death.[27] Louis's betrayal of Commynes is the filtering event which separates the narrating present from the narrated past. First, without Commynes's betrayal of Charles the Bold, there would be no story to tell, no *Mémoires* of Louis XI. Then, Louis's betrayal provides the framing lens through which that story will be told. Each of the two obliges us to think about subjectivity and subjection; about the nature of political betrayal and loyalty to the king, his crown, or the State; and about the legacy of Commynes's narrative.

THE IMPOSSIBLE QUEST TO DEFINE BETRAYAL

There are so many ways of discussing betrayal that only their insufficiency is certain.[28] Defining betrayal is, in practice, more a matter of defining the limits of a chosen approach. The desire to define betrayal cannot be separated from the desire to master the anxieties that betrayal awakens in each human being. The shipwreck of many distinct attempts lets us see two or three ribs that shape every approach to the question. We need to bring these observations to the forefront of our thoughts: much depends on them. These points are as true and relevant to the historical and political dimensions of betrayal in fifteenth-century France as they are to a more philosophical or literary approach to the topic. The English historian Frederic William Maitland stated, "Treason is a crime which has a vague circumference and more than one centre."[29] The sentence has become proverbial, but it might not be amiss to imagine the great scholar throwing up his hands in despair as he formed the words.

The difficulty of forming a fixed, objective definition for betrayal begins as soon as we recognize that betrayal exists only through the interpretation given by its would-be victim, or, on rarer occasions, by its perpetrator. The phenomenon of betrayal is above all a linguistic one. No deed is treacherous but that speaking makes it so.[30] Next, popular and scholarly authors concur that before there can be a betrayal some expectation of loyalty must exist between the parties concerned.[31] The treacherous deed must be unexpected if it is to be perceived as a betrayal.[32] As soon as one party expects that the other intends harm, his aggression ceases to constitute betrayal. Thus betrayal is a quality which describes the character of a separation between self and other. One broader and more formal way of stating the same premise is that betrayal occurs as the rupture in a contract. The smaller the circle of its partners, the greater the stakes of the intimacy forged, the more violent the betrayal detonated from within.

Betrayal is a frame which confers intelligibility on inchoate experience. The tropes of betrayal have political associations as well, the historical consequences of whose rhetoric are each unique. Betrayal is both trans-historical and constantly self-reproducing. The word "betrayal" evokes a narrative of ethical violation, ruptured union, and lost harmony. Betrayal is always the product of a retrospective vision, always and necessarily an event situated in the past. Betrayal exists only as a function of remembrance, and is inextricably dependent on memory, whether individual or collective.

Betrayal is a pervasive facet of intersubjectivity and one of the principle archetypes in human experience.[33] We cannot separate subjectivity from betrayal nor betrayal from subjectivity. Language itself is the crucible where each is forged and where they are joined. However, if subjectivity cannot be separated from betrayal, it may be possible to shift the terms through which we try to articulate the relations between the two. For betrayal to transcend its habitual status as a literary theme, we need a methodological approach to betrayal grounded in language itself. We can try to untangle how subjectivity casts the language of betrayal, and how betrayal recasts the language and possibilities available to the subject. Approaching the question of betrayal in this way reframes what had been a problem of affective perception in narrative terms. We shift our attention to the language through which betrayal signifies, to the architecture of enunciation.

BETRAYAL, TRAUMA, THE GEOGRAPHY OF NARRATION

Let us begin from the appreciation that betrayal is a traumatic event. The specificity of betrayal as a kind of trauma comes from its concrete relational aspect. Betrayal is fundamentally dyadic, even when its dynamics are influenced by the presence of a third party or term.

We might hazard a working definition of betrayal as the abrupt and traumatic reversal of relational values within a dyad.[34] In their *Vocabulaire de la psychanalyse,* Laplanche and Pontalis define trauma as,

> Evénement de la vie du sujet qui se définit par son intensité, l'incapacité où se trouve le sujet d'y répondre adéquatement, le bouleversement et les effets pathogènes durables qu'il provoque dans l'organisation psychique. En termes économiques, le traumatisme se caractérise par un afflux d'excitations qui est excessif, relativement à la tolérance du sujet et à sa capacité de maîtriser et d'élaborer psychiquement ces excitations.[35]

A trauma is, by definition, something one cannot talk about, an event that remains unhealed in memory. The specificity of betrayal as a kind of trauma comes from its inherently intersubjective, relational nature.[36]

Trauma, like memory, has come to occupy a central place in critical debate within the humanities over the past thirty years.[37] As an area of inquiry, trauma has a rare capacity to engage both practical and theoretical approaches from a broad spectrum of disciplines. The eye of this storm concerns how trauma is remembered and recalled, by the body or in language, and thus the relations between trauma, narrative, and mimesis.[38] The matter has implications which are individual and private, but also shared and historical. One of the earliest, but still most important of these studies for literary scholars was the 1992 book *Testimony: Crises of Witnessing in Literature, Psychoanalysis, and History,* by literary critic Shoshana Felman and psychiatrist Dori Laub. Felman and Laub explored "how issues of biography and history are neither simply represented nor simply reflected, but are inscribed, translated, radically rethought and fundamentally worked over by the text," and demonstrated the potential for a cross-disciplinary approach to trauma and narrative.[39]

When we talk about trauma and narrative we trace a map both literary and psychological, universal and particular. Like a substantial portion of recent writings about trauma, memory, and history, Felman and Laub's book concentrated on the historically specific trauma of the Shoah. Writing about responses to the Shoah by way of Mallarmé, Felman observes, "Both free verse and free association undergo the process of a fragmentation – a breaking down, a disruption and a dislocation – of the dream, of verse, of language, of the apparent but misleading unities of syntax and of meaning. The passage through this fragmentation is a passage through a radical obscurity."[40] Silence, the unspeakable, is twice enfolded into betrayal. He who betrays nurtures the precise moment of rupture in secrecy; the moment of betrayal's realization hatches from this incubating silence. For those betrayed, however, this silence is of another quality, and the question posed is whether or not the shock of its discovery can enter the order of language. The failure of language of which Felman and Laub speak – what they so evocatively call its fragmentation and radical obscurity – conveys the subject's experience of being *inside* of the trauma. Felman's phrase identifies with those to whom it lends its voice. Felman and Laub bring the therapist's empathy to the literary critic's eye for structure. The process they analyse involves the subject's "passage through" – that is, his emergence from – the fragmentation and radical obscurity of historical trauma into narrative. Cathy Caruth poses this question in explicitly universal terms when she contemplates Freud's reading of Tasso: "[L]iterature, like psychoanalysis, is interested in the complex relation between knowing and not knowing. And it is at the specific point at which knowing and not knowing intersect that the language of literature and the psychoanalytic theory of traumatic experience precisely meet."[41] This fault line between knowing and not knowing defines the *Mémoires'* narrative of an emergent political "self" in a psychoanalytically grounded way. It also defines Commynes as a historical subject whose biography was riven by both geographic exile and the intellectual tremors of a world in upheaval.

Do we dare, like Felman and Laub, to read with empathy? The phrases Commynes forms about the great ruptures in his biography do the best job they can to spackle over the cracks in what he is saying. The political nature of both betrayals in Commynes's past makes the external consequences of speech potentially acute. Since Commynes's manuscript circulated during his lifetime among those near to him, his first audiences knew what he had been through. I believe that Angelo Cato, to whom Commynes addresses the *Mémoires*, played a so-called therapeutic role in enabling Commynes to give voice to his narration. (I will develop this point more fully in my final chapter.) Twice, Commynes confesses and resists in a single gesture. Twice, the same words veil and unveil. Betrayal both provides the material to be narrated and troubles the capacity to narrate. Commynes has been so often accused of wilful deceit. What if we read, instead of "I don't want to talk about it," "I cannot talk about it"? Instead of viewing the narrator's words through a lens of truth and falsehood, deception, and concealment, I would suggest that Commynes's words are so sparse because he has no language and no frame of reference adequate to his experience.

A BRIEF MANIFESTO ON LANGUAGE, BETRAYAL, NARRATIVE

Intersubjective relations are always grounded in language. We mark our alliances in the words we address to our friends or enemies. We speak in a private language to our intimates, a *parole* embroidered with allusions, ironies, secret codes; even our grammar and syntax is marked by this difference. This language is the living expression of a fluid nexus of constantly reconfirmed relations. Commynes reminisces about how Louis liked to whisper in his favourites' ears, and the days when he would whisper to Commynes, saying: "il me dist en l'oreille" (he whispered in my ear [271]); or again, "me dist en l'oreille que ce qu'il avoit pensé luy estoit advenu" (he whispered in my ear that what he had been waiting for had happened [294]). During a moment of potential crisis, Commynes alone dared to interrupt the silence of Louis's spiritual retreat (284). And, Commynes remembers, he lent the king his voice when the palsied king could not speak on his own (462; see chapter 7).

There are also moments of nostalgia or bitterness. "Comme vous sçavéz, Monsr de Vienne, nostre Roy parloit fort priveement et souvant a ceulx qui estoient plus prochains de luy, comme j'estoie lors et d'autres despuis, et aymoit a parler en l'oreille" (As you know, Monsieur de Vienne, our king spoke very privately and frequently to those who were closest to him, as I was then and others have been since, and he liked to whisper into [a persons's] ear [270]). When one person betrays another, the language between them fractures irremediably. Intimacy and secrecy are betrayed, the meanings of words perverted, and promises broken. The betrayer turns outwards, away from the other. Betrayal is the abrupt, unexpected, and unilateral severance of an implicit or explicit contract of expectations between two individuals. Language actively shapes human relationships, and so serves as the foundation of their contractual dyad. Therefore, betrayal is a rupture in the language of the dyad, or rather, in the *parole* through which the dyad exists. Betrayal severs the fluid ribbon of conversation. Betrayal is what is left when the answering partner in conversation has turned away. To narrate a betrayal compels the speaker to re-enter a subjective position from which he has been alienated. He writes about a person and in a *parole* from which he has been exiled. To emerge from the radical obscurity of this dislocated and fragmented language, he must somehow narrate the violent end of that common tongue.

To confront betrayal is also to confront a fundamental misreading of what has come before, a misreading of the past itself. In this sense, our very possession of the past is troubled by the revelation of a deception. The discovery of betrayal produces a schism of "before and after" in our experience of time. This splitting gives rise to two rival narratives, one based on lived-experience but now mistrusted in its every detail, the other a new-born fantasy of terrifying otherness.[42] This *after* (the present) consumes *before* (the past), cannibalizing its coherence and integrity, and poisoning its victims with bitter knowledge of their own misprision.

In the aftermath of a traumatic betrayal, narration seeks a psychic space of re-encounter with the lost other, and with a self now lost in time. This psychic space may be inflected with rage, nostalgia, or longing. The force of the psychic conflict, and hence the resistance, this traumatic severance inspires may even render that reimagined subjective position inaccessible. The reader encounters betrayal as a moment of narrative crisis – a symptomatic, highly cathectic moment of unresolved signification. The narration of the trauma takes place in the language of the trauma. In writing about a betrayal he has experienced, the narrator again speaks from within that private language.

Betrayal thus serves as an organizing principle governing the symbolic economy in a sense loosely inspired by Freud's theorization of the *Traumarbeit* and by Lacan's readings of Freud. The content of the dream is not its work, but only the vehicle through which signifying structural transformations can be realized. It is the shape given to the dream's content that matters. Similarly, I propose that the text does not have to appear to be "about" something in order to be determined by it.

Structural transformations provide its true work: the form is the content. What a narrative is "about" and what its "work" is need not be identical. In the traditional sense of the term, Commynes's *Mémoires* are "about" the reign of Louis XI and his contemporaries Charles the Bold and Edward IV, as these lend themselves to an analysis of the theory and exercise of political power. The "work" of his narrative is to reconcile the experience of having been reborn in Louis's image as his subject and the annihilation of that identity. Commynes labours in the *Mémoires* to construct his individual relationship with Louis XI as unique. His writing both reflects and attempts to realize a fantasy that the author was at the centre of the king's gaze. "There is something in a historical masterpiece that cannot be negated," wrote Hayden White in "The Historical Text as Literary Artifact," "and this non-negatable element is its form, the form which is its fiction."[43] Immediately, in the first sentences of his prologue, Commynes declares his unique intimacy with Louis – what he calls his "plus continuelle residance avecques luy"(1). He then plainly explains that his memory has been sharpened by the pain he has experienced since that time. The words come as part of his written address to Cato, but Commynes himself did not write them. It is very clear that Commynes "wrote" by dictation. The scene of enunciation is thus a complex one, in which Commynes speaks aloud a doubly deferred confessional discourse. First, his voiced confession addresses an absent other.[44] Is this other Cato, an empathic, listening third-party, or might it be the grieved-for king himself? His enunciation is deferred also, not only because of the complex play of absence / presence between written sign and spoken word, but quite materially, in the sense that we do not know how or if Cato ever received Commynes's text. Ultimately, Commynes's enunciation sheds this context, and declares its own sufficiency – its emergence from – the radical obscurity of trauma into narrative.

Betrayal is only possible as a rupture within a closed, contractual circuit. In the case of Commynes, the dyadic relationship ruptured by the betrayal is a historically specific one between king and subject. This relation is not symmetrical: the subject has only one king, but the king has many subjects. A relationship which is unique and privileged on one side is not so on the other. How can we see the disruption and dislocation in Commynes's narrative and not see that his words try in vain to stitch over a moment of terrible rupture? There are several characters who logically ought to appear on the *Mémoires'* pages but do not.[45] Commynes's critics have frequently reproached him for these silences, and cited the way he silences the names of his so-called enemies as proof of his mendacity. I submit that their enmity is a red herring: this pattern of silences concerns Commynes's rivals for the king.

FROM *TRAHISON* TO *LÈSE-MAJESTÉ*

In order to be a useful tool for reading the *Mémoires*, this conceptualization of betrayal and narrative must also work in a way that deepens our understanding of Commynes's narrative in relation to its historical context. The consolidation of the territory and notion of the French state in its modern form, under a strong monarch, did not occur uniquely during the twenty-two years of Louis XI's reign. Nonetheless, the period 1461–83 constituted a significant turning point. Charles VII, Louis's father, had inherited a kingdom in the throes of civil war. France had been so ravaged that one imaginative scholar compared the Norman countryside to Hiroshima.[46] When Louis XI ascended to the throne in 1461, his subjects were still fragile from old wounds. He faced historical and material obstacles to his rule in the form of enduring fatigue and poverty, legacies of the long civil war that marked the first half of the century. The Crown's power was held in check by an allied resistance led by the Dukes of Brittany and Burgundy, whose real menace and equally real weaknesses were epitomized in the 1465 Guerre du Bien Public. The importance of the territorial imperatives and fiscal resources wielded by these representatives of the aristocracy was made still more menacing by the risk of a renewed English (military) alliance. During the twenty-two years Louis XI reigned, he carried out a ruthless campaign of territorial acquisitions, wresting final control of remaining outposts such as Calais from the feuding English; seizing Roussillon from Spanish hands; and browbeating René de Sicile and the Dukes of Savoy in pursuit of sovereignty over their lands. When Charles the Bold, Louis's greatest adversary, died outside Nancy, aristocratic resistance to the Crown was driven underground, if not defeated.

In the transformation from medieval to Renaissance France, there is perhaps no single evolution so essential as the appropriation of Roman imperial law by the French Crown. The divide between medieval and Renaissance law, and therefore the medieval and Renaissance French state and society, can be handily represented by the transition from customaries which essentially preserved the traditions of local oral law to the imposition of a single, written, prescriptive law grafted from the written legal traditions of the late Roman empire. The French kings of the Middle Ages increasingly sought both justification and the pattern for their exercise of sovereignty in the legislating emperorship of late antiquity. Writes Jacques Krynen:

> Bien sûr, la découverte des compilations justiniennes impose partout en Occident l'image du prince législateur. Le moment est décisif. Tandis que le Moyen Age considérait jusque-là le droit comme une création de la vie collective, toute réglementation positive n'étant jamais que consécration d'un usage accepté, voici que le droit peut désormais résulter de la volonté unique et délibérément créatrice du titulaire de l'*imperium*. *Lex animata*, le *princeps*, empereur ou roi, est habilité, si le bien commun ou la nécessité publique l'exige, à établir des règles nouvelles et contraignants: "*Quod principi placuit legis habet vigorem*" (D. 1,4,1). Ce que le prince juge à propos a force de loi. En France, on aperçoit bien la montée en puissance d'un fort courant absolutiste, dont une des armes favorites consista dans la proclamation tous azimuts des formules romaines de l'omnipotence. Au Conseil du roi, dans les Grands corps de l'Etat, dans les bailliages, les partisans du *princeps legibus solutus* (D., 1,3,31) n'ont pas manqué de se faire entendre, et les protestations indignées qu'ils suscitèrent en retour attestent la réelle efficacité des maximes impériales.[47]

To begin thinking about the issue of betrayal in a historically determined, but extra-juridical context we need to begin by taking a careful look at what this embrace of Roman law meant to those who experienced its consequences.

Louis was able to realize the triumph over aristocratic resistance that remains his prime legacy because he effected a series of transformations that altered the very architecture of loyalty between himself and his subjects. Treason law provided him with the means to effect this transformation.[48] "In the hands of Louis XI the law of treason was devastating weapon," reflected Simon Cuttler in his *The Law of Treason and Treason Trials in Later Medieval France*.[49] Treason was such a devastating weapon in Louis's hands because he used it as an instrument of power – as an active, constant means of repression.

We use a special word to describe an individual's betrayal of the State: treason. The etymology of this English word arrives in our mouth directly from the French *trahison*. In French, however, the word *trahison* fills the broad lexical space occupied in English by the word betrayal. The expression whose use in French most closely corresponds to the English "treason" is *lèse-majesté*, a term derived directly from the Latin *laesa maiestas*, meaning an affront against the majesty of the emperor.[50]

Lèse-majesté is something of a catchall term which can be applied to everything from attempted regicide to counterfeiting. The range of crimes categorized as *lèse-majesté* reflects the breadth in the notion of majesty itself. The discourse of *lèse-majesté* thus realizes an important decorporalization and diffusion of power towards the realm of discourse. The king, in his incarnation as legislating prince, forms the anchor and absolute centre of this discursive tissue.

In France, those who opposed the king's will found themselves increasingly confronted with a conception of majesty, and thus of *lèse-majesté*, imported directly from Roman law. Over the later fourteenth century the word *trahison* gradually disappears from charters, edicts, or ordinances concerning royal powers, replaced by *lèse-majesté*.[51] In the transcripts of high-profile royal prosecutions of traitors to the Crown such as the *connétable* Saint-Pol (1475), whose case we will examine in chapter 6, the word *trahison* has been replaced entirely by *lèse-majesté*. Krynen is emphatic: "L'expression souvent utilisée de 'renaissance du droit romain' est impropre. Ce qui se produit, à la fin du Moyen Age, c'est bien plus la naissance d'un droit scientifique qui, grâce surtout à une persévérant travail d'adaptation des *leges* romaines, s'impose comme le foyer d'une nouvelle rationalité au service de la régulation sociale."[52] The key phrase here is "la régulation sociale."

There can be no discussion of the power struggles inherent to the discourses of betrayal without consideration of the nature of loyalty, as well. To understand how something has been severed, we must first see how it was once joined. In the background of this discussion of the imposition of Roman law remains the oral, customary, and often specifically local law, and the feudal structures that it pushed aside. The label "feudalism" proclaims its most defining element: the promise of fealty, that is, loyalty.[53]

> The key element in the relationship between unequal holders of power in a vassalic situation was, then, the oath of personal allegiance. This was a sworn contract obliging both vassal and lord to be mutually faithful ... The obligations created thereby were permanent but nonetheless conditional; resistance was legitimate if fidelity was breached (*diffidatio*) by one of the parties.[54]

The vassal's relationship with his lord is based on a fundamentally two-directional model of loyalty and service. These oaths bound specific individuals in personal bonds of loyalty. This personal quality is one of the lessons evident in feudal investiture ceremonies. The contracts these ceremonies brought into existence required repeated affirmation in rituals involving face-to-face encounter and physical contact. It is far more than a coincidence that the decay into bastard feudalism and clientelism was accompanied by a dilution in these rites.[55]

The idea of sovereignty which the French Crown, and especially Louis XI, was forging for itself was fundamentally incompatible with betrayal. The late antique model at the root of the legal codes from which French sovereignty drew inspiration called for the ruler to be dreaded, graciously good, and majestic.[56] Majesty is monologic; betrayal is, by definition, dialogic. To acknowledge oneself as betrayed is to deliberately occupy a position of vulnerability. The being or entity who declares himself betrayed identifies himself as wounded and vulnerable. Neither are compatible with true sovereignty, for the concept of majesty admits no discourse which might cast a shadow over its own absoluteness. Majesty is an immutable principle; it can neither betray nor be "betrayed." Majesty remains forever unaffected by human contingency, including the specific contingency of the man possessing or possessed by its crown. Majesty is indifferent to the uniqueness of the individuals it concerns.

The displacement of the word betrayal by the adjacent lexical field of *lèse-majesté* is thus both necessary and essential to the reconfiguration of power implicit in the French Crown's self-fashioning. Like the word "treason," the notion of *lèse-majesté* posits the implicit but necessary existence of a State, and a vaguely theocratic one at that. The distinction between the two words could not be more vital, whether for the French state, the French Crown, or those who lived within the French state under the French Crown. The lexical shift from *trahison* to *lèse-majesté* corresponds exactly to the transition from feudal to sovereign structures of power and governance in France, and can be considered instrumental in that transformation. The shift from a discourse of *trahison* to a discourse of *lèse-majesté* provides a key index to the renegotiation of the bonds, whether "discursive" or "real," between individual, Crown, and state in later medieval France. In writing about the transition from a lexicon of *trahison* to one of *lèse-majesté* we are observing how a discourse of betrayal can be wielded as a strategy of power.[57]

The subject's relation to an imperial Crown, for such was the precedent upon which Louis XI based his political construct, is based not in service but in obedience. Where the vassal owes loyalty, the subject owes obedience. The relation between sovereign and subject is uni-directional, imbued with the attributes of Christological kingship, and predicated on absolute obedience and submission. Subjection recasts loyalty as obedience; or rather, subjection conceives of no loyalty, no value, other than that of obedience. If it is possible to talk of the feudal contract of vassality or of a contractual loyalty which results, the notion of such a contract does not apply under the Roman model of sovereignty. Models of obedience borrowed from the Roman empire push aside feudal notions of a contract of personal, reciprocal loyalty between vassal and lord. Louis's father, Charles VII, had vassals. By the time of his death, Louis XI had subjects. In the enduring formula of one French historian, "la sujétion éclipse la vassalité"; subjection extinguishes vassalage.[58]

Textuality and Textual Cultures

The *Mémoires* crystallize an image of written cultures in radical transformation. Notes historian Henri Dubois, "si la génération de Charles VII scelle toujours ... à la génération suivante, celle de Georges Flavart, maître de requêtes à l'hôtel de Louis XI, on signe sans sceller."[59] Under Louis's reign reading and writing, objects written and printed, grew ever more inextricably linked with the exercise of power. The juridical tissue of individual identity and social cohesion increasingly depended on writing and written objects. The absolutist strains of Louis's idea of royal power were realized in the written documents through which Louis made his will known in absolute ways. The *Mémoires* participate in and critique the role that reading, writing, and written objects play in the production of royal authority. Where the chroniclers against whom Commynes defines himself detail jousts and banquets, the *Mémoires* tend to the pen-and-paper nitty-gritty of governing: writing letters, drawing up treaties, authorizing donations. Signets, seals, relics, and oaths, but most of all, letters – the *Mémoires* give voice to a critique of the texts through which power writes itself.

THE WEIGHT OF AUTHORITY

The literary and historiographic landscape of France was profoundly marked by the anxieties particular to Louis XI's reign. Several distinct tendencies in historiography emerged under his rule. The king himself broke with his predecessors and ended the relation between the Crown and the chronicles of Saint-Denis.[60] The Burgundian court patronized the production of its own "official" historical narratives. Elsewhere, writers occupying a variety of social functions began to write their own accounts of the history taking place around them.[61] As the notarial class gained in size and importance, its members used the literacy which secured their power in continuously more varied ways. Evidence of this renaissance in historiography at the dawn of the Renaissance goes far beyond the work of Commynes. Franck Collard, speaking of "la fécondité historiographique des années 1480–1520," calls the moment "un tournant incontestable de la production historique française."[62] In all times and places, literature has responded to the pressure of authority with a flowering of innovation. Where one path to expression is thwarted, another opens. Periods of intense political transformation produce historiographic renewal, brought about by the need to respond to the challenges and pressures of near-intolerable authority.[63] In these conditions the passage from a potentially self-contained theoretical reflection on betrayal and narrative to the material realization of that theory through the writing of the *Mémoires* becomes historically logical and even necessary.

The importance of the relations between Louis XI and Commynes comes from their simultaneously prescriptive normativity and their affective rarity. Commynes announces a new model of idealized royal subject. Half-banished, half-exiled from Burgundy, Commynes becomes, from the moment he arrives at Louis's court, entirely dependent on the king for every aspect of his identity. Commynes's historical project owes its specificity to an extreme tension between political identity and private identity. Indeed, the different facets of Commynes's biography or his legal fortunes present themselves to us as a stark but fruitful way to think about the emergence of the "private." Commynes's very existence depends on Louis XI and this absolute dependence cannot be separated from the character of their intimacy. The relation between the human person of the king and his transcendent crown was for the chamberlain an intersubjective issue more than a theoretical one. The extension of royal power and the strengthening of its absolute quality were the salient forces in his life course. The *Mémoires* give voice to a critique of the language of royal authority, but this critique also provides the narrative architecture of remembrance (*un lieu de mémoire*) where the encounter between king and servitor dwells.

We are at the heart of a situation that Hayden White describes as the matrix from which subjects, narrative, and historical narration are all born. "The reality which lends itself to narrative representation," he theorizes, "is the conflict between desire, on the one side, and the law, on the other. Where there is no rule of law, there can be neither a subject nor the kind of event which lends itself to narrative representation."[64] The sixteenth-century renewal in historiography that emerges as a direct legacy of writings by Commynes occurs side by side with a completely new position for history as a genre of belles-lettres. The birth of the memoir as a literary genre, a genre whose modern form was forever stamped by Commynes, coincides with the birth of the political subject of an impersonal state. During the same years in which political identity was being progressively reshaped via Roman treason law, the authors of historical narratives began to write "I," and to see their personal experiences as the basis for universal reflections on the nature of history. As the voice of the political subject was progressively eclipsed, the voice of the historical narrator came forward. The voice of the private subject begins to speak just as the political and social context which made possible its birth seeks to silence that voice. From the outset, the historical memoir – Commynes's *Mémoires* – must be understood as a genre of resistance and of subjective affirmation.

Chapter 1 begins with one of the most controversial episodes in the *Mémoires*, the summit at Péronne, where Commynes first met the king he would later serve. Chapters 2 and 3 highlight the complexities of a narrative whose poetic richness has not often been savoured. Each study takes the polysemic word "enseigne" (sign) as the point of departure from which to examine how the body, naked or clothed, signifies within the economies of loyalty, betrayal, and remembrance. By drawing attention to the importance of the relation to (an)other's body in the narrative construction of self, they tie together this study's autobiographical and political concerns. At the same time, these readings lay the groundwork for my excavation of Commynes's writing about the body of Louis XI in the book's final chapter. Two interlocking issues are at stake in chapter 4; one concerns the nature of the bond between king and counsellor, the other concerns the written objects at the heart of that union. Chapter 4 contemplates what it meant to be Louis's subject, and gives historical ballast to our attempt to understand the centrality of texts and textuality in the violent union and rupture between king and servitor. Chapters 5 and 6 further explore the roles that texts play in the construction and shaping of political subjectivity. These chapters introduce two characters at the core of the *Mémoires*' broader historical account of royal domination: Mary of Burgundy and Louis de Luxembourg, *connétable* de Saint-Pol. Commynes's roles as a diplomat and spy-boss mean that he was a professional writer long before he became an author of history. In chapter 5, I look at the *Mémoires* in dialogue with Commynes's diplomatic correspondence, much of it cloak-and-dagger secret dispatches. Chapter 6 dissects a corpus of texts which circulated between Louis XI and those at his court who preferred to plot against him. This chapter argues that reading and writing construct the political subject as a subject conscious of his own subjection. These studies expand our understanding of Commynes's context, and of how the *Mémoires* act as a textual mirror in which Commynes contemplates his own reflection. Chapter 7 takes us back deep into the remembering, lyrical narration of self and lost other. I show how the *Mémoires* develop an autobiographical structure which, in both plot and work, portrays the narrator as realized in and through a resurrected union with his king.

Chapter One

The Black Box of Péronne, or Commynes and the Canon

peu de choses y a secrete en ce monde, par especial de celles qui sont dictes
— Commynes, *Mémoires*

Betrayal can never be reduced to one cause, one motive, or one reason. With betrayal, we are faced with the greatest tragedy of human relations: the fact that the other is unknowable.
— Gabriella Turnaturi, *Betrayals*

Face to Face: The Encounter at Péronne

The fateful encounter with Louis XI that would reshape Commynes's destiny came in October 1468, at the town of Péronne, some fifty kilometres east of Amiens on the river Somme. The significance of the diplomatic crisis that played out in Péronne in the autumn of that year remains, like Commynes's role in its events, a subject of contention.[1] In 1468, the dust had only just settled on the negotiations that calmed the Guerre du Bien Public. The more energetic of Louis's opponents continued to swarm around the king's younger brother, Charles de Guyenne, seeking renewed leverage against the king. As was and remained the case for many years, Charles the Bold and his most powerful ally against the Crown, François II of Brittany, were feigning to be most loyal to whomever was standing directly before them, toying with Louis XI, but also with one another. The encounter at Péronne presents itself as the condensation of everything that is at stake in the *Mémoires*, distilling fifteen years of Franco-Burgundian manoeuvres, strategies, personalities, and ambiguities into a single, sprawling episode. (For convenience, I will talk about the diplomatic crisis at Péronne as if the meeting that took place there and the events that led up to and followed from that climactic encounter could be easily extracted from a larger sequence. It would be more nuanced, but also more awkward, to talk about an interlaced series of actions and consequences that form the heart of Book II.) The event's capacity to signify at an abstract level precedes our knowledge of its proceedings. Up until the fall of 1468, Charles the Bold and Louis XI had repeatedly met face to face. After Péronne, they never again saw one another.[2] Commynes's first encounter with Louis XI was Charles's last.

One reason Péronne matters to my understanding of the *Mémoires* is because of its place in the mythology that surrounds Commynes and his king. In this mythology, everything that followed had its origin in this first encounter. Commynes's account of the events that brought him face to face with Louis XI has served as a lightning rod for polemical responses to the *Mémoires* and their author. Over the course of their 500-year history, the *Mémoires* have been edited and translated, annotated, analysed and appropriated, criticized and praised by some of Europe's most influential writers. Péronne has repeatedly proven a litmus test of attitudes towards Commynes. Critical engagement with Péronne provides an identifying, indexing site through which both methodology and ideology make themselves visible. The three topoi of ethics, rhetoric, and political subjectivity coalesce in the reception of Commynes's *Mémoires*, and especially in the polemical reception of the Péronne episode. The relationship between these three domains of ethics, rhetoric, and political subjectivity has been a topos since Cicero's *De oratore*. As regards the *Mémoires*, the ethical value accorded to Commynes's rhetoric has served as a flashpoint for discussions of language, self, and State since the early Renaissance. This chapter analyses Commynes's narration of Péronne and explores the fascination his account has frequently exerted.

Behind Closed Doors

Commynes's dramatic handling of Péronne brings together an ensemble cast from Louis's reign, and puts each man's most defining trait forward, as if in caricature. The conniving cardinal Jean Balue, soon afterwards to be imprisoned for treason, pockets the money Louis XI gives him for lining others' pockets. Charles is all bombast and bluster: on the final night of his stand-off with the king, "ne se despoulla oncques; seullement se coucha par deux ou trois foyz sur son lit, et puis se pourmenoit ... Sur le matin, se trouva en plus grand colere que jamais, en usant de menasses, et prest a executer grand chose" (never once got undressed; he only lay down two or three times on his bed, and then paced ... In the morning, he was more enraged than ever, threatening things, and ready to carry out some great deed [134]). The king, shrewd, "faisoit parler a tous ceulx qu'il pensoit qui luy pouvoient aider et ne failloit pas a promettre" (had everyone he thought could help him speaking on his behalf and did not fail to make promises [133]). The king transforms a moment of mortal danger into a demonstration of his superiority over Charles. Charles shakes from the effort of restraining his temper in front of the king: "la voix luy trembloit, tant il estoit esmeu et prest de se courroucer. Il fit humble contenance de corps, mais sa geste et sa parolle estoit aspre" (his voice shook, he was so agitated and ready to let out his wrath. He gave his body a humble posture, but his gestures and his words were harsh [134]). One need not be partisan to observe that in Commynes's narration, Louis XI shows his very best traits, and the duke shows his worst.

We can join Commynes's narrative in media res, at the moment when Louis XI announces that, since he is in the neighbourhood, he will drop in for a visit with Charles. "Ainsi fut conclud que le Roy viendroit a Peronne, car tel estoit son plaisir, et luy escripvit ledict duc une lettre de sa main, portant seurté d'aller et tourner bien ample" (So it was decided that the king would come to Péronne, since this was his desire, and the duke wrote him a letter in his own hand, offering abundant guarantees to go and come in safety [117]). The king comes, "et n'amena nulle garde, mais voullut venir de tous poinctz a la garde et seureté dudict duc" (and he brought no guards, but wanted to come in every way under the guard and safety of the duke [118]). Charles puts him up in the receiver's handsome lodgings, right next to the castle. This is when the king begins to lose control of the situation, and Commynes to ratchet up the narrative suspense. "La guerre entre deux grans princes est bien aisee a commencer, mais tres mauvaise a appaiser" (Warring between two great princes is very easy to start, but very hard to resolve [118]). What happens at Péronne between Charles and Louis has everything to do with whether or not the violence of their animosity can be held in check. Will the chaos of a royally provoked Liegeois rebellion against Charles trigger a chain reaction? Will the duke cede to the fatal temptation to follow the *voie de fait*, to take matters with Louis XI into his own hands? Is either man fully in control of what he has set in motion? The deep structure in Commynes's narrative of Péronne comes from the tension between violent disintegration and what might be called "finding the centre."

Guests begin to show up for the party almost as soon as Louis has settled in under Charles's protection. First come two men the king once held in prison, Monsieur de Bresse and Monsieur de Lau, along with two others, all of them wearing the emblem of Burgundy's ambitions, the Saint Andrew's cross (119). Monsieur de Bresse puts a fine point on it: he asks for Charles's protection against the king, and reminds the duke that all four men in his band "estoient prestz a le servir envers tous et contre tous" (were ready to serve him against any and all [120]). This formula will return again and again on the pages of this book: it contains a promise of loyalty bar none; in this case, not even bar the king. It promises – maybe – to be faithful even to the point of treason, or regicide. Commynes tightens further the springs of his narration: learning that enemies surround him, Louis decides he would feel safer lodged directly with Charles, and asks to move into the castle. "Ledict duc en fut tres joyeulx ... et l'asseura fort de n'avoir nulle doubte" (The duke was very happy about this ... and assured him heartily to have no fears [120]). This is now the third time that the narrator has reminded the reader of Charles's promises to the king, and the tone has turned ominous.

Abruptly, Commynes turns away from this tense situation and launches into a sustained digression about the importance of learning from the examples of treachery, perjury, and deceit that one reads about in history books. "En tous endroictz est grand avantaige aux princes d'avoir veu des ystoires en leur jeunesse, esquelles se voient largement de telles assemblees et de grandes fraudles et tromperies et parjurements que aulcuns des anciens ont faict les ungs vers les aultres, et prints et tuéz ceulx qui en telles seuretéz s'estoient fiéz" (In every situation, it is a great advantage to princes to have read histories in their youth, in which one can see many such meetings and the great frauds, deceits, and false oaths which men in ancient times committed against one another, and how those who had trusted in such promises were captured and killed [120–1]). In a few more pages, Commynes will reveal that Louis is right on the spot where Herbert II once kept the Carolingian king Charles the Simple prisoner.[3]

After three or four days, when the two sides are in the thick of negotiations, and Louis XI is lodged in the castle, news arrives from Liège. Some of the townsmen have revolted and seized the bishop. They have cut up an archdeacon's body, and have been throwing the pieces at each other while the bishop looks on. "Ilz tuerent ledict maistre Robert, present ledict evesque, et en firent plusieurs pieces qu'ilz se jectoient a la teste l'un de l'autre par grand derrision" (They killed this Master Robert, with the bishop right there, and they cut him into several pieces which they threw at one another's heads out of great derision [124]). A stream of messages begins to arrive about the spreading rampage, and some of them report that the bishop and one the duke's ablest courtiers, the Lord of Humbercourt, have also been killed by the rebellious townsmen. "Et certiffioyent avoir veu les ambassadeurs du Roy en cest compaignee, et les nommoyent. Et fut compté tout cecy audict duc, qui soubdainement y adjousta foy et entra en une grand colere, disant que le Roy estoit venu la pour le tromper" (And they swore to having seen the king's ambassadors among this gang, and gave their names. And all of this was told to the duke, who suddenly believed it and entered into a great anger, saying that the king had come there to trick him [125]). The duke invents a flimsy excuse to close all the gates to the castle and the town, and to reinforce the guard. Louis XI has been caught red-handed inciting the duke's subjects to rebel right at the moment in which he is most thoroughly at the duke's mercy. Moreover, he is "logé rasibus d'une grosse tour ou ung conte de Vermandoys fit mourir ung sien predecesseur roy de France" (lodged right up against a fat tower where a count of Vermandois had killed one of the kings of France before him [125]).

Until this point, Commynes has been guiding the reader through events more or less visible, and more or less diplomacy- and governance-related, such as the affronts between Charles and the town of Liège, or the dynamics within Louis's attempts to pry loose the alliances between the Dukes of Brittany and Burgundy, events spread out or dispersed in space. Now the stage shrinks, and what follows becomes a largely psychological drama, played out at point-blank range. Commynes casts himself in an ambiguous role, alternately portraying himself as an exceptionally privileged witness-participant and drawing elaborate rhetorical curtains in front of the reader's eyes. "Pour lors j'estoie encores avec ledict duc et le servoye de chambellan et congnoissoye en sa chambre quant je voulloye, car telle estoit l'usance de ceste maison. Ledict duc, comme il veit les portes fermees, fit saillir les gens de sa chambre, et dist a aulcuns que nous estions que le Roy estoit venu la pour le trahir" (At that time I was still with the duke and I served as his chamberlain, and I was as familiar in his room as I wished, because that is how things were done in that house. The duke, when he had seen that the doors [to the town] were shut, made the people in his room go out, and said to those of us that remained that the king had come there to betray him [125]). Notice how the narrator has evoked Charles's mounting anger twice, back to back, in a manner that reminds this reader of *laisses similaires* in the *Chanson de Roland*. The first time, Charles closes the gates of the town and declares Louis has come to trick him, "le tromper." The second time both elements are intensified. Charles closes the doors to his rooms, and declares the king's intention to betray him, "le trahir." Leaving the reader in a tête-à-tête with the enraged duke ("terriblement meu" [126]), cocked to kill or imprison Louis at the slightest encouragement (126), Commynes turns to what is happening outside. "Toust aprés, tint aulcunes de ces parolles a plusieurs, et coururent par toute la ville et jusques en la chambre ou estoit le Roy, lequel fut fort effroyé"; then Commynes adds, significantly, "et si estoit generallement chascun, voyant grand apparence de mal" (Shortly afterwards, [Charles] said some of these things to other people, and they were repeated through the whole town and reached the room where the king was, and he became quite alarmed; so did just about everyone else, seeing the likelihood of a bad outcome [126]). Then, maddeningly – brilliantly – the narrative cuts away to a didactic segment on how meetings between princes have a way of going wrong.

Few critics have appreciated Commynes's talent for telling a story, but one early twentieth-century biographer of Louis XI recognized the runaround. "With all his opportunities as an eye-witness, it must be owned that Commines is a most tantalizing chronicler. At the critical moment of the story, when we hold our breath in suspense, he calmly goes off into two long tedious dissertations on general principles."[4] These "tedious dissertations" are in fact some of the most famous passages in the *Mémoires*, and they are very artfully placed. The first concerns the benefits of reading history for princes, the second why summitry does more harm than good.[5] Finally, three and a half long-lined folio pages after he first left the reader dangling, Commynes returns to the crisis playing out at Péronne. As readers, we have been waiting with such bated breath that we barely realize Commynes has just put one over on us. The narrative of Péronne offers a pivotal example of the split between narrative content and narrative work, and demonstrates with exceptional clarity how attention to this split relocates meaning within the *Mémoires*. The content of the Péronne episode concerns a moment when the fear that France would again be hurled into civil war was briefly reignited, a moment that might be irreverently compared to a fifteenth-century Bay of Pigs. The episode's *work* is to construct a point of origin for the author's relationship with Louis XI. But, the origin Commynes inscribes is both rhetorically and referentially aporetic.

Commynes's digression is a sleight of hand, a diversionary tactic of the most flagrant sort. While the reader has been receiving Commynes's admonishments about the jealousy, mockeries, and hatred that grow from having two princes in one place, three days have gone by at Péronne – three days of locked doors, round the clock secret counsels, bribes, and rumours. Three days of falling and rising emotions. Must the safe conduct pass Charles has given Louis be honoured? Some think the king should be summarily taken prisoner, with no pretences of doing otherwise. ("Aultres vouloient sa prinse rondement, sans cerimo-nie" [133]). Or should the king be irrecoverably humiliated, forced to sign away his kingdom to the league of Charles's allies, in a "paix bien adventageuse pour tous les princes de France" (a peace strongly advantageous to all the princes of France [133])? Commynes, in his role as narrator, has directed the reader's attention away from all these tense happenings; away from where his younger self, face to face with Louis XI, is committing the most important and dangerous acts of his life.

The Dark Years, 1468–72

Four years after his first encounter with Louis XI, on the night of 7–8 August 1472, Commynes snuck away from Charles's court. Charles discovered his favourite's absence before the sun ever rose. By six in the morning, the duke had already given all of Commynes's belongings to someone else: "Lesquels droits ensemble tous les biens quelconques d'icellui messire Philippe, nous sont échus par droit de confiscation, au moyen de ce que il s'est, aujourd'huy, date de cestes, distraict hors de nostre obeyssance, et rendu fugitif au party à nous contraire" (The rights to which, together with all and every possession of the said Messire Philippe, have come to us by right of confiscation, for the reason that he has, today, on the date of these letters, torn himself from obedience to us, and become a fugitive with the party to us opposed).[6] The dawn summons to a court secretary and the familiarity of the first-name only description "icellui messire Philippe" give some inkling of the duke's rage. This leaves us with a question that has repeatedly gripped readers' imaginations, sometimes feverishly: What happened between Louis XI and Commynes when they met at Péronne? Commynes met Louis XI in October 1468, but he only left Charles in August of 1472. Then, one summer night, suddenly, he was gone. Three weeks later, he reappeared

400 kilometres away, at Louis's court.[7] In the *Mémoires*, Commynes writes of this mysterious episode only, "envyron ce temps, je vins au service du Roy" (around this time, I came into the king's service [226]).

Commynes's role at Péronne – and the place of Péronne in deciding the author's betrayal – have elicited contradictory assessments.[8] The narrator deals coyly with his own role as an intermediary between Louis XI and Charles. From the moment when Charles first empties his rooms of courtiers, dramatically shuts the door, and declares that Louis has come to trick him, Commynes is at his side. In the flare of this first reaction, he calms the duke's anger as much as he can: "nous ne aigrismes riens, mais adoulcismes a nostre pouvoir" (we didn't let anything ferment, but rather softened what we could [126]). When the *Mémoires'* narrative returns from its didactic interlude to the scene at Péronne, Commynes is still in the duke's rooms, having explained to the reader, "le servoye de chambellan et congnoissoye en sa chambre quant je voulloye" (I served as his chamberlain and I was as familiar in his room as I wished [125]).[9] A few pages later, when Charles is too agitated to sleep, Commynes is there, pacing with him in the middle of the night ("et me pourmenay avec luy plusieurs foiz" [134]). Whereas Charles's chambers are repeatedly named, the place of Commynes's conversation with the king remains vague. "Le Roy eut quelque amy qui l'en advertit, l'asseurant de n'avoir nul mal" (The king had some friend who warned him, and guaranteed him that he would come to no harm [134]) says Commynes. Then he adds, "Aultresfoiz a pleu au Roy me faire cest honneur que de dire que j'avoye bien servy a ceste pacification" (Long ago it pleased the king to do me the honour of saying that I had served well in that arrangement [135]). The words are heavily coded. "Avoir un ami," "assurer," "servir" – these are terms we will find again and again in the coming chapters. Some people have believed that Commynes singlehandedly saved Louis XI's life; others have called that idea nonsense; some have said he spied for the king for all the years in-between; others have believed, or tried to believe, that he was wholly loyal to Charles, until the duke's cruelty drove him away. The division between the two attitudes tends to be clear cut. Those who prefer to imagine a loyal and heroic Commynes praise the modesty with which he alludes to having saved the king's life, and then recall how Charles burned down whole villages in Normandy.[10] Those who tend to view him as a traitor nearly always say he betrayed at Péronne, and sometimes intimate that his entire tale of the episode is inflated and self-serving. In the eyes or imaginations of those inclined to paint him as a traitor, Commynes became entangled in Louis's web at Péronne, and then acted as the king's spy at the Burgundian court for more than four years afterwards, only revealing himself when threatened with exposure if he did not immediately come to the king's court.[11]

Affection for the idea of Commynes as a "traitor" to his feudal lord is not only a matter of nationalisms and romantic longings, whether Burgundian or French. It is also an arguably anachronistic and / or reactionary view. Commynes's change in loyalties – his defection or his betrayal – falls juridically within a murky zone. The interpretation depends on the interpreter's views of the feudal or sovereign nature of Charles's and Louis's respective authorities, and, similarly, on his view of the feudal, sovereign, or rival nature of the relationship binding Charles and the king to one another. Commynes's choice of the king lays bare the whole of the apparatus of the French state and the Burgundian *pays* (country), along with all the uncertainty of the legal and social relations between them. Going with Louis XI recognizes – or creates an illusion of having recognized – who will win the Cold War–style struggle in which Charles and Louis are locked. Going with Louis XI is a modern choice because it looks forward to the shape of the institutions the king was building. To this end, there exists a necessary link between the twin tropes of betrayal and modernity attached to Commynes, since the question of his so-called betrayal concerns the relations of obligation or necessity binding individual, Crown, and nascent French State. Thus – and this is a central premise of my arguments in this chapter – the anxieties that have surrounded Commynes's betrayal must be conceived of in relation to the emergence of the modern French State, as well, with all that implies.

Commynes's departure has been slandered as avarice and treachery, and praised as an act of moral courage. In truth, a number of more sociological factors must be taken into account in order to arrive at a more nuanced historical understanding of Commynes's act. The political and economic aspects of Commynes's passage from one court to the other fit into a recognizable framework. The shifting balances of men and loyalties, the flow of information and alliances between Louis and Charles provide the basic plot of Louis XI's reign. Contrary to what was once received opinion, many people did move between Burgundian and royal circles, and sometimes back and forth between them.[12] A nuanced appreciation of Commynes's "betrayal" requires that we balance an ethos in which such revisions were common features in the careers of many of Commynes's contemporaries, against the darker circumstances that surrounded his own departure from Burgundy. Commynes's claim to an exceptional position among this coterie stems from the role of confidant he played to each ruler. Few at the king's court were so deeply involved in the backroom dealings through which Louis waged his war of espionnage-over-arms against the Burgundian duke and his allies. Until he joined the king's service, few at Charles's court were as close to the duke. The memorialist's value to Louis XI was the direct result of his former intimacy with Charles. These factors, combined with Commynes's three-week-long disappearance, contribute to the impression of a dramatic rupture, an "affaire Commynes." We thus have a legally ambiguous situation, further complicated by a series of potentially anomalous behaviours. Three years later, in 1475, Charles excluded Commynes from the amnesties accorded by the Treaty of Soleuvre, making him one of only four men to whom the duke refused forgiveness.[13] Commynes remained a fugitive in exile from the country of his childhood.

What motivated Commynes to go to Louis's court? Almost certainly, the king made promises. Commynes says that of all the many princes he met, Louis XI was "le plus saige pour soy tirer d'adversité" (the wisest at getting himself out of a difficult spot [61]), and the one who "plus travailloit a gaigner ung homme qui le pouvoit servir ou qui luy pouvoit nuyre" (worked the hardest to win over a man who could be useful to him or do him harm [61]). A more provocative question would thus be, what did Louis see in Commynes that he wanted for himself? Unlike the Commynes who narrates their encounter so many years later, the Commynes who was present at Péronne in 1468 had no experience of the world. His first, bungled missions to Calais were still three years into the future. The barely twenty-something Commynes Louis gazed upon at Péronne in 1468 was all unrealized possibility and unformed talent. Whatever happened between them transpired at the level of intuition and affect. We ought not to forget the importance of the age difference between the two men, neither in our attempt to understand their first interview, nor for all that came afterwards. The king, born in 1423, was exactly old enough to be the orphaned Commynes's father.

Why did Commynes pass from one master to the other? It is not that we cannot answer the question; it is relatively easy to produce not just one but many answers. He went to Louis XI because of legal obligation: the king was his liege lord; the king was his sovereign. He left Charles because the duke had become cruel and erratic. He left because he succumbed to the temptation of easy riches. If these answers satisfied those who have read the *Mémoires*, Commynes's betrayal would be a footnote to his value as a historical source, a paragraph in an editor's introduction – no more. Instead, Commynes's betrayal has been, if not the constant obsession of his readers for nearly five hundred years, then, at the least, the gnawing anxiety that returns, over and over again, to the mind and imagination. It is easy enough to account for the legal and social frameworks that give Commynes's actions their context. It is far more difficult to account for the effects that this action has had on the historical imagination. Emille Dupont, one of Commynes's most sensitive readers, notes that doubtless Commynes, "dut contracter l'un de ces engagements dont les témoignages écrits subsistent rarement, et dont les faits accomplis viennent seuls fournir les preuves."[14] And this is the crux of it. The "engagement" between Louis XI and Commynes escapes us. Neither the perception of Commynes's modernity nor the lingering unease with his betrayal can be separated from that which is most elusive about the author's relation to Louis XI, and all that remains obscure in his words.[15]

"Truth, Whose Mother is History"

Two tropes dominate readings of the *Mémoires*: modernity and betrayal.[16] Both terms belong to the domain of archetypes and myth-making. "In literary criticism myth ultimately means mythos, a structural organizing principle of literary form."[17] (The assertion belongs to Northrop Frye's *Anatomy of Criticism*.) Modernity is one such myth-structure; betrayal is another. The two have in common a formal structure dependent on a defining cleavage between Now and the (lost, forgone) Past. Both the modern subject and the traitor / betrayed define themselves temporally in relation to a moment of schism. Both modernity and betrayal are frames which enable us to give order to a narrative of rupture. Says Frye, "The allegorization of myth is hampered by the assumption that the explanation 'is' what the myth 'means.' A myth, being a centripetal structure of meaning, can be made to mean an indefinite number of things, and it is more fruitful to study what in fact myths have been made to mean."[18] This second panel in my examination of Péronne traces how the cleavage that provides this common element between betrayal and modernity comes to be located in the relationship between rhetoric and ethics. The claims of my argument concern Commynes and his *Mémoires*, but I do not exclude their relevance on a broader scale.

Voltaire, A Turning Point

The reception of the *Mémoires* takes a very definite turn at Voltaire's 1756 *Essai sur les moeurs*, a galloping universal history first begun for his mistress, Emilie du Chatelet. Voltaire draws on Commynes as a source throughout his narrative of the struggle between Louis XI and Charles the Bold. The phrase that stuck in posterity's memory, however, comes from Voltaire's blurred account of Louis XI's prosecution of Jacques d'Armagnac, Duke of Nemours. Commynes played some part in the Nemours trial, and he reaped material rewards for his effort, but he never mentions it in his *Mémoires*.[19] Voltaire identifies him as "ce Philippe de Commines, célèbre traître qui, ayant longtemps vendu les secrets de la maison de Bourgogne au roi, passa enfin au service de la France, et dont on estime les *Mémoires*, quoique écrits avec la retenue d'un courtisan qui craignait encore de dire la vérité, même après la mort de Louis XI."[20] I am not the first of those who have written about the *Mémoires* to spotlight the influence of Voltaire's well-turned phrase. Emille Dupont sputtered, "de quel témoignage contemporain est-elle étayée? d'aucun" and called the accusation an "outrage" against the truth.[21] As if in sympathy, Frédéric Chabaud noted, "Ce jugement sommaire traverse tout le XIXe siècle pour rejoindre, à peine nuancé, 'notre' époque."[22] I am not sure, however, that anyone previously has stopped to consider what it is about Voltaire's words – beyond their sharp wit – that posterity has found so compelling.

The early modern reception of the *Mémoires* possesses a dense, reticulated, history; arguably, no other single text was as important to political discourse.[23] Three great currents run through Commynes's reception during the two and a half centuries leading up to Voltaire's words: the quest for a national historiography; arguments over the shape and limits of royal power; and finally, evolving notions about the ideal relation between rhetoric and historiography. It is the last of these which concerns us especially, although the three cannot be entirely separated. The sixteenth-century canonization of Commynes's *Mémoires* took place in the context of a multifaceted Renaissance quarrel between "Ciceronian" and "anti-Ciceronian" schools.[24] The Ciceronian school emphasized oratory. The anti-Ciceronian school argued that history should be grounded in knowledge of the world rather than book learning. Those who have made history should write it, and they should write it in a naked and unadorned style. Commynes was their exemplary author, and his ghost animates every discussion of what it means to write a "pure and true" narrative of history from the preface of Johann Sleidan's 1545 Latin translation onwards.[25] To French royal historiographer Denis Sauvage, French was Commynes's "naturel" – the word could be taken to mean either his mother tongue or his naked, unadorned (textual) body.[26] Commynes's abandonment still smarted for some living under Habsburg rule (like Jacques Meyer, whom we will meet shortly), but it is legendary that Holy Roman Emperor Charles V, great-grandson of Charles the Bold, kept a copy of the *Mémoires* at his bedside.

Early in the seventeenth century, Pierre Matthieu, in a defence that combines many of the topoi just alluded to, wrote the following reflection on Péronne, the duke's rage, and Commynes's change of heart, in his *Histoire de Louys XI Roy de France*.

> Le Duc demeura trois jours en de grandes alteres, et passa la troisiesme nuict en telle inquietude qu'il ne se despoüilla point, se couchant sur son lict, puis tout soudain se levant, se promenant & parlant à Philippes de Commines son Chambellan, la probité & moderation duquel servit à calmer ces orages impetueux qui agitoient son ame. Il estoit tout François & délors on croit qu'il fit resolution de se retirer en France. Mais il n'est pas croyable qu'il y eust de la trahison en son faict. La candeur & la sinceritè si apparente en ses escrits en oste le soupçon. S'il eust eu ce blasme d'infidelité & d'ingratitude, vices qui sont la dissolution de l'humaine societé, le Roy ne luy eust pas fié tant de grands & importans affaires.[27]

Matthieu wraps things up neatly: Commynes's probity and moderation calmed the duke; if afterwards he decided to join Louis XI, this was only right since he was "entirely French" to begin with; in any case, a traitor could never write with Commynes's candour.

Voltaire's contrasting accusation has a comfortably worn tone to it – Commynes spied for Louis XI at Charles's court. In many ways, Voltaire embroiders on a legacy usually associated with the sixteenth-century Flemish patriot Jacques Meyer (1491–1552). Meyer was among the first to put the accusation of Commynes's betrayal down on paper, although even patriotism does not blind him to Charles's cruelty: "Crudelis visus hic Carolus & animus turbato: crediturque quosdam ex familiaribus habuisse parum fideles, ex quibus hauddubie erat Philippus ille Cominius ortu Flandrus, Dominus Ruscurii, qui hoc anno transfugit ad Regem" (Charles appeared cruel and his reason disturbed: it is believed that some of those close to him were not entirely loyal, among whom was doubtless that Philippe de Commynes, born in Flanders, Lord of

Renescure, who that year crossed over to the king).[28] To the Flemish Meyer, all those who left Burgundy for Louis's service would have earned the right to be called traitor. The matter is juridical and political. However, if Voltaire read Meyer, I have not found traces of it in his library.[29]

Voltaire plucks at a different string. Voltaire does not accuse Commynes's text; he does not say that Commynes lies, nor that his text is not reliable as a historical source. Voltaire brings together the "celebrity" of Commynes's betrayal and his (rhetorical) behaviour as a "courtesan." Meyer calls Commynes's text full of lies: "scripsit plane mendaciter, multaque dicenda infideliter reticuit" (he wrote mendaciously and much that was to be said he disloyally silenced).[30] Voltaire does not impute the reliability of the *Mémoires* as a source of information about Louis's reign; he says their author is full of lies. For Voltaire, the idea of Commynes-the-traitor sits on the fault line between individual-as-individual and individual-as the-subject-of-a-king, that is, as a political subject. In the turn of Voltaire's phrase, Commynes's actual treachery takes a subordinate position to his servility, a point his syntax makes clear: the information that Commynes sold state secrets is literally presented as a subordinate clause. Voltaire hangs his accusation of Commynes's rhetorical duplicity on the relations between the author and the Crown, rather than on Commynes's purported espionnage. His phrase carries within it the fully formed notion that political subjectivity lies in what we might call a consciousness of self in relation to power. This consciousness of self-in-relation-to-power exists as the awareness of a cleavage, and this internal cleavage is the site of a lie. It is the site of baseness and deception. The individual, faced with the absolute power of a king is, at heart, a traitor. Voltaire's Commynes possesses an internal consciousness which is at the same time inscrutable and divided. Voltaire gives to his accusation an expression that significantly changes its terms. His *Essai sur les moeurs* can be pinpointed as the moment at which responses to Commynes's passage from Charles's service to the king's detach themselves from an easily decipherable relation to the debates of a particular moment and instead attach themselves to Commynes's betrayal, transforming that action into the centre of gravity in their reception. This is the moment when myth takes hold, and Commynes becomes a traitor.[31]

Early modern reception of the *Mémoires* had always focused on the political value of their rhetorical style. In Voltaire's judgment, language ceases to be the index of virtue and becomes instead the artful mask of its absence. This reversal is more than a shift in relation to the rhetorical debates of the sixteenth century; it is a reversal in the values attached to Commynes as a political subject. A century before, Pierre Matthieu had believed in the transparent relation between Commynes's words and his ethical integrity, saying "il n'est pas croyable qu'il y eust de la trahison en son faict. La candeur & la sincerité si apparente en ses escrits en oste le soupçon."[32] Sixty-five years before the first edition of Matthieu's history, Sleidan had held Commynes's "pure and true" history aloft. For Sleidan or for Matthieu, Commynes's political subjectivity was grounded in the unity between ethics and rhetoric, and his narrative offered proof of his integrity. What Voltaire says about Commynes opposes ethics and political subjectivity. Voltaire's Commynes is a craven sycophant, made abject by his relation to royal power.

The Endurance of Myths

"Is Commynes a modern writer?" These are the first words of Jean Dufournet's 1966 La Destruction des mythes dans les Mémoires de Philippe de Commynes.[33] After pointing out a handful of those who have also chosen Commynes's modernity as their touchstone, and giving a quick survey of the commmonplaces habitually used to reference the later Middle Ages, Dufournet comes clean.[34] "Aussi, notre propos est-il de dégager, dans une oeuvre apparemment objective et impassible, les intentions secrètes derrière les desseins avoués."[35] Dufournet answers a question about modernity with an assertion about textuality, interpretation, and authority. Moreover, he does so through a sustained demonstration of the politically motivated manipulation of rhetoric. Dufournet locates the modernity of Commynes's text in its rhetorical duplicity.[36] What Dufournet does is parallel to but not identical with what Voltaire does. Dufournet makes betrayal the explanation for rhetoric, and, simultaneously, he implicitly situates the Mémoires' modernity in that rhetoric. This is to say, Dufournet locates Commynes's modernity in what he claims betrayal does to language. For Dufournet, Commynes's status as a traitor is of a piece with the unreliability of his narrative. "En 1472, Commynes abandonna Charles de Bourgogne pour rejoindre Louis XI: ce fut le fait capital de sa vie, d'autant plus important qu'il fut un traître à ses yeux et aux yeux des autres, et qu'il ne cessa de se le reprocher, plus ou moins consciemment."[37] In Dufournet's view, Commynes's narration is calculated to demonstrate, obliquely but tirelessly, the perfidy of his peers, in an attempt to justify and exonerate Commynes's own perfidy in "betraying" Charles the Bold.[38] "Les *Mémoires* constituent une véritable anthologie de la trahison ... La trahison est un cancer qui ronge tous les êtres."[39] To prove his thesis Dufournet assembled a collage of contrasting contemporary sources, chipping away little by little at the veneer of Commynes's affirmations. *La Destruction des mythes* might have realized a study of irony as Commynes's dominant mode. Riveted instead on the intentionality of his implied author, Dufournet conjures a Commynes of unending rancour.

La Destruction des mythes appeared at almost exactly the same time as the first volumes of Karl Bittmann's *Ludwig XI und Karl der Kühne: die Memoiren des Philippe de Commynes als historische Quelle* (1964–70).[40] Bittmann's study sought to realize what one scholar delicately labelled, the "minutieuse et impossible entreprise de vérification du contenu des 'Mémoires.'"[41] The first volume (out of a projected five) covered just two episodes: the Guerre du Bien Public and the Péronne summit. Bittmann managed two more volumes before collapsing from exhaustion.[42] In his review of the work, historian Richard Vaughan noted with approval that Bittmann's "analysis fully confirms what one has long suspected: that Commynes is one of the greatest liars in the history of historical writing."[43] Other reviewers were surprised to discover that neither scholar knew of the other's work. Indeed, the two fit together with rare coherence: Dufournet compared the account given by the *Mémoires* against contemporary narrative sources, while Bittmann carried out a similar process using archival sources. It is disconcerting to realize that both of these studies appeared during structuralism's blossoming, since both seek to "pierce through" rhetoric and textuality, and both clutch at the author's devious intentions.[44] The concentrated attention both Bittmann and Dufournet train on the Péronne episode confirms its centrality to the textual trouble stirred up far and wide by Commynes's *Mémoires*. The two works coincide in more than method. Each privileges Péronne as the locus of Commynes's betrayal of Charles the Bold, and of his paradigmatic deception of the reader. What interpretations present themselves for this strange coincidence of ambitions to exhaustivity? From the perspective of this very "literary" reading of Commynes's portrayal, these two studies appear in many ways like acts against interpretation. In their distinct manners, each exposes a "truth" scoured until it admits no ambiguity – which is to say, until all of its possible signification has been scoured away.

In recent years, the work of historian Joël Blanchard has displaced that of Dufournet. Blanchard argues strenuously against the historical appropriateness of seeing Commynes as a traitor. In fact, he attempts to undermine the very term "betrayal" as it might be applied to the courtiers caught in the middle of Louis XI's skirmishes with Charles the Bold or François II of Britanny. His work, especially a 2009 article bearing the title "Commynes n'a pas 'trahi': Pour en finir avec une obsession critique," offers a rigorous consideration of the legal and documentary evidence surrounding Commynes's case and many useful comparisons with his contemporaries. We are left to wonder, however, whether such vehemence does not perpetuate the same mythology against which it strains. Blanchard wants to convince us that Commynes was not a traitor, but begins from the premise that there is an objectively definable thing called a "traitor." My own position is that there cannot be a "truth" of Commynes's betrayal, only different constructions of an event, whose only certain and knowable facts are Commynes's whereabouts, and by implication, his self-positioning in a field of competing power structures. Understanding how and why the view of the *Mémoires'* author as a traitor came to exert such a hold on readers' imaginations is arguably as compelling as the dilemmas hidden within the case's legal aspects.

It is a truism that each generation rewrites the past through the filter of its own present moment. It is nonetheless striking how readings of the *Mémoires* so forcefully enact the hopes or anxieties of each age surrounding the relations between individual and State. *La Destruction des mythes* argues that Commynes was ashamed of his treachery and wanted to show that everyone else shared the same moral corruption, too. Can this preoccupation with hidden betrayal and shame be detached from the legacy of the Occupation, which inevitably hung over the years of Dufournet's childhood?[45] The methodological coincidence between Dufournet and Bittmann rests on their common belief that the surface of Commynes's narrative is but a sinister concealment of a darker plot, a master plan to manipulate the truth. Can such a critical project be separated from the Cold War context in which each wrote? In turn, Blanchard's *Commynes l'Européen* appeared in 1996, and must have been written directly after the 1992 Treaty of Maastricht. The Commynes Blanchard conjures is a man for whom there are no more frontiers, a man who moves across a map whose lines are fluid, and whose limits are ever-shifting. In *Commynes l'Européen* the title of Blanchard's very first chapter tells the reader that Commynes is "un homme sans frontières."[46] The Commynes that Blanchard imagines is no less manipulative, greedy, or spiteful than the Commynes conjured by Dufournet or others before, but he is not a feudal traitor. He is a businessman, steeped in the ethos of profit, an early investor in the Medici's international banking schemes.

These are speculations and imaginings, at the outer edges of historical knowledge and the limits of epistemological certitude. We see Commynes in a mirror of our own imagining. The discourses of betrayal are necessarily preoccupied with authority and transgression. There is no way to talk about betrayal which is not politically freighted. The history of Commynes's reception is inscribed with the traces of ideological struggle. What fingerprints of the decade which has followed September 11th will someday be seen on these pages?

A Tarot Deck

The canon is an uncanny allegory of the state and its discontents, which grips us, often against our taste and will, because it tells the story of our coming to the untenable site of subjectivity we occupy. The canon is an allegory whose code has been misplaced, or, more precisely, repressed.

– Peter Haidu, *The Subject Medieval/Modern*

To see Commynes as a traitor is to see in him the cipher of unknowable subjectivity, perhaps our own. The polemics that have surrounded his betrayal may be something of a red herring. Commynes's portrayal of his first encounter with Louis XI evades any clear response to the reader's many questions, and thus pushes us to contemplate our own deep, and deeply divided, relationship to the abstracted and mythic faces of authority. Ultimately, the preoccupation with Commynes's betrayal obscures a much more frightening question, that of how we fantasize our own relation to power. The traitor exposes the fault lines within our own loyalties, and forces us to think carefully about who "we" are. His actions expose fractures within the self. Every reader of Commynes's text must struggle with this tension, whose most profound gesture is one of turning away and internal division. Commynes's narrative presents a matrix of the condition of the modern political subject. The implicit subject running through the *Mémoires* is none other than the constitution of political subjectivity.

At the level of abstraction, Commynes's narrative of Péronne questions whether violence can be contained or if it must overflow. This is not a moral lesson or principle, but rather the uncertainty that hangs over events as they develop. Can the centre hold? Where or in whom does that centre reside? In an immediate and nearly literal sense, the question concerns whether Louis will triumph or whether Charles will carve the monarch's fragile nation into "a peace advantageous for all the princes of France" (133). These are the political stakes of Péronne, but they come out in a series of suggestive narrative details. On the side of concentration and confrontation, we see gates shut, rooms emptied, doors locked. Yet, all of this risks being torn apart, exploding into anarchy. Voices shake from the effort of restraint. The archdeacon's body is dismembered. Later, when Charles has obliged the king to help put down the Liège rebellion he provoked, townsmen on a raid rush forward over the rubble of razed walls.

Commynes's account of Péronne boils down to a series of intimate encounters, in which character and chemistry are everything. The heart of the episode plays out behind closed doors, in two distinct but interdependent *huis clos*, or what we might call in English "locked room" plots. The first opposes Charles and Louis XI, who try to outwit or overpower each other, testing who possesses the greater force. The second *huis clos* is both more explicit and more oblique, and concerns Commynes's presence in each of the two men's rooms, and his movement as a privileged messenger shuttling between them. Commynes says a little and holds back much, so that the reader is both inside these locked rooms with Commynes and metaphorically "outside" them.

Commynes's narrative of the meeting at Péronne is well-stocked in the formal building blocks of literature's capacity to produce meaning. It contains, in fact, a staged microcosm of universal themes. If one grasps the writing of history as a kind of mythologizing, Péronne brings a stew of many ingredients together in one pot. Péronne has a huge cast of characters, a hornet's nest of opposing interests great and small. Vengeance, fear, ambitions, rivalries, revolts, battles, ruses, fear, anger, suspense, secrets, power, dreams of empire – it is all there in the mix. Alongside this list is a veritable Tarot deck of archetypes: towers, money, prisoners, king, death, battle, locked rooms. There is suspense: the king's enemies are all around, prowling for trouble. There are big emotions: the duke's barely controlled anger, the king's fear. The episode shows the meeting between two powerful rivals. During their time together, a series of more and less explicit challenges permits Commynes to measure duke and king against one another. The confrontation between the two plays out over time, in a choreography that translates the depth and complexity of the struggle between them. Never entirely effaced, the power relation which defines them becomes destabilized, and risks capsizing. Péronne can be read as a tremor in French history, a brief moment in which the shaky balance between Louis XI and Charles the Bold shudders. France's future shape becomes for a moment uncertain; the whole map of Europe is in play.

The episode of Péronne in its ensemble occupies a central position in a mythography of modernity. Within the details of Commynes's narrative there is another myth-structure still to be read. In a poetic image which has become proverbial, the Burgundian *rhetoriqueur* Molinet compared the king to a siren from Greek mythology whose voice fatefully seduces men. Seduction is a key word: seduction implies a before and an after. Earlier in this chapter I evoked Northrop Frye's articulation of myth as a structure which enables signification. Like betrayal, the structure of modernity involves a backwards gaze at lost innocence. The generations that lived through or just after the Revolution remembered or imagined the lost past reflected in Louis XI's reign.[47] Michelet evokes popular fantasies of Louis XI as modernity's ravenous mask, greedily drinking children's blood to prolong his own life, or letting Nemours's blood pour from the scaffold onto the bodies of his sons below; yet these images were born long before the guillotine gave them new resonance.[48]

The structure of Frye's *Anatomy of Criticism* enables him to approach a subject such as myth from several angles. "In terms of narrative," he explains early on, "myth is the imitation of actions near or at the conceivable limits of desire."[49] When Frye writes this, he is thinking of the unchecked sexual rapacity one finds in Ovid's *Metamorphoses*. That text is a fitting one to remind us that seduction is also a kind of fall – a fall from innocence, a fall from virtue, a fall from an irretrievable past. Remember the blank screen made by Péronne's closed doors. I think that what people react to in Commynes's account of Péronne is the image of a naive teenager going into the king's room, and a besmirched, lying, deceitful, corrupted spy coming out. Before and after. Corruption and unknowability. These are the keystones in the arcs of mythologizing which surround the encounter between Commynes and his king. Post-Voltaire readings of the *Mémoires'* portrayal of Péronne tend to reinforce one another. In every case, whether anchored to political content and the nascent State, to rhetoric and the ethical subject, or to the quest for a "truth" about Commynes's betrayal, we encounter an implied author who has been cast in essentializing ways as both a traitor and an unreliable narrator. Both this implied authorial persona and the recurrent coupling of his betrayal of Charles the Bold to the truth of his narrative derive from an essentializing belief that Commynes was a "traitor."

Seduced by Louis XI, Commynes betrayed Charles. Now he seduces his readers and betrays them with his treacherously mendacious narrative. Two schema combine in the projections that superimpose themselves over the meeting between Commynes and Louis at Péronne. The vaguely traced outline of a "fall" combines with an equally fantasy-rich notion of "union" with the king. Together, a sketched outline appears in which we see the coupling of Commynes's inner being to the apparatus of a terrifying state power. In short, did Commynes throw himself into the open gullet of the State? Are we afraid that we, too, will fall in?

Chapter Two

Enseignes: What History Writes on the Body

Il desiroit grand gloire, qui estoit ce qui le mectoit plus en ses guerres que nulle autre chose, et eust bien voulu ressembler a ses anciens princes, dont il a esté tant parlé après leur mort.

– Commynes, *Mémoires*

Le corps: surface d'inscription des événements (alors que le langage les marque et les idées les dissolvent), lieu de dissociation du Moi (auquel il essaie de prêter la chimère d'une unité substantielle), volume en perpétuel effritement. La généalogie, comme analyse de la provenance, est donc à l'articulation du corps et de l'histoire. Elle doit montrer le corps tout imprimé de l'histoire, et l'histoire ruinant le corps.

– Michel Foucault, "Nietzsche, la généalogie, l'histoire"

Commynes entered Charles's service as a teenager and by every indication quickly became one of the count's favourites. Then Commynes abandoned Charles for reasons which can never be fully known, and which Charles never forgave. For his part, Commynes says nothing, only, "envyron ce temps, je vins au service du Roy (et fut l'an mil CCCCLXXII)" (around this time, I came into the king's service (and it was the year 1472) [226]). Commynes's silence forces the reader to confront the inscription of indeterminacy not only as *a* function of the narrative but as *the* function of narrative itself. The braided readings on the following pages seek to shift consideration of how the *Mémoires* portray Charles away from the relentless *plaidoyers* for and against Commynes's deed, and towards the lyricism of private remembrance steeped in forceful and often contradictory emotions. Commynes talks about Charles's body in mediated and fragmented ways that blur the frontier between vision and imagination, forcefully insisting on the filaments that connect memory, desire, and nostalgia to narrative representation.

We begin by seeking to share the gaze of the boy that once was. Vision gives way to the memory of sensation. The polyvalent word *enseigne* offers a point through which to make visible the conflictual encounter between different moments in the narrator's memory. This word *enseigne* (sign) flowers in Commynes's text. Banners, livery, graffiti, signet rings, and scars all form part of a non-verbal textual rhetoric. The *Mémoires* are unencumbered by the kind of self-conscious literary flourishes and postures often associated with the Burgundian court. Their force comes from relatively austere effects of symmetry, repetition, and inversion.

Linguists Olivier Soutet and Claude Thomasset distinguish three levels of subjectivity in the narrative voice of the *Mémoires*: "avouée, masquée, cachée."[1] In ways deliberate and less so, Commynes manifests more or less self-consciousness about his presence in events narrated and his role as their narrator. The relation between the narrator and his own enunciation is not stable. At moments Commynes veils the relation between his experiences and their narration, at others he clearly accepts the responsibility of witnessing. A psychoanalytically informed approach to Commynes's narrative incorporates and builds on Soutet and Thomasset's linguistic observation. Memory's hand plucks from the past those elements on which time has bestowed a greater importance. (This thematic coherence signifies in part because it escapes from authorial intent, and hence from the ability to control or limit meaning.) The end helps us to understand the beginning. Although neither transparent nor unmediated, narrative detail communicates value as it is retrospectively perceived through the filter of time. The details Commynes recalls, and the way he recounts these details, construct a larger field of intratextual signification, modulated through the refractions of narrated and narrative time.

How Young I Was: The Desacralized Body

In July 1465 Louis XI, Charles, and the assembled armies of their supporters faced off on the fields of Montlhéry. Commynes tells the reader that this inconclusive battle was his first military experience. Biographic importance accompanies the moment's political significance. The moment brought an anticlimactic climax to the aristocratic campaign known as the Guerre du Bien Public. The dukes' armies then laid siege to Paris until, one rebelling nobleman at a time, Louis vanquished them all with promises of lands and offices. As each man pursued his own personal advantage, resolve against Louis's unpopular reforms fizzled away. "Le bien publicque estoit converti en bien particulier" (The public good was transformed into private goods [70]). Recalling his debut in these worldly affairs, the older, narrating Commynes remembers the wide-eyed bewilderment of his younger self with piercing cynicism. On the day of Montlhéry,

> me trouvay ce jour tousjours avecques luy, ayans moins de crainte que je n'eu jamais en lieu ou je me trouvasse depuys, pour la jeunesse en quoy j'estoye et que n'avoye nulle congnoissance du peril; mais estoye esbaÿ comme nul se osoit deffendre contre ce prince a qui j'estoie, estimant qu'i fust le plus grand de tous les aultres. Ainsi sont gens qui ont poy d'{experience}. (26)[2]

> [I was beside him the whole day, less afraid than I have ever been in any place I have found myself since, because I was so young and didn't have any notion of the danger; instead I was astonished that anyone dared to fight against this prince to whom I belonged, believing that he was the greatest of all of them. That's how people are when they lack experience.]

Commynes's narrative, marked by a recurrence of indirect free speech, allows this distance between innocence and experience to undulate throughout the narrator's account of the battle and its aftermath. The narrator speaks of how his first innocence was lost, but the self whose disillusionment he recounts appears to him, so many years later, as a vision of innocence.

Commynes's depiction of Montlhéry is characterized by a series of moments which, risking the burlesque, debunk the attitudes and iconography of chivalric glory. In one famous passage a corps of scouts spend all night frightened out of their wits, only to realize with the sun's rise that the row of spikes they had taken for upright lances are in fact thistles.

> Le temps estoit fort obscur et trouble, et noz chevaucheurs ... bien loing oultre eulx veoient grande quantité de lances debout, se leur sembloit ... et ceste ymagination leur donnoit l'obscurté du temps ... Ilz s'en aproucherent le plus qu'ilz peurent, et le jour estoit ung peu haulsé et esclarcy. Ils

trouverent que c'estoient grands chardons ... et en furent honteux ceulx
qui avoient dit ces nouvelles, mais le temps les excusa. (66–8)

[The weather was very dark and foggy, and our scouts ... saw a good way
off a large quantity of upright lances, so it seemed to them ... and this
imagining came to them from how dark the weather was ... They came as
close as they could, and the day had risen a little and cleared. They found
that it was giant thistles ... those who had given the report were ashamed,
but the weather excused them.]

The glory of battle is an illusion; being there is about feeling cold, wet,
and terrified. Although the thistles-for-lances incident takes place at
night, Commynes blames the weather for the scouts' inability to see
clearly. They are engulfed in the cloudy vapours of their own confusion.
Their error and its discovery contain a loose *anagnorisis*, the surprised
recognition which provides one of the plot structures in tragedy.
Commynes's story is about sight and knowledge, and the vulnerability
of each. The scouts' ordeal presents itself not as comic anecdote but
rather as the emblematic, ironic misprision of a whole enterprise. This
incident is one of the most often recounted from the *Mémoires*. The concern with disillusionment is the seed that provides its piquancy, and its
paradigmatic value.

Commynes's account of events at Montlhéry reprises all the confusion
of the battle itself. The fantasied image of a unified corps surging forward to meet the enemy while a gold-embroidered *enseigne* (banner)
flutters against the blue sky gives way to a sequence characterized
by frenzy, absurdity, and dismemberment. In his zeal to vanquish the
king, Charles effectively compels his foot soldiers into a forced march;
they arrive for battle already exhausted. So little order reigns in the
Burgundian forces that it was "comme se on eust voulu perdre a son
essiant" (as if we had been trying to lose [24–5]). Already Commynes's
use of the ambiguous pronoun "on" shows signs of tension: "on eust
voulu" and "son essiant" blur the relation between the speaker and his
subject in two conflicting directions. Who is "on"? Is it we or Charles?
Commynes seems to use it simultaneously for both, as if he were trying
to distance himself from the content of his phrase. Breaking ranks, the
archers "rompirent eulx mesmes la fleur de leur esperance" (themselves
crushed the flower of their hopes [26]). The wing Charles leads encounters no resistance, so the duke plunges ever further ahead, as if he
were driving back enemy soldiers. Ignoring repeated admonishments,

Charles charges after the king's soldiers nearly all the way to the edge of the enemy camp. Finally one of the older courtiers who had served Charles's father when he was duke, "luy dist semblablement et si audacieusement qu'il estima sa parolle et son sens et retourna tout court; et croy que s'il fust passé oultre deux gectz d'arc, qu'il eust esté prins comme aulcuns aultres qui chassoient devant luy" (told him so and did so boldly that he understood the words and their meaning and turned straight back around; and I think that if he had kept going two arrow flights further he would have been captured like some of the others in front of him [28]). This scolding puts the glorious duke in his place as little more than a rambunctious little boy.

Even as he retreats, however, Charles continues to play at being a hero. He will be injured twice as he retreats from his own private cavalry charge. "Et passent [passant] par le villaige, trouva une flote de gens a pied qui fuyoient; il les chassa, et si n'avoit pas cent chevaulx en tout. Il ne se tourna que ung homme a pied, qui lui donna d'ung vouge parmy l'estoumac; et au soir s'en veit l'enseigne" (And crossing through the village he found a wave of foot soldiers who were fleeing; he chased after them; there weren't even a hundred horses in all. Only one man on foot turned around, and he stabbed [the duke] with a halberd in the stomach; and in the evening we saw the mark [28]).[3] L'enseigne: the mark, the scar. This enseigne carved into Charles the Bold's body comes not from single combat against a sword or lance-wielding knight or nobleman, but from the vulgar jab of a foot soldier. Further ahead, a line of the king's archers waits, blocking the duke's path forward. Charles veers, looking for an open space. (I have been calling Charles "the duke," but Commynes calls him by the title he wore at the time, comte de Charolais.)

> Vindrent courre sus quinze ou seize hommes d'armes ou environ … et d'antre{e} tuerent son escuyer trenchant, qui portoit ung guydon de ses armes … Et ledict conte fut en tres grand dangier et eut plusieurs coups, et entre aultres ung a la gorge d'une espee, dont l'enseigne luy est demouree toute sa vie, par deffault de sa baviere qui luy estoit cheute et avoit esté mal atachee des le matin, et luy avoie veu cheoir. (28)

> [Fifteen or sixteen men at arms came running at him … and straightaway they killed the squire who cut his meat, who was carrying a small banner with his arms … And the count was in great danger and received several blows, and among others one to the throat with a sword, of which the scar

stayed with him his whole life, since he didn't have the beaver [face guard]
which had fallen because it had been ill-attached since morning, and I saw
it fall off him.]

This scar, this specific *enseigne*, is an essential clue to understanding
the work of Commynes's *Mémoires* in the sense discussed in my introduction in relation to trauma and witness, and to the "work" of narration. We will return to it – or it will return to us – much later in
Commynes's narrative.

During his lifetime, Charles was renowned for his physical stamina,
which often left those around him exhausted. Commynes's narrative of
Montlhéry begins by presenting a fantasy: Charles is invincible; the surface of his virile, martial body cannot be penetrated by pique or halberd,
sword or lance. Each of the *enseignes* Commynes locates on the duke's
body defaces the heroic image the young narrator has of him. Charles
begins as a glorious, idealized embodiment of warrior masculinity. The
duke's "fort sanglant" disfigured neck represents a violation of the in-
violable. There are thus two distinct gazes discreetly layered into this
moment. The first belongs to the page bursting with pride over the idealized man with whom he identifies ("ce prince a qui j'estoie"). The
second belongs to the older voice of the narrator, who contemplates the
unscarred young man that he once was. Desire is remembered, but its
articulation is twice mediated by the filter of other memories of disillusionment and marking.

Charles has just acquired two *enseignes* in short order: one from a
random foot soldier and the other because his helmet had been shoddily
attached. The word *enseigne* returns again to refer to the insignia-bearing
standards soldiers carry into battle. The *guydon* that the squire is carrying when he is killed is also a kind of banner or *enseigne* ("d'antre[e]
tuerent son escuyer trenchant, qui portoit ung guydon de ses armes").[4]
The colours and emblems embroidered on those *enseignes* function as
extensions for the men whose identity they represent. Clothing and banners become synecdoches of the body. Commynes carries this series
further. The two sides pull back from one another; a band of the duke's
allies are huddled nearby. Charles, "fort sanglant, se retira a eulx, comme
au meillieu du champ. Et estoit l'enseigne du bastard de Bourgongne
toute despessee, tellement qu'elle n'avoit pas ung pied de longueur; et
l'enseigne des archiers dudict conte. Il n'y avoit pas quarante hommes
en tout, et nous y joignismes, qui n'estions pas trente, en tres grand
doubte" (very bloody, withdrew to them, like in the middle of the field.

And the banner of the Bastard of Burgundy was all cut up, so that it wasn't a foot long; and [same] with the banner of the count's archers. There weren't forty men in all, and we who joined them weren't thirty men, and all very frightened [29]). In highlighting this sequence and its development, I mean to point out how the text simultaneously negotiates issues of memory and of representation. The foundational layers in Commynes's narrative of self are, from their beginnings, concerned with violence and inscription. The narrative progresses from the *enseigne* left by the pike jabbed at Charles, to the felled squire, to the gouge on the duke's neck, to the blood that covers him, to the shredded banner. Commynes describes a graduated series of physical and symbolic scars. On the space of one folio side, he uses the word *enseigne* three times interchangeably as mark, wound, scar, banner, or, most literally and most starkly, sign.[5]

Let us rejoin Commynes on the battlefield where, as if still breathless, the narrator looks around, taking his bearings. "Nostre champ estoit aussi ras, ou demye heure devant le blé estoit si grand, et la pouldre la plus terrible du monde, tout le champ semé de mors et de chevaulx, et ne se congnoissoit nul homme mort pour la pouldre" (Our field was totally flattened, where half an hour before the wheat had been so high, and the dust was the worst in the world, the whole field strewn with the dead and with horses, and you couldn't recognize any of the dead men because of the dust [29]). Dust, "the most terrible in the world," erases all. Commynes's words twist the conventional piety that all men are equal in death into another, more horrific vision. The dead who lie on the battlefield have been erased: their faces, the sign of their individual existences, cannot be read. The description can be read as realistic and apocalyptic all at once. The word *poudre* can also mean *cendre*, ash, so Commynes's words contain an index to their own potential allegorization.

At evening's fall,

> monsr de Charroloys beut et mengea ung peu, et chascun en son endroit, et luy fut adoubee sa plaie qu'il avoit a la gorge. Au lieu ou il mangea, fallut oster quatre ou cinq hommes mors pour luy faire place; et y eut l'on deux boteaulx de paille ou se seist. Remuant ung de ces pouvres gens nudz, commença demander a boire: on luy gecta ung peu de ptisanne en la bouche, de quoy ledict seigneur avoit beu; le cueur luy revint et fut congneu, et estoit ung archier de corps dudict seigneur, fort renommé, appelé Savarot, et fut pensé et guery. (32–3)

[Monsieur de Charolais drank and ate a little, each at the appropriate time, and the wound he had on his throat was dressed. In the place where he ate, four or five dead men had to be moved out of the way to make room for him; and there were two bales of hay where he sat. While they were pushing aside one of those poor naked people, the man began to ask to drink: they threw some herbal tea that the count had drunk in his mouth; he revived and was recognized; he was an archer in the count's corps, very famous, named Savarot, and he was bandaged and healed.]

Commynes directs the reader's thoughts away from the duke who takes a seat, and towards the piles of bodies that have to be shoved aside to make room for him. Already pillaged and stripped naked, "ces pouvres gens nudz" piled next to where the duke eats wait to become a meal for wolves and vultures. The archer, from the duke's own corps, remains unrecognized even though Commynes reputes him "fort renommé." The reader learns his name not on account of heroic deeds but because he was found alive in a pile of cadavers. Louis, *roi thaumaturge*, heals the scrofulous. Charles, his rival, revives the (almost) dead – after clearing them out of his way. Instead of Eucharistic wine, Charles uses herbal tea to achieve miracles. The moment teeters between burlesque and tragedy. Its irony plays on the sacrality of an elected, anointed body (royal or holy), and the profanity of human flesh.

Throughout his account of Montlhéry, Commynes underscores his own presence as a witness to events. He points to each mark on Charles's body, and explains its origin: the pike in the stomach and the sword that catches him on the neck, leaving a lifelong scar. The narrator comes forward to claim his experience. Soutet and Thomasset observe,

Nous ne ferons qu'entrevoir cette apparition d'un moi qui serait antérieur à tous les autres, moi passif et inapte à la lecture de l'événement. Il cède immédiatement la place à *l'observateur et à l'interlocuteur privilégié*. L'habilité de Commynes consiste très souvent à passer sans transition des faits d'observation aux faits qui relèvent de *l'information*. Mais la technique est sûre pour signaler la présence qui réordonne, authentifie, justifie *a posteriori* une suite d'événements. Que la bavière de Charles le Téméraire tombe, parce qu'elle était mal attachée, Commynes est présent pour l'attester – "et luy avoye veu cheoir" – événement qui ne trouve sa signification que dans la carrière malheureuse du prince.[6]

Soutet and Thomasset mean that Charles's recklessness at Montlhéry foreshadows the reckless obstinacy of his final campaigns. In my own reading, the duke's fallen helmet finds a slightly different retrospective significance. The *enseigne* on Charles's neck serves as an index of a single event (the battle), but it also performs a more complex representative function as a symbol of the grandeur and decadence which follow. The sign cut into the duke's body begins a process of textualization, a process through which Charles's flesh becomes the legible surface on which history is written.

I Did Not See Him Fall

The end of Charles the Bold's ambitions came on a bitterly cold day in January 1477. News of the duke's defeat outside Nancy reached Louis XI swiftly, but the first letters could not say where he was. There were rumours he had fled and was still alive. It took several more days to confirm Charles's death. The victorious René de Lorraine sent a small search party out onto the battlefield to look for him. The duke's body, trampled and pillaged, lay naked and anonymous. Dogs or wolves had eaten away part of his face, and the mutilated corpse had to be pried free from the frozen mud.[7]

In the *Mémoires*, Commynes explicitly says he does not want to talk about the way Charles died. "Y mourut sur le champ ledict duc de Bourgongne. Et ne veulx point parler de la maniere, pour ce que je n'y estoie point" (The Duke of Burgundy died there on the field. I don't want to talk at all about how, because I wasn't there [355]).[8] The structure of his narrative forcefully enacts this avowed resistance. At the brink of relating how Charles was defeated in battle, Commynes postpones that pivotal event to describe a naively conceived trip by the Portuguese king. He then moves from a concise report on Charles's defeat and death, to a meditation on a pendant the duke used to wear, and back to the tense ambiance at Louis XI's court, before finally arriving at his account of how the news arrived that Charles's body had been found.

Like his description of Montlhéry, Commynes's portrayal of the duke's death is both abstract and cinematographic. Both episodes describe what the mind's eye sees, but one emerges from the recollection of experience, while the other takes shape out of imagining. In the passage below describing Charles's defeat, Commynes's narration progresses through a series of displaced and unresolved viewpoints, moving in and out of "close-up." (Note that Commynes writes the date of 1476, based on a year beginning and ending at Easter; *nouveau style*, the year was 1477.)

> Assembléz qu'i furent les deux armees, la sienne qui ja avoit esté descon-
> ficte par deux foiz, et qui estoient peu de gens et mal empoint, furent in-
> continent tournéz en desconfiture et tous mors ou en fuyte. Largement se
> saulverent; le demeurant y fut mors ou prins, et entre aultres y mourut sur
> le champ ledict duc de Bourgongne. Et ne veulx point parler de la maniere,
> pour ce que je n'y estoie point; mais m'a esté compté de la mort dudict duc
> par ceulx qui le veirent porter par terre et ne le peurent secourir parce
> qu'ilz estoient prisonniers; mais a leur veue ne fut point tué, mais par une
> grande foulle de gens qui y survindrent, qui le tuerent et le despoullerent
> en la grand troupe, sans le congnoistre. Et fut ladicte bataille le cinquiesme
> jour de janvier l'an M CCCC LXXVI, veille des Roys. (355)

> [When the two armies came together, his, which had already been
> defeated twice, and which was made up of a few, poorly equipped men,
> was immediately defeated and scattered and everyone in it killed or
> routed. Many ran away; the rest were killed or captured there, and
> among others, the Duke of Burgundy died there on the field. I don't want
> to talk at all about how, because I wasn't there; but the duke's death was
> told to me by those who saw him fall to the ground and who could not
> help him because they were prisoners; he wasn't killed while they were
> watching, but rather by a great surge of men who came afterward, who
> killed him and stripped him along with everyone else, without recogniz-
> ing him. And this happened on the fifth day of January in the year 147[7],
> on the eve of the Epiphany.]

When Commynes talks about Charles's helmet-piece at Montlhéry, he says outright, "I saw it fall." His description of Charles's defeat at Nancy reverses this witnessing position. The narrator recuses himself from every personal responsibility. About Nancy he says, "I didn't see him fall. I don't want to talk about it. I wasn't there; I didn't see; I can't say." The negation is forceful; each time he repeats, "ne ... point." Paradoxically, although there is not a single visual description of surface, arrangement, or landscape in these sentences, the effect is grippingly cinematic. This effect comes from the relay of interposed gazes through which Commynes frames Charles's fall for the reader. The reader sees through the eyes of those who watched the duke fall down from his horse, and then from a distance saw the mob that swarmed over the fallen. We begin to realize that this distanced gaze is also the site of a conflict. The scene Commynes gives his reader depicts a group of people watching powerless. "I didn't see him fall," he says in effect. "Other people saw it," he says, "but they couldn't help him, either." There is something in his words that evokes the paralysis of a dream state. The prisoners' report only concerns seeing him fall. Those who come and strip his body do not recognize him. The phrases are as desolate as the duke's own body gripped by the icy mud. There are, in fact, no witnesses to Charles's death in Commynes's account. No one sees him die.

The long breath of this passage exhales fully on the date, "eve of the Epiphany." Immediately, the narrator draws a new breath, and launches into a sustained reflection on princely houses, moral conduct, and taxes, expounding at length on good governance and divine equilibrium. His narrative cuts away from the passages just cited about Charles the Bold's death into a sweeping panorama of history as a long series of falls (359). The articulation which joins the individual (his)story that is Charles's death and the immense vision of limitless human striving into which the narrator now propels himself pivots on the recollection of a *signet* the duke once wore. This remembrance cuts across time and space, from Nancy to Milan to Burgundy, and from the naked bodies strewn on an open expanse of muddy field to the architecturally defined interiors of court life, before landing again in the moment of telling. We find ourselves caught in the dissonance and unresolved harmonies between images.[9]

A leur veue ne fut point tué, mais par une grande foulle de gens qui y survindrent, qui le tuerent et le despoullerent en la grand troupe, sans le congnoistre. Et fut ladicte bataille le cinquiesme jour de janvier l'an M CCCC LXXVI, veille des Roys.

J'ay depuis veu ung signet a Millan, que maintes foyz avoye veu pendre a son pourpoint, qui estoit ung aneau, et y avoit ung feuzil entaillé en ung camayeu, ou estoient ses armes; lequel fut vendu pour deux ducatz audict lieu de Millan. Celluy qui luy ousta luy fut mauvais varlet de chambre. Je l'ay veu maintes foiz habiller et deshabiller en grand reverence, et de grans; et a ceste derniere heure luy estoient passees ses honneurs. Et perit luy et sa maison comme j'ay dict, au lieu ou il avoit par avarice consenti de bailler le connestable, et peu de temps aprés. Dieu luy vueille pardonner ses pechéz! (355–6; punctuation slightly altered)

[He wasn't killed while they were watching, but rather by a great surge of men who came afterward, who killed him and stripped him along with everyone else, without recognizing him. And this happened on the fifth day of January in the year 147[7], on the eve of the Epiphany.

I have since seen a small pendant in Milan, which I had many times seen hang from his doublet, which was in the form of a lamb, and it had a briquet carved in cameo showing his arms; this was sold for two ducats there in Milan. Whoever stripped it from him was a bad chamber valet. Many times I watched him dressed and undressed in great reverence and by important men; and at this final hour he received no honours. He and his house perished like I said, on the spot where he had consented out of avarice to hand over the *connétable*, and not long afterward. May God forgive his sins!]

Commynes was long familiar with this pendant when he was the duke's companion. He saw it again after the duke's death, and remembers both moments now. Twice he now confesses his own role as a witness to this pendant. In answer to the callous, molesting hands of those who strip dead bodies naked on the battlefield, Commynes remembers gestures of caressing reverence. He remembers the duke's whole and regal body adorned with the insignia (the *enseignes*) of his glory.[10] Recoiling from the cosmic obscenity of the duke's final nakedness, Commynes remembers the ritualized intimacy of clothing his living body. Human touch provides the common thread between these two images of desolation and privilege. Rhetorical, political, and theological topoi condition Commynes's reflections, yet they also possess a powerful lyric quality. Commynes addresses his reader directly. Having placed every obstacle between himself and seeing Charles die, Commynes now speaks to us, urgently and without veils, of the pleasure he once felt at watching others pay homage to the duke's body, at watching him be dressed, and, though he does not say so outright, perhaps at dressing Charles with his own hands.

The cameo *signet* in which Commynes lodges the whole tragedy of the house of Burgundy carries the *enseigne* of the Order of the Golden Fleece, the chivalric order founded by Charles's father in 1430. This symbol of the luxury and beauty of Charles's court is sold for two ducats. The difference between the priceless value of the duke's *signet* and its tawdry price neatly signifies the devastation wrought. Commynes subtly places reading and literature at the root of Charles's obstinate military pursuits, and hence of his self-destruction.[11] Indeed, Duke Philip's naming the Order of the Golden Fleece after the memory of Jason is itself a culturally modulated act of emulation towards a literary hero, one that set a prescriptive agenda for his son. As for Charles, "il desiroit grand gloire, qui estoit ce qui le mectoit plus en ses guerres que nulle autre chose, et eust bien voulu ressembler a ses anciens princes, dont il a esté tant parlé aprés leur mort" (he desired great glory, which was, more than any other thing, what caused him to go to war, and he would well have liked to resemble those ancient princes, who have been so talked about after their deaths [357]). The "anciens princes" Commynes alludes to include Caesar and Alexander. Charles loved to listen as tales of their deeds were read to him night after night.[12] The passage again recalls the interdependence of textuality, spectrality, and desire. Charles longs to resemble the heroes in one kind of narrative, but ambition unseats him.

Earlier in the *Mémoires*, Commynes says that reading histories helps keep a prince from being "ignorant" (121) and "peu entendu" (122). "Dieu ne peult envoyer plus grand playe en ung pays que d'un prince peu entendu, car de la procedent tous aultres maulx. Premier en vient division et guerre ... Et de ceste division procede la famyne et mortalité et les aultres maulx qui deppendent de la guerre" (God cannot send worse suffering on a people than a prince who is unwise, because all other evils come from that one. First come disputes and war ... And from those rifts come famine and plague and the other evils that follow war [122–3]). But the duke has gotten grandiose ideas in his head from listening to the fantastic exploits of ancient princes. Commynes suggests that one can be a bad reader, and not know how to read between the lines of genre and convention. He warns that a book full of illustrious deeds and fancy illustrations is alluring, but also potentially dangerous. Desiring to be like the hero of a book, Charles has brought war, famine, and division to his people, and destroyed his own house.[13] Books have made him "peu entendu" instead of "lettré." Through his misreading he comes to be the hero in a different kind of narrative. The lost *signet* of the Golden Fleece thus further becomes an *enseigne* of reading and desire as well, and an admonition against the hunger of impossible ambitions.

The Very Wicked Count of Campobasso

My reading of the way that Commynes represents (and silences) Charles's death in the *Mémoires* requires that we take a detour through the *Mémoires* and then through two other texts. This peregrination will take us into the ways that what it is impossible to say nonetheless inhabits what is said.

Commynes offers both cosmic and proximate causes for Charles's death. The cosmic cause is the avarice that made him hand the two-timing *connétable* de Saint-Pol over to Louis XI, against his promise and knowing that the *connétable* would be killed. (We will return to the *connétable* in chapter 6.) The proximate cause of Charles's death lies in the treachery of Cola di Monforte, "conte de Campobasse, du royaulme de Naples, partissant de la maison d'Anjou, homme de tres mauvaise foy et tres perilleux" (Count of Campobasso, from the kingdom of Naples, a partisan of the house of Anjou, a man of very bad faith and very dangerous [244]).[14] Campobasso, says Commynes, was the agent of God's vengeance against Charles; Charles dies in the same spot where two years previously he had betrayed Saint-Pol.

If there is a single, dastardly villain in the *Mémoires*, it is Campobasso. The *Mémoires*' treatment of Campobasso is unsettled and unsettling from the outset, and for reasons that can be only partially explained away. Commynes mentions Campobasso repeatedly, and just as the Gospels do with Judas, each time Commynes reminds the reader of the danger he represents. Campobasso is a landless outcast, "tres mauvais pour son maistre" (very bad for his master [309]). Almost as soon as he enters Charles's service, "commença a machiner la mort de son maistre, comme j'ay desja dict, et continua jusques a celle heure dont j'ay parlé" (he began to engineer the death of his master, like I said before, and he continued up to the time I spoke about [342]). After several unsuccessful attempts to find a buyer for his treachery, Campobasso finally reaches an agreement with René de Lorraine.[15]

While Campobasso is going back and forth negotiating with René, however, it happens that Charles catches a group of men from his camp trying to sneak outside messages into the besieged city. Charles wants to hang the men, claiming that they are "dignes de mort par les droictz de la guerre" (deserving of death by the laws of war [343]). One of them, Siffredo [Siffron] dei Baschi, pleads to be given an audience with Charles, promising to tell him a secret that "qu'il ne v{o}uldroit pour une duchié qu'il ne le sceust" (he wouldn't want him to go without knowing for a duchy [344]). Charles's men have pity on the captive, and want the duke to grant his request. Only Campobasso, says Commynes, remained unmoved. Campobasso is convinced that Siffredo means to expose him to Charles as the traitor he has seen in René's camp, and so he snarls that the prisoner is just trying to weasel out of a tight spot. While all of Charles's men plead for mercy on his behalf, Campobasso alone presses the duke to hang the man without delay. "Et finablement ledict Siffron fut pendu, qui fut au grand prejudice dudict duc de Bourgongne" (Finally this Siffredo was hanged, which was to the great disadvantage of the Duke of Burgundy [344]). Charles hangs Siffredo dei Baschi and assures his own death, all because he listens to the treacherous Campobasso's evil counsel.

Commynes weaves a dramatic story around Campobasso, but his account drags behind it a train of earnest debate. The thing is, only Commynes attacks Campobasso in quite this way.[16] For hundreds of years, Commynes's portrait of Campobasso was taken at face value. Then in the 1930s, Benedetto Croce demonstrated that Commynes's narrative maligns Campobasso without cause.[17] His study set in motion a revised examination of the case which has still not been resolved.[18] Commynes's narrative account of Campobasso's betrayal appears in a very different light when it is situated within a larger constellation of texts. On the following pages I will immerse myself in the silence of things Commynes does not say in the *Mémoires*. In doing so I will take risks with the limits of knowledge and interpretation.

The *Chronique de Lorraine*: The Heroic Campobasso

A very different version of what happens between Campobasso, Charles, and the captured Siffredo dei Baschi appears in the *Chronique de Lorraine*.[19] The Lorraine chronicler spins a picturesque, pathetic account of heroic suffering and rightful vengeance around the "bon maistre d'hostel Chiffron [Siffron, Siffredo]" that turns Commynes's execration of Campobasso on its head.[20] In the *Chronique de Lorraine*, Campobasso is just as responsible for arranging the circumstances of Charles's death, but he is no traitor.

The *Chronique de Lorraine* shares the same cast of characters and the same premise as the *Mémoires*: Charles captures dei Baschi and wants to hang him. The Lorraine chronicle's episode begins when the small towns all around the besieged city of Nancy send out messengers to get help for René (René II d'Anjou, Duke of Lorraine).[21] Siffredo, who "xv jours avoit que les fièbvres trembloit" (has been shaking with fever for two weeks), has the idea to sneak into the city of Nancy and, "comme un léal serviteur" (like a loyal servitor), cheer the siege victims with news that help is on the way.[22] Slower and weaker than his healthy companions, Siffredo alone gets caught and is brought to Charles. Despite every plea from the duke's own men, Charles "jura sainct Georges que incontinent pendu seroit" (swore by Saint George that he would be hanged right away).[23] Up to this point, the *Mémoires* and the *Chronique de Lorraine* are in alignment, but listen to how the Lorraine chronicler presents Campobasso's intervention.

> Por prières ne pour requeste, pitié de luy ne volt [le duc] avoir. Dict le comte de Campebese: Monsieur, il a faict comme léal serviteur; si un de nous estoit prins, en vous servant {et} on nous pendoit, vous ne seriez pas content, je vous certiffie que se morir le faictes, de vos gens mourront pour luy. Li duc, quand il veit que le comte assy fièrement parloit, le duc airmé estoit, en ses mains ses gantelets avoit, haussit la main, à comte donna un revers; le comte plus ne dict mot, ne tous les altres assy.[24]

> [Neither prayers nor entreaties could move the duke to pity for him [Siffredo]. Said the Count of Campobasso: "Monsieur, he acted as a loyal servitor; if one of us was caught while serving you and they hanged us, you wouldn't be happy, I promise you that if you have him killed, your men will die for him." The duke saw that the count was speaking quite proudly; the duke was armed, he had armoured gloves on his hands; he raised his hand and struck the count across the face; the count said not a word more, nor any of the others, either.]

After striking Campobasso, Charles has Siffredo hanged pre-emptively – although not so pre-emptively that the narrator cannot fit a pitiful soliloquy into his mouth. One cannot help but be charmed by the Lorraine chronicler's nostalgia and literary ambition. After all, his characters are not Frankish vassals and lords, but rather wage-driven Swiss mercenaries and Italian condottieri. The Lorraine chronicler restores some of the old polish to his material. For his betrayal scene, Campobasso delivers a speech in direct discourse, in which he recounts how he lost his lands in Sicily for being a good servant to René's predecessors, and asks to keep the lands received from Charles in exchange for delivering the duke to him.

Let us stay with the *Chronique de Lorraine* a moment longer since what happens next puts into play textuality, inscription, and the semiotics of the (dead) body. Siffredo's body is returned to Nancy and buried. The burghers of Nancy avenge themselves by hanging one of their Burgundian prisoners. The situation escalates until the Lorraine camp hangs all their Burgundian prisoners, more than 120 of them. To be sure the point is clear, they put a tag around each dead man's arm, saying "NOUS MOURONS POR LA MORT DU MAISTRE D'HOSTEL CHIFFRON."[25] The connection between writing and body is reinforced at the siege's end, when the starved burghers line up the bones of the animals they have eaten on the town square, all the way down to the last rat. These bones become legible signs through which René reads the record of their sufferings.[26]

Returning now to Campobasso as he appears in both the *Mémoires* and the *Chronique de Lorraine*, we can begin to compare these two contrasting versions of a single episode. Both Commynes and the Lorraine chronicler present what is basically a set piece in which a ruler receives political counsel. Although he does not use any fancy Latin words to say so, the *Chronique de Lorraine*'s virtuous Campobasso warns Charles that he is about to breach *ius gentium*. If he kills dei Baschi, he crosses into a lawless savagery. Commynes, also, alludes to the "laws of war," the practices of different peoples, and to what constitutes cruelty (343).[27] Each version centres on an implicit debate about the divide between justice and violence, and each turns on Campobasso's persuasive talents. In Commynes's version, however, there are no good guys. Campobasso argues furiously against mercy, and wants to have a man killed to protect his own planned crimes. Charles, who was known for his tendency to solicit and then disregard sound advice, here ignores every plea for mercy and heeds the cruelest words spoken.[28] Not even Siffredo dei Baschi is above reproach. Commynes says that dei Baschi is the middleman in Campobasso's negotations with René, pinpointing him as, "Sifron, lequel conduisoit tous les marchéz dudict conte avecques le duc de Lorraine" (Siffredo, who handled all the count's negotiations with the Duke of Lorraine [343]). Commynes's Siffredo promises Charles information worth a whole duchy, information which Campobasso is afraid will expose his plotting against the duke. But there is a further nuance to this offer; if dei Baschi reveals Campobasso's plans, he also extends the siege. Commynes's Siffredo eagerly offers to betray his companions and prolong a whole city's suffering in order to save his own life. In stark contrast, the Lorraine chronicler's Siffredo dei Baschi is a loyal burgher and folkloric hero. Not even fever can keep him from coming to the aid of his compatriots. In the *Mémoires*, Campobasso is trying to conceal a betrayal which has already taken place. In the *Chronique de Lorraine*, the noble and compassionate Campobasso, who "poinct oblyé n'avoit la buffe que li duc donnée luy avoit" (had not at all forgotten the blow the duke had given him), approaches René de Lorraine as a direct result of the duke's violence.[29] Once Charles strikes Campobasso across the face with his chain mail glove, he has severed the obligation between them symbolically, and perhaps legally also.

There is one further and very important inverted resemblance between the *Mémoires* and the *Chronique de Lorraine*. Irony is the dominant trope in each. Using a turn of phrase that recurs at pivotal moments throughout his history, Commynes writes that if Charles had listened to Siffredo dei Baschi, he might still be alive and his dynasty thriving. "Luy eust myeulx vallu n'avoir esté si cruel et humaynement ouy ce gentil homme; et par aventure, que s'i l'eust faict, qu'il fust encores en vie et sa maison entiere et de beaucop acreue" (It would have been better for him to not be so cruel and to have humanely listened to that gentleman; and maybe, if he had done so, he would still be alive and his dynasty whole and greatly strengthened [344]). The words that the *Lorraine* Campobasso speaks to Charles in counsel voice the same wisdom in a prophetic tone: "I promise you that if you have him killed, your men will die for him." The duke's slap creates irony where there had been none. Campobasso intends only to safeguard the duke's men; instead his words become an omen of the duke's own imminent death. Irony makes interpretation possible.

"La Tête Bottée"

The contrast between these two stories about Campobasso's betrayal turns out to be the keyhole through which we can see something much larger. The story the *Chronique de Lorraine* tells about Campobasso struck across the face resembles a gossipy story told about Commynes himself from the earliest days of his service to Charles, when Charles was still Count of Charolais. The story shows up in print for the first time in the sixteenth century, and has followed Commynes's reputation ever since. By the time that Antoine Le Pippre's *Intentions morales, civiles et militaires* was published in Antwerp in 1625, its author was able to present no fewer than five versions, of which I cite only one below.

> Ce que j'ay ouy conter autrement, avec plus d'apparence, à un ancien gentilhomme qui disoit de l'avoir aprins de son père: à sçavoir que, retournant un jour de la chasse fort fatigué et las, il [Commynes] s'endormit en la chambre, demy courbé et appuyé sur le lict du comte qui l'y surprint; de

quoy messire Philippe tout honteux se cuyda excuser, quand le comte luy dict: "Non, non, demeure: je ne veux pas que tu bouges; mais tu n'es pas à ton aise avec tes bottes, car il faut que je te les oste." Et, demy par force, et jaçoit que l'autre contesta au contraire, il le débotta; puis, prenant les bottes, luy en donna contre la teste, avec ceste reproches: "Va, coquart, qui permis à ton souverain te débotter."[30]

[Which story I heard told otherwise, with a greater semblance of truth, from an old gentleman who said he had learned it from his father: to wit, that returning one day from hunting very tired and worn out, Commynes fell asleep in [Charles's] chamber, half slumped over and propped up against the bed of the count, who caught him there, for which monsieur Philippe all ashamed tried to excuse himself, when the count said to him: "No, no, stay: I don't want you to move; but you're not comfortable with those boots on, I have to take them off you." And, half by force, and despite the other's protest to the contrary, he unbooted him; then, taking the boots, hit him across the head with them, with this reproach: "Get out, knave, who let your sovereign take off your boots."]

For this reason, so the story goes, Commynes was known as the "tête bottée." Although this retelling of the tale does not do so, other versions Le Pippre recounts specifically mention the spurs attached to the boot. The "tête bottée" story offers the same exculpatory motivation for Commynes's betrayal as the Lorraine chronicler advances to explain Campobasso's "betrayal": Charles hit him.[31] Symmetrical narratives portray Charles striking both Campobasso and Commynes across the face.

The flamboyance in this and other versions of Commynes's "tête bottée" give it a fictional aura. This apocryphal colour was not lost on those who passed it on. "I neither reject this little story as unbelievable, nor do I guarantee it as true" (Quam narratiunculam neque ut incredibilem respuo, neque ut certam assevero), says Jacques Marchant, apparently the first to include it in his published history.[32] Le Pippre does not want to pass judgment on the reliability of his story, but he is firm in asserting that Commynes was taunted with the nickname "la tête bottée." "Si est-il certain que l'on en fit, à son blasme et dérision, une chanson en la cour qui lors estoit en ceste ville de Lille."[33] If Le Pippre then says that Commynes was the butt of mockery at Lille with such confidence, I find it likely that he knew these songs directly, perhaps from sources which have since been lost. Maybe Le Pippre did not think graffiti tags or rondeaux fitting material to include among the lofty subjects of his volume. Despite the variations between them, the different versions of the "tête bottée" display an admirable coherence. The story's persistence; its consonance with numerous other, documented reports of Charles's violence towards his servitors; its consistent association with Commynes and Commynes alone; and the clarity of its events as judged against the generic plots of popular legend all provide additional reasons to intuit its roots in an event that actually took place. However exuberantly apocryphal the "tête bottée" story may first sound, it has every trapping of truth.

Despite many reasons to believe in its veracity, there is something more important than knowing whether or not the "tête bottée" story is objectively true. It is more important to grasp an ensemble of elements circulating around Commynes in their textual truth and, going further, to understand how they function together. The coincidence between Commynes's calumny of Campobasso as a traitor, and his erasure of a story in counterpoint to one told about his own betrayal is glaring. Jean Dufournet spotlighted this similarity in his *La Destruction des mythes dans les* Mémoires *de Philippe de Commynes*.[34] There he stated that Commynes's hostility towards Campobasso derives from transferred hostility towards a man he perceives as his own double. "L'un et l'autre auraient été souffletés par le duc, et humiliés publiquement. Commynes ne dit mot de la gifle qu'aurait reçue le condotierre, et que signale la *Chronique de Lorraine*."[35] Dufournet interprets this silence as part of Commynes's effort to distance himself from someone whose treachery was well known, and with whom, Dufournet claims, Commynes already felt too identified, "tous deux ayant subi les effets de la violence aveugle de leur maître."[36] He then suggests that "en Campobasso, Commynes découvrait le double haï de son propre personnage."[37] I agree with the hypothesis that, learning of the scene that played out in Charles's counsel over the fate of Siffredo dei Baschi, Commynes felt the identification Dufournet suggests. In my reading, however, this identification is of a different nature, dominated by shame, and strictly speaking, entirely distinct from the act of betrayal with which Dufournet identifies it.[38]

Charles's temper was notorious. Richard Vaughan introduces his portrait of the duke saying, "Certain traits of character emerge prominently from the welter of contemporary evidence. He was violent and cruel."[39] According to Richard Walsh, there is no independent second source for the *Chronique de Lorraine*'s story about Campobasso and Siffredo dei

Baschi.[40] Out of all the many sources that identify Campobasso's betrayal, only the *Chronique de Lorraine* and Commynes include the Siffredo dei Baschi episode. Commynes's role at the head of Louis's intelligence operations guarantee that he was informed, in one way or another, not just about events, but also about personalities and dramas at Charles's council. The powerful symmetry between Commynes's account of the Siffredo dei Baschi episode and the version in the *Chronique de Lorraine* dramatically strengthens the likelihood that such a scene took place.[41] The key to this ciphered, inverted symmetry lies in the blow that Charles gives Campobasso with his heavy glove, because this is the element that disrupts their symmetry.

In the *Chronique de Lorraine*'s story about Campobasso, the slap takes place during a moment of counsel. It has a clear political context and bolsters two points made repeatedly about the duke: he refused to listen to anyone else's opinion and he was prone to outbursts of violence. The glove symbolizes contractual obligation and loyalty. Charles does violence to that bond when he strikes his condottiere. A political reading, enriched by the many tropes that surround rhetoric, counsel, and the gages of feudal vows, satisfies. Commynes's humiliation in the "tête bottée" story takes place against a background of homosocial privilege, in private chambers, on a bed. The legend presents the signifying image of a relationship at its limits, and of the limits of a relationship. Whether these limits are of intimacy between lord and servitor (Commynes lies down on the duke's bed) or of a power relation hollowed out by its own performance of domination and submission (Charles abases himself and then humiliates Commynes) is not as easy to say. Where the glove has feudal, political overtones, the boot has intimate, sexual ones. Was there a sadomasochistic element to the relations between the teenaged or twenty-something Commynes and his idolized lord?

Commynes's description of Péronne includes the mention, "j'estoie encores avec ledict duc et le servoye de chambellan et congnoissoye en sa chambre quant je voulloye" (I was still with the duke and I served as his chamberlain, and I was as familiar in his room as I wished [125]). The contemporary Flemish monk Adrien de But described Commynes as Charles's "most secret secretary" (secretissimus secretarius ducis Karoli).[42] Richard Walsh has recently published a letter in which a Milanese ambassador reports a letter of August 1472 from Charles confiding that "era fugito … el più caro et secreto creato ch'el havesse" (the dearest and most private servitor that he had … had run away).[43] I have translated the word "creato" used to describe Commynes with the sober "servitor," but the word also means someone cherished, a political pro-tégé, or even a son.[44] Where Charles's father, Philip the Good, was an incorrigible ladies' man, Charles seems to have dreaded the company of women, even including his own wife, with whom he spent only a couple weeks in 1473 and 1474, and saw for only a few days during the final two years of his life.[45] In November 1470, a nobleman named Jean de Chassa fled Charles's court; the duke accused de Chassa of plotting to assassinate him with poison. De Chassa countered with a statement alleging he had preferred to abandon everything ("ai trop mieux aimé laisser tous les biens, Terres & Seigneuries") rather than continue to endure the duke's sexual advances ("les très-viles, très-énormes & de-shonnestes choses, que ledit Charles de Bourgogne, lorsque j'étois de-vers lui fréquentoit & commettoit contre Dieu, contre nature & contre nostre Loi; en quoi il m'a voulu attraire & faire condescendre d'en user avec lui").[46] How far or how deep did the relationship between Charles and Commynes go? Commynes was appointed chamberlain in January 1468; at the time, he would have been between twenty and twenty-three years old.[47] After reprinting de Chassa's statement, Lenglet Dufresnoy imagines fear of sexual assault as Commynes's first motive for leaving Burgundy, "sur-tout à l'âge qu'avoit alors Comines, & avec la familiarité où il vivoit auprès de ce Prince."[48]

Let us dare for a moment to read with empathy. There is no mention of the physical consequence of Charles's violence on Campobasso's body in the *Chronique de Lorraine*. Not so with Commynes: Le Pippre and others mention the cuts and bruises he suffered at Charles's hands. At least one later author specifically alludes to his bloody, disfigured face. Although Charles strikes his favourite behind closed doors, his violence leaves an enduring sign (*enseigne*) on Commynes's visage. As Commynes moves through the court, this legible trace of his story moves with him. His body becomes the first text through which the tale is disseminated. The gash on his face is both the index of a particular event (Charles struck him) and the symbol of something much more difficult to pin down: the intimate and explosive relationship between Charles and "el più caro et secreto creato ch'el havesse."[49] Le Pippre assures us that a popular song was sung in Lille about the "tête bottée." In a moment we realize that the subject that has court and town singing amounts to the taunt that Commynes is Charles's "bitch." The tale changes from a bit of dubious salon trivia to the trace – the *enseigne* – of a spectacular abjec-tion. We return again to the spectral, remembered body, on which we see the stinging red mark across each man's face. If we dare or if we are able, we might imagine the way a cheek burns. We might feel the *enseigne* of where the duke's blow landed, a burning mark that can be seen, read, and interpreted by all around us.

By allowing myself to bring empathy and imagination into the process of interpreting I do not mean to imply belief in a recoverable real but rather the opposite: the importance of fiction and the fictional to our apprehension of truth. The *enseigne* is the sign through which the text bears witness to both memory and desire. I do not mean to suggest that the "tête bottée" incident is a hidden secret which explains Commynes's departure from Charles's court. Nor, I emphasize, do I mean to reduce Commynes's hostility towards Campobasso to an act of displaced self-hatred. My point is that there is a significance and a pattern to the things Commynes silences. These narratives have in common a preoccupation with marking violence and the male body. They bear witness to an obstacle, a site of resistance, within a relation, past and "real" or remembered and fantasized.

Let us return to the paradigmatic scene of contact between the two bodies of *seigneur* and servitor. The contract of loyalty between them is not an abstraction; it is an obligation of the body. It is the obligation to be close by on a battlefield when cavalry is charging, the privilege of sleeping in the same room, the ritualized banality of taking off a shoe. To strike someone – to hit them across the face – is also an intense physical contact: an abrupt way of touching another body. Campobasso bears the brunt of a virulence found nowhere else in the *Mémoires*. I would suggest that what makes the condotierre so intolerable is something apart from politics, money, social hierarchy, landlessness, or even betrayal. I submit that the intolerable lies in the fantasized spectacle of Charles's violence against Campobasso. This hypothesis calls on us to return again to seeing and being seen, and to the question of the legibility of the human body as a textual surface. The *enseigne* that unites the two figures, and that defines the relation between each man and Charles, lies in the mark left on the face of a man struck with a spurred boot or a pair of metal gloves.

Enseignes: What History Writes on the Body

In the immediate aftermath of the battle at Nancy, it was not at all clear what had become of Charles the Bold. The first letters came swiftly, "mais nul n'accertenoit, par les premieres, de la mort, mais aulcuns disoient que on l'avoit veu fouyr et qu'il s'estoit sauvé" (but none, among the first letters, gave assurances of his death, but rather some said that he had been seen to flee, and that he had escaped [360–1]).[50] After a few days, Louis XI sent Commynes on a mission to find information. "Nous n'eusmes point faict demye journee que nous rencontrasmes ung messaige, a qui nous feismes bailler ses lectres, qui contenoient comme ledict duc avoit esté trouvé entre les mors par un paige ytalian et par son medicin appellé maistre Louppe" (We had not gone even half a day when we encountered a messenger whom we made hand over his letters; these contained how the duke had been found among the dead by an Italian page and by his doctor named Master Louppe [363]). Commynes says nothing about persistent rumours that the duke was alive and plotting his return.[51] He says nothing about the circumstances in which Charles was found, and nothing about his burial. Other sources are more forthcoming.[52]

Here is the *Chronique de Lorraine* on the search for Charles's body:

> Tous les morts estoient tout nuds et tout engealés, à peine les pouvoit-on connoistre. Le paige véant deçà et delà, bien treuvoit de puissants gens et des grands et des petits, blancs comme neige ... Le paige commencea à chercher, tous les retornoient ce que dessus, dessoubs, les ungs avoient le dos dessus, les altres le ventre dessoubs. Entre les altres treuva Monsieur de Bourgoigne. – Hélas! vecy mon bon seigneur et maistre.[53]

> [All the dead were completely naked and completely frozen; they were barely recognizable. The page looking here and there found powerful men and great ones and humble ones, [all] white like snow ... The page began to search, turning them all over; some had their backs up, others their stomachs down [*sic*]. He found Monsieur de Bourgogne with the others. – Alas! Here is my good lord and master.]

Jean de Roye gives the following description of the body they found:

> Fut icellui page mené à grant compaignie de gens de guerre au lieu où ledit de Bourgongne gisoit mort et tout nu. Et, en icellui lieu, le mardi ensuivant de ladicte bataille, au matin, ledit page monstra clerement ledit de Bourgongne mort et tout nu, et environ lui xiiii {cens} hommes tous nuz, les ungs assez loings des autres. Et avoit ledit duc de Bourgongne ung cop d'un baston nommé halebarde à ung costé du milieu de la teste par dessus l'oreille jusques aux dens, ung cop de pique au travers des cuisses et ung autre cop de pique par le fondement. Et, fut congneu manifestement que

c'estoit ledit de Bourgongne à six choses: la première et la principale fut aux dens de dessus, lesquelles il avoit autrefois perdues par une cheute; la seconde fut d'une cicatrice à cause de la plaie qu'il eut à la rencontre de Montlehery en la gorge, en la partie dextre; la tierce, à ses grans ongles qu'il portoit plus que nul autre homme de sa court ne autre personne; la quarte fut d'une plaie qu'il avoit en une espaule à cause d'une escharboucle que autrefoiz y avoit eue; la cinquiesme fut à une fistule qu'il avoit au bas du ventre en la penillere du costé dextre; et la sixiesme fut d'un ongle qu'il avoit retrait en l'orteil du pié senestre. Et, ausdictes enseignes donna son jugement pour tout vray ung sien médecin portugalois nommé maistre Mathieu, que c'estoit ledit de Bourgongne son maistre; et aussi le dirent pareillement ses varletz de chambre, le grant bastard, messire Olivier de la Marche, son chappellain, et plusieurs autres de ses gens prisonniers dudit Monseigneur de Lorraine.[54]

[The page was brought in a great company of soldiers to the place where the Duke of Burgundy was lying dead and utterly naked. And in that place, the Tuesday following the battle, in the morning, the page pointed out clearly the Duke of Burgundy dead and utterly naked, and round him fourteen [hundred] men all naked, some a good distance from the others. And the Duke of Burgundy had a blow from a pike called a halberd on one side from the middle of his head above the ear to the teeth, a blow from a pike across his thighs and another blow from a pike from the backside. And it was known certainly that it was the Duke of Burgundy from six things; the first and the principle were his upper teeth, which he had previously lost in a fall; the second was a scar from the wound he received at Montlhéry on his throat, on the right side; the third, his long fingernails, which he wore longer than any other man at his court or than any other person; the fourth was a wound that he had in one shoulder because of a carbuncle [pustule] he had once had there; the fifth was a fistula which he had at the base of his abdomen in his groin on the right side; and the sixth was an ingrown toenail he had on his left foot. And, by these signs a Portuguese doctor of his named Master Matthew gave his utterly truthful judgment that this was his master the [Duke of] Burgundy; and his chamber valets, the Grand Bâtard [Antoine de Bourgogne], Messire Olivier de La Marche, his chaplain, and several others who were prisoners of Monseigneur de Lorraine made the same statement.]

When he introduces the list of identifying traits on Charles's body, de Roye calls them things ("choses"), but when he comes to establishing the link between these marks and knowing that this cadaver is indeed Charles, he returns to the word "sign" – the Portuguese doctor recognizes him "ausdictes enseignes." Those closest to Charles recognized his mangled and partially faceless body by its strangely long fingernails and missing teeth, by an abcess and an ingrown toenail, by a fistula in the groin area, and by the scar Charles received at Montlhéry when his helmet-piece fell. These were the *enseignes* of his identity.

De Roye's description possesses a certain grotesque quality. To begin, this list of ingrown nails, fistulas, and abscesses necessarily speaks of corrupted flesh. There is also the difficult unsentimentality with which de Roye tells how the duke's skull was split apart from temple to jaw, or that a pike had impaled him "from the backside" ("par le fondement"). Last but not least, there is the narrator's unsparing, almost clinical gaze. As Commynes does when describing the duke's mortal fall, de Roye calls upon a series of interposed "see-ers" as witnesses. Where Commynes wrote of a body dressed and undressed in reverence, de Roye displays that body in all its graphic destruction for the collective, voyeuristic scrutiny of Charles's brother, his chaplain, his valets, several others who were prisoners, and not least, for the reader.

The description of Charles's body brings us back to the male body in its military glory or the spectacle of its humiliation. Commynes does not mention the *enseignes* by which Charles's body was identified, but there is no doubt that he knew about them. Setting aside the matter of Commynes's place in the hierarchy of Louis's intelligence service, Molinet gives the same list, and they appear in precise detail in several documentary sources, also.[55] Since Commynes names those who found Charles's body, it is evident that his silence is purposeful. There can also be no doubt that, learning how Charles had been found, Commynes would have recognized these identifying *enseignes* from his time in Burgundy. When he heard how the duke had been found and recognized, how many of these marks did he remember? How many had come about during the four and a half years since his departure? (And is there not an equal intimacy in contemplating how a naked body has changed over time and in remembering how it once was?)

The anonymity of Charles's body lying among a tangle of cadavers from whom all identity has been crossed out reprises the story Commynes tells about the man revived at Montlhéry, the one buried under an indistinguishable heap of bodies. Commynes silences the marks on the duke's physical body that made it possible to identify him among the anonymous dead. One is the very scar that Charles receives at Montlhéry, and which Commynes writes about. When Commynes tells the reader he was there when that *enseigne* was written onto Charles's body during his narration of Montllhéry, he already knows that reading that sign is part of how the duke will later be found and recognized. At Montlhéry Commynes cannot believe that any would dare oppose Charles the Bold. At Nancy, his hero lies frozen into the mud, the jewelled emblem of his glory hocked for a pair of coins, all the *enseignes* of his might erased.

The memory of the signet that hung from the duke's doublet joins past and present. The narrative moves associatively back to touching the duke, to dressing him and undressing him, to the rituals and privileges whose corruption is told in the story of the "tête bottée." The *enseigne* can also become a *point de fuite*, the locus of a charged absence. It is the emblem of contact between one man and another: between Commynes and Charles, or more abstractly between Commynes and Campobasso, or between Charles and those who struck him down. The *enseigne* can be an emblem of silence: the red mark left by a gesture that cannot be seen, but from which the imagination cannot free itself. In these readings the word *enseigne* has indexed banners and cameos, but the meanings that have returned again and again are of wound and scar. Commynes says nothing about being called "la tête bottée"; he says nothing about Campobasso's humiliation; he says nothing about being hit by Charles, or about the marks it left. He says nothing about his own body in relation to the duke's. When Commynes comes to narrating Charles's death, he cannot bring himself to name the scars and wounds which history has written into his body.

Beyond Rhetoric and Exemplarity

Charles, says Commynes, "eust bien voulu ressembler a ses anciens princes, dont il a esté tant parlé aprés leur mort" (357), that is, he wanted to be remembered like one of the exemplary, epic heroes whose likeness adorned the walls and mansucripts at the Burgundian court. The duke has ambitions to "overwrite" the mortality of his actual body with the perfection of a literary hero's timeless, immaterial one. Posterity has given a bitter satisfaction to his desire. In the carbuncle in his shoulder and the fistula in his groin, the duke's body reveals its material vulnerability to (lived) history. Foucault writes of the body imprinted, ruined by history. Could he have meant this so literally as a face whose features have been gnawed away?

In my introduction, I asked about memory and the spectral body. Although the scar received at Montlhéry is the only physical wound Commynes mentions in relation to the duke, the word "plaie" appears rarely but meaningfully in the *Mémoires*, a total of four times. The first instance is at Montlhéry (33); the second in a passage also quoted in this chapter, about how a prince "peu entendu" is a great "playe" for his people (122). Commynes then uses the word just twice more, both times in a single passage of Book V, where he again describes the harm that can come to a country when it has a foolish prince. In this passage the word "plaie" evokes the desolation of a country at war, especially civil war (418). In these reflections, the trope of falling – of literal and meta-phorical falls – recurs in the text, and is explicitly linked to the action of divine justice. Although we will not receive an answer, we still must ask to what extent the insistent return of the word "plaie" in Commynes's meditations (direct and oblique) on the consequences of Charles's death for his people should be seen as the return of the word silenced or re-pressed in his telling of that death.

Commynes's silences are the silences of history itself, and the *Mémoires'* narrative turns on what it is possible to know or say. The pattern that emerges reveals history as a series of dislocated signs, all im-perfectly apprehended. Commynes's narration traces the limit of how it is possible to know, think, remember, or write history.

Chapter Three

Enseignes: Crosses and Coins, Bridges and Fences

This chapter examines two episodes in which the nature and limits of loyalty are put on graphic display. It thus shares a number of concerns with the preceding chapter, including writing on the body, the filters of memory, and the tension between the narrator and his younger self. The word *enseigne* returns again, this time as part of the author's reflections on writing, power, and authority.[1] Commynes's narrative explores two simultaneous ideas about loyalty made manifest in the dynamic circulation of coins, livery, and graffiti. First, there is something ineffable and lawless about the bonds between individual men. A human loyalty exists which cares nothing for politics or law. This is a loyalty that we might say is all "depth." The loyalty that one sees – the performance of wearing someone's livery, for instance – is a matter of pomp and circumstance: it is all "surface." The contrast between these two calls on us to consider both the troubled nature of community and the deceptive nature of the sign. The explicit content in Commynes's narration concerns the rather conservative development of a series of exempla. The closer one examines these exempla, the more ambiguous and ambivalent they appear. Another current begins to emerge within Commynes's imagery. The reflections on the *enseignes* of loyalty that run through the *Mémoires* seem to question the boundaries between loyalty and possession. The different passages I examine on the following pages are united thematically by insignia and writing. They are united at the level of structure by an ongoing and unresolved interrogation of the (loyal or deceiving) self as interior and surface.

The Exemplary Loyalty of Treacherous Captain Wenlock

Commynes's place first at the Burgundian court, and later at the royal court, gave him a front-row seat on the Wars of the Roses.[2] Although

Charles the Bold's mother, Isabella of Portugal, was descended from the Lancasters, in 1468 Charles married the sister of the English king Edward IV, Margaret of York. One of Commynes's earliest diplomatic missions was as Charles's envoy to the English garrison at Calais. In Book III, he gives his own up-close account of the zigzagging power plays between Edward IV and Richard Neville, Earl of Warwick ("the kingmaker"), including Warwick's flight to France in March 1470, his successful return and grab for power in October of the same year, and Edward's final recapture of the throne in March through May 1471. Commynes's narrative focuses on the rapid and intricate realignment of loyalties – feigned and true – that accompanied "the most dramatic volte-face in the whole history of these wars."[3]

In the spring of 1470, Edward IV, his suspicions of Warwick's plotting against him confirmed, met and defeated the earl in battle. When Warwick fled, he fled first to Calais, taking his family with him, including his pregnant daughter Isabelle and her husband, Edward's own brother, the Duke of Clarence. Soon what began for Commynes as a low-level assignment to an ally's outpost escalates in importance. Commynes's story about Yorks, Lancasters, and the Earl of Warwick becomes a coming-of-age story about the encounter with a "monde neuf" (a new world [196]). "Tout cecy m'estoit bien nouveau, car jamais je n'avoye veu des mutations de ce monde" (All this was very new to me, because I had never seen such upheavals in the world [196]), he confesses. Commynes himself describes this experiences as a loss of innocence, which is to say, as an awakening into a new consciousness of history and self. "Ce fut la premiere foiz que j'euz jamais congnoissance que les choses de ce monde sont peu estables" (It was the first time that I ever understood that the affairs of this world are unstable [198]). The disposition of kingdoms and offices, or of the human heart, are made up of a succession of potentially incompatible truths. The *Mémoires* reflect on the nature of this instability through three intertwined developments on the themes of loyalty and betrayal, surface and depth, writing and being written off. The (anti)hero of Commynes's tale is a man who at first seems to be a minor character, a man named Lord Wenlock. (His name appears transcribed in Commynes's text as "Waucloe" or even "Vaucloe"). Wenlock proves to be a master of dissimulation, a word that appears repeatedly in the *Mémoires*, and without which, Commynes intones, "les ouvraiges ne se sçauroient passer" (nothing would work [187]).

To follow the play of misrepresentations that make Commynes's story possible we need to know that, among his great number of lands, titles,

and offices, Warwick holds the captainship of Calais.[4] Wenlock is lieuten-
ant of the garrison in Warwick's place. When Warwick and his party
arrive at their would-be port outside Calais, fresh from defeat at Edward
IV's hands, Wenlock begins an elaborate charade of loyalty to Edward.
Warwick is anchored off-shore, but Wenlock acts as if he does not want
Warwick to receive any help from the Calais outpost. "A grand peyne
voulut consentir ledict seigneur de Waucloe que on luy portast deux
flaccons de vin" (Wenlock would barely consent to have him brought
two bottles of wine [183]). At this point, Warwick's daughter gives birth
on board the boat, and Commynes enters the scene as Charles's ambassador. Commynes plays his role with great seriousness, unaware that the
play is a farce. It takes months before he discovers that when Warwick
presented himself at Calais, Wenlock, "qui estoit tres saige, lui manda
que, s'il y entroit, qu'il estoit perdu ... et que le meilleur pour luy estoit
qu'il se retirast en France; et que de la place de Callais, qu'il ne s'en sou-
ciast, et qu'il luy en rendroit bon compte quant il seroit temps" (who was
very wise, sent him a message saying that if he entered [Calais], he would
be lost ... and that the best thing for [Warwick] to do was to withdraw to
France; and that he shouldn't worry about Calais, that he would give a
good account of it when the time came [185]). Warwick followed this
advice, and lived to fight another day.

To reward Wenlock for his rigorous treatment of Warwick, Edward IV
grants him the captainship of Calais – Warwick's own office, and a very
handsome prize. Charles is almost as joyful to be free of Warwick as is
Edward IV. He sends Commynes to receive homage from Wenlock and
his men, offering the new captain a one-thousand écu pension to boot.
Wenlock "feit serment en l'hostel de l'estaple a Callais, entre mes mains,
audict roy d'Angleterre, envers et contre tous; et semblablement tous
ceulx de la garnison et de la ville" (made an oath in the Staple House at
Calais, with his hands between mine, to the king of England, against any
and all; and all those in the garrison and the city did the same [184]).
Notice how Commynes repeats the legal formula, "envers et contre
tous," so central to the nomenclature of treason, and the ritually precise
mention of holding Wenlock's hands between his own. Meanwhile,
Warwick finds refuge, financing, and men with Louis XI. Edward IV,
confident that England is his, enjoys himself hunting, and brushes
aside Charles's increasingly emphatic warnings about Warwick's re-
surgent force. Soon it is obvious to everyone except the debonair and
leisurely Edward IV that Warwick is poised to sail back to England,
pull Henry VI out of prison, plant that addled monarch back on the
throne, and reclaim a seat next to it for himself.

The whole time that this situation has been brewing, Commynes has been making frequent trips to Calais to press Wenlock to expel men known to be Warwick's from the garrison, and Wenlock has been courteously ignoring him. This is precisely the kind of tactical dissimulation the mature Commynes advocates, but his younger self never catches on. Wenlock at last pulls Commynes aside and, opening a parallel discourse of personal confidences, assures the rookie "qu'il demourroit bien le maistre en la ville" (that he would very well remain master of the town [188]). Wenlock even tries to pass a warning on to Charles through Commynes that the duke should not get caught on the wrong side when the tables turn. "Or j'estoye a Callais pour entretenir mons[r] de Vaucloe, a l'heure de cest appareil; et jusques lors n'entendiz sa dissimulation, qui avoit ja duré trois moys" (Now I was in Calais to meet with monsieur de Wenlock during all these preparations, and at that point I didn't understood his deception, which had already been going on for three months [187]). Shortly afterwards, Warwick sails to England, plucks Henry VI from prison, and routs Edward. Only after the stupefied Edward has jumped onto the nearest ship at hand with only the clothes on his back, does Commynes understand what Wenlock had been hinting at all along. Wenlock has been loyal to Warwick throughout. Wenlock is Warwick's man.[5]

Wenlock "servit tres bien son cappitaine, luy donnant ce conseil, mais tres mal son roy (quant audict seigneur de Warvic, jamais homme ne tint plus grand loyaulté), veu que le roy d'Angleterre l'avoit faict cappitaine en chief, et ce que le duc de Bourgongne luy donnoit" (served his captain very well, giving him this advice, but very poorly his king [as for Lord Warwick, no man was ever more loyal], seeing as the king of England had made him head captain and what the Duke of Burgundy was paying him [185]). Commynes's remark seems to have troubled his readers. The phrase bears the traces of several copyists' efforts to make sense of the memorialist's sentiment. Both Galliot du Pré's 1524 edition of the *Mémoires* and Denis Sauvage's of 1552 replace loyalty with disloyalty.[6] In his recent edition, Blanchard has used parentheses to separate out the two sides of this observation. His intervention makes the phrase clearer but imposes a subordination of one idea to the other which the manuscript original pointedly lacks. It would be best to hear two separate, conflicting yet interlocking and equal appraisals: Wenlock ill served Edward and Charles considering how much money they were paying him; Wenlock's counsel served his captain well, no man was ever more loyal. In other words, the sentence juxtaposes two distinct kinds of loyalty. One is a rational economy of service and reward, official duty, and honour. The other, the one that made Wenlock unbuy-able, was the irrational, personal keenness of the bonds between one man and another.

Warwick pulls Henry from the Tower of London "ou aultresfoiz i l'y avoit mis, et y avoit bien long temps, criant devant luy qu'i estoit traistre et crimineulx de lese majesté, et a ceste heure l'appelloit roy" (where he had once imprisoned him, a long time before, proclaiming that he was a traitor and guilty of *lèse-majesté*, and now he was calling him king [195]). How can the same man be both traitor and king? Warwick's deed poses two problems, one related to loyalty and betrayal, the other to language, and both philosophical. If anything and its opposite are pos-sible, then the notion of essence is undermined. If Warwick can both depose and crown the same man, then the election of a king loses its divinity. Any man can be king if he wears a crown, and the crown can fall from any head (or be knocked from it). A crisis lurks in the shadows of the narrator's tale. Either the ability of language to signify truly is terribly compromised or, to put it in highly anachronistic terms, loyalty is a social construction. Loyalty and betrayal cease to be divinely or-dered virtues, and become only profane, situational behaviours. There are no absolute values, only relative senses. Warwick's use of language, and Wenlock's also, expose the priority of the signifier over the signi-fied. In this lesson, meaning becomes contingent. Power comes to those who recognize the plasticity of language as a mode of access to it. If you call something a rose, it will begin to smell sweet. If you call it a relic, you can make it holy.

While Commynes arguably does not approve of what Warwick does, it is far from clear whether he condemns Wenlock. Early on, Commynes claims he is telling this story about the two,

> pour ce qu'il est besoing d'estre informé aussi bien des tromperies et maulvaistiés de ce monde comme du bien, non point pour en user mais pour s'en garder, et vueil declarer une tromperie ou habilité, ainsi qu'on la vouldra nommer, car elle fut saigement conduicte; et aussi vueil que on entende les tromperies de nous voisins commes les notres, et que partout il y a du bien et du mal. (185)

> [because it is necessary to be informed about deceptions and evil deeds in this world as well as about the good, not so as to imitate them but to keep oneself from them, and I want to explain one deception or skilful deed, whichever one wishes to call it, because it was wisely carried out; and

I would also like people to understand our neighbours' deceptions and
our own, and that there is good and evil everywhere.]

The explanation Commynes gives for including his story touches on a
long-standing debate among medieval writers over the value or danger
of a negative example. He begins from the posture of a commonplace,
"I'm warning you so you can stay away." But then things get more complicated. The first couplet pairs "tromperie" with "maulvaistiés"; then
the second couplet juxtaposes "tromperie" with "habilité," something
manifesting skill and competence. The narrator then refuses to decide
which of the two words should be used ("ainsi qu'on la vouldra nom-
mer"), since the deed was "saigement conduicte," wisely handled. The
narrator admires the very thing he warns against. Confusion seeps in
between two competing value systems. In one, skilled deception is a sin;
in the other, it is a form of wisdom.[7] At the end, Commynes admits that
good and evil can be found "partout." The apparent meaning of this
sentence is that examples of good and evil can be found at home and
abroad. A more subtle interpretation is also possible, however: "there
are elements of good and evil in everything." The narrator once more
avoids passing judgment on whether what Wenlock did was good or
evil, and instead seems to question whether good and evil can be fully
separated from one another. Although many other potential lessons
might also be suggested from Commynes's episode, one of the most
important concerns the ambiguous loyalty between Wenlock and
Warwick. The teaching Commynes derives begins with a platitude and
culminates in an amazing declaration of moral ambiguity.

I described this episode as a coming-of-age story, and that description
implies that the narrator must experience both knowledge and disillusionment. When Charles hears of Warwick's triumph, he has Commynes
turn around and head straight back to Calais. The turning point in the
autobiographical story about Commynes contained within this historical episode begins with his arrival in the now-enemy garrison. As soon
as he arrives, he begins to lie. "Je leur respondoye a tous propos que le
roy Edouard estoit mort et que j'en estoie bien asseuré, nonobstant que
j'en savoye bien le contraire" (I answered all their queries with the information that King Edward was dead and that I was certain of it, even
though I knew the opposite was true [198]). With these lies, Commynes
simultaneously takes his first step towards political wisdom and reveals he has begun to understand something about the upheavals of
this new world ("ce monde neuf" [196]). The ability to produce a false

representation represents a leap forward in the mastery of the unstable play of difference between *être* and *paraître* so necessary to the diplomat.[8] To lie is also to create a conscious division between interior and exterior, depth and surface, to model a tiny interior space, an inner "I" out of which subjecthood is born. This is to say that subjectivity begins in duplicity. By giving a false sign the subject brings into being a self born of the ironic capacities of language.

In chapter 1 we discovered Voltaire's influential role in shaping Commynes's modern legacy. My reading of the above passage implies, however, that the ideas which blossom in Voltaire's attack – the idea that the self is brought into existence in the act of lying, and that rhetoric masks and protects this self – are latent in Commynes's own narrative. The notion of the fractured self articulated by Voltaire is a foundational one within debates about the constitution of a "modern political subject." If this idea is present in Commynes's own text, then Commynes is, indeed, far more modern than he has been given credit, no matter how "medieval" the narrative traditions he brings to final bloom. This is not to imply belief in a premodern unity of self. It is rather to complicate ideas about the subject and subjectivity present in the *Mémoires*, and to highlight ways that earlier philosophical debates about language and the subject find their way into Commynes's political philosophy.

Heads and Tails

Commynes's initial portrayal of Wenlock's ruse deals primarily with the obscure nature of personal fealties, the performance of deception, and the relations between language and political truth. Warwick's triumph and Edward IV's exile initiate a second stage in these events, in which the text is largely preoccupied with the interdependence between power and the production or circulation of signs (*enseignes*).

We left Edward as, fleeing Warwick, he jumped onto the first ship at hand. Commynes makes it sound like Edward runs straight from the battlefield up the boarding plank. The passage below introduces an expression Commynes repeats throughout his discussion of English affairs: *pille et croix*. The phrase refers to the images on either side of a coin, so I have translated it as "heads or tails." Commynes uses it throughout to mean coinage, money, or wealth.

Ainsi fouyt ce roy Edouard l'an M CCCC LXX, avecques ces deux hulques et ung petit navyre sien, et quelzques sept ou huyt cens personnes avecques luy, qui n'avoient aultre habillement que leur habillement de guerre. Et si n'avoient ne croix ne pille, ne n'y sçavoient a grand peyne ou ilz alloient. (192)

[That is how this King Edward fled in the year 1470, with two hulk ships and a smaller boat of his own, and some seven or eight hundred people with him, who had no clothes but the ones they were fighting in. They had neither heads nor tails, and they barely knew where they were heading.]

A fleet of Easterling (Hanseatic) ships chase him all the way to Holland. Landing is no better; Louis de Bruges, seigneur de Gruuthuse, has to pay the ship's captain and cover Edward's expenses the rest of the way to safety (194). The king is dazzlingly broke. Commynes says so twice, once right after the other, first as Edward runs from England and again when he arrives on Dutch shores. Both times he repeats the same expression, "n'avoir ne croix ne pille"; Edward has neither "heads nor tails." Just as coinage presents a metonymy of authority and its circulation, so Edward's collapse expresses itself in monetary terms. He is without throne and without *enseignes*, without any capacity to represent or impose his authority; he is too nil to be represented. He possesses neither the front nor the back side of the authority he figures. It is not simply that he cannot put gold or silver images of himself into circulation, but rather that he himself has no currency and literally cannot circulate. When his men followed him on board ship, "they barely knew where they were heading."

Duke Charles is horror-struck – "merveilleusement effroyé" (194) – by the diplomatic fiasco his brother-in-law has propelled him into, "et eust beaucop myeulx aymé sa mort, car il estoit en grand soucy du conte de Warvic" (and he would have much preferred his death, because he was very worried about the [Earl] of Warwick [194]).[9] It is difficult not to read what follows as a kind of punch line. The duke "faignit en public de ne luy bailler nul secours, et feist crier que nul n'alast a son aide; mais soubz main et secretement il luy fit bailler cinquante mil florins a la croix Sainct Andri" (in public he pretended not to give him any assistance, and he had it publicized that nobody should come to his aid; but underhandedly and in secret he gave [Edward] fifty thousand florins stamped with the cross of Saint Andrew [201]). The cross of Saint Andrew is Burgundy's emblem, so it is fair to say that these florins have Charles the Bold's name written all over them. Although no legal obligation or ties of vassalage unite them, every time that Edward IV spends one of the gold coins the Burgundian duke has given him, he puts Charles's *enseignes* into circulation in lieu of his own. Everything the English "king" does will be stamped "paid for by Burgundy." The irony or humiliation of the situation gets an added punch from its graphic aspect. Edward's English coins bore crosses that looked like this: ╫.[10] The Burgundian cross of Saint Andrew looks like a letter "X." The pivot from the English "long cross" to the cross of Saint Andrew takes the hands of a clock and resets the hour. In the substitution of one for the other, Charles the Bold "knocks over" Edward IV. Edward has not a cross to his name, nor does he any longer have his own cross. Similarly, the English coins, unlike the Burgundian ones, depicted the king himself, so the irony is still sharper. Saint Andrew has taken Edward's place. This metaphorical gesture of re-visioning and re-writing plays itself out in literal ways, also. After hesitating over what to do with the existing treaties bearing Edward's name, it is eventually agreed that all the terms will remain identical, but that Edwards's name will be crossed out and Henry's written in its place (199).[11]

Arriving in Calais after Warwick's triumph in the company of two Burgundian companions with known Lancastrian sympathies, Commynes alone is left to fend for himself. No one comes out to greet him; at the city gates, he is offered wine but not lodging. In town, every man in the garrison wears "la livree de mons^r de Warvic" (monsieur de Warwick's livery [197]). Wenlock graciously invites Commynes to dine.

> Ledict de Vaucloe me manda a disner, qui estoit bien acompaigné, et avoit le revastre d'or sur son bonnet (qui estoit la livree dudict conte), qui est ung baston no[ué], et tous les aultres semblablement; et qui ne le pouvoit avoir d'or, l'avoit de drap. Et me fust dict a ce disner que, des que le passagier fut arrivé d'Angleterre, qui leur avoit porté ceste nouvelle, que en moins d'un quart d'heure chascun portoit ceste livree, tant fut ladicte mutation hastive et soubdayne. (197–8)[12]

[Lord Wenlock invited me to dinner, which was well attended, and he had a gold *ravestre* on his hat (which was [the image represented on] the earl's livery), that is, a ragged staff, and all the others had the same; and whoever couldn't afford one of gold had one out of cloth. And I was told at that dinner that, as soon as the messenger who had brought them the news from England had arrived, that in less than a quarter of an hour everyone was wearing that livery, so hurried and sudden was the change.]

In Commynes's vocabulary, the word "mutation" summons all the instability of the human world; it means here "fracturing, upheaval, dissent." Each man has adorned himself – written onto the surface of his clothing and wrapped his body – in the enseigne of his new loyalty. They have literally "turned their coats," and shown the other side of the medallion [coin].[13] Notice also, the element of time and disruption here: Commynes spent three months going back and forth to Wenlock's garrison before catching on to what was afoot, and it took Edward several days to flee from London to Holland. But reordering these *enseignes* took only fifteen minutes.

When Commynes returns from dinner he finds the outside of his lodgings covered in graffiti. "A la porte de mon logis et de ma chambre me firent plus de cent croix blanches et des {rymes}, contenants que le roy de France et le conte de Warvic estoit tout ung. Je trouvay tout cecy bien estrange" (On the door of my lodgings and of my room they drew more than one hundred white crosses and rhymes about how the king of France and the earl of Warwick were united. I found all this very strange [197]).[14] As with long crosses that slump into the cross of Saint Andrew, attitude is everything. Saint Andrew's cross has been twisted into the French royal white cross. Like Mona Lisa with a moustache, authority has been relegated to derision with a single, well-angled stroke. This perversion of form enacts a kind of symbolic violence. Commynes used to have the authority to make marks, for instance, to imprint the duke's seal. Now he has become a "marked man."

This graffiti breaks out like a rash. The door's open surface has become something to be abhorred and filled. The surfeit of scrawled *enseignes* proves that power is the ability to saturate the spaces of representation. Commynes pointedly remembers that every single man in the garrison donned the new livery. Presumably, Wenlock's men wore another livery before putting on the ragged staff. Were these previous livery emblems all alike? When every man wears Warwick's livery, the insignia they sport erase all differences and thus thwart meaningful interpretation. The glut of signifiers confounds all difference or indeterminacy. The soldiers' sudden change of costume foreshadows how diplomatic uncertainty will be cured by crossing out Edward's name and writing Henry's in its place (199). There is danger in a naked door, unlabelled clothing, or a white page. Indeterminacy makes private interpretation possible, and the internal conscience from which interpretation emerges is inherently subversive.

The repeated play of crosses and crossing-out offers one of the most poetically fertile series of images in the *Mémoires*. Power is marked by semiotic fecundity. Whether florins *à la croix Saint André*, a flush of white crosses scrawled onto a door, or the scurried handing round of cloth badges bearing Warwick's livery, one *enseigne* chases another. Paper or parchment, wooden door or metal coin, each receives the imprint of a new *enseigne*. Each support is saturated by a sign which at once refers to and perverts the sign that preceded it. This is potentially the most subversive aspect of Commynes's tale. What is crossed out is crossed out. Legitimacy is not portable. Power confers the authority of its own legitimacy, and that legitimacy is identical to the aggressive fecundity of its symbols.

Coins, doors, seals, letters – in each case surface is at a maximum and depth at a minimum. A specific kind of opposition is also implicated in these objects: *pille et croix*, heads and tails, inside and outside. Letters also place on one side their destination and, concealed on the other side, the contents of their message.[15] This coincidence between the re-inscription of a sign which retrospectively voids the value of its predecessor, and a semiotically saturated support resembles what will happen to Commynes when he leaves the duke for the king. On the night in which Commynes joins the king, he changes name and home, never to be allowed to return again. Back to back stand two equally whole "sides" of his life.

Bridges and Fences

In the final reading in this chapter I will examine Commynes's remembrance of the Picquigny summit between Louis XI and Edward IV.[16] There are a number of compelling reasons to consider the episodes surrounding Calais and Picquigny together. Both highlight exemplary political successes brought about in defiance of chivalric ideals, and both feature Edward IV. Both share certain thematic concerns as well. Most important, both articulate sceptical, ambiguous critiques of loyalty and rewriting.

At the end of August 1475, Louis XI and Edward IV met to confirm an alliance between the French Crown and the English. The treaty they signed together at Picquigny healed a Franco-Britannic alliance severed almost 150 years before and, depriving Burgundy of its most powerful ally, stifled what remained of Charles's chances of dethroning Louis's power. It was Charles who had brought Edward's armies across the Channel, but then the duke exasperated his would-be ally by refusing to set aside his Eastern campaigns, letting the season trickle away. Louis XI seized the opportunity presented by English disgruntlement to seek his own arrangements with Edward IV. For Commynes, the moment was an uncanny one; the Picquigny summit brought him face to face again with the English king.

One of Commynes's best-known political views is that princes should avoid summitry; it always turns out badly. "Grand follie a deux princes qui sont comme esguaulx en puissance, de s'entrevoir, sinon qu'ilz fussent en grand jeunesse, qui est le temps qu'ilz n'ont aultres pensees que a leurs plaisirs!" (It is great folly for two princes equal in power to see one another, unless they are very young, because at that age they have no thought but to enjoy themselves! [126–7]). Commynes knows this first hand, having participated in several such royal get-togethers. He has seen how, in the best cases, the two sides develop a lasting contempt for one other. They decide, for instance, that Spain's King Enrique IV is a fop and the Holy Roman Emperor a skinflint, as the French courts did after meeting those two rulers (126–32). Louis XI fared no better; the Spanish found his hat ugly and his cheap clothing ridiculous (129). These are best-case scenarios, warns Commynes. The worst case was Montereau, and nobody needed to be reminded of how it went wrong. There, on 10 September 1419, the then dauphin Charles VII – Louis XI's father – stabbed to death John the Fearless, Charles's grandfather, reigniting the cycle of violence begun by John the Fearless's 1407 assassination of Louis d'Orléans, and setting in motion some sixteen more years of civil war. Charles VII used the pretext of reconciliation and peace-making to lure John the Fearless out to the place where he would be killed. The two met on a bridge, with a double-gated fence between them. When the duke crossed to the other side to pay homage to the dauphin, "Incontinent fut tué et ceulx qui estoient avecques luy, dont est advenu depuys assés de maulx, comme chascun scet" (He was immediately killed, along with the people with him, from which many evils have since come, as everyone knows [288]).[17] Louis XI reminds Commynes of Montereau as the two are preparing for Louis to meet with Edward IV, and Commynes reminds his reader. "Cecy n'est pas de ma matiere, pour quoy je n'en diz plus avant, mais le Roy le me compta, ne plus ne moins que je vous diz, en ordonnant ceste veue" (This isn't my subject, so I won't say more about it, but the king recounted it to me, neither more nor less than what I am telling you, in setting up this meeting [288]). "Everyone knows" what happened there, but Louis reminds Commynes, and Commynes reminds the reader. Montereau and its trellised bridge are, for Commynes, for Louis, for all of France in the fifteenth century, a *lieu de mémoire* in every possible sense of the phrase.[18]

The bridge constructed for the encounter between Louis XI and Edward IV rewrites the staging of Montereau. Commynes served as one of the location scouts for the French side, and he carefully explains what went into the arrangements behind the meeting of the two kings. The place chosen beside Picquigny cannot be forded but it is not too wide for a bridge to span. A dinghy can ferry one or two men at a time from one side to the other. The bridge itself cannot be crossed because a sturdy fence divides it into two halves. "Et au meillieu de ce pont fut faict ung fort treillis de boys, comme on faict aux caiges de ces lyons: et n'estoient point les troux entre les barreaulx plus grans que a y bouter le bras a son aise ... et comprenoit le treilliz jusques sur le bort du pont, afin que on ne peult passer de l'un cousté a l'autre" (In the middle of this bridge a strong wooden trellis was made, like they make for lion cages: and the gaps between the bars were no bigger than to be able to stick an arm through comfortably ... and the trellis reached to the edges of the bridge, so that one couldn't cross from one side to the other [287]). The bridge and its gates have a practical purpose as security measures. They also represent the danger of encounter, mistrust, and the potential for violence. The metaphors of political alliance and enmity materialize into tangible signs. The significations of this gated bridge so transcend its functional architecture that it may properly be thought of in terms of a sculptural installation set into the landscape.

Commynes's description of the English king reminds the reader that he and Edward knew one another at the Burgundian court. "C'estoit ung tres beau prince et grand, mais ja commençoit a s'engresser, et l'avoye veu autresfoiz plus beau, car je n'ay pas souvenance d'avoir jamais veu ung plus bel homme qu'il estoit quant monsᵣ de Warvic le feist fouyr d'Angleterre" (He was a very handsome and tall prince, but he was already beginning to get fat, and I had once seen him looking better, because I don't remember ever having seen a man more handsome than he was when monsieur de Warwick made him flee England [290]). Commynes's words refract this particular moment into a prismatic reflection of past, present, and future. "Once" Commynes knew him to be handsome, but he was "already beginning" to get fat. Each time Edward IV makes an appearance in the *Mémoires*, Commynes alludes to the English king's handsome good looks and to his popularity with the ladies. This creates a ricochet effect within the text, since in effect Commynes is always praising Edward's beauty while announcing his decline, or commenting on his decline while recollecting his former beauty. The effect is particularly notable in his narration of Picquigny.

These markers set the limits of a "now" predicated on a remembered future in which the king will grow dissipated and hugely fat. Edward died in April 1483, so "ja commençoit" points to the beginning of a development whose final conclusion is known to the narrating Commynes, but could not have been seen by his younger self.

At a certain moment, Louis XI and Edward IV send away their respective suites and stand alone together at the middle of the bridge, facing each other through the bars. They summon Commynes to stand with them as a third man. Then Louis asks Edward if he remembers Commynes, and the English king "respondit que ouy, et dit les lieux ou il m'avoit veu, et que d'autresfoiz m'estoie empesché pour le servir a Callais, du temps que j'estoie avecques le duc de Bourgongne" (answered yes, and named the places where he had seen me, and how once I had worked hard to serve him at Calais, during the time when I was with the Duke of Burgundy [292]). The bridge and platform constructed for the summit at Picquigny had multiple diplomatic and historic parallels, but their structures also mime the metaphorical architecture of memory and self-in-time. The duality inherent in bridge and fence reprise the meeting's autobiographical content. The fence presents a metaphor for division or encounter, or for both at once. The *Mémoires* relate Edward IV's exile during the period of Lancastrian rule as a virtual parable of exile. Between the time when Commynes first saw Edward far from England and dependent on others' mercy, and when they meet at Picquigny, Commynes's fortunes shifted also. Between the time that Commynes met with Edward at Picquigny and the moment when he recalls that meeting, both men have been around Fortune's wheel again. Indeed, this moment in the *Mémoires'* narrative brings together three distinct historical moments – the 1470–1 events Commynes experienced through his mission to Calais, the 1475 summit that forms the narrated "now," and the moment, some fifteen years afterwards (i.e., circa 1490), when the narrator sets out to portray this history.

This episode at Picquigny thus contains two distinct but interdependent *mises en abyme*, each of which concerns memory and loyalty. The first concerns the relationship between Montereau and Picquigny and the bond between collective memory and landscape. After all, the memory of Montereau, like the memory of Picquigny, concerns a place. This setting offers itself as a materially realized rewriting of history. In the passage from one generation to the next, the meeting at Picquigny reenacts the past and transforms history's promise. The second *mise en abyme* describes the relations between the three biographical moments in Commynes's life that come together in narrating this scene. The narrated Commynes looks across a physical gate at a king he knew when he was a young man in a different life. In turn, the narrator remembers the past self that stood on the bridge at Picquigny from across a metaphorical, fenced bridge-in-time. The moment squares off contradictory identities and moments in Commynes's life. The fence itself presents a graphic image of the barrier against which narration and memory press. In this kaleidoscopic vision, there are not one but several fences, real and metaphorical, all superimposed in memory. Which barrier is foremost – the fence built at Picquigny or the memory of the Montereau fence? The metaphorical fence that separated the "now" of Picquigny from a Burgundian "then"? Or the metaphorical fence that separates the memory of Picquigny from the "now" of narration?

Text and Genealogy: The Fleur de Lys

Commynes receives a unique honour for this face-to-face conversation between Louis and Edward. "Le plaisir du Roy avoit esté que je fusse vestu pareil de luy ce jour" (The king's pleasure had been that I be dressed just like him that day [289]). When Commynes writes of wearing robes identical to Louis's, he exposes the contradictions, tensions, and signifying potential inherent to their relations. The moment thus lends itself to multiple, potentially contradictory readings. Dressing a courtier in the king's clothing is essentially theatrical. It is both spectacular and specular. Commynes's description of the privilege Louis grants him conveys pleasure and the gratification of a certain fantasy of fusion. Moreover, this satisfaction would have been performed for all who saw the two side by side. Commynes's narrative again puts his privileged relation with the king on display for all to see.[19] To be dressed like the king is to be made his double, his reflection. This is mimetic desire expressed as a desire for mimesis.[20]

Commynes says that Louis XI "avoit acoustumé, de long temps, d'en avoir quelc'un qui s'abilloit pareil de luy souvent" (had long had the frequent habit of dressing somebody like him [289]), but Commynes mentions it only this once. It is possible that this was the only time that Commynes was the one dressed this way. It seems more likely, given the long reign of Commynes's favour, that he now brings the detail forward in his narration for other reasons. Commynes comes to the fence at Picquigny clothed in clothing identical to the king, clothing which prominently displays his royal, French identity. The word "identity" comprises two distinct meanings whose relationship to one another is potentially paradoxical. Both significations come into play in these matching garments. The *Oxford English Dictionary* gives the word's first meaning as "the quality or condition of being the same in substance, composition, nature, properties, or in particular qualities under consideration; absolute or essential sameness; oneness."[21] The second meaning includes the definitions, "the condition of being a single individual; the fact that a person or thing is itself and not something else; individuality, personality."[22] Commynes's mention seeks to portray a (textual) filiation, as if to emphasize a resemblance capable of naturalizing his identity beside the king.[23] This process works through two slightly different mental sequences. First, the resemblance between their clothing gives material form to the more abstract resemblances that sustain Commynes's place among the king's favourites. Simultaneously, Commynes portrays his abstract proximity to the king by emphasizing the material resemblance between them. Genealogy is a relation of both continuity and resemblance, one in which metaphor is often thicker than blood.[24] I would suggest that Commynes's inscription of the identity between himself and the king at Picquigny, in particular, reveals the extent to which Commynes rewrites his past through his performance of the present. His relationship with Louis XI crosses out individual history as a kind of vertical descent shifting from one self into the next. In lieu of this temporal, deep notion of self, the identity of Commynes's robes and the king, reinscribes identity as surface. When Commynes chooses the encounter with Edward at Picquigny as the moment in his narrative where he will explicitly tell the reader that he was the king's double, he obscures his own (doubly) problematic relation to his own past. He rewrites his own identity by re-inscribing the symbolic and semiotic nature of his relation with Louis.

On such an occasion, the king's garments were surely emblazoned with the fleur de lys, the sign of the French Crown. Commynes thus wears the *enseigne* of the king as well. This unmentioned fleur de lys drives home difficult lessons. Commynes's belonging to the king is literally "written" all over him. Another way of saying this is that Louis has covered Commynes with the marks of his possession. Wenlock and his men suddenly changed their livery after Warwick's return to power, but we might wonder whether Commynes does not now go a stage beyond just wearing his master's *enseignes*. I would suggest that Commynes is a living enseigne of the king. Commynes did not just come to the king's court from that of his rival; he passed from one bedchamber to another.

Louis captured his favourite chamberlain from deep behind enemy lines. Commynes's presence in Louis's service is the sign of all the king's ambitions and their realization. In an admittedly abstract sense, Commynes has crossed from one shore to another; he has turned his own vest. But in doing so, he has revealed the lining of his most exemplary, that is to say, potentially propagandistic, identity. The *enseigne* on that metaphorical lining is the fleur de lys. (By using the metaphor of lining, I mean to emphasize the hidden face of identity at the same time as I emphasize the importance of surface to the Freudian "I.") Commynes displays an individual privilege: he alone has been chosen for this display of proximity. He also displays how royal possession displaces and overwrites individual identity. Commynes becomes the surface on which the fecundity of Louis's capacity to create signification is written. Commynes becomes, to stretch a metaphor, the door on which Louis graffitis the *enseignes* of his power.

Chapter Four

The Prince of Talmont

Commynes's narrative conceals two foundational secrets about his relationship with Louis XI. The first concerns how he came to join the king in the late summer of 1472, having disappeared completely for three weeks, and during that time, travelled 400 kilometres from Upper Normandy to Ponts-de-Cé outside Angers. The impassioned judgments so many writers have brought to bear on this journey rely on little more than conjecture. Commynes himself says only, "envyron ce temps, je vins au service du Roy" (around this time, I came into the king's service [226]). The second secret hides within Commynes's narration of the king's death in the allusion to a "commandement extraordinaire." With the help of court transcripts, it is possible to excavate the betrayal buried in this second passage of the *Mémoires*. The two moments counterbalance one another exactly: each pivots on a betrayal that remains muted within Commynes's narrative. Each acts as a structuring pillar in the architecture of the *Mémoires*. Where one alludes to Commynes's union with the king, the other struggles with the rupture between them. When this betrayal of Commynes, buried within some of the best-known pages of the *Mémoires*, is exhumed, and when this second betrayal is understood in counterpoint to the author's 1472 defection, the result is a transformed perception of the architecture of the *Mémoires*.

Of Lands and Letters

From his first arrival at the royal court in 1472 until Louis XI's death in August 1483, Commynes enjoyed a position of power in Louis's entourage, at moments one of unrivalled power. In one often-cited letter the Milanese ambassador Francesco da Pietrasanta wrote to Galeazzo Maria

Sforza, "Solus, il gouverne et couche avec le roi. C'est lui qui est tout *in omnibus et per omnia*. Il n'y a personne qui soit un si grand maître, ni d'un si grand poids que lui."[1] The vividness of the bond between king and servant endures and as such, provides a unique, defining trait to their long relationship. Baron Kervyn de Lettenhove conceded that the chemistry between the two men defies the archives' muting dust: "Comines aima peut-être Louis XI, et à coup sûr il l'admira."[2] His acknowledgment that the relationship between the two men was marked by a rare affective intensity coloured by desire is all the more powerful when one considers the Belgian scholar's frequent distrust of his subject.

Even before Commynes's 1472 arrival at the royal court, Louis had six thousand *livres tournois* placed for Commynes with his trusted Jean de Beaune in Tours.[3] Upon his arrival at the royal court, a yearly pension of the same amount assured substantial revenues.[4] Appointments as the captain of Chinon and the seneschal of Poitou rounded out this income. A marriage was arranged to Hélène de Chambes, daughter of a wealthy and prominent member of the Potevin nobility, and with the bride came the barony of Argenton.[5] Yet the largest of Louis XI's gifts to Commynes were the "principautez de Talmont, baronnies, chasteaux et chastellenies, terres et seigneuries dudict lieu, Aulonne, Curzon, Chasteaugontier et la Chaulme, assises en nostre pays de Poitou" (the principalities of Talmont, the baronnies, chateaux, and chatellanies, lands and seigneuries of the stated place, [together with] Aulonne, Curzon, Chasteaugontier and La Chaulme, situated in our land of Poitou).[6] Philippe de Commynes, once the seigneur de Renescure, an orphaned inheritor of debts, now became the Prince of Talmont.[7]

Reflecting on these facts, Emille Dupont wrote, "Commynes, sans doute ... dut contracter l'un de ces engagements dont les témoignages écrits subsistent rarement, et dont les faits accomplis viennent seuls fournir les preuves."[8] The best place to begin examining the contract between Commynes and Louis XI is in the letters by which the king first granted the principality of Talmont and its dependent properties to Commynes. These letters provide the second panel in a diptych whose first leaf was formed by the duke's letters confiscating Commynes's lands and belongings in Burgundy. Those ducal letters, with their raw fury, might be seen as the site of a violent severance. Louis's letters become a new textual site, one in which the union of Commynes to Louis XI is at once performed and enshrined.

At first glance, little distinguishes these particular *grandes lettres patentes* from other royal acts emerging from Louis XI's chancellery.[9]

However, the more closely we read them, the more ambiguous the narrative they tender appears. What begins as an apparently simple donation gradually comes to seem like the veil over a fierce and violent union. The Talmont letters construct the first encounter between Louis and Commynes as a moment of intense and potentially dangerous complicity, and then confer upon this moment the status of a privileged origin. The bond forged between the two at Péronne took root during secret conversations when the king was Charles's prisoner, conversations whose words have never been revealed. With the donation of Talmont, this bond is brought out of the silences of individual affinities and into the open, performative realm of royal authority. The words sent forth by the king in his open letters echo and modulate irretrievable words once spoken between the two in the king's rooms at Péronne. These written words function as a kind of exegesis to the events that once occurred there, clarifying what was once obscure. Louis's letters cast the gift of Talmont and its surrounding fiefs as the inevitable, necessary consequence of events at Péronne.

Drafted at Amboise in October 1472, that is, just one month after Commynes's arrival at the royal court, the preamble to the Talmont donation begins by describing Commynes's love of the king, the "grande et ferme loyauté et la singuliere amour qu'il a eue et a envers nous" (great and firm loyalty and the singular love which he had and has for us).[10] Commynes possesses a perfect devotion to the Crown; despite "les troubles et divisions qui ont esté ... tousjours ait gardé envers nous vraye et loyalle fermeté de courage" (the troubles and divisions which have existed ... he has always maintained towards us a true and loyal resolve).[11] Open letters, narrated in the king's own voice, summon the whispered secrets of their first encounter out of individual, private recollection and into the immortality of textual remembrance, for all to see and know.

> Lors que estions entre les mains et sous la puissance d'aucuns de nosdicts rebelles et desobeissans, qui s'estoient declarés contre nous comme nos ennemis, et en danger d'estre illec detenus, nostredict conseiller et chambellan, sans craint du danger qui lui pouvoit alors venir, nous advertit de tout ce qu'il pouvoit pour nostre bien, et tellement s'employa que, par son moyen et ayde, nous saillismes hors des mains de nosdicts rebelles et desobeissans ... et au dernier a mis et exposé sa vie en avanture pour nous, et sans crainte ne consideration du danger de sa personne ne d'autre chose quelconque a abandonnée et perdu tous ses biens, meubles et immeubles,

chevances et heritages, terres et seigneuries pour nous venir servir, et à present nous sert continuellement à l'entour de nostre personne, au fait de nos guerres et autrement, en plusieurs manieres, en très grande cure, loyauté et dilligence.[12]

[When we were in the grip and power of those who are rebellious and disobedient, who had declared themselves against us as our enemies, and in danger of being held [prisoner] there, our counsellor and chamberlain, without fear of the danger which could come to him from it, warned us of · everything he could for our well-being, and so exerted himself that by his means and help, we emerged from the hands of those who are rebellious and disobedient ... and most recently he hazarded his life for us, and without fear nor consideration of the danger to his person nor any other thing, abandoned and lost all his possessions, both movable and fixed, domains and inheritances, lands and lordships, in order to come serve us, and now he does so continually in matters surrounding our person, our wars, and otherwise, with very great care, loyalty, and diligence.][13]

In the interstices of chancellery protocols and rhetorical formulae, two intertwined narratives of redemption emerge. Commynes's skilful rescue of Louis from the menace he faced at Péronne provides the first. The second concerns Commynes's own deliverance from rebellious lands, those "lieux où il a conversé, qui, par aucun temps, nous ont esté et encore sont contraires, rebelles, et desobeissans" (the places that he frequented, which, for some time, have been and still are contrary, rebellious, and disobedient to us).[14] Royal donations are not normally known for the exuberance of their prose, but these letters tell a story of reciprocal election and salvation, a story made possible by singular love. The word *singulier* means extraordinary, rare, precious, and unique, all definitions now archaic in English. A singular love has no second object, so this sovereign description also answers the Burgundian motto, "autre n'aurai" (I will have no other). Phrases like "in the hands or grip," "under the power," and "held prisoner" seem to clutch at the king or at the reader himself, creating an impression of imminent violence. The repeated phrase "rebellious and disobedient" sounds a coda emphasizing chaotic lawlessness and danger, while "saillismes" – to leap, to gush, to burst forth – rings with echoes of biblical exodus from oppression. From the cruel oppression of a Pharaonic duke, Commynes has made his way across a desert to the promised kingdom of France.

The language of these letters foregrounds the physical bodies of the individuals in question and so confirms the significance of their encounter within the contingencies of the individual and human, as well as within a metanarrative of French providential history. Commynes exposed his life to protect the king; he did so without thought to the physical pain or danger that Charles's anger would bring ("a mis et exposé sa vie en avanture," "sans crainte ne consideration du danger de sa personne"). He now serves Louis so closely as to care for his physical person ("continuellement à l'entour de nostre personne").[15] These words, insistent on the vulnerabilities of the flesh, reinforce the element of specific, human agency in a text one might initially be inclined to read at an abstract level. Commynes has rescued Louis from the menace of bodily imprisonment and harm; he has risked the destruction of his own life and limbs; and he has accepted the annihilation of the body of lands that were his in Burgundy. The king's donation text alludes to the physical dangers that would come from being caught by Charles, dangers the reader of this book has glimpsed already.[16] Louis XI rewards Commynes's acceptance of bodily danger with lands, thus tightening the link between one kind of body and the other, one kind of service and the other.

These letters also point to an abstract danger, the danger of risking who one is, stretching the limits of one's loyalties and thereby of one's self. The danger to Commynes's person is existential as well as physical. The Talmont donation becomes the narrative of a transformational encounter between Louis XI and Commynes. The king's letters frame Commynes's renunciation of his Burgundian past and his embrace of a new, royal identity as a conversion narrative. Having shed one body, Commynes receives new lands, a new life, and a new name from Louis. The swathes of coastline, forest, town, and field now possessed by Commynes fulfil this promise of rebirth.

To explore the narrative of the Talmont donation through the lens of individual salvation is by no means to negate the energy with which the same text enacts an aggressive political agenda. Indeed, it is one of the guiding hypotheses of this book that in Commynes the individual or private and the political or State-oriented coalesce into a single narrative. Contrary to nineteenth-century characterizations of Commynes's defection as a shocking rupture from feudal mores, Commynes was only one of many individuals who sought to cultivate their own fortunes in a context dominated by the frictions between royal, ducal, and other competing alliances. Commynes stands not as a lone individual acting in defiance of a communal ethos, but rather as one among many engaged in the perilous negotiation of rival loyalties. As such, his life exposes the tensions produced by the continued redefinition of royal authority and its limits. The documents which surround Commynes's arrival in Louis's service exemplify the rhetorical construction of a new model of political subjectivity. The discourse used in these Talmont letters to describe Commynes's behaviour constructs a new model for what it means to be loyal to the Crown or to love the king.

Donating Talmont to Commynes in fact served several purposes in Louis XI's greater political agenda, including, first and foremost, his efforts to expand and strengthen royal presence in the west. The domains given to Commynes formed a geographic and political buffer between Breton ducal lands to the north, and Albret and Armagnac lands to the south. They represented a substantial block of land tenure, effectively extending royal control along a key frontier in Louis's ongoing struggles against the French nobility. Commynes's presence in Poitou was a reminder of Louis's presence there, intended to subdue an aristocracy reinforced in its pretensions by a too-comfortable distance from the royal court. We will see below to what extent the Talmont holdings were politically fraught, long before Louis placed them in Commynes's hands.

Another aspect of the political agenda driving the Talmont donation appears in Louis's expressed desire to "recompenser et remunerer [Commynes], comme en nostre conscience nous y sentons tenus et obligez, et à ce que ce soit exemple à tous nos subjets, sous quelques princes et seigneurs qu'ils soient, d'abandonner tous autres pays pour nous servir comme leur souverain seigneur" (to recompense and remunerate [Commynes], as in our conscience we feel ourselves obligated to do, and so that it may be an example to all our subjects, under whatever prince or seigneur they may be, to abandon all other lands in order to serve us as their sovereign lord).[17] With these words Louis invites those living under his ducal rivals, most notably François II of Brittany and Charles the Bold of Burgundy, to recognize the obligations they hold to their sovereign lord. Yet in calling upon "tous nos sujets" to "d'abandonner tous autres pays pour nous servir," Louis betrays the fragility of his imperium. These words, implying both that Burgundians are subjects of the Crown and that Commynes has come from another land, illuminate the plurality of significations attached to the word *pays* in this particular time and place, the delicate balance between regional and proto-national sentiments, and the centre's uncertain hold.[18] Eighty years later, Denis Sauvage will write confidently of Commynes as French, and speak of his "natural" tongue. The Talmont donation seeks, by a multitude of rhetorical sallies, to make what remains awkward and uncertain look like it is natural.

Donations to foreigners were typically made solely for the lifetime of the recipient. To bequeath (*leguer*) is the privilege of the legitimate subject.[19] The Talmont donation pointedly includes Commynes's heirs and successors, perpetually and forever: "pour en jouir par ledict Philippe de Comines, ses hoirs, successeurs et ayans cause, perpetuellement et à tousjours" (so that they may be enjoyed by Philippe de Comines, his heirs, successors, and other rightful claimants, perpetually and forever).[20] These terms affirm the Burgundian Commynes as a royal subject, implicitly identifying the Duke of Burgundy as Louis XI's feudal vassal, and refusing to recognize a de facto political situation in which the Frenchness of Burgundian subjects was not always so readily evident. To treat Commynes uncomplicatedly as a French subject is to engage in a deft rhetorical and juridical parry. The phrasing of the Talmont donation thus repeatedly affirms the coherence between Commynes's specificity as a Burgundian émigré and the Crown's ongoing pursuit of absolute sovereignty in the Roman model.

At the same time, this rhetoric constructs a relation between Commynes and Louis XI that declares itself at once exemplary and singular. The letters take pains to present Commynes as the recipient of the king's loyalty in a manner that, by its promise of personal and reciprocal service, evokes an idealized relation between liege lord and vassal. In this manner, the donation holds forth the promise of a relationship based on personal contact and one-to-one mutual loyalty between subject and sovereign. The praise and rewards lavished upon Commynes promise that each subject will become partner to an encounter as personal and as sanctified as the one described, and thus subtly promised, by the donation text. The text thus constructs Commynes's position as utterly unique and, however paradoxically, promises an identical uniqueness to all those who, following his example, abandon other *pays* to serve their sovereign king Louis XI. The king, as we saw in chapter 1, did plenty to foment collective rebellions among Charles's subjects, but here he calls on those living under his rivals, not collectively, but rather one by one. Pushing aside the hierarchies of vassalry and subvassalry, these phrases summon each individual subject to rebel against the lawlessness of his rebellious feudal lord, and to become a true and loyal subject in a direct, unmediated relation with his king.[21] The narrative of these letters looks towards a new era, indeed, inaugurates an immanent political order, grounded in and exemplified by the singular bond between Louis XI and Commynes. Commynes becomes the exemplary model of the new, idealized royal subject.

By virtue of its construction of an ideal, exemplary political subject, the Talmont donation provokes a series of broader questions about the symbiotic relations between political and individual subjectivity. The uncertain or elusive meanings attached to the word *pays* again prove significant. In a society for whom identity is anchored by investiture in a body of lands – both vertically through time and horizontally across space – where is now Commynes's *pays*, his home? From whence does his identity come? Put very bluntly: Can the Talmont lands really replace the homeland Commynes has fled or forsaken? That is the fiction which this donation asks its intended public to believe. It is in this sense that we can truly say that the identity bestowed upon Commynes by his sovereign king Louis XI glimmers with the promise of subjectivity through subjection. Since Commynes's evasion from Charles's court left him unable to return to Burgundy, we today might see him as being in (political) exile. Through the Talmont donation, Louis XI declares that Commynes has arrived home. Commynes's service to Louis, especially his service to Louis's physical person, pretends to reconcile the tensions between different facets of human experience: the bodily, tactile, particular, and individual on the one hand; the political and social on the other. What Commynes epitomizes is nothing less than the individual alternately erased and brought into existence through the law which emanates from and is incarnated by the person of the king. This observation has far-reaching consequences for our understanding of the *Mémoires*.

Between Personal and Institutional Histories

Alongside its trumpeting of a new era, the Talmont donation also includes a rather startling clause.

> Et combien que le donateur ou donateresse ne soient tenus de porter gariment [garantie] de chose donnee, toutefois, attendu que le don et transport que faisons presentement à nostredict conseiller et chambellan desdictes terres et seigneuries est pour recompense des grans services qu'il nous a faits, et aussi de la perte de ses biens meubles et immeubles, qu'il a eu et soustenu pour nous ... avons promis et promettons par ces

presentes, pour nous, nos hoirs et successeurs, garantir et defendre perpetuellement à icelui Philippe de Comines, ses hoirs, successeurs et tous
ceux qui lui auront cause, envers et contre tous, de toutes evictions, empe-
schements, troubles, molestations et perturbations quelconques.[22]

[And however it may be that the giver is not obligated to guarantee the
thing given, nonetheless, since the gift and conveyance of these lands
which we here make to our counsellor and chamberlain is in recompense
for the great services which he rendered us, and also for the loss of his belongings and lands which he sustained for us … we have promised and do
promise by these letters, ourselves, our heirs and successors to guarantee
and defend perpetually the named Philippe de Comines, his heirs and successors and all similarly interested parties, against any and all, from any
eviction, hindrance, trouble, molestation, and disturbance whatsoever.]

The rhetoric in this paragraph hits several different notes, in essence
making two arguments at once. The donation first asserts a sovereign's
right to give what he wishes to whom he wishes. It then offers to protect
that gift by assuming the posture of a feudal lord promising to defend a
vassal's rights. Moreover, its wording contains several highly charged
expressions such as "être tenu"; these are phrases we will see again, and
come to see in a different light. The phrase "envers et contre tous" here
signals that Louis XI is placing his vows to Commynes above and against
claims his other subjects might make on him. The king's promise gains
force in the letters' emphatic *clauses dérogatives*, clauses which command
obedience regardless of any possible contradictory or anterior dispositions, conventions, or laws.[23] These dispositions awaken the reader's
suspicions. The word "guarantee," in particular, gives pause, since this
word describes the feudal lord's legal, procedural role in the defence of
his vassal in court.[24] The narrative tendered, of a pure, true, and irrevocable gift made in reward for great services rendered, becomes more
ambiguous. Ironically perhaps, the security of Commynes's feudal identity was anchored to the triumph of the imperial, absolutist strains in
Louis's rule, and his status as the subject of a sovereign guaranteed by
the practices of feudalism. Louis's reward to Commynes amounts to
placing the new arrival in a situation of debt and dependence.

Not content to promise the king's own protection, the sentences which
follow catalogue, in exhaustive detail, the extermination of any possible
path of resistance to Commynes's ownership of Talmont and its dependencies (see immediately below). Louis does not simply abolish and

extinguish all rival claims to the property, he annihilates them. As for those who would claim otherwise, let no court receive them. If there is recompense to be made, it will come from the king, and it will not include returning said lands, all rival pretensions to which the king himself, confident in his certain knowledge, special grace, full power, and royal authority has foreclosed and rejected. The text possesses a certain heaving insistence in these passages, an urgency which seeps through despite the plodding repetition and bombastic tone of its legal formulae.

> Et au cas que pour l'avenir il y eut aucuns qui voulsissent donner quelque empeschement à nostredict conseiller et chambellan en la jouissance desdictes terres et seigneuries, soit en tout, ou en partie, ou contre lui intenter quelque action, petition, ou demande, à cause de la proprieté ou possession d'icelles, ou autrement en quelque maniere que ce soit le troubler ou molester: Nous, considerees les causes dudict don et transport, que presentement faisons, de nostre certaine science, grace especiale, pleine puissance, et autorité royale, toutes lesdictes actions, et autres droits que personnes quelconques voudroient ou pourroient pretendre sur lesdictes terres et seigneuries dessus declarees, avons esteint et aboly, esteignons et abolissons, et mettons du tout au neant par ces presentes, sans que jamais ceux qui ont quelque droit et y voudroient pretendre en puissent rien demander sur lesdictes terres et seigneuries, ne intenter contre nostredict conseiller et chambellan, ne ses successeurs et ayans cause, ne qu'ils puissent jamais estre à ce receus en quelque cour ou jugement que ce soit ; mais que ceux qui quelque chose y voudroient pretendre, ayent leur action contre nous et nos successeurs, pour en avoir recompense, si trouvé estoit que faire se deust, non pas pour rien avoir ne distraire desdictes terres, dont, par tant que mestier est, de nostredicte certaine science, grace speciale, pleine puissance et auctorité royale, nous les avons privés, forclos, et deboutés, privons, forcluons et deboutons par cesdictes presentes.[25]

> [And in case in the future someone might wish to present our counsellor and chamberlain with obstacles to the enjoyment of these lands, in whole or in part, or to undertake against him any action, petition, or request, related to the property or possession thereof, or otherwise in any way, shape, or form trouble or molest him: We, considering the causes of this gift which we are here making, by our certain knowledge, special grace, complete power, and royal authority, have extinguished and abolished, do extinguish and abolish, and annihilate by these letters all said actions and other rights which any person would or could pretend to over the above-named

lands, such that those who [might pretend to] some right and would aspire to do so can never request anything from the named lands, nor undertake legal action against our counsellor and chamberlain, nor against his successors or related parties, nor can they ever to such an end be received in any court or jurisdiction whatsoever; but let those who wish to make some claim take their action against us and our successors to obtain recompense, if it should be found that such is due, but not by possessing or taking away anything from the said lands which, as it fits our office, by our certain knowledge, special grace, full power, and royal authority, we have deprived them, foreclosed, and rejected, we do deprive, foreclose and reject by these letters.]

The king calls upon his Parlement, bailiffs, seneschals, "et à tous nos autres justiciers et officiers, ou leurs lieutenans presens et à venir, et à chacun d'eux" (and all our other dispensers of justice and officers, or their present and future lieutenants, to each of them) to ratify his gift, so that those who would pretend to a claim on these lands can never trouble Commynes in his possession "ne qu'ils puissent jamais estre à ce receus en quelque cour ou jugement que ce soit" (nor that they ever be received for such purpose in any court or jurisdiction).[26] It would be difficult to more clearly signal the anticipation of a full-blown legal challenge than does the wall of belligerence erected here.

Louis XI's donation of such a large and controversial gift to the Burgundian refugee he has chosen as his exemplary subject initiates a high-stakes game. The *dispositif* of the Talmont donation emphatically proclaims the lands to be given, granted, acquitted, conveyed, and delivered by pure, true, and irrevocable donation to Commynes and his heirs ("par la teneur de ces presentes, donnons, cedons, quittons, transportons et delaissons par pure, vraye et irrevocable donation audit Philippe de Comines pour lui, ses hoirs, successeurs et ayans causes, les principautez de Talmont [etc.]").[27] Commynes is to enjoy possession of Talmont,

> tout ainsi et par la forme et maniere, et à tous tels droits que feu Pierre d'Amboise ... les avoit et tenoit ... et qu'elles vindrent par succession entre les mains de feu Louis d'Amboise, son neveu. Et avons cedé, quitté, transporté et delaissé audict Philippe de Comines et les siens tout tel droit, nom, raison, action, proprieté, possession et seigneurie que nous avons et avoir pouvons et qui nous peut competer et appartenir esdictes terres et seigneuries ... soit par confiscation et forfaicture dudict Louis

d'Amboise, obligations, transports ou autrement, à quelque titre, ou par quelque maniere que ce soit.[28]

[in precisely the same form and manner and with all the same rights as the late Pierre d'Amboise ... possessed ... and as they came by inheritance into the hands of the late Louis d'Amboise, his nephew. And we have ceded, acquitted, transported, and relinquished to the said Philippe de Comines and his relations all such rights, names, reasons, actions, property, possession and lordship which we have and which we could have and which could depend on or belong to said lands ... whether by confiscation and forfeiture from Louis d'Amboise, obligations, conveyances or otherwise, for any reason or in any manner.]

With these words we begin to see the outlines of what lies behind the proverbial curtain: forfeiture and confiscation, rights and inheritance, generational conflict. The menace that Louis XI's words seek so insistently to quash has its roots in a quarrel between the Amboise family and the house of La Trémoïlle. Talmont owes its disputed possession to a family feud featuring as many twists and turns as one could hope for in a tale involving spurned bridegrooms, vengeance, debauched old men, and nuns. The intricacies of this conflict, however, pivot very precisely on a series of betrayals, on the uses of treason as a political lever, and on the currents of royal will.

Four decades previously, around 1430, Louis d'Amboise decided to marry his eldest daughter, Françoise, to the heir to the duchy of Brittany. This decision did not sit well with Louis d'Amboise's neighbour, Georges de La Trémoïlle, who had desired that Françoise marry his own son. La Trémoïlle, a favourite of Charles VII, convinced the king that Louis d'Amboise's action constituted *lèse-majesté* – i.e., treason – since Louis d'Amboise had not obtained the king's permission in contracting his daughter's marriage. Eventually, in 1438, d'Amboise was pardoned and the confiscated Talmont lands returned to him. D'Amboise then agreed to marry his younger daughter, Marguerite, to Georges de La Trémoïlle's previously slighted son, Louis I de La Trémoïlle.[29] Louis d'Amboise included Talmont and its dependencies in Marguerite's *dot* (dowry), but withheld the property for his own usage until his death. In January 1459 d'Amboise was placed under guardianship at the request of all three of his daughters, who charged that their father was squandering his fortune in debauchery. Arriving on the throne in 1461 Louis XI overturned the ruling of guardianship made by his father. In

September 1462 he arranged to buy the Talmont lands from Louis d'Amboise, agreeing to reserve his own possession of the properties until after d'Amboise's death, just as had been stipulated in the original terms of Marguerite's *dot*. Louis d'Amboise, vicomte de Thouars, passed away on 28 February 1470; Louis XI was standing by to take immediate possession of the long-coveted lands.[30] The king immediately granted the title vicomtesse de Thouars to his favourite daughter, Anne de France, the future Anne de Beaujeu. Two years later, he awarded Commynes the lands and title of prince de Talmont.

When Louis XI, as in the above-cited *lettres de don*, expressly identifies Talmont as his to donate, whether by confiscation and forfeiture from Louis d'Amboise, obligations, conveyances, or otherwise, for any reason or by any manner, he asserts a double right. He bases one element of his claim on his purchase of the lands from Louis d'Amboise (i.e., by obligations, conveyances, or otherwise).[31] The other pillar in his argument revisits the 1430s' accusations of treason levelled against d'Amboise under Charles VII. On this account, Louis XI asserts that the Talmont lands entered royal domain through confiscation and forfeiture from Louis d'Amboise. In such circumstances, the king's gift to Commynes falls under the rubric of "aliénation du domaine" and is subject to approval by the Chambre des comptes.[32] The task of certifying the legitimacy of a confiscation and the entry of the concerned lands into the royal domain fell to Parlement, whose approval was also required when the circumstances of a given confiscation had to be examined before the land could be considered eligible for donation.[33] The king's attempts to steamroll this process of review and double-checks begins in the Talmont letters when he declares the donated lands conveyed to Commynes,

> non obstant que declaration fust ou eust esté faite desdictes confiscations ou forfaicture, et que soubs couleur de ce on voulust dire les terres à nous avenues par declaration de confiscation estre venues à la couronne et estre nostre domaine, et les ordonnances sur ce faites par nos predecesseurs Roys et nous, que ne voulons quant à ce avoir lieu, ni prejudicier au contenu et effet de ces presentes: ains, attendu la cause desdicts cession et transport, qui est pour la redemption de nostre personne et eviter l'eminent danger et peril d'icelle et, par ce moyen, de tout nostredict royaume, nous, de nostredicte certaine science et grace speciale, pleine puissance, loy et autorité royale, y avons … derogé et derogeons par cesdictes presentes.[34]

[regardless of whether a declaration was or might have been made concerning the stated confiscation or forfeiture, under the rubric of which it might be said that lands which come to us by declaration of confiscation have come to the Crown and are of our domain, and [are thus subject to] the ordinances on this matter made by the kings who preceded us and by ourselves; since we do not want [those ordinances] to have any bearing or prejudice on the content and effect of these letters, but rather, given the reason for this transfer and conveyance, which is because of the redemption of our person and the avoidance of imminent danger and peril to ourselves and, by this means, to our entire kingdom, we, by our certain knowledge, special grace, complete power, law and royal authority, have ... waived and do waive [those ordinances] by [virtue of] these letters.]

In the text of the donation itself, the king explicitly commands Parlement, the Chambre des comptes, and royal officers in Anjou, Maine, and Poitou as well, to obey his will. Each is to do his part to ratify Louis XI's donation at each and every level, in thorough and complete form "sans aucun refus, contredict, ou difficulté, nonobstant ... quelconques autres ordonnances, mandemens, restrictions, ou defenses à ce contraire" (without refusal, contradiction, or difficulty, regardless of ... any other ordinances, commandments, restrictions, or prohibitions to the contrary).[35] Despite these royal admonitions, the king's letters were sent first to Parlement and then to the Chambre des comptes. Louis XI's actions acknowledge that Parlement has something to say about the matter as well as the Chambre des comptes; that is to say, he implicitly concedes that the confiscation itself will be examined. In this sense, the Talmont donation exposes Louis XI's broader struggle for legislative authority over and in spite of the traditional roles occupied by Parlement and the Chambre des comptes, and over and in spite of the modes of resistance available to those institutional bodies or to interested individuals. For Louis XI to present the Talmont donation to Parlement and to the Chambre and then to seek, simultaneously, to circumvent their respective roles is to disrobe them of their legislative authority, in practice if not in theory.

It would be impossible to summarize the degree to which legislative authority fell to Parlement or exclusively to the Crown because this question forms the heart of the conflict which shapes not only our study of Commynes's fortunes, but also the development of the monarchy and of French institutions throughout the fifteenth century.[36] More than any of his predecessors, Louis was inclined to view his will as pre-emptive over all other considerations, legal precedents, or processes. Royal will to legislate was neither entirely sufficient nor consistently insufficient in and of itself, whether in practice or in theory. The Talmont donation thus stages a virtuoso performance of Louis XI's skill as a manipulator of royal prerogative. Louis seems to attack the La Trémoïlle family and raise Commynes in a single, efficient gesture. Moreover, he does so in such a way that the issue becomes directly focused on the question of royal authority, or rather, on the obedience of the king's officers to that authority. By donating contested lands and by insisting on his right to alienate them, Louis XI leverages the Talmont letters into a high-wire performance of his own absolute sovereignty. The Talmont donation puts to the proof whether or not *quod principi placuit legis habet vigorem*, whether what the ruler desires has the force of law.[37] The donation text penned at Amboise plays on Louis's sovereign authority and power through the narrative given of Commynes's actions, in the explicit lesson drawn from those actions, in the "pure and true gift" bestowed in recompense, in the legislative power which enables the giver to bestow the gift, and finally in the pretension to demonstrate the sufficiency of royal will to effect that gift. The narrative contained in the text of the Talmont donation constructs a particular vision of sovereignty and of the sovereign subject. Commynes, loyal to the Crown although oppressed by the rule of a seditious prince, becomes the ideal subject; his reward provides a signal demonstration of Louis's sovereign authority.

Administrative Delays

On 15 November 1472, only a month after the royal letters to Commynes were issued and most likely as soon as word reached him, Louis II de La Trémoïlle, acting as champion of his family's interests as heirs to Louis d'Amboise, wrote to Parlement in an effort to delay the ratification (*entérinement*) of the king's letters.[38]

> Très chiers et espéciaulx amis … Aucun de mes amys m'ont fait savoir que, puisnaguères, le roy a donné à ung sien mignon … la terre et seigneurie de Berye, menbre de la vicomté de Thouars, et la terre et seigneurie de Thalemond, qui est du mariage de feu ma femme, dont Dieu ait l'âme. Je vous prie que aiez le soing de vous donner garde quant on vouldra faire enterinez les lettres dudit don en la court de Parlement et ès chambres des comptes des généraulx et ailleurs où il est costume de les faire enterinez, et que, à l'expédicion et enterinacion des dites lettres, vous vueillez

opposez pour moy et en ce pour la conservacion de mon droit faire tout ce
que vous savez mieulx qu'il est de faire en la matière.[39]

[Dear and special friends … Some of my friends informed me that the king
has recently given to one of his minions … the land and seigneurie of Berye,
part of the viscounty of Thouars, and the land and seigneurie of Talmont,
which is from the marriage [dowry] of my late wife, may God keep her
soul. I ask you to take care to be on your guard when they try to have the
letters for this gift ratified in Parlement and in the Chambre des comptes in
Paris and elsewhere where it is custom to have them ratified, and that you
please oppose the expedition and ratification of these letters on my behalf
and that for the protection of my rights you do all that you know it best to
do in the matter.]

Although the sexual connotation later attached to the word "mignon"
during the sixteenth century remains in the future, the label does not
flatter. The king's minions are favourites whose self-interested voices
drown out the counsel necessary for good kingship and the health of the
kingdom.[40] The oppositional pair "amis" and "mignons," with their respective nuances of alliance, trust, and shared interests versus corruption, abuse of power, and exclusion, frame La Trémoïlle's petition in "us
versus them" terms. La Trémoïlle suggests his own solidarity with the
members of Parlement, perhaps on the basis of their shared victimization
as objects of the king's harassment. His rhetoric angles to cast his family's
particular conflict with the Crown as representative of Louis XI's tyran-
nical oppression of all his subjects. The letter campaign had begun.

In February 1473, with his gift to Commynes still floating in juridical
limbo, Louis XI sent lettres de jussion[41] to Parlement demanding that his
lettres de don ceding Talmont to Commynes be duly lues, publiées and
enregistrées "sans attendre d'en avoir second ou tiers commandement,
et ne nous y faire un seul refus, delay ou difficulté, pour quelconque
autre cause ou occasion que ce soit" (without waiting to be ordered to
do so a second or third time, and without making any refusals, delays,
or difficulties, for any cause or excuse whatsoever).[42] A note in Louis XI's
own hand concludes: "Vous pouvés cognoistre le grant desir que j'ay
que ceste matiere soit bien expediée, et à mon entencion, et les causes
qui à ce me meuvent; et, pour ce, gardés que vous n'y faites point de
difficulté, et n'en renvoyés point devers moy" (You know my great desire to see this matter taken care of and in the manner I intend, and the
reasons motivating me; on this account, take care that you do not make

things difficult, and don't send it back my way).[43] Still the Chambre des comptes hesitated. On 25 April 1474 an impatient Louis XI wrote again:

> Noz amez et feaulx, vous savez assez comme, pour la verificacion et finelle expedicion du don que avons fait à nostre amé et feal conseillier et chambellan le sire d'Argenton, vous avons tant de foiz escript et par diverses foiz fait savoir nostre entencion et voulenté, et encores n'en avons peu avoir la fin, qui ne nous a esté ne n'est chose plaisante … et ceste foiz pour toutes, vous prions, tant acertes que povons … aussi, se faulte y a, tenez vous seurs que nous n'en serons pas contens.[44]

> [Our dear and faithful, you well know how, for the verification and final expedition of the gift which we made to our dear and loyal counsellor and chamberlain the Lord of Argenton, we have written you repeatedly and by various means made known our intention and will, and still we have not been able to conclude the matter, which has not been nor is it amusing to us … and this time once and for all, we ask you, as firmly as we can … [And] also, if you fail to do so, you can be sure that we will not be happy.]

Did the members of Parlement read this letter and fear for their wealth or their persons? At last, on 13 December 1473, fourteen months after the letters were first signed at Amboise, Parlement registered the Talmont donation.[45] A further five months elapsed before the Chambre des comptes followed suit in May 1474.[46] Many letters and nearly two years after Louis XI, with "certain knowledge, special grace, complete power, and royal authority," first bestowed Talmont on his counsellor, Commynes's possession of the Talmont properties was at last cemented. Or so it would seem. The day following its registration of the Talmont donation, Parlement inscribed in its ledgers that its capitulation had been forced.[47] In the eyes of its members, the donation remained legally unsound and non-binding. Parlement had lost and was now sulking over its forced submission. For the time being, their protest remained more symbolic than effective.

The resulting calm would prove to be temporary. In 1480 Louis de La Trémoïlle mounted a new legal challenge. Although the king's own *procureur général*, the crown prosecutor, represented Commynes in court, the court ruled in favour of La Trémoïlle, restoring to him a number of Talmont's dependent properties. Louis XI lost no time expressing his irritation. "[P]ar ce moyen ait nostre dict conseiller, par ledict arrest et execution d'icelui, esté desappointé et evincé desdictes terres d'Aulonne, la Chaulme et Curzon, *et lui soient nosdictes lettres de don, quant à ce, demeurees illusoires,* à nostre desplaisance" (And by means of the stated judgment and enactment our counsellor has been disappointed and evicted from the said domains of Aulonne, la Chaulme, and Curzon, and *our letters of donation have, on this account, remained illusory to him,* to our displeasure).[48] The word "desplaisance" alludes to a transgression against *quod principi placuit,* so that both the legality of the donation and the basis on which legality can be established are once more brought into play. This time, the king's letters brought swift results. The court reversed its decision; Commynes remained in full possession of the original gift.[49] These letters between Louis XI and Parlement would prove, however, to have a prophetic quality.

How aware was Commynes of the La Trémoïlle family's claims when he received Talmont? He could not have remained ignorant of them for very long. Yet even if Commynes had known fully of their dispute, he would not have been free to refuse the king's gift. Commynes was effectively a refugee; he needed the lands Louis offered him. Talmont provided Commynes with the basis for a social identity in France and served as the foremost expression of the king's engagement with his counsellor. Furthermore, Talmont arguably bound Commynes and Louis XI together more strongly than a legitimate donation could have done. Talmont remains in Commynes's possession through the use of verbal and juridical violence, with the threat of physical violence never far away. This latent violence reinforces both the intimacy and the constraint binding donor and donatee. The private secrets embedded in the Talmont donation guarantee the security of the political secrets the king shares with Commynes. The consequences to Commynes of any breach of Louis's confidence are absolute. His control of Talmont, and as such, his very social existence, remains entirely dependent on the king's favour. By awarding the contested Talmont to Commynes, Louis assured himself of Commynes's absolute and total dependence on the Crown, and thereby his absolute and total obedience. Commynes depends entirely on the king; therefore the king may depend entirely upon Commynes.

Death and Consequences

Louis XI passed away on 30 August 1483. He was buried one week later, on 6 September, in funeral ceremonies that lasted three days, concluding on 8 September. On 9 September the La Trémoïlle family renewed its petition for the restitution of Talmont.[50] The first depositions were heard on the very same day. The ensuing legal battle between Louis II de La Trémoïlle and Commynes – or, to be more precise, this final act in the ongoing struggle over possession of Talmont – would not reach a final conclusion until July 1491. The stages in the escalation of the Talmont debacle over these eight years (1483–91) are well known to historians. Dupont published extracts from their transcripts among the documentation supporting her 1840–7 edition of the *Mémoires*. Since then scholars from Kervyn de Lettenhove to Joël Blanchard have frequently cited the episodes that marked what Jean Dufournet evocatively called "le naufrage, ou Commynes sous Charles VIII" – the shipwreck of Commynes.[51] From the early days of Anne de Beaujeu's de facto regency, when Commynes occupied a seat on the fifteen-member *conseil*, to his political isolation and arrest in January 1487 for "intelligences, adhésions et pratiques, par paroles, messages, lettres de chiffre et autrement avec les rebelles et désobeissants sujets du roy" (secret agreements, support and dealings, by words, messages, coded letters and otherwise, with rebellious and disobedient royal subjects),[52] to his gradual return to court affairs in the early 1490s, Commynes's legal fortunes and his political fortunes are one.[53] In the *Mémoires*, Commynes remains resolutely silent about these years. Only an embittered remembrance of how the Duke of Lorraine "m'avoit aidé a chasser de la court avecques rudes et folles parolles" (had helped to chase me from court with rude and wild words [517]) lets slip his resentment.[54]

It is beyond dispute that Louis II de La Trémoïlle, through his leading role in the defeat of the Orléaniste camp and the subsequent Breton submission, came to enjoy a place of rare favour in Anne de Beaujeu's eyes.[55] It is equally beyond dispute that Commynes's increasingly desperate part in Louis d'Orléans's repeated bids to siphon power away from the unofficial Beaujeu regency did very little to endear him to the woman known as "Madame."[56] Jean de Bourbon's reconciliation with the Beaujeu regents in 1486 and the interception of seditious letters implicating Commynes marked the end of that path for the disgraced counsellor.[57] At the same time, Commynes's reconfirmation as seneschal of Poitou in October 1483,[58] his presence on the *conseil royal* during the early years of the new reign,[59] the inconsistent application of Charles VIII's royal ordinance revoking his father's numerous *aliénations du domaine*,[60] and Anne de Beaujeu's personal implication in the Talmont affair[61] all indicate that Commynes's shipwreck was not politically inevitable.

It has long been a habit to explain the seizure of Talmont as a conse-quence of the increasing hostilities between Commynes and Anne de Beaujeu, whose rivalry for Louis XI's confidence and whose similar tem-peraments left them ill-suited as close companions. In other words, it is traditional to see Commynes's Orléaniste alliances in a causal relation to his loss of the Talmont estates. I would argue the contrary: Commynes's increasingly incautious gestures were driven by his attempts to retain the Talmont lands and the identity their possession made possible.[62] The La Trémoïlle revindication of Talmont provided an easy focal point for a broader backlash against the excesses that marked the final years of Louis XI's reign, and to this extent, the struggle for Talmont remains one nakedly concerned with wealth and power. The La Trémoïlle legal posi-tion, however, was not invulnerable. The surviving documents reveal a tangle of conflicts, some material, others more difficult to pin down. The Talmont affair enables us to explore ideas of contract and rupture, in particular as they are anchored in ambivalent attitudes about the letter as a locus of power and ideological encounter. We must take seriously the contents of this trial, and heed the deeply felt words there spoken, words whose import is greater than the specifics of this particular case. What were the attitudes and beliefs that propelled the Talmont trial? What went wrong for Commynes in the aftermath of Louis XI's death and how or why was it so irremediable?

In the prologue to his *Mémoires* Commynes asserts,

> nul n'en devroit avoir meilleure souvenance que moy [de Louis XI]; et aussi pour les pertes et douleurs que j'ay receues despuis son trespas, qui est bien pour estre revenue a ma memoyre les graces que j'ay receues de luy, combien que c'est bien chose accoustumee que, aprés le decés de si grant et puissant prince, les mutations sont grandes, et y ont les ungs perte et les aultres gaigne, car les biens et les honneurs ne se despartent point a l'apetit de ceulx qui les demandent. (3)

> [no one should remember him better than I do, because the losses and suffering I have known since his trespass are also good for bringing back to my memory the graces I received from him, however much it is a well accustomed thing that, after the death of such a great and powerful prince, there are great upheavals, and some lose and others profit, for wealth and honours are not distributed according to the desires of those who seek them.]

These sentences allude to but do not name the disgrace in which Commynes finds himself at the moment he begins to write. The word "trespas" that Commynes chooses as a synonym for death comes from the sense of crossing over the threshold between life and death. Now obsolete in English, this is the only meaning the word retains in modern French. During Commynes's lifetime, however, the French *trespasser* meant to die (i.e., *trespasser de ce siècle*), and it also meant to transgress an order or commandment, and, still further, could mean *omettre, passer sous silence*.[63] In order to begin to hear the silence within Commynes's narration, we must turn to his description of the king's "trespas" in Book VI of the *Mémoires*.

During the king's final days,

> Ledict seigneur se jugea mort, et sur l'heure envoya querir mons^r de Beaujeu, mary de sa fille ... et luy dist plusieurs bonnes choses et notables. Et si en tout ledict seigneur de Beaujeu eust observé son commendement, ou en partie (car il y eut quelque commendement extraordinaire et qui n'estoit de tenir), mais si en la generalité il les eust gardés, je croy que ce eust esté le proffit de ce royaulme et le sien particulier, veues les choses advenues depuys. (486–7)

> [The king knew himself to be on his deathbed, and immediately sent for monsieur de Beaujeu, his daughter's husband ... And if the seigneur de Beaujeu had observed his commands or partly so (for there was one that was extraordinary and wasn't to be heeded), but if in general he had honoured them, I think it would have been for the good of the realm and for his own in particular, considering the things that have happened since.]

These are astonishing words – harsh and bitter. Throughout the *Mémoires* Commynes dwells on what pushes men to make the choices they do, and the consequences those decisions have on their lives. In these judgments, "s'il eust" spans the distance between the ideal – what might have been – and the historical – what was.[64] This distance embraces all the tragedy, suffering, and folly that characterize mankind's fallen state, and each individual man's inevitable fall. The refrain "s'il eust" announces some of Commynes's most strongly felt judgments about the engines of history, bringing to bear all the clarity of hindsight on human weakness.

A few sentences later Commynes continues his description of the king's final words to his entourage, describing how Louis XI sends each of those who come to his bedside onwards to "the king" – Charles VIII – with parting words. "Et tous ceulx qui le [Louis XI] venoient veoir, tout envoyoit a Amboyse devers le Roy [Charles VIII], leur priant le [Charles VIII] servir bien. Et par tous luy mandoit quelque chose et par especial par Estienne de Vers [Vesc]" (And all those who came to see him, he sent onwards to Amboise where the king was, asking that they serve him well. He sent some message with each of them and especially with Etienne de Vesc [487]). Commynes again dodges revealing what the king ordered while calling attention to Louis's particular command to Etienne de Vesc.[65] What was the unnamed extraordinary command that was not to be heeded (this "commendement extraordinaire et qui n'estoit de tenir")? And what request was made especially to Etienne de Vesc?

Antoine de Jarrye, "ecuyer, conseiller et premier ecuyer d'ecurie de monsieur de Beaujeu, agé de 27 ans" (squire, counsellor, and first squire in charge of the stables of Monsieur de Beaujeu, aged 27 years) was among the witnesses called by La Trémoïlle on the very first day their petition was received in the court after the king's death.[66] De Jarrye's deposition tells us something that Commynes can only allude to in the *Mémoires*.

Le jeudi 28 aoust dernier passé, environ l'heure de trois heures après midi, lui estant ou chastel de Montils lez Tours, en la chambre en laquelle le feu Roy Loys estoit malade, après son reveil de dormir demanda ledict feu Roy à un des gens de sa chambre si Estienne de Vez, bailli de Meaux, estoit là; et lors ledict Estienne, qui estoit dans ladicte chambre, se presenta devant ledict seigneur, et incontinent que ledict seigneur l'eust apperceu, lui dict les paroles qui s'ensuivent: 'Estienne, dictes à monsieur le dauphin que j'ai tenu la viconté de Thouars, que j'ai baillee au seigneur de Bressuyre, en laquelle je n'ai aucun droit, mais appartient aux enfans de la Tremoille; et dictes lui que je lui prie qu'il la leur rende et le plus tost qu'il pourra, car j'en sens ma conscience chargee, et si je estoye en prosperité je la leur bailleroye; aussi Tallemont que j'ai baillé au seigneur d'Argenton. Je lui ai promis deux mille livres de rente; il est estranger, est un honneste chevalier et homme de bien, et m'a bien servi: pour ce je vous prie dictes à monsieur le dauphin qu'il m'en acquitte, et qu'il lui baille lesdictes deux mille livres de rente, car je vueil que Tallemont leur soit rendu.[67]

[Thursday, the 28th of this past August, around three o'clock in the after-noon, while he [Antoine de Jarrye] was at the chateau of Montils-les-Tours,

in the room in which the late King Louis was sick, after he awoke from
sleeping, the late king asked one of his chambermen if Etienne de Vesc,
bailiff of Meaux, was there; and then Etienne, who was in the room, presented himself before the king, and as soon as the king saw him, the king
said the following words to him: 'Etienne, tell the Dauphin that I held the
viscounty of Thouars, which I gave to the seigneur de Bressuire, in which
I have no right, for it belongs to the La Trémoïlle children; and tell him that
I ask him to return it to them as quickly as he is able, because I feel my
conscience burdened by it, and if I were in good health I would give it to
them; and Talmont also, which I gave to the seigneur d'Argenton. I promised him two thousand pounds in rents; he is a foreigner, he is an honest
knight and a good man, and he served me well: and that's why I ask you
to tell the Dauphin to settle this for me, and that he give [to Commynes]
these two thousand pounds of rents, because I want Talmont returned to
them [the La Trémoïlle family].]

The court secretary takes down de Jarrye's account in third-person
indirect discourse, but writes out de Jarrye's quotation of Louis XI's
speech in direct discourse. De Jarrye's role is described; that of Louis XI
is dramatically re-enacted. With each reading the king again commands
the listener to obey. Louis disavows the same same *lettres de don* whose
absolute sufficiency he had previously compelled Parlement to recognize. These same letters were at stake when in 1480 the *cour de Parlement*
produced its short-lived judgment in support of the La Trémoïlle case
against Commynes. At that time the king had reacted violently to the
suggestion that his letters could be illusory ("et lui soient nosdictes lettres
de don, quant à ce, demeurees illusoires, à nostre desplaisance").[68] Now
he himself declares them so. The words "I want Talmont returned to
them" and "he is a foreigner" ring in the listener's ears. With these words
the king for whom Commynes betrayed homeland, wealth, family, even
the name to which he had been born, now betrays Commynes. Here then,
are the words spoken to Etienne de Vesc. Here then, is the *commendement
extraordinaire* uttered by the king on his deathbed.

The dismissal "il est estranger" – he is a foreigner – provides the
strangest moment in this apparent disavowal.[69] Reading the narrative
tendered in the Talmont donation, we noticed the ambiguities attached
to the notion of *pays* in that text. However, whatever barriers between
Burgundian, royal, and Breton subjects may effectively have existed,
official discourse considered them all equally as subjects of the sovereign French Crown. In response to one argument that Commynes's acts

of devotion to the king made him exceptional, the lawyer for La Trémoïlle had responded some years before that, "se le dict de Commynes avoit revelé aucunes conspiracions faictes contre le Roy ... dont par ses dictes lettres estoit faicte mencion, il n'avoit faict que ce qu'il devoit faire, attendu qu'il estoit *né de ce royaume:* autrement de l'avoir cellé en deust avoir esté pugny comme crimineulx de crime de leze majesté" (if Commynes revealed a conspiracy against the king ... as is mentioned in his letters, he only did what he was obligated to do, given that he was *born of this kingdom:* to have otherwise concealed it he should have been punished as guilty of treason [*lèse-majesté*]).[70] Twenty-seven of those to serve on Louis XI's council were "estrangers" of the same sort as Commynes.[71] When Louis XI declares, Commynes an "estranger" the words are performative rather than descriptive. The king purges himself of a foreign substance. The revulsion has nothing to do with the memorialist's Burgundian roots: Louis XI, and all those who will repeat the word during the trial, are casting him out for a transgression that has irrevocably made him into an Other.

To seize Talmont from Commynes was to undermine the foundations of his identity in France. Two thousand pounds represent only a fraction of either Commynes's yearly revenues from the Talmont properties or of his 6000-*livre* pension under Louis XI. Moreover, during his years of ownership Commynes had invested large sums into developing both the estates and the commercial potential of his Talmont holdings. In contemporary documents, Commynes is most often called *monseigneur d'Argenton*. In fact, the Argenton lands, like the Talmont lands, trailed a long history of contested ownership and legal wrangling.[72] Dreux, where Commynes spent his years of confinement after he was released from prison, did not properly belong to him either.[73] Talmont was the patrimony that Louis XI, desiring to reward his privy counsellor and as an example to all his subjects, gave to Commynes, his heirs, and successors to use and enjoy, fully and in peace ("sesdicts hoirs [et] successeurs" to "jouir et user pleinement et paisiblement").[74] Deprived of Talmont, Commynes will have no home and no homeland.

"Au Feu"

De Jarrye's deposition ends with words that would become a refrain cycling through the testimony given by the prosecution's witnesses. The ailing Louis XI confessed that giving Talmont to Commynes "est tout ce que [*sic*] dont je en tiens plus ma conscience chargee" (is everything that most weighs on my conscience).[75] Why would Louis XI consider the Talmont donation the greatest burden on his conscience? This is the same king whom posterity credited with placing Jacques d'Armagnac's children under the scaffolding where their father was being beheaded so that his blood would wash over them. Compared to such acts, there was truly little exceptional in the struggle between the Crown and the d'Amboise / La Trémoïlle family. Furthermore, while the king acknowledged that granting the seigneur de Bressuire the use of Thouars weighed on him, it is only the Talmont donation that he calls his conscience's greatest burden.[76]

Another secret waits to be uncovered, and within this secret hides a betrayal of another kind. At its most simple, this final secret explains Louis XI's deathbed repentance. At a more elusive level, this final secret exposes the engine of a deep rift between the memorialist and his peers, and a deep ambivalence within the king.

Two simple, interrelated questions lay at the root of the contestations between the La Trémoïlle family and Louis XI. The solidity of Louis XI's possession of Talmont, and thereby of his gift to Commynes, depended on their answers. First, had Charles VII authorized the marriage of Françoise d'Amboise to Pierre de Bretagne? Second, had Charles VII returned the confiscated property of Talmont to the La Trémoïlle family?[77] Ever since Louis XI had given Talmont to Commynes in 1472, the La Trémoïlle family had based their claim to rightful ownership on the assertion that letters to both these effects had been issued. Commynes's control of Talmont rested jointly on the legal sufficiency of the king's *lettres de don* and on the premise that Charles VII had never issued any such letters. The La Trémoïlle archives were at the chateau de Thouars, making them inaccessible to the family, since Louis XI's faithful executor, the seigneur de Bressuire, had controlled all access to the chateau since the viscount's death in 1470. A cursory inventory had been made of the chateau archives at that time, but in 1476 the king dispatched a small party to draft a second, more detailed inventory. Their mission was clear: to assure that the La Trémoïlle case was as unfounded as Louis XI intended and desired.[78]

It was late January 1484 when a fresh inquest began hearing witness testimony in the La Trémoïlle case against Commynes.[79] Some were clerks once employed at Thouars who described in detail letters they had copied. The most damning testimony came from those sent to Thouars with Commynes in 1476. One after the other they told a single story.[80] Letters had indeed been found in the armoires and trunks at Thouars, letters from Charles VII to Louis d'Amboise, some authorizing the marriage of his daughter and others restoring to him his once-confiscated lands. The seigneur de Bressuire's testimony came on the penultimate day of January 1484. He himself never read the letters found,

> mais bien entendit qu'elles contenoient ce que dessus a dit par ceulx qui les lisoient et disoient: "Ceste cy nous est bonne, ceste cy ne nous est pas bonne"... Lesquelles lettres de restitution et permission ainsi eslues et choisies, furent mises ès mains de il qui deppose, et lors ledict de Commynes dit à il qui deppose: "Le Roy veult que ces lettres icy soient jettees au feu," et les print d'entre ses mains et les jetta au feu. Et alors maistre Jehan Chambon dit telles paroles ou semblables: "Quel deable est cecy? c'est mal fait, il ne les faut pas jetter au feu." Et adoncques ledict qui deppose ou ledict maistre Jehan Chambon retirerent les lettres qui estoient deja dedans le feu; lesquelles il qui deppose print et les porta au feu roy Loys qui alors estoit à Cande, ainsi qu'il lui avoit mandé: et eulx estant à Cande, monsieur de Commynes dit au Roy telles paroles ou semblables: "Sire vecy monsieur de Bressuyre qui a des lettres qui ne servent pas bien à nostre matiere;" et ledict Roy demanda à il qui deppose: "Où sont elles, sieur de Bressuyre?" lequel lui respondit: "Sire, ve les cy." Et adonc le Roy les print et les jetta dedans le feu, et puis dit: "Je ne les brusle pas, c'est le feu" ... Et fit faire le Roy serment à ceulx qui estoient là presens de ne reveler point qu'elles eussent esté jettees au feu, et qu'ils s'en gardassent bien de riens en dire.[81]

[but he understood that they contained what he said earlier from those who were reading them and who said: "This one here is good for us, this one here is not good for us" ... When these letters of restitution and permission had in this way been decided on and selected, they were put in the hands of the witness, and then Commynes said to the witness: "The king wants these letters here to be thrown into the fire," and he took them in his hands and he threw them into the fire. And then master Jean Chambon said these words or similar ones: "What the devil is this? That's not right, they shouldn't be thrown into the fire." And then the witness or master Jean Chambon pulled out the letters that were already in the fire, and the witness took them and brought them to the late King Louis who was then at Candes, like the king had ordered him to do: and when they were at Candes, monsieur de Commynes said to the king the following words or similar ones: "Sire, here is monsieur de Bressuire who has letters which do not serve our business well"; and the king asked the witness: "Where are they, monsieur de Bressuire?" And he responded: "Sire, here they are." And then the king took them and threw them in the fire, and then he said: "I am not burning them, the fire does it" ... And the king made those who were present swear never to reveal that the letters had been thrown in the fire, and [warned them] that they should take care not to say anything.]

Now the very heart of the secret betrayed by Louis XI is revealed. The single, audacious sentence, "Ce n'est pas moi qui la brusle, c'est le feu" (It is not I who burns [the letter], the fire does it) returns over and over again from one deposition to the next.[82]

What is the validity of letters which it is commonly agreed do not exist, at least, not any more?[83] At a later hearing, Regnault du Noyer, Louis XI's *procureur du Roy en Poitou*, testified that the letters found at Thouars regarding Talmont "n'estoient verifiees, publiees ne enregistrees par ladicte court de parlement ne autres: et en a bien memoire, parce que dès lors en fut parlé entre les dessus dicts et il qui parle ainsi qu'ils visitoient lesdictes lettres" (were not verified, published, or registered by the *cour de Parlement* nor any other: and he remembers it well, because the witness and the men with him discussed the issue at the time, while they were examining the letters in question).[84] Without evidence of this ratifying process, the letters alleged by La Trémoïlle would have been of dubious force. Similarly, du Noyer recalled seeing letters granting Louis d'Amboise permission to marry his daughter but could not recall who the authorized bridegroom was. "Et semblablement ne scet se lesdictes lettres de congié estoit escriptes en forme de lettres closes ou patentes, en papier ou en parchemin" (And similarly he doesn't know if these letters giving permission were written as open or closed letters, on paper or on parchment).[85] If the found letters had never been registered by Parlement and if even their material description remained hazy, did they need to be destroyed in order to be illusory?[86]

The destruction of the La Trémoïlle family letters raises questions about the textual, human, or institutional locus of authority, and about where the law resides. In counterpoint to the way that Louis XI used texts to expand and enforce royal power, the expansion of written law supported the protection of private property. Whereas the monarchy used writing and texts to expand and enforce its control over individuals, written documents also conferred a new level of coherence on the individual as a legal entity. Legal historian John Gilissen sees "le rôle grandissant de l'écrit dans le droit, comme manifestation de l'individualisme à l'époque de la Renaissance."[87] Private self and private property go hand in hand. Written law, with its attention to the property interests of individuals, as opposed to traditional rights of groups or collectives, reflects the shift towards new modes of thinking.[88] The Talmont case puts into play both of these contradictory tendencies at a threshold moment in French legal history. The Talmont trial reveals written documents to be both sites of coercive violence and sites where violence can be resisted.[89] The violence latent in one set of written documents (the Talmont donation) is brought to intolerable levels when another (the La Trémoïlle family's letters) are burnt. By Louis's own idea of his rights as king, it was his will that made the letters' contents illusory or performative. They were his to burn or honour. Yet clearly his actions crossed a taboo that even he could not break. Louis repents on his deathbed less of granting Talmont to Commynes than of burning the letters found at Thouars.

The testimony given in this contest for Talmont possesses a twofold value. Each man bears witness to the uncertainty of justice as regards possession of the property, and to the certainty of the injustice committed when the Trémoïlle letters were burned. The Talmont trial lays bare the breadth and limits of the king's moral power over men and the contradictory, violent attitudes that surrounded the written object during a moment of radical transformation in both written and legal cultures. Some eleven years earlier, Louis XI's *lettres de don* brought into public discourse the bond forged between king and servant at Péronne. The king's letters proclaimed that encounter transformative and exceptional, and they did so in words which acknowledged a shared, secret experience. The Talmont donation translated a moment of transgressive complicity long nurtured in silence into a new identity. Burning the La Trémoïlle letters repeats just such a moment. The shared act of destroying the letters undermining Commynes's possession of Talmont might be seen as a ritualistic re-enactment of the contract between Louis and Commynes. The other men present became not only party to a secret, but participants in a very particular crime. Burning letters that were court evidence provides the first layer of this crime. At another level, each man is forced to witness at close range the violence at the heart of the bond between Louis XI and his minion.

A Promise Fulfilled

Commynes first came to the witness stand on 19 July 1484. Asked if he recalls the letters in question, his replies taunt credulity.

Pour le present, il n'a pas bonne souvenance d'avoir lors veu lesdictes lettres, et requiert delay d'y penser, afin qu'il en puisse mieux dire la verité.

Dit, par le serment qu'il a fait, que le delay qu'il demande, il ne le demande pour eviter d'en dire la verité; mais est seulement pour y penser, pour en scavoir plus seurement parler: et pour toute souvenance qu'il ait pour le present, dit que audict chasteau de Thouars furent regardees plusieurs lettres, et les aucunes par eux emportees, mais ne scet depposer, comme dit a, pour le present, se lesdictes lettres faisoient mention de ladicte restitution et congié de mariage, et requiert derechief delay, s'il plaist à la court, d'y povoir penser afin d'en respondre plus certainement.[90]

[For the moment, he doesn't have a clear recollection of having seen the letters in question, and requests a delay to think about it, so that he can better tell the truth.

He says, by the oath he took, that he isn't asking for the delay he requests to avoid telling the truth; but only to think about it, to better know how to speak surely: and as for what he remembers, at the moment the only thing is that at the chateau de Thouars several letters were looked at, and some were taken away with them, but right now he doesn't know what to testify, as he said, as to whether those letters mentioned the restitution and permission to marry in question, and he asks again for a delay, if the court pleases, to be able to think in order to answer more surely.]

This is the same strategy Commynes recommends in politics – wear out the opponent in side plays. The court was not duped, and acceded to only a brief delay.

Called again to testify (28 July 1484), Commynes can no longer deflect the questions he faces. No longer does he play metaphysical word games over the sequence of actions debated in the remainder of the hearings. The king, insists a weary Commynes, threw the letters into the fire of his own will, and of his will alone ("de soy mesme, sans prieres de lui, ne d'autres").[91] In a lengthy harangue, the La Trémoïlle family's lawyer had insinuated that Commynes, not the king, was to blame for all that had occurred. Even dampened by its transposition to indirect discourse, Commynes's response resonates with the awkwardness of his situation.

[Ce] qui plus est, jamais il qui parle [Commynes] ne demanda audict feu roy Loys lesdictes terres dont il est question; mais les lui bailla sans

demander, de soy mesme, estant moins de plus grant somme dont il estoit
tenu envers lui,[92] et les lui promit garantir envers tous et contre tous: et
n'eust point voulu ledict feu Roy que s'il y eust eu aucunes doubtes ès
dictes terres, que il qui parle en eust esté adverti, pour crainte que il qui
parle ne se feust apperceu lesdictes terres n'estre pas seures, et que, par ce
moyen, ledict qui parle eust eu cause de s'en retourner dont il estoit venu,
et de laisser ledict feu Roy.[93]

[And what's more, the witness [Commynes] never asked the late king
Louis for the lands in question; but [the king] gave them to him without
him asking, on his own, that being the greatest amount for which he
[Louis?] was obligated to him [Commynes?], and the king promised to
guarantee them against any and all: and the late king would not at all have
wanted there to be any doubts about the said lands, or that if there were
any, the witness be made aware of them, out of fear that the witness would
perceive that the said lands were not securely his, and that, on that account, the witness might have had cause to go back to where he came
from, and to leave the king.]

The expression "être tenu envers" which Commynes uses to describe
his receipt of Talmont from Louis XI is the same one which we will see
Commynes use about the treasonous Saint-Pol, and then again to tell
how he tended to the king during the paralysis which followed Louis's
first stroke (chapters 6 and 7). "Etre tenu envers" goes directly to the
nucleus of the union between the narrator and the king. A pair of secret
epistolary transgressions lay at the heart of the contract between
Commynes and Louis, first in the violence used to enforce Louis's *lettres
illusoires* and then in the burning of the La Trémoïlle letters. If the core
issue in the Talmont inquest pivots on the destruction of those letters, if
the trial confronts the nature of written documents and unwritten contracts of loyalty, then it lies close indeed to the heart of the *Mémoires*,
which are, after all, the product of one man's attempt to bear witness,
in writing, to his king.

The king's deathbed remorse broke the seal on a long-kept secret. In
betraying this secret, he betrayed Commynes. Commynes was "tenu
envers" the king because these secrets lay at the heart of his position in
France. When the king confessed that his conscience was burdened by
these secrets he betrayed the foundations of Commynes's identity in his
adopted land. The king's dying words constitute a repudiation of the
contract established between himself and Commynes in 1472, a contract

whose terms included the exchange of one loyalty for another, sealed by the exchange of one set of lands for another, and resulting in the shedding of one identity for another. In bestowing Talmont upon Commynes the king paid his servant in forged money, offering him letters in which a multitude of secrets, and thus of potential betrayals, lay ripening. Indeed, the king's *commendement extraordinaire* might be seen, not as the repudiation of his contract with Commynes, but rather as its fruition.

Chapter Five

Paper and Parchment

Qui non laborat non manducet[1]
(Whoever does not work, let him not eat)

Le monde n'est qu'abus[2]
(The world is nothing but deception)

Realpolitik: Beyond the Mystical Textuality of Royal Justice

At the top of a document from the chancellery of Charles V, a historiated initial encloses an ink drawing of the king seated on his throne, sceptre in hand.[3] The letter, a C, has been decorated with architectural details to resemble the *lit de justice*, so that its arching canopy shelters the king's crowned head. The image of Charles V which adorns these patent letters is meant to depict how the king embodies Justice.[4] The material parchment text offers the physical embodiment of a mystical relation. The parchment letter, agent of the king's will as law, affirms through this drawing the solidity, stability, and permanence of the several intertwined symbolic relations through which the king, in flesh and blood, but especially in voice and presence, inhabits the Law. This is the tradition against which we must measure the ideologies and practices that shape Commynes's experience of writing, and his representation of letters, the law, or Louis XI's uses of authority.[5]

Secret diplomacy offers a first key to understanding how Commynes could burn the La Trémoïlle family letters. Secret diplomacy proves as well an important conceptual framework through which to approach the *Mémoires'* narrative; this holds true both theoretically and historically.

The narrative contained within the Talmont donation, secretly burning the La Trémoïlle letters, and writing *Mémoires* about Louis XI all place a textual relation at the heart of a human one. The *Mémoires* can be understood as a sustained meditation through one kind of writing, on another. Constant and often complex reflections on the nature and limits of textual authority, the nature of authorship, and the difficulty of being a wise reader reverberate through the *Mémoires*. At the same time, Commynes's own letters offer new insights into the stakes and paradoxes inherent to writing and written objects. Burning the La Trémoïlle family archives and writing a historical narrative are not the same thing, but they both require us to think carefully about the multiplicity of potentially conflicting values and behaviours attached to written objects. Diplomatic activity establishes deep-rooted attitudes and practices around writing. Commynes's own letters highlight this praxis and suggest its capacity to construct an authoring, reading subject. Commynes was writing the *Mémoires* at a moment when the textual dramas examined in chapter 4 were still fresh in his memory. Some of the most intriguing portions of the *Mémoires* from a literary point of view articulate, in ways alternately brutal and subtle, a critique of the confluence of writing, justice, and violence. In this chapter and the next, I will begin by examining a corpus of texts against and through which we can better understand Commynes's relation to writing and the written objects around him. I will then conclude each study with sustained close readings of the *Mémoires* themselves.

The *Mémoires* bristle with anxiety about writing and the written, and especially about letters.[6] The readings in this chapter examine both the portrayal of letters in the *Mémoires*, and letters which Commynes himself wrote and sent. These letters have little to do with permanence, justice, or the institutional; they are not official, chancellery documents meant to be read *in coram nobis*, in open, assembled court. They are "closed" letters, written in – and intended to be read in – private cabinets, alone. Commynes was an adept of the coded, dissimulating letter, intended to be read and then burned. The strange rite in which the king and his henchman burned the La Trémoïlle letters can be best understood as a collision between a traditional, quasi-mystical ideology of legal texts as monuments inseparable from royal authority, and an ethos in which burning letters held a quite different meaning. We need to understand better the ideas that Commynes had about writing letters, about textuality as a set of functions, and about the danger inherent to the letter as a material object. When we understand these things we seize the drama of Talmont more fully. We immerse ourselves in this book's broader arguments about textuality, political subjectivity, and narrative, and prepare ourselves for the intertextuality of chapter 6. Finally, we squint at how Commynes himself might have understood what it meant to write about his king in the *Mémoires*, and thus begin to prepare ourselves for this book's final chapter.

Diplomacy and Ideology: A Historical and Material Context

Commynes was at the forefront of the economic and political practices associated with the arrival of the Italian Renaissance in France. He was the official and preferred interlocutor of the Milanese ambassadors at Louis's court – the very first resident ambassadors in France and among the first anywhere.[7] In the years following Charles the Bold's 1477 death, Commynes became ever more involved in Louis XI's Italian affairs. In 1478, Louis XI chose Commynes as his ambassador to Florence following the Pazzi conspiracy. This mission introduced him to Lorenzo de Medici. The encounter marked a re-orientation of Commynes's professional energies, and a turning point in his personal fortunes as well.[8] After the *Mémoires* of Louis XI were written, Commynes returned to Venice as Charles VIII's ambassador there during the First Italian War. Many of the *Mémoires*' best known passages on statecraft would be inconceivable without the influence of the diplomatic and mercantile milieu he encountered during his travels in Milan, Florence, and Venice.

Few patches of human history have been studied as extensively as these Italian courts in whose ambit Commynes spent the final decades of his career. The rise of Renaissance diplomacy and its institutions, first in Italy, and then in France and beyond, has been a focal point for discussions of modernity at least since Jacob Burckhardt's *The Civilization of the Renaissance in Italy*. Indeed, a great deal of scholarly energy has been devoted to exploring the interdependence of humanism, diplomacy, modernity, statehood, and the nebulous awakening we call the Renaissance. The figure of the ambassador, in particular, has been at the heart of scholarly debate about literary cultures and their economic contexts, rhetoric and law, or statecraft.[9] Commynes was deeply marked by his experience of Italy and Italian diplomats.[10] On this basis alone, we begin to better understand the paradoxical blend of attitudes, ideas, and behaviours – one part Christian, medieval, and provincial, one part cosmopolitan, modern, and universal – that characterizes Commynes's ideas of history and the world. Already, for these reasons, we understand something about the troubling modernity of the *Mémoires*. But these answers are not enough. Commynes was deeply immersed in this world, and yet this was not his world.

To appreciate the conflicts that inhabit Commynes's claims to authority, we must shift our attention away from the Latin learning, formal treatises, and institutions where high-minded notions of rhetoric and statecraft were taking root. Commynes, we shall see below, proclaims adamantly that these are not what is real. In any case, he did not have enough Latin learning to run in those circles.[11] To understand Commynes in his cultural context we need to step back from the public performance of honours and rituals, entries, processions, gifts, or speeches, and to look for what these displays conceal: rumours, information gathering, letter writing, influence peddling, artful confusion, and deliberate deceit.[12] Recent scholarship has deepened our recognition that official diplomacy and secret diplomacy or paradiplomatic missions were often braided together. In a 2008 volume of the *Journal of Medieval and Early Modern Studies,* John Watkins emphasized the variety of practices involved in medieval and early modern diplomacy, and called on literary scholars and art historians, in particular, to join in a renewed, multidisciplinary theorization of diplomatic practices.[13] Timothy Hampton's 2009 *Fictions of Embassy* explored the impact of diplomatic practices on early modern literature, challenging scholars to recognize the extent to which "the cultural implications of diplomatic action are inseparable from the problematics of *writing*."[14] Hampton's analysis of the cross-pollination between literature and diplomacy highlighted the literary importance of theoretical issues of representation, ethics, and selfhood.[15]

Commynes was keenly attuned to textual circulation as the circulation of knowledge and information, power and authority. His letters make this clear and help us to better understand the implications of such an assertion. A deepened understanding of Commynes's letters as both objects and events substantially enriches our appreciation of the relationships between Commynes's experience of diplomacy and the *Mémoires*. The relevance of Commynes's letters for our appreciation of the *Mémoires* is above all ideological.[16] Through Commynes's own letters we grow to recognize all that is at stake in the letters that he writes about in the *Mémoires*. When we see these fragments from a very particular life in letters as *texts* – when we grant their narratives the same rhetorical attention we grant the *Mémoires* themselves – we are able to transform our understanding of Commynes's narration.

The Literature of Experience

At the very end of Book VI, Commynes describes himself as "homme qui n'a aucune litterature, fors quelque peu d'experience" (a man who has no literature except for a little experience).[17] By asserting that his "literature" is "experience," Commynes calls himself learned in the book of the world. He makes use of a particularly literary metaphor to assert his lack of literary credentials. Elsewhere Commynes alludes to "ceulx qui voiront cecy … au temps ad venir" (those who will see this … in times to come [217]). He even says that "bestes ne simples gens s'amuseroient point a lire ces *Memoires*, mais princes ou gens de court y trouveront de bons advertissemens, a mon advis" (brutes and simple people wouldn't take enjoyment from reading these *Mémoires* but princes or courtiers will find good advice in them, in my opinion [210]). These statements show that Commynes, whatever he may say in his prologue, came to imagine the endurance and autonomous circulation of his text beyond his lifetime.[18] They also stretch a filament between Commynes's own conception of the *Mémoires* as an enduring work and the textuality of diplomatic experience.

The "proofs" appended to eighteenth- and nineteenth-century editions of the *Mémoires* include more than one letter written by Commynes, and many more in which his name appears. Yet it was only in 2001 that Commynes's extant correspondence was brought together in a single volume.[19] Scraps of paper scribbled with the most formulaic of *laissez passer* abut letters rich with information about Commynes's private affairs and diplomatic missions; the minutes of ambassadorial reports alternate with unsigned, autograph letters written in code, or still bearing traces of sealing wax.[20] Their editor, Joël Blanchard, hypothesizes a date of 1476 for the earliest surviving letter.[21] The other seventy-eight date from July 1478 or later. Simply put, this means that all Commynes's surviving letters come from the final, "Italian" period of his life.

This material heritage complicates our understanding of the relations between diplomacy, Commynes's professional persona, and either the Talmont debacle or the emergence of the *Mémoires*. The preponderance of Italian correspondents among what survives is not terribly difficult to explain. On the other hand, this material legacy overwhelms and suffocates Commynes's "Burgundian" period. This material legacy also obscures the extent to which Commynes's first fame (or infamy) and a good deal of his early modern legacy derive from his notoriety in, and in relation to, Burgundy. During the years between his arrival at Louis's side in 1472 and the death of Charles the Bold in 1477, Commynes exercised his talents for persuasion and discretion at the head of Louis's clandestine campaigns against his Burgundian rival.[22] Commynes writes in the *Mémoires* of his espionage against Charles and his network of allies. However, in this domain we have not a single scrap of paper from all those that Commynes surely sent. Evidence of Commynes's activity in service to Louis XI's secret campaigns against Charles and Burgundy has all been carefully made to disappear. This is one important reason to remember the Burgundian letters: they are all lost to us, and their destruction signifies.

Eighteen of Commynes's extant letters are described as written in his own hand; we can gain a number of insights from considering which ones.[23] The matter of autograph or secretary-drafted letters turns out to be quite revealing of another facet in Commynes's complex and contradictory relation to writing.[24] The quick succession of relatively informal missives Commynes drafted represents the very opposite of the carefully composed and executed, formula-thick, chancellery-produced charters one associates with medieval diplomacy. Here we reach an important disjunction, rooted in the courtly, and also budget-strapped, education received by the orphaned Commynes. Commynes received no clerkish training; he was not raised to write. Commynes repeatedly alludes to his illegible handwriting. Based on the large, broken, angular shapes he traced, I suspect that he probably had such extremely poor handwriting because the manual gestures of writing were awkward for him. Commynes occasionally writes letters in his own hand for expediency, and he does so frequently for the sake of secrecy. Most importantly, Commynes offers handwritten letters as a mark of esteem. This is most evident in the relatively long, autograph letters he sends to Lorenzo de Medici. Despite apologies for the difficulty of reading his handwriting, five of the ten letters to Lorenzo included in the 2001 edition are entirely autograph. "Je vous usse escript de main, mes ja n'ois, pour que vous ne susés lire ma lettre" (I would have written in my own hand, but I didn't dare, because you wouldn't have been able to read my letter), he adds at the close of a sixth.[25] This respect for writing in one's own hand shows Commynes's investment in the material letter itself as an object of care, and not only the vehicle of communication.

"I Throw All Your Letters into the Fire"

From our first glance at Commynes's letters, we are caught up in a swift-moving current. I quote below the earliest of Commynes's letters printed in the 2001 edition. It addresses Francesco da Pietrasanta, one of the

Milanese ambassadors at Louis XI's court, and would seem to have been written in 1476. Commynes wrote this letter in his own hand – proof of its secrecy and of the familiarity between the two men,.and an opportunity to see Commynes's very personal spelling habits.

> Monsegneur l'ambassadeur, je sray bien tost devers le roy, et y pence estre avant trois jours ou iiij, ou, a l'aventure, bocoup plus tost bref, car j'atens d'eure en eure qu'i me mande. Il y a deux ans que je ne fus icy, pour coy il faut que vous me tenés pour escusé, et ne vous soufrés en rien des besonges de vostre mestre; car y ne se fra riens ou vostre mestre ait honte ny doumage, et ne parlés de vos besonges a personne jusques a ma venue. De la main de tout vostre, Commynes.[26]

> [Monsieur Ambassador, I will very soon be where the king is, and think I will arrive within three or four days, or, maybe, even sooner, since I expect him to send for me any hour now. It's been two years since I was here, so you'll have to pardon me, but don't worry at all about your master's affairs; nothing will be done that would cause your master shame or harm, but don't talk about your business to anyone until I get there. From the hand of your, Commynes.]

It takes a few minutes to untangle what is so unsettling about a letter so sparse and that purports to deliver so simple a message. The paragraph is a masterpiece of spring-loaded tension, offering a coy mixture of evasiveness and manipulation. Commynes speaks directly, without formality or formula. The letter's allusive terms chase after one another, and then slip away from any stable, anchoring point of reference. The very first sentence promises Commynes's arrival by marking a series of temporal limits – "soon," "within three or four days," "maybe sooner." Each one hedges closer and closer to the *now* of writing, and in so doing turns the screw of anticipation a bit tighter. Then comes the final phrase, an unresolved and anxious location of that *now* of writing in a posture of unrelieved tension: "from one hour to the next." The letter is also full of veiled contradictions which begin as grammatical but swell into something ominous. Commynes simultaneously says he will "soon" be "there" and that he "has not been here" in two years: it is as if he were both anticipating and explaining something retrospectively. These shifting, contradictory terms effectively make it impossible to locate the narrating voice on either a geographical or metaphorical plane. He then twice uses the conjunction "et" – "and" – to prepare a negation. The second instance is especially noticeable, resulting in a startling double-speak. Everything is fine; say nothing, or else.

For the twenty-first century reader, the tropes of Commynes's correspondence are the stuff of fiction. Certain letters, and many scenes in the *Mémoires*, evoke the taut menace of a well-wrought thriller or the moody anxiety of film noir. It is evocative to talk of dark alleys and midnight rendez-vous, but the mentions come from the letters themselves. Commynes often includes information about where and when he is writing, especially when he is on the move, or if he is writing about situations in rapid evolution, for example. This practice has obvious pragmatic purposes; transit times could vary, messengers could cross paths or fail to catch up with a letter's intended recipient. It also has interesting poetic implications. One 1478 letter to Antonio di Bernardo de Medici, one of Commynes's early Medici contacts, concludes, "Escript a Hasti a mi de nuyt, ce vendredi xxviij d'ost" (Written at Asti at midnight, this Friday, twenty-eighth of August), thus anchoring the letter in a very precise here and now.[27] Another letter to the same correspondent, written less than two months later, vividly captures the moment's urgency.

Anthoine, annuyt, qui est le xiiᵉ de ce mois, ay trouvé ung clerc du seigner Robert qui est François … Ledict clerc m'a monstré le double de deux lettres … Ledict clerc m'a dit en secret que le seigneur Robert [Roberto di Sanseverino] a appointement avec le pappe et le roy Ferrand … et m'a dit ledict clerc qu'il a quelque intelligence en Lombardie et qu'il doit partir bref de Jennes pour y aller. Monstréz ces lettres a messire Chicque [Cicco Simonetta] et puis les gettéz au feu. Je seray demain au lever du roy. Escript en haste au Pont de Saudre, ce xiiᵉ d'octobre.[28]

[Antoine, last night, which was the 12th of this month, I found a clerk of Robert's who is French … This clerk showed me the duplicate of two letters … the clerk told me in secret that Roberto [di Sanseverino] has an understanding with the Pope and king Ferdinand … and this clerk told me that he [Robert] has a network of allies in Lombardy, and that he is supposed to leave soon from Genoa to go there. Show these letters to Cicco [Simonetta], and then throw them in the fire. I'll be at the king's *lever* tomorrow. Written in haste at Pont de Saudre, this 12th of October.]

The words fairly thrum with anxiety. Anticipation pulses through the next lines, which seem to accelerate with each phrase. Sanseverino will leave "soon"; Commynes will be "tomorrow morning" at the king's chambers. Now he writes "in haste," that is, his hand moves with uncomfortable speed; the material object receives a kinetic charge. The letter tumbles forth in a cascade of secrets exposed and confidences betrayed. First Commynes finds a clerk willing to turn informant. The informant has leaked letters, and then spilled two more secrets – Sanseverino has made deals with powerful people, and he has friends in Lombardy he is going to meet. Commynes is categorical: "Show these letters to Cicco, and then throw them in the fire." How does such a letter survive? The final secret exposed – and the final confidence betrayed – is Commynes's. Whether by intent or lucky accident, neither de Medici nor Simonetta burned the missive as asked.

Commynes manifests a persistent anxiety about the traces his own writing could leave behind, and he repeatedly exhorts his correspondents to burn his letters. His letters are, in fact, peppered with references to their destruction. I know of no original, extant letters addressed to Commynes; he was more diligent about destroying letters than were his interlocutors. Another letter from him reassures Francesco Gaddi, "Fransisco, Jaques m'a escript que vous en allés mecquerdi et que vous usés bien avant vollu parler a moy. Je n'y puis estre juques vendrcdi matin, mes vous me poés escripre surement par se porteur, *car je gette toutes vous lettres au feu*" (Francesco, Jacques wrote me that you are leaving on Wednesday and that you would have liked to talk with me. I can't be there before Friday morning, but you can write me safely by this courier, *because I throw all your letters into the fire*).[29] Commynes's reassurances to Gaddi point to two recurrent concerns, the messenger's reliability and the letter's capture. To protect against the dangers of getting caught, messengers travelled in disguise. Letters were folded until they were only the size of walnuts, then encased in wax. If a messenger was intercepted, he was supposed to be able to swallow his contraband whole.[30] A disguised messenger's clothing and equipment offered dozens of hiding places. Letters could be secreted inside saddles, sewn into the lining of clothing, or hidden inside walking canes. The only thing more surprising than these locations is the apparent nonchalance with which one after another exposed hiding place is listed.[31]

I have called Commynes a kind of spy boss; he says as much himself in the *Mémoires*, and with evident pride. News of Charles's defeat at Grandson in March 1476 reaches Louis's ears quickly "car il avoit maintes espies et maint messages par pays, la pluspart depeschee par ma main" (since he had a large number of spies and messengers in the countryside, most of them sent by my hand [321]).[32] To hamstring the duke, Commynes "envoyoit vers ces ligues d'Almaigne, et a grand difficulté pour les chemyns, et y falloit envoyer mendians et pellerins, semblables gens" (sent to the German leagues, and with great difficulty on account of the routes, and we had to send beggars and pilgrims, and people like that [321]). In the same season, Louis XI catches René II and his sister Yolande, Duchess of Savoy, playing a double game when he seizes one of their messengers loaded with 20,000 écus (324–5). But the king is also playing a double game. He also does not want to declare his part in Charles's struggles openly, and "craignoit bien encores qu'il fust nouvelles de ses messaiges qu'il envoioit par pays" (he was very fearful word would get out about the letters he was sending out into the countryside [322]). The king, as much as anyone else, is afraid of getting caught.

The most remarkable of Commynes's letters to survive falls outside what may strictly be considered diplomacy.[33] Commynes wrote this letter in his own hand in June 1486, during the time of his troubles with the Beaujeu regency, using coded allusions to *the bishop, the chaplain, the cantor, and the deacon* (*l'evesque, le chapelain, le chantre,* and *le doien*).[34] These codes, like the mysterious identity of Jacques, continue to protect the names of Commynes's friends. A mysterious postscript further alludes to the unnamed identities of those present at a secret meeting. Commynes intended his letter for Jean Tiercelin, seigneur de Brosse, but it is clear the letter never arrived. On the back, someone has written,

Ces presentes me furent baillees par ung passant que je ne congnois, il y a environ huit moys … depuis lequel temps je les ay gardees et depuis que j'ay oÿ les nouvelles dudit d'Argenton qui presentement courent, je les ay baillees a monseigneur le Chancellier de Bourbonnoys, maistre Charles de La Vernade et monseigneur le general de Languedoc, pour en faire pour le bien du Roy ou qu'ilz verront bien estre.[35]

[These letters were given to me by somebody passing by that I don't know, about eight months ago … and since that time I have kept them and after I heard the news about d'Argenton [Commynes] now going around, I gave them to monsieur the Chancellor of Burgundy, master Charles de La Vernade and monsieur the General of Languedoc, to use them for the good of the king however they see best.]

One could spend a long time wondering what exactly the note written on the back of Commynes's letter is trying to hide, or how suspicious its evasions would have been at the time. We do not know who wrote this note, nor for what motives its author would have held on to Commynes's letter for eight months without transferring it forward to either its intended courier or the Crown. Clearly its possessor's decision to disclose the letter's existence is linked to the "nouvelles dudit d'Argenton qui presentement courent." Like the English Captain Wenlock (see chapter 3), the author of this piggy-backed letter has played his cards carefully.

Commynes's correspondence reminds us that the fear letters could provoke was a powerful one. Writing to Anne de Bretagne in 1505, after his return to diplomacy, Commynes implores, "Je vous suplie, madame, rompre sez lettrez" (I beg you madame, tear up these letters).[36] In another autograph, unsigned letter to Gaddi written most likely in December 1480, Commynes had begun by writing "Je ne vueil point que l'on chase [sache] que je ly aie escript (I don't want it known that I wrote him)." Then, thinking better of it, he crossed out the word "escript," and filled in "fait savoir" (let him know) between the lines.[37] If one letter goes astray, it is still better not to reveal that there have been others.

These relics from Commynes's correspondence show that there are risks to writing a letter; danger is frequently part of the epistolary pact. Between Commynes and his correspondents, burning a letter can be an act of great loyalty, the act by which one proves trust. A letter that asks to be burned and is not is a letter betrayed: in this universe, the ideal missive vanishes and leaves no trace. When it comes to Commynes and diplomacy, the destruction of the letter is one of the essential stages in epistolary circulation and signification. The material letter can play a role in establishing complicity, but the letter's destruction ratifies the most important of communications. The secret letter is consummated as it is consumed – as it is burned or, in desperation, swallowed whole, to be slowly absorbed into the body itself. This notion that for a select community a letter might only be fully consummated when it is destroyed necessarily bears on our understanding of the events that took place between Commynes, Louis XI, and the witnesses who saw them burn the La Trémoïlle family's papers.[38]

On Letters of Credence

Several of Commynes's surviving letters are letters of credence (*lettres de créance*).[39] The *Mémoires* also allude frequently to messengers giving their credence. Letters of credence serve as the most basic and omnipresent guarantors of an oral message or of its messenger. They provided a hedge against the risk that a messenger would be arrested and his letters confiscated.[40] They also protected against impostor messengers, and certified the trustworthiness of the messenger. Some may have contained signs through which to confirm the bearer's legitimacy.[41] Letters of credence are omnipresent, and for this very reason, they are the most banal and the most fascinating of letters. The interest of such letters goes beyond the official information they smuggled from place to place. Letters of credence serve as keystones in the elaborate poetic architecture that surrounds and supports diplomatic practices (and, in a broader sense, the epistolary itself). They are a catalyst through which presence and absence, voice and writing, are confounded.

Commynes carried letters of credence from Louis XI the first time he visited the Florentine court after the Pazzi conspiracy in April 1478. In them the king addresses Lorenzo the Magnificent, saying,

> abbiamo pensato di mandare verso Vostre Signorie il nostro amato e fedele consigliere et cameriere, el signor d'Argenton, siniscalco del nostro paese de Poitou, che è oggi uno degli uomini che noi abbiamo, nel quale abbiamo maggiore fidanza, per farvi sapere bene a lungo la nostra intenzione, che vi dira e esporra più cose toccante questa materia, preghiam voi che di tutto quello vi dice da nostra parte, che gli vogliate credere e prestargli attenta fede, quanto voi faresti alla nostra persona.[42]

> [we have thought to send to Your Lord our beloved and faithful counsellor and chamberlain, the Lord of Argenton, seneschal of our lands in Poitou, who is currently one of the men in whom we have the greatest confidence, who will inform you of our intentions at length, and who will tell and show you more regarding this matter; we pray that you believe and have confidence in everything he will say to you on our behalf as you would do our own person.]

Compared to these elaborate formalities, Commynes's letters are brisk and no-nonsense. One letter addressed to Gaddi reads, in its entirety, "Fransisco, je me recommande bien fort a vous; je vous prie que vous croiés se porteur, mon secretere, de se qu'i vous dira de par moy, comme moy meismes. Et a Dieu" (Francesco, I bid you warm greetings; I ask that you believe this porter, my secretary, regarding what he will tell you on my account, as if he were me myself. God bless).[43] Both of the above letters fulfil the same function, using a variation on the same, ritualized and ritually necessary phrase. The poetic core of the phrase "as if he were myself" lies in the mystical fiction of its capacity to summon one who is absent. The uses given to this fiction help to give diplomatic letters their specificity. Donald Queller alludes to "letters of Edward II in 1309 requesting the pope hear the very voice of the king in the speech of his envoys. On another occasion the recipient is asked to believe 'as if I were speaking to you with my own mouth.'"[44] Author and recipient join, briefly, in a vicarious experience of presence. Letters of credence minimize the monumental aspect of writing in favour of evenemential possibility. The letter as object creates the possibility of the letter as event. The letter's realization depends on the conjuncture, in time and in space, of a material key (the letter), a site (the intended recipient), and a catalyst (the speaking messenger).

Letters serve as the catalysts for encounter and union, but also carry within the potential for subversion and deviation. To Ludovico Sforza, Commynes writes that his messenger is a man that "le roy a bien pour recommandé. Je luy ai chargé vous dire aucunes choses de ma part. Je vous prye que vostre plaisir soit le vouloir croire" (the king has taken under his wing. I have asked him to tell you a few things on my behalf. I pray that your pleasure will be to believe him).[45] The messenger carries two messages, and the letter a double or dual message. He delivers an official communication from Louis XI, and, in addition, a second one from Commynes. What secrets does this second message hold? Does Commynes whisper advice for dealing with Louis XI into Sforza's ear? Does the second message perhaps subvert official discourse in favour of another, more personal, agenda? Commynes asks that Sforza receive the messenger "as myself," that is, as a representation and agent of Commynes's authority. This relation duplicates and extends the relation between Louis XI and Commynes, who writes to Sforza in his own capacity as representation and agent of the French king's authority. We know nothing about the relation between these two messages. The few words scratched onto the messenger's credence stand in for one or more narratives. Between the material letter and its two unknown and unknowable potential narratives a dynamic field of possibility opens. The relation of delegation and representation between king and ambassador, author and messenger, carries within it possibilities both creative and destructive. In thinking about the relation between deferral and presence, voice and text, we realize that these letters hollow out an interstitial space that makes individual (political) subjectivity possible and simultaneously renders any such subjectivity potentially transgressive.[46]

Letters and Letter Writing in the Mémoires

The continuity between Commynes's letters and the *Mémoires* is manifest through issues of style, content, and ideology. Letter writing is not simply a theme in the *Mémoires*. It is a major influence on their genesis, narrative, and modes of signification, and one of their principle subjects. *Unes lettres, blancs signés, lettres de créance*, and *sauf-conduits* all appear frequently on the *Mémoires'* pages. These are the very loom on which Commynes's text is woven. Joël Blanchard has proposed a very literal meaning for my metaphor: he believes that Commynes drafted the *Mémoires* with the aid of letters and documents in his possession.[47] I submit that the passage from letter into *Mémoire* involves a continuous "glossing" of distinct forms of writing. A critique of writing and of what can be done with written objects runs through the *Mémoires*. Much of this critique concerns the production and uses of authority, and the violent consequences of their exercise. Letters are commodities to control or be controlled by, at one's own peril; this is the constant lesson in Commynes's words.

Let us begin with a relatively straightforward example, one that is almost anecdotal to the larger episode from which it is extracted. In the summer of 1465, during the Guerre du Bien Public, the Breton vice-chancellor, Jean de Rouville, came to meet Charles the Bold at Saint-Denis outside Paris, acting as an agent for François II, Duke of Brittany. "Tous les seigneurs du royaulme" (All the lords of the kingdom [15]) were supposed to be there, "pour remonstrer au Roy le mauvais ordre et justice qu'il faisoit en son royaulme" (to reprimand the king for the disorder and injustice he was causing in his realm [10]). Instead, their gathering is falling apart before it ever comes together: no one is making any firm decisions and several of Charles's would-be allies have not shown up as promised. The moment is a critical one. If the dukes and their companies advance and are rebuffed, there will be no place for their armies to retreat. Rouville "avoit des blans signés de son maistre, et s'en aidoit et faisoit nouvelles et escriptz comme le cas le requeroit. Il estoit Normand et tres habille homme; et besoing luy en fut pour le murmure qui sourdit contre luy" (had signed blanks from his master, and he helped himself to them and manufactured news and letters as needed. He was Norman, and a very wily man; he had to be, considering the rumours that circulated about him [15]). The liberty Rouville possesses to produce documents in the duke's name exemplifies his ascendancy over François II. The next day he displays letters he claims come from the dukes of Berry and Brittany, who are strangely missing in action from this rendez-vous. Rouville "monstroit lectres d'eulx, mais il les avoit faictes sur des blans, et aultre chose n'en sçavoit" (showed letters from them, but he had fabricated them from blanks, and knew nothing else [16]).[48] In layman's terms, Rouville is bluffing. Herein lies both the genius and the treachery of Rouville's character, and the proof of Commynes's carefully chosen word, *habille*, which describes a wisdom more useful than honest.

To control the flow of letters and information is to wield power. Louis has control of his land and a firm grip on his throne precisely to the extent that he controls the vast spaces of his realm. The struggle between Louis XI, Charles, and François II hangs on this battle to control the flow of letters between the two dukes. The reach of royal power expresses itself in material ways, through the success or failure of Louis's attempts to block their letters' passage through the Crown's lands. Remembering Louis XI's passion for the hunt, we might ask, "How fine is the king's net?"[49] Louis makes it impossible for either man to send messengers by land, forcing them to use longer, slower, and more perilous sea routes, and thus putting a serious wrench in their ability to coordinate their efforts against him.

> Tou{s}jour{s} se traictoient choses secretes et nouvelles entre ces princes. Le Roy estoit tiré entre le duc de Bourgongne et le duc de Bretaigne et avoient lesdictz ducs grand peyne pour avoir nouvelles les ungs des aultres, car souvent avoyent empeschement leurs messagers, et en temps de guerre failloit qu'ilz vinsent par mer. (92)

> [There were always new and secret things being discussed between those princes. The king was smack in-between the Duke of Burgundy and the Duke of Brittany and the two dukes had a terrible time getting news of one another, because their messengers were often stopped, and when there was fighting they had to go by sea.]

Louis's surveillance was so tight that at least one messenger sent by the Duke of Brittany "n'estoit que ung homme a pied" (was only a man on foot [173]). Time itself becomes a strategic weapon. It was a risky gambit to be the messenger carrying a letter across enemy lands. The valet Louis XI picks out as the right man to penetrate the English army, Commynes notes, "se jecta a deux genoulz devant moy, comme celluy qui cuidoit estre desja mort" (threw himself on two knees in front of me, like somebody who believed himself already doomed [271]).[50] In Book VII, from Commynes's later historical writing about Italy, Ludovico Sforza has the messenger Isabella of Aragon attempts to send to her father drowned. This is the signal proof of Isabella's powerlessness: she can't get communication past her husband's uncle (535).

So inseparably tied together are the letter and its circulation to the exercise of power that at the end of his life, they are the supreme prop in Louis XI's charade of health (see chapter 7). The first sign of the king's recovery from his stroke is to ask after the letters that have come and gone during the ten days of his illness. "Et vouloit veoir les lectres closes qui estoient arriveez et qui arrivoient chascune heure. L'on luy monstroit les principalles et je les luy lisois. Il faisoit semblent de les entendre, et les prenoit en sa main et faisoit semblant de les lire, combien qu'il n'eust nulle congnoissance" (He wanted to see the closed letters which had arrived and which were arriving by the hour. They showed him the most important ones and I read them to him; he pretended to understand them, and he took them in his hand and pretended to read, even though he had no capacity to do so [464]). Letters depart in every direction from the king's sickbed. In England they tease Edward IV with the prospect of marrying his daughter to the dauphin; to Spain they offered "toutes parolles d'amytié et d'entretenemens" (all words of friendship and talk of the future [474]). Most famously, Louis sent letters far and wide to satisfy his appetite for exotic animals – dogs and horses, but also ostriches and a leopard, moose, and reindeer with giant antlers.[51] However far the king's letters can reach, there his presence will be felt. "Et en effect il faisoit tant de telles choses semblables qu'il estoit plus crainct, tant de ses voisins que de ses subjectz, qu'il n'avoit jamais esté" (And in effect, he did so many things like this that he was more feared, by both his neighbours and his subjects, than he had ever been before [475]). The letters' ostensible purpose – to collect a curious dog or puff daydreams into Edward IV's mind – is trivial next to their true intent. Their true intent is to make sure that everyone remembers that he, Louis XI, still wears the crown of France.

Commynes constantly points out his own skills, especially where those skills are keenest, that is, at the margins where decisions are brokered, in hallways and antechambers, on horseback or in secret nighttime conversations, far from the theatrical ritual of open court audiences. His narrative shifts constantly between what is apparent and official, and what transpires far from any observer's eyes. One of Commynes's most important lessons is that what happens in open court is not "real."[52] The real is what you do not see. Often the people dispatched on a mission do not themselves know how their role fits into the king's larger plans.

> Mais il y a de bonnes gens qui ont ceste gloire qu'il leur semble qu'ilz con-
> duyront des choses la ou ilz n'y entendent rien, car quelques foiz leurs
> maistres ne leur descouvrent point leurs plus secretes pansees. A la com-
> paignee de telz comme je dictz est que le plus souvent ne vont que pour
> parer la feste, et souvent a leurs despans, et va tousjours quelque humblet
> qui a quelque marché a part. Ainsi au moins l'ay je veu par toutes ces
> saisons dont je parle, et de tous les coustés. (84)

> [But there are some good folks who have the glorious idea that they will
> arrange matters about which they understand nothing, since sometimes
> their masters don't in the least share their most secret thoughts with them.
> And in the suite of those ones I'm talking about who are only along for
> decoration at the ceremonies, and often at their own expense, there is al-
> ways some minor figure who has some private deal in the works. At least
> that's the way I've always seen it go, in all these seasons I'm talking about,
> and on every side.]

What is really going on is happening behind closed doors, in private sessions, with the knowledge of as few people as possible. The pomp and circumstance taking place in open court can sometimes be a sleight of hand by which one manoeuvre disguises another. The important negotiations are being carried out in muffled tones just out of view. Power and agency are to be found in the margins.

This layering of apparent mandates over concealed agendas could sometimes involve the deployment of several distinct textual directives. In one convoluted example, Commynes's reader learns that if the king's brother Charles de Valois (Duke of Guyenne) had not died,[53] and if Louis XI had actually signed the treaties with which he spent months teasing Charles the Bold, then Louis's terms were set to require that Burgundy's ambassadors take copies of the signed treaties to the Duke of Brittany, and show François II how Charles the Bold had forged an alliance with the king at Brittany's expense. However, says Commynes, at the last minute a second Burgundian ambassador was going to produce a second, secret set of letters, reassuring the Duke of Brittany that the signed treaties were all part of an act, and that Charles had not really deserted him (219–20). Such hedged bets and double dealing were par for the course between Brittany and Burgundy. Shortly afterwards, the reader learns that, having done the flagrant opposite of what the two had agreed upon together, François II of Brittany writes letters reassuring Charles of Burgundy that he is only faking it. "Et disoient que autresfoiz les avoit il habandonnés par lectre, que par tant ne s'estoient point departiz de leur amytié" (And these said that if he had once abandoned them in letters, that nonetheless he had absolutely not taken leave of their friendship [229]). Once more we see how distinct kinds of letters work with and against each other in ways that emphasize the contradictions inherent to diplomatic strategy. The official discourses of open letters conceal a far more ruthless, knotted set of motivations and loyalties.

The opposition between open and closed, visible and concealed, spoken and intimated, is a structuring one in the *Mémoires*, declined in myriad ways throughout the narrative, beginning with the contrast between *lettres ouvertes* and *lettres closes*, official, public "letters" – treatises, alliances, agreements, decrees, and other forms of administrative documents – and folded, sealed missives that circulate between individuals. Open letters – like those from the chancellery of Charles V bearing a drawing of the king on his *lit de justice* or those claimed by the La Trémoïlle family – are forever and for everyone's eyes. Closed letters are another matter. Closed letters are the ones that Louis XI asks to see as soon as he is able to, as part of his charade of recovery. They are the kind that Commynes wrote, and that he mostly writes about. These missive letters Commynes wrote were literally folded sheets of paper or parchment, sealed with wax to protect their contents from prying eyes. During a meeting of the Société des antiquaires de France, a certain Monsieur Gasnault pointed out that "les lettres closes étaient scellées par des cachets qu'il fallait bien entendu briser pour pouvoir prendre connaissance du contenu, ce qui explique qu'ils aient été très endommagés ou aient même complètement disparu" (closed letters were sealed by cachets which of course one had to break in order to learn of the contained contents, which explains that they [the wax cachets] were extremely damaged or even disappeared completely).[54] Closed letters thus lead us again to reflect on how apparently mundane details can sometimes contain the keys to poetically resonant truths. To read one, you have to break the seal and tear the folded pages apart. Without this act of violence, the letter cannot be read. Reading a closed letter requires a small act of destruction. The revelation of meaning latent within the material text depends on an act of banal, quotidian violence. The object's violation and the realization of its purpose cannot be separated. A letter is a secret whose contents wait to be exposed. Its pages bear the scar of their own existence.

Mary of Burgundy: The Bride Stripped Bare

The final portion of this chapter analyses the *Mémoires'* narrative of Mary of Burgundy humiliated by Louis XI during the months after her father's death. Mary of Burgundy is one of the few female characters in the *Mémoires* for whom Commynes shows unquestionable sympathy. Commynes almost certainly knew Mary when she was a child and he was a young favourite in her father's service. Between the moment narrated in the episode at hand and the moment when Commynes completed the *Mémoires*, Commynes would almost certainly have also known Mary's daughter, the future Marguerite d'Autriche, since Commynes's wife, Hélène de Chambes, was one of Marguerite's ladies-in-waiting when she came, half child-bride, half hostage, to reside at the French court during her years of engagement to Charles VIII.[55] Like the *connétable* de Saint-Pol whom we will meet in the next chapter, Mary becomes the victim of letters she has written. Commynes's writing about each of these two figures grapples with the relations between betrayal and the letter; the secret, confession, and writing; and Louis's capacity for cruelty. Commynes's reflections on these characters show how Louis XI could also use letters as an instrument of domination in a way even more raw than the legislating, legalistic uses explored in chapter 4.

Commynes's account of Mary's humiliation condenses and dramatizes a series of events which took place between February and April of 1477, during the upheaval that followed Charles's defeat at Nancy.[56] The duke's death had created a void in which the long-standing power struggles between city guilds and the ducal court flourished. Without a husband, the not-quite-twenty-year-old Mary struggled to impose her rule. In Commynes's stylized rendering of the spring that followed, Mary's devastation explodes out of Louis's calculated exposure of a set of secret letters. Commynes's narrative transformation of real historical events becomes so intensely charged as to function independently as an inset narration within the larger body of the *Mémoires*. Although he never touches her or sends one man into battle, the king uses letters as a devastating weapon, against Mary and against all of Burgundy. The story Commynes tells is about letters and violence, about the consequences of secrets betrayed, about suffering and stubbornness in

Commynes's childhood home, about the death of a man he admired, and about the irremediable destruction of (political) innocence.

The engine for this tragic theatre begins when the *échevins* of Ghent send their delegates to negotiate with Louis XI, supposedly under Mary's authority. The encounter between them escalates through a series of diplomatic misjudgments, blunders, gaffes, and failures – all of them on the *échevins'* side. Louis XI is a model of shrewd malevolence throughout. When the *échevins* arrive, they do not know that Louis has already received "aulcuns ambassadeurs de la partie de madamoiselle de Bourgongne, ou estoient des plus grans et principaulx personnaiges dont elle se pouvoit aider" (some ambassadors on behalf of mademoiselle of Burgundy, including the most important and principal persons on whom she could rely [379]). That mission had dispatched Guillaume Hugonet, the Burgundian chancellor; the Lord of Humbercourt, whom Commynes calls a wise man and well suited for important affairs; Louis de Bruges, seigneur de Gruuthuse, whom we met in chapter 3; and several others, representatives of all three Estates ("tant nobles que gens d'eglise et de bonnes villes" [380]). Mary's handling of this earnestly ill-conceived embassy is the first error; although it is a forgivable one, it will soon lead to more serious consequences.

As soon as Louis XI receives the townsmen's delegates, he begins to toy with them, exploiting their gross inexperience and his knowledge of their long-standing quarrels, "car ce n'estoient que bestes ceulx a qui il avoit affaire" (because the people he was dealing with were only stupid creatures [388]). When the burghers declare that Mary is determined to follow the wishes of the "trois Estatz de son pays" (three Estates of her land [388]) – by which they mean themselves and their wishes – Louis tells them point blank that they do not know what they are talking about,

> et que eulx se trouverent desavouhéz. Dont lesdictz ambassadeurs se trouvoient fort troubléz, et, comme mal accoustumés de besongner en si grans matieres, respondirent chaudement qu'ilz estoient bien seurs de ce qu'ilz disoient, et qu'ilz monstreroient leur instruction, quant besoing seroit. On leur respondit qu'on leur monstreroit lectres, quant il plairoit au Roy, escriptes de telles mains qu'ilz les croyroient, qui disoient que ladicte damoiselle ne vouloit conduyre ses affaires que par quatre personnes. (388)

[and that they had been repudiated. The said ambassadors found themselves very confused by this, and since they were ill-accustomed to handling such important matters, they responded heatedly that they were quite sure of what they were saying, and that they would show their instructions, if necessary. We answered them that if the king agreed, we would show letters in handwriting that would convince them, saying that the lady (Mary) wanted to manage her affairs through just four people.]

This is the second blunder. Showing letters of instruction is not unlike beginning a poker game by showing your cards to the whole table. An experienced envoy would never rashly offer to show letters not intended for that purpose. (Later ambassadors carried two sets of instruction letters, one for the ritualistic demonstration of good faith, the other, a secret set of real directives.)[57] The *échevins'* offer exposes them as rank amateurs, while Louis's ploy comes disguised as an ally's gesture of goodwill. Outclassed and increasingly agitated, the *échevins* do, in fact, proceed to show Louis their instructions. The king then seduces them completely by showing them Mary's letter. Commynes's description of this letter is so very precise that there can be no doubt he knew it well, and that he had reason to think about it often afterwards.

> Lors leur feist le Roy monstrer une lectre que le chancelier de Bourgongne et le seigneur de Humbercourt avoient apportees a l'autre foiz qu'ilz avoient esté a Peronne [to see the king during a preceding embassy], lesquelles estoient escriptes partie de la main de ladicte damoiselle, partie de la main de la duchesse de Bourgongne, doueyriere … et partie du seigneur de Ravastin … Ainsi estoit ceste lectre escripte de trois mains, mais elle ne parloit que au nom de ladicte damoiselle; mais il estoit faict pour adjouster plus grand foy. (389)

> [Then the king had them shown a letter which the Burgundian chancellor and the Lord of Humbercourt had brought the preceding time when they had been to Péronne, which was written one part in the handwriting of the said princess, one part in the handwriting of the dowager Duchess of Burgundy… and one part by the Lord of Ravenstein … The letter was written like this in three hands, but it only spoke in the name of the said princess; but it was done like this to give it greater authority.]

We notice immediately that Mary's letters are autograph ones. This in itself clearly identifies them as privileged and out of the ordinary; it also gives them a higher priority than any secretary-drafted credentials the *échevins* might possess. Mary's autograph letters say that only that letter's authors and Humbercourt are authorized to act on her behalf. When the townsmen see these letters which are indeed in Mary's hand-writing, they forget everything else. This is a third blunder, and a more serious one. "Quant ces Gantoys et aultres depputéz eurent veu ceste lectre, ilz en furent fort marriz" (When the men from Ghent and the other deputies had seen this letter, they were very angry [389]). Louis XI has hamstrung Ghent's delegation in a single gesture. He then stokes the men's feelings of humiliation, turning their naivety to his own advantage. "Finablement ladicte lectre leur fut baillee, et n'eurent aultre depesche qui fut de grand substance; et il ne leur en challut gueres, car ilz ne pensoient que a leurs divisions et a faire ung monde neuf" (Finally the said letter was given to them, and they didn't receive any other message of real substance; but they barely cared about that, because they were only thinking about their own disputes and about making a new order [389]). The townsmen have acted foolishly in showing their letters, but their far more dangerous error has been to fall into Louis's trap.

The Ghent ambassadors return home, and council is called so that they can make their report. When they get to the point in their story where Louis proclaims they have no authority, Mary "soubdainement meue et courroucee, dist sur le champ: 'Il ne seroit,' cuident estre seur que ladicte lectre n'eust esté veue" (suddenly changing colour and piqued, said immediately, "Impossible," since she was sure that her letter had not been seen [392]). What happens next has far-reaching consequences. "Incontinent celuy qui parloit ... tira de son sein ladicte lectre, et devant tout le monde la luy bailla ... Il ne fault pas demander si elle eut grand honte, car a chascun avoit dict le contraire" (Right away the one who was speaking ... pulled from his bosom that very letter, and presented it to her in front of everybody ... You don't have to ask if she was ashamed, because she had told everyone the contrary [392]). Pausing for a minute over this denunciation, we realize that Mary's letters have now been deployed three separate times. Each time, they have been ceremonially presented. The first time the letters are shown for their intended purpose authorizing Humbercourt and his colleagues; the second time Louis XI exposes them in a move to unsettle the Ghent ambassadors; this third time one of those ambassadors shocks the court by producing proof that Mary has deceived them. The *échevins'* behaviour precisely rehearses the French king's. Did Louis not also stun his disbelieving interlocutors by showing these very same letters? The *échevins* become agents of someone they are not supposed to represent after failing in their role as Mary's delegates.[58] When they go to Louis, the Ghent *échevins* have their minds set on their own preoccupations; they fail to represent their ruler. Upon their return, however, they proceed to represent Louis doubly: first by the striking repetition they make of his deed, and then by virtue of how their behaviour advances the king's interests. Having failed to establish an authentic or successfully mediated symbolic relationship to the duchess, they unwittingly fulfil a role as the king's ambassadors – they are Louis XI's agents now.

That night, the townsmen seize Humbercourt and Hugonet, and after the semblance of a trial, haul them out to the public square and execute them.[59] When they are hauled out from prison, Humbercourt has been beaten so badly that he cannot stand, and a chair must be brought for him at the scaffolding.[60]

> Par avant ladicte sentence, ilz les avoient fort gennés sans nul ordre de justice; et ne dura point leur procès plus de six jours. Et nonobstant ladicte appellation, incontinent qu'ilz les eurent condempnéz, ne leur donnerent que trois heures de temps pour les confesser et panser a leurs affaires, et, le terme passé, les menerent sur leur marché, sur ung eschaffault. (395)

> [Before the sentence was given, the townsmen had beaten them badly without any semblance of justice; and their trial didn't last more than six days. And despite their appeal, as soon as they had been condemned, the townsmen gave them only three hours to confess and put their affairs in order, and when the time was up, brought them out to the market square, and onto the scaffold.]

In what is for him a scene of extraordinary empathy, Commynes writes of how Mary pleads with the townsmen to spare these two men.

> Alla sur le marché, ou tout le peuple estoit ensemble et en armes, et veit les deux dessusdictz sur l'eschaffault. Ladicte damoiselle estoit en son habit de dueil et n'avoit que ung couvre chief sur la teste, qui estoit humble et simple et pour leur faire pitié par raison. Et la supplia audict peuple, les larmes aux yeulx et toute eschevelee, qu'il leur pleust avoir pitié de ses deux serviteurs et les luy vouloir rendre. (395–6)

> [She went to the market square, where all the people were gathered and armed, and she saw the two men on the scaffold. The damsel was in her mourning clothes and was only wearing a headscarf, which was humble and simple so that they would be reasonable and have pity. And there she

begged the people, with tears in her eyes and her hair dishevelled, that they please have pity on her two servitors and return them to her.]

Mary comes to the square and begs for their lives, but to no avail. Commynes is telling such a powerful story we almost forget how simple and how cruel its premise is: Mary writes the names of men she trusts in a letter, and they are killed for it.

With Humbercourt and Hugonet dead, the townsmen pry Mary's other advisors away from her, too. "Et prindrent de tous pointz l'auctorité et la maistrise de ceste jeune pouvre princesse: car ainsi se pouvoit elle bien appeller" (And they took total command and control over this poor young princess, as she could well be called [396]). Only the intended groom's sudden death saves Mary from the townsmen's plan to force her into marriage with Adolf of Egmond, Duke of Guelders, a man she despises, and one of the *Mémoires'* blackest villains (241).[61] In their great hatred, the Ghent burghers do as much to convert Charles's subjects to royal obedience as Louis does himself (399).

There is something stark and also indulgent in Commynes's narrative about the harm that comes to Mary from this exposure of her letters. Stark in that the longer one reflects on the episode, the more one comes to see Louis XI as the perpetrator of an atrocious violence – Louis XI, and not the Ghentish townsmen who are his willing executioners.[62] Indulgent in that the episode is styled in terms that brush against the romanesque. Its narrative more deliberately seeks the tropes, artifices, the poetic revelations of fiction than any other portion of the *Mémoires*.[63]

The tale of Mary's humiliation functions as a metonymy for the ravaging of all of Burgundy. Mary of Burgundy's political vulnerability depended greatly on her condition as a woman. Charles's death left Burgundy with no heir except his virgin daughter. It is rare that the sexual commerce inherent to dynastic ambition shows through so crudely as it did in the early months of 1477.[64] The drama that faced Mary and all of Burgundy pivoted on who would marry her and reign over her lands. The appropriate groom would take possession of her lands and wealth by taking possession of her body. So long as he was alive, Charles had never wanted to marry his daughter to any of the many suitors who clamoured for the richest dowry in Europe. Although he pretended otherwise, the duke did not aspire to marry his daughter advantageously; he wanted to use her as bait. Even in the context of imperial ambitions and matrimonial politics, Charles's behaviour garners harsh words from Commynes: "Ledict duc de Bourgongne

monstroit tousjours y vouloir entendre, mais jamais n'en eust le vouloir, mais en vouloit entretenir chascun, comme j'ay dict" (The Duke of
Burgundy was always acting like he was interested [in marrying her],
but he never had the intention of doing so, but instead wanted to string
each [suitor] along, like I've said [206]). Louis XI especially dreaded an
alliance between his younger brother Charles de Valois and Charles the
Bold. But, says Commynes, this would never have happened: Charles
did not want a powerful son-in-law; he wanted to "marchander de ce
mariage partout" (get something from everybody out of this marriage
[206]). Charles resembles a literary archetype: the king who wants
to keep his daughter all for himself. In folklore, this archetype is that
of the incestuously desiring father. Literature and medieval legal history coincide in their assessments of the vulnerabilities inherent to this
situation. Lineage can falter; the virgin daughter can be abducted or
raped by a man who wants to leverage a claim to her hand, and thereby
her inheritance.[65]

Commynes's richly fictionalized account of the urban uprisings that
ripped across Mary's lands transforms their history into a fiction rooted
in the mediated and sexualized violence enacted by Louis XI on Mary
using her handwritten letters. This confusion is made possible through
a series of slippages between the metonymy through which Mary of
Burgundy represents her lands; the metaphor through which Louis is
the Father of his kingdom; and a doubly charged synecdoche through
which the letters that circulate stand in for both Mary's inexperience –
her innocence or virginity – and for Louis's aggression. In fact, Louis XI
was Mary of Burgundy's godfather. In the very first letters the king
writes after learning of Charles's defeat, even before he is certain of the
duke's death, Louis XI alternately reminds his subject that Mary is his
goddaughter and expresses his desire to conclude her marriage to the
dauphin.[66] Commynes also repeatedly employs a vocabulary resonant
with sexual politics, romanced and otherwise. When the townsmen hear
they are "désavoués," they become "fort troublés"; their disarray causes
them to respond "chaudement"; confronted by the princess's letter they
can only be "fort marriz." The same phrases might describe the poor
behaviour of a rejected suitor. The Ghentish ambassador pulls Mary's
letter suddenly out from concealment and brandishes it in front of the
assembled court with the intent to harm. Mary is then "soubdainement
mue" – she changes colour – "et courroucee" – she loses her composure
and becomes angry. Se muer, especially, belongs to the corporal language
of courtly love, where ladies change colour from extreme emotion,

whether anger, pleasure, or surprise. Words like "erreur," "honte," and "vilain," punctuate Commynes's account; these tend to produce an impression of latent criminal sexuality in the actions of the princess's commoner adversaries, described as "bête," "déraisonnable," and "très mauvais." Each time Commynes designates Mary he uses descriptors which emphasize her sexual eligibility, calling her "demoiselle" and "jeune demoiselle." At other moments, the appeal for pity is more direct, and he calls her a "pauvre princesse." Commynes then uses the words "constraindre," "tenir," and "prendre" to describe the townsmen's power over her, even while he continues to insist on their bestiality ("ce n'estoient que bestes" [388]). Commynes synthesizes months or years worth of deep-rooted political rivalries and economic interests, not to mention one of the single most influential moments in European dynastic politics. But this extratextual scope does not alter the fact that what he writes about is a once beloved and carefully guarded young princess, now held "in the hands of" a group of lower-class men, free to do as it pleases them. "Pour l'heure de ce siege d'Arras estoit madamoiselle de Bourgongne a Gand, et entre les mains de ces gens tres deraisonnables, dont luy ensuyvit perte, et prouffit au Roy" (At the time of this siege of Arras mademoiselle de Bourgogne was at Ghent, in the clutches of those very unreasonable people, on account of which grief came to her, and profit to the king [385]). The Ghentish townsmen pursue their rebellious agenda "a leur plaisir, pour ce qu'ilz tenoient ladicte damoiselle entre leurs mains" (as they pleased, because they held the damsel in their grip [387]). How many times must he write this phrase before the reader begins to visualize fingers curled around an arm? It is true that Commynes gives free reign to the class prejudice through which he perceives the Ghent *échevins*. However, class prejudice is not sufficient explanation: the story also involves a child Commynes once knew, the mother of another child he has known. In a final, damning precision, Commynes writes that when Mary comes out onto the square wearing only a modest scarf on her head, she weeps and she is "toute escheveelee." This scene is entirely of Commynes's invention, but its fictions contain little that is pleasant. Weeping and undone hair, as both legal scholars and art historians have demonstrated, belong to a highly codified set of conventions surrounding rape and its representations.[67]

The emotion that so characterizes this episode of the *Mémoires* does not fade as the narrative moves beyond the events of 1477. Instead, Commynes repeats several more times how Mary hates Louis XI specifically because of what he has done to her with these letters. "Ladicte damoiselle avoit conceu hayne contre le Roy, a cause de sesdictes lectres, qui luy sembloit avoir esté occasion de la mort de ces deux bons personnaiges dessus nommés et de la honte qu'elle receupt quant publicquement luy furent baillees devant tant de gens, comme avéz ouy" (The damsel had conceived a hatred for the king, on account of her letters, which seemed to her to have been the cause of the death of the two good men named above and of the shame she received when they were given to her publicly in front of all her men, as you have heard [436]).

What does Mary of Burgundy represent for Commynes? Does she symbolize a lost home or does she command his personal, individual loyalty? The drama that plays out between Mary of Burgundy and Louis XI, the drama of Burgundy, is a family drama for Commynes. The dealings between Mary and Louis XI lead us to confront a violence grounded in the figure of the Father. Louis XI, Father of France, takes on the allure of a substitute father-figure in relation to Mary at the same time that he continues to occupy the role of aggressor against her (now dead and absent) father. Louis XI occupies, at several, simultaneous levels, the role of protecting father and dangerous rival. Louis kills the father and then occupies his role. Louis XI, because of what he does to her with letters, becomes Mary's ravager.

Our readings of the attitudes that surrounded the material life of closed, diplomatic letters in the first half of this chapter have made it possible to understand how Commynes could have burned the Talmont letters with such confidence. At first glance, the Talmont affair examined in chapter 4, the study of closed letters in the first half of this chapter, and Commynes's portrayal of Mary's humiliation might appear to us as very different faces of textuality, epistolarity, and remembrance. However, the trait these episodes share is also the trait that defines their importance to Commynes. To varying degrees, all three bring out the universal and visceral fear that one's secrets will be exposed. All three pivot on the ways that letters can be used to exercise control over someone. In the *Mémoires*, Louis has exposed Mary's secrets, he has alienated people she once trusted, he has made her powerless and dependent on her enemies. Louis XI's deathbed betrayal did to Commynes precisely what Commynes portrays the king doing to Mary.

Chapter Six

The Treasonous Saint-Pol

L'oiseleur parle bien doucement pour prendre les oiseaux.

The Birder and the Birds

Louis de Luxembourg, Count of Saint-Pol, *connétable* of France, was sentenced to death for *lèse-majesté* on 16 December 1475, and publicly decapitated three days later, 19 December, on the Place de Grève. Two hundred thousand people attended his execution.[1] Saint-Pol is among the most important characters in the *Mémoires*, and Commynes appears to have had detailed, first-hand knowledge of Saint-Pol's attempted betrayals. Like Mary of Burgundy, Saint-Pol became a victim of letters he himself wrote. Several of the *Mémoires'* revelations about Saint-Pol's treason concern his efforts to turn the marrying of Mary of Burgundy to his own advantage. In this sense, the historical plot threads surrounding these two characters begin together. More important is the common symmetry of their relation to Commynes's own story of letters and loss, a story which we have seen remains untold in the *Mémoires*. Commynes's narrative uses both characters as frames through which to explore Louis XI's use of letters as instruments of domination. If the episode of Mary's humiliation provides an allegory through which to mourn a lost homeland, the radically dispersed telling of Saint-Pol's downfall displaces and so makes possible a meditation on what it means to live in exile.

In this chapter I will examine a mosaic of texts including the letters used to condemn Saint-Pol, a bound presentation copy of the deposition the *connétable* gave during his trial, and Commynes's writing about Saint-Pol in the *Mémoires*.[2] Considered as an ensemble, this corpus offers a naked vision of how writing, textuality, political subjectivity, and narrative coalesce under Louis XI's reign. My arguments concern the ways that acts of reading and writing are bound up with the subject's relation to power, real or fantasized. Intertextuality becomes a mechanism through which this relation to power becomes destabilized and rewritten, sometimes literally so.

"The birder talks sweetly when he wants to catch the birds." The line comes from the immaculate pages of a manuscript made for Chancellor Pierre Doriole. The manuscript contains the deposition given by Saint-Pol, over whose trial and condemnation Doriole had presided. The *greffier* who first wrote the line, in a hand less neat and on a page less pristine, was transcribing words spoken by one of the men the king had charged to interrogate Saint-Pol. The interrogator was himself reading from another text, a letter Saint-Pol had written years earlier. The way he goes on citing at length and with precision makes it clear that, as he speaks, he holds Saint-Pol's letter in his hand. This letter is addressed to Louis XI's younger brother, Charles de Valois, Duke of Normandy and then of Guyenne, the same brother Louis was rumoured to have poisoned. It continues, "l'oyseleur parl[e] bien doulcement pour prendre les oyseaulx et qu'il ne se fyast en chose que le roy lui promeist" (The birder talks sweetly when he wants to catch the birds, and he shouldn't believe in any of the king's promises).[3] When Saint-Pol hears his words read back to him aloud, Charles de Valois is long dead, and he is the bird caught in Louis's net.[4]

Saint-Pol's condemnation was made easy for the Crown by the abundant paper trail he left in his wake. Saint-Pol was not only two-timing the king; he was also attempting to play Charles the Bold and Edward IV off one another. All this scheming made for a thick packet of letters. Louis XI seized the ones Saint-Pol could not destroy in time; Charles and Edward handed others over to the king. "Le roy d'Angleterre envoya au Roy les deux lectres de creance que ledict connestable luy avoit escript, et manda toutes ses parolles qu'i luy avoit jamais mandees. Et ainsi povéz veoir en quel estat il s'estoit mys entre ces trois grans hommes, car chascun des troys luy vouloit la mort" (The king of England sent the king the two letters of credence which the *connétable* had written to him, and conveyed to him all the words that Saint-Pol had ever given him. And so you can see what a mess he had gotten himself into between those three great men, because each of the three wanted him dead [298]). More than once, Commynes seems to marvel at the catastrophe Saint-Pol prepared for himself. "A Paris fut commencé le procés dudict connestable; et bailla ledict duc tous les seellés qu'il avoit dudict connestable et ce qui pouvoit servir a son procés" (In Paris the *connétable*'s trial began, and the duke handed over all the sealed agreements he had from the *connétable*, and everything which could be of use in his trial [310]). The letters used against Saint-Pol in his trial have not survived, but the terms of his interrogation provide a running inventory of their recipients, contents, and occasionally details of their material description.[5]

Saint-Pol is at the core of the *Mémoires'* broader history of royal domination. No other strand in Commynes's narrative quite so subtly expresses what Louis XI's authority meant to those who lived under its shadow. In my introduction, I discussed the interlocking history of treason law and royal claims to sovereignty in fifteenth-century France. I highlighted the passage from a discourse of *trahison* to one of *lèse-majesté*, and showed how essential this lexical shift was for the mutation of loyal vassals in reciprocal relations of service with their lords into subjects obedient to a sovereign king. In a study devoted to the doctrinal and theocratic aspects of majesty, Jacques Chiffoleau writes that the history of *lèse-majesté* "nous aide enfin à approcher le mouvement de ce qu'on pourrait appeler, de façon pédante, 'l'intériorisation de la domination.' Car, nous le savons biens, ce n'est pas seulement, et peut-être surtout, parce que nous avons peur de la sanction que nous obéissons à la Loi, c'est aussi parce que nous aimons cela."[6] Chiffoleau's appreciation touches at the psychological ambivalence that saturates Commynes's writing about Louis XI. Saint-Pol's role in the *Mémoires* opens a vista on the relations between their narrative and contemporary discourses surrounding the nature of loyalty and betrayal (on the one hand) or the status of the written (on the other).

In reaching for the ghost of Saint-Pol we touch at the core of Commynes's reflections on subjectivity and subjection. His portrait of Saint-Pol provides several of the *Mémoires'* most powerful reflections on human experience. In passages about Saint-Pol we are able to see Commynes writing his way through questions of contingency, the nature and limits of human experience, or the tension between the demands of history and the individual. The story Commynes weaves around Saint-Pol explores what we might anachronistically call the tragedy of identity. (The significance of this phrase will unfold as we follow the peripeteia of Saint-Pol's struggles.)[7] Saint-Pol's story is both his own and universal. It is Commynes's own story, seen through a glass darkly.

The Making and Unmaking of the *Connétable* de Saint-Pol

Louis XI's reign stands out as a pivotal moment for the use of treason law and the theatre of treason trials in service to the expansion of royal power. Saint-Pol's trial and execution stand out in turn as a pivotal moment within Louis XI's reign. Saint-Pol's historical significance is both practical and symbolic.[8] Saint-Pol's trial had practical significance because it exposed the sprawling network of alliances that united France's nobility in plotting against the king. Saint-Pol was the ringleader of this conspiracy and its first to fall. His confessions likewise paved the way for the arrest of Jacques d'Armagnac, Duke of Nemours, whose trial and execution quashed what remained of aristocratic resistance to Louis's tyrannic ways. The exemplary symbolic value of his trial comes from the legal apparatus in which the *connétable* perished. The treasonous *connétable* was executed for *lèse-majesté*, not *trahison*. The judgment against him never uses the word for betrayal in its broader human or feudal meanings. Instead, "ladicte court a declairé et declaire ledict messire Loys de Luxembourg crimineux de crime de leze magesté" (the court has declared and declares the said monsieur Louis de Luxembourg guilty of the crime of *lèse-majesté*).[9] As promised in the introduction to this book, the lexicon of *lèse-majesté* has completely displaced the lexicon of betrayal.

Before looking at how Saint-Pol's letters, the manuscript of his trial deposition, and the *Mémoires* fit together or call one another into question, some contextualization is needed. Saint-Pol's far-flung domains were spread across France and both the Flemish and francophone Netherlands. He even held a title from the kingdom of Naples. The tragedy of Saint-Pol's identity begins here, in the double bind inherited with these scattered fiefs.[10] Saint-Pol held lands from, and owed loyalties to, both Charles and Louis. "Combien que le Roy fust lors son maistre, si avoit il la pluspart de son vaillant et ses enfans soubz ledict duc" (Even though the king was then his master, most of his possessions and his children were under the duke [171]). The scale of this not-uncommon situation was grander for Saint-Pol than for most of his contemporaries. Historian Pierre-Roger Gaussin has estimated that, including the 24,000 *livres tournois* Saint-Pol received from Louis XI as *connétable*, Saint-Pol's revenues were close to 50,000 *livres tournois* in 1471, the last year before his situation began seriously to deteriorate.[11] Married to Marie de Savoie, Saint-Pol had Louis XI for a brother-in-law.[12] His older sister was mother-in-law to the English Edward IV.[13] One of the *connétable*'s children had the French king for godfather; another very nearly had Charles the Bold for his.[14] The honour itself is a conventional one, but the fact of being so close to both Charles and Louis reveals the schism Saint-Pol was called upon to straddle. Such a position combines both rare influence and extreme vulnerability, and required a constant balancing act. It was easy to be too close for comfort to either Louis or Charles. Saint-Pol was too close for comfort to both.

Saint-Pol's strategy for personal and political survival emerged from this position astride and in-between two reigns. Charles and Louis's expectations of Saint-Pol were almost completely incompatible. Proof of loyalty to either could come in no other form than active, visible disloyalty to the other. It was in Saint-Pol's interest to foment a constant, low-level military engagement between Charles and Louis so that their attention and their troops would be directed elsewhere. As long as Louis XI and Charles are occupied by one another, they will, so Saint-Pol's logic goes, leave him more or less alone. If either Charles or Louis has any respite from the other, or worse, if one should triumph over the other, then the victor's next move would likely be coming after him, Saint-Pol. He therefore worked out a deliberate, desperate, strategy to keep Charles, Louis, and Edward IV at bay by nurturing their respective grievances against one another. "Il vouldroit bien qu'on eust tant a besongner ou royaume qu'on le lessast en paix" (He would much like for there to be enough to do in the kingdom that he be left in peace).[15] To prove two mutually exclusive loyalties, Saint-Pol maintained a dizzying, almost schizophrenic jig of espionage and counter-espionage.[16]

Reading in the *Mémoires* about Saint-Pol's almost ten years of double-dealing is apt to produce the same flabbergasted sensation that accompanies televised reports of men arrested after decades of unlicenced surgical practice, extravagant bigamy, or spurious investment management. One hesitates between incredulity over the lies told and incredulity that anyone believed such lies. On the pages of the *Mémoires* and in the narrative spun by his own confessions, Saint-Pol comes across as at first confident in his ability to finesse anything, and then later exhausted by the theatrical exuberance required to finesse his own narrow escapes. With time, each side grew increasingly suspicious of his repeated excuses. Louis XI and Charles eventually set aside their own differences and made capturing Saint-Pol their common goal, agreeing that whoever caught him would hand him over to the other for trial. Although Commynes usually avoids mentioning Louis's interference in matters of justice, he acknowledges the pressure Louis XI placed on the court to resolve Saint-Pol's case quickly. "Le Roy pressoit fort la court (il y avoit gens pour la conduicte du procés), et aussi veu ce que le roy d'Angleterre avoit baillé contre luy, comme avez oÿ cy dessus; et aussi ledict connestable fut tost condampné a mourir, et tous ses biens confisqués" (The king put a lot of pressure on the court (he had [his] people running the trial), and also seeing what the king of England had handed over against him, as you have heard already; and so the *connétable* was quickly condemned to die, and all his belongings confiscated [310]).[17] Found guilty of *lèse-majesté*, the *connétable* should have been quartered. He got off with decapitation.[18]

All Politics Are Textual

Political subjectivity begins as a textual relation. The corpus of texts that connects Saint-Pol, Commynes, and others makes visible the primacy of the textual in resistance to Louis XI, the extent to which the repression of that resistance was textual, and the interdependence between the circulation of politically valued texts and the production of normative or transgressive subject positions. Saint-Pol's trial is about texts and textuality; the *connétable* is guilty of reading and writing about the king.

Although imperfect, the trial transcript holds a mirror to the gradated vocabulary of alliance and protection used in Saint-Pol's letters. Werner Paravicini notes, "par le vocabulaire employé dans le procès du connétable, on saisit bien les différences qui existaient entre intelligence ou entendement, amitié, et amitié fermée ou alliance."[19] Letters are the material anchors for the "amitié" and "recommandation" between correspondents. The words have none of the neutral politeness they possess today. The *Trésor de la Langue Française* defines the word *recommandation* as the "acte par lequel un homme libre se constitue l'homme d'un seigneur en s'engageant sous serment à le servir à vie en échange de la protection de celui-ci."[20] In a context where fear of royal displeasure is so pervasive, it becomes difficult to untangle acts of disloyalty to the Crown from acts of loyalty to a fellow subject. Letters become the material guarantors of each. It is commonly remarked that one of feudalism's great weaknesses came from its relative lack of "horizontal" social bonds. The tissue of alliances that surrounds Saint-Pol brings the bonds between comrades to the fore. At a time when Louis XI was quashing the obligations of feudal reciprocity beneath the language of imperial sovereignty, his subjects were reaching for that feudal vocabulary as armour against royal pressure. The greater the disloyalty towards the

Crown, the greater the danger, the tighter the bond between each sei-
gneur, and the more exalted each morsel of written communication.[21]
Each letter has the potential to forge a connection with another subject.
Every such connection acts as a potential obstacle to royal obedience.

What is the relation between the conspiracy of which Saint-Pol stands
accused and his letters? We find ourselves confronted with an essential
textual problem. Saint-Pol's interrogation tests the limits of our ability
to distinguish between notions of the text as the representation of an
extratextual real, and of the text as producer of the real. Our first inclina-
tion might be to see Saint-Pol's letters as referring to a conspiracy against
the king. In truth, however, his letters *are* the conspiracy. The letters
presented in court are fragments of a polyphonic narrative made from
many more such letters. In their ensemble, this body of letters forms a
larger tapestry of resistance and alliance. Writing is what Saint-Pol is
guilty of; the prosecution is eager to get at the details about his correspondence precisely because these produce the opposition to which
they refer. Saint-Pol's letters are fragments of history as text. Saint-Pol
and his "amis" do not, in the end, take up arms against Louis XI as they
had in 1465. They never do poison Louis XI or try to kidnap him or stab
him. They write letters, letters which thus truly constitute both texts and
events. We shift from an idea of Saint-Pol's letters as the proof of an
extra-textual "real" towards the recognition that acts of reading and
writing are themselves subversive activities.

The *connétable*'s epistolary networks are part of a more porous textual
economy. Especially in Paris, the *connétable* became a favourite subject
for defamatory texts of every sort, oral and written. These constitute
another element in the mosaic surrounding Saint-Pol. Most insult the
connétable and so first come across as expressions of royal propaganda.
It is likely that some were so, but their popular character is, in my view,
more important. These most ephemeral texts can be understood as part
of a popular, public discourse about royal power and government abuses. They give proof that the textual dynamics at stake in this book were
not limited to Louis XI's conflicts with the upper nobility. Graffiti, rondeaux, slogans, and ditties of all sorts incarnate the extreme unruliness
of the textual-political relation. During his interrogation, Saint-Pol
described himself as "fort troublé des escripteaux qu'on avoit attachés
contre les paroiz en diffamacion de lui" (very upset by the graffiti that
had been written on the walls to his dishonour).[22] The *connétable* goes
from writing to being written about: he loses the power to be an author
and becomes a character. One element in this popular cacophony, a

complaint poem written after Saint-Pol's death in a style imitating the *rhétoriqueurs*, included the memorable call: "Petits enfans, dont guerre occist les peres, / Menez liessee au ventre de vos meres, / Car par ma mort vous vivrez en repos; / Povrez femmes qui les larmes ameres / Avez jettées pour les maris & freres, / Muez le dueil, prenez joyeux propos" (Little babies, whose fathers war slayed / Rejoice inside your mothers' wombs, / For by my death you will live in peace; / Poor women who bitter tears / Did shed for husbands and brothers / Cast off your mourning, talk of cheerful things).[23] This is the vox populi, and it has an agency all its own.

Saint-Pol's letters produced consequences far beyond their author's ability to limit the damage caused. Louis XI appropriates the texts intended as weapons against his domination, and, in a process which both proves and reinforces his own greater power, absorbs that power and turns it against Saint-Pol and his allies. Each scrap of paper is a catalyst that can set in motion a potential reordering of power relations. The same letters the *connétable* wrote to protect himself against Louis XI and Charles became the means of his own destruction. The arms of resistance and the arms of coercion are one. One can obey a text that originates with the king, or one can assume a textual identity that opposes and resists his authority. Writing, especially writing in secret, carves out a subjective position which is essentially oppositional. In December 1477, Louis XI issued a royal ordinance declaring it treason to conceal knowledge about treasonous activities.[24] In other words, one does not have to be the author of a letter to be guilty of treason; knowing of the letter's existence becomes in itself dangerous. In chapter 5 we read the letter inscribed, poetically enough, on the reverse side of Commynes's ciphered missive by the man who handed it over to the king. It is not necessary to wait until after 1477 to observe the acute fear that contact with potentially subversive letters could inspire. During Saint-Pol's trial, his son wrote to the president of the Chambre des comptes, Jean de la Driesche, whom Saint-Pol had once helped in an hour of need. But de la Driesche refused to open the letters addressed to him except in the presence of Chancellor Doriole and the royal council. The messenger who brought the letters was arrested, and not released until after Saint-Pol had been executed.[25] That is how powerful and how dangerous a letter can be – one man goes to jail for having carried it; another is too afraid to read it.

Saint-Pol's letters are the shards of an imperfect narrative. Obliged to find more than perhaps is there to be found, the men Louis has charged to interrogate the *connétable* pick away at his replies, reminding him that, "la chose du monde par quoy il peut plus contenter le roy et lui monstrer qu'il a bon vouloir a lui et a son royaume est de lui declarer franchement ceulx qui estoient malcontens de lui et qui pratiquoient contre lui et qui escripvoient ou mandoient nouvelles" (more than anything in the world, he could best make the king happy and show his good intentions towards the king and his kingdom by frankly naming those who are unhappy with him and who are conspiring against him and who are writing or sending news).[26] A conspiracy inquiry should tell the dramatic story of disaster averted, a king saved just in time. The bits and pieces should fit together in a neat whole; political plots, like any others, need a beginning, a middle, and an end.

The standard edition of Louis XI's letters is strangely mum for the weeks surrounding Saint-Pol's arrest.[27] However, a justly famed letter from Louis XI to Jean de Blosset, seigneur de Saint-Pierre, written while the Duke of Nemours was under arrest, lays bare the violence involved in producing a satisfactory narrative.[28] In this letter Louis accuses Chancellor Doriole of having rushed Saint-Pol onto the scaffold in order to keep his own name from coming out in the *connétable*'s confession. He explodes with irritation that Blosset's men have been letting Nemours out of his cage to interrogate him, and that he has been allowed to hear Mass where women are present. (Worse still, they have taken off his leg irons and failed to transfer guards who were complaining about their wages.) This must stop, writes the king. Only let him out of his cage if it is to beat and torture him.[29] Louis begins and ends with the same exhortation: Blosset must get Nemours to produce a detailed story. The letter opens in a tone of irritation:

> Monseigneur de Saint Pierre, j'ay receu voz lettres.
>
> Il me semble que vous ne avez que à faire une chose, c'est de savoir quelle seureté le duc de Nemoux avoit baillée au connestable d'estre tel comme luy pour faire le duc de Bourgongne régent, et pour me faire mourir et prandre Monseigneur le daulphin et avoir l'aucthorité et gouvernement du royaume, et le faire parler cler sur ce point et le faire gehenier bien estroit.[30]

> [Monsieur de Saint Pierre, I received your letters.
>
> It seems to me you have only one thing to do, that is find out what guarantee the Duke of Nemours had given the *connétable* so that he would go along with him to make the Duke of Burgundy regent, and to kill me and

kidnap Monsieur the Dauphin and take over the authority and governance of the kingdom, and to get him to speak clearly about this matter
and to beat him up thoroughly.]

Louis concludes by returning to the letter's opening command. "Si
vous avez jamais voulenté de me faire service, que vous le me faites
bien parler" (If you ever desired to fulfil your obligations to me, make
him talk well).[31] Voluminous or sparse, each trial can be thought of as
a sustained negotiation of textual power dynamics, in service to the
unwilling production of a tell-all account. Each day that Saint-Pol is
brought before his "jury" traces an ever-widening circle of names.
Reading the whole of Chancellor Doriole's manuscript from one end
to the other produces a surprising fatigue, along with the impression
that the *connétable*'s plotting, no less than his interrogators' attempts to
produce acceptably clear and shocking revelations, could be drudgery.
Unlike the whirlwind of Saint-Pol's three-week examination, the trial
of Jacques d'Armagnac, Duke of Nemours, lasted many months and
generated hundreds of folios containing numerous interrogations.[32]
The two partake in a similar quest, the quest to exhaust what there is
to know.

  Saint-Pol's trial stages a confrontation between the *connétable*'s desire
to produce and disseminate texts while concealing them from the
Crown, and the Crown's quest to impose its textual dominance. The
connétable and his cronies rebel by sending scheming letters back and
forth. The letters presented in court are pieces in a larger puzzle made
from many more such letters. Each of Saint-Pol's letters is both an act
complete in itself and one fragment in a larger narrative woven from all
the letters the *connétable* sent or received. Saint-Pol's trial helps to fill in
and expand a broader narrative from these epistolary fragments. By
appropriating Saint-Pol's letters Louis XI takes control of the *connétable*'s
narrative and rewrites its ending. Louis XI puts an end to the *connétable*'s
scribbling, and then demonstrates his own power by exposing these
letters to his own exegetical prowess. His interrogation of the *connétable*
scrapes clean every possible recess of meaning from the confiscated
letters, and answers their address with his own definitive sentence.

From *Greffe* to Book

Chancellor Doriole's manuscript copy of Saint-Pol's interrogation serves
as the keystone in an elaborate intertextual architecture. In the first place

are the *connétable*'s letters, those he managed to have destroyed and those that fell into the hands of the king. The original *greffe* of the *connétable*'s interrogation provides the next piece. This spontaneous copy of the *connétable*'s confession gives way to a group of more carefully recopied versions. Louis XI appears to have ordered the court *greffe* copied into a neat hand on folio pages intended for reading and circulation. Paravicini has suggested that Louis XI then offered these presentation copies as gifts.[33] Based on the recurring coincidence between the *Mémoires* and the revelations made during Saint-Pol's trial, Commynes seems to have known Saint-Pol's deposition very well. Could Commynes, like Chancellor Doriole, have been the recipient of a book copy of Saint-Pol's deposition?[34]

The triangulation between the *Mémoires'* narration, Saint-Pol's deposition (within which the reader hears several braided voices), the neat recopying of that deposition, and the *connétable*'s perished letters, produces a kind of kaleidoscope of partial texts. Physical preparation of the *connétable*'s confession into a proper "book" transforms its contents. Oral record becomes literary narrative; document becomes text. The deliberate reproduction and circulation of the trial transcript in codex form adds another all-important facet to the textual architecture that surrounds Saint-Pol. One might argue that either Saint-Pol or the *greffier* Guillaume de Cérisay is the author of the original *greffe*, but Louis XI is the author of this "book of Saint-Pol." The king now controls the production, content, and circulation of the *connétable*'s story. It is Louis XI who has written the story's end. Genre also shifts in this reconditioning. Chancellor Doriole's copy, Bibliothèque nationale manuscrit français 3869, might more justly be seen as a persuasive text. In the words of Wolfgang Iser, meanings in literary texts are "mainly generated in the act of reading; they are the product of a rather difficult interaction between text and reader and not qualities hidden in the text."[35] For Chancellor Doriole, Commynes, or Saint-Pol's contemporaries the manuscript of Saint-Pol's confession tells part of a story about which the reader may well know more than just what he reads. The reader knows how to interpret this story because he is himself one of its missing, untold pieces. The recipient is a part of the tale he reads, whether or not his name appears on the page. Herein lies the terrible message within Louis XI's gift. By offering the "book of Saint-Pol" to his subjects, the king reminds the recipient that he could become the "hero" of a similar narrative. As the recipient reads this presentation copy of Saint-Pol's trial, he remembers who the real author(ity) is. If he is a good reader, he understands the warning not to do too much writing or reading for his own good.[36]

Saint-Pol in the *Mémoires*

Commynes's portrayal of Saint-Pol in the *Mémoires* typifies all that is most elusive and most powerful about his narrative. Commynes alludes several times to his own far-reaching knowledge of Saint-Pol's treachery. The *connétable*'s double-dealing is the hidden cause that Commynes reveals behind many of the events he narrates. Surprisingly, however, relatively little has been said about Commynes's portrayal of Saint-Pol. This likely has to do with the way that Saint-Pol haunts the *Mémoires*' narrative. Commynes tells Saint-Pol's story in a manner that hews closely to its gradual unfolding. Revelations about what Saint-Pol was writing and to whom are woven into the cloth of his narrative. The stages of Saint-Pol's machinations and eventual self-destruction marble Books II, III, and IV of the *Mémoires*, carrying Commynes's narrative a good portion of the way from the Guerre du Bien Public through to Charles's final defeat outside Nancy. However, when one goes to pluck the red thread of Saint-Pol's betrayal and downfall from the *Mémoires*, one realizes how diffused his presence is within the narrative. We get a different understanding of Commynes's reflections on the *connétable* by making ourselves receptive to the images and phrases in Commynes's narrative. The affective tenor of these passages in the *Mémoires* holds up a further textual mirror to both Saint-Pol's story and Commynes's own. Commynes's depiction of the *connétable* is steeped in ambivalence. Saint-Pol surfaces constantly, but Commynes's portrayal of him also characterizes all the most elusive aspects of the *Mémoires*' narration.

When Saint-Pol's trial was taking place, Charles was still alive, and Commynes was as close as could be to Louis XI. By the time that Commynes wrote the *Mémoires*, however, many things had happened during the intervening decade which may have complicated how Commynes thought or felt about the *connétable*'s duplicity, his restiveness, or his fate. When he writes the *Mémoires*, Commynes is no longer a royal favourite possessing exceptional knowledge or power. He is a man who has been betrayed, felt persecuted, has plotted and conspired, and been at grave risk of becoming the hero of his own trial for *lèse-majesté*. He, like Saint-Pol, has clung to lands which assured his survival and promised his destruction. He has contemplated fleeing, and been unable or unwilling to turn his back and leave while there was still time.

He has been confronted with secret letters in his own hand, and he has known himself to be written about.

In order to appreciate the rhetoric of Commynes's portrayal of Saint-Pol in the *Mémoires*, it is useful to return for a moment to the historical context of Saint-Pol's case. Our sensitivity to the linguistic resonances within Commynes's narrative depends on knowledge of these circumstances. Few themes resume so succinctly the relations between Burgundy and the French throne as the *villes de la Somme*, the Somme River towns.[37] In 1435 Charles VII ceded them to Philip the Good as part of the Treaty of Arras. In 1463, under the influence of the powerful Croÿ family, Philip allowed them to be repurchased by Louis XI. The sale caused a durable rupture between Charles and his father and planted the seed of Charles's hatred of the king. Regaining possession of the Somme River towns provided Charles with one of his most violent preoccupations. Charles recovered Saint-Quentin and several other towns from Louis XI as part of the negotiations that brought a close to the 1465 Guerre du Bien Public.[38] It was during these same negotiations that Louis de Luxembourg, who had fought with Charles against the king, acquired the office of *connétable*.[39] Despite having been obliged to return the town of Saint-Quentin to Charles, Louis XI remained focused on regaining control of it. Using his position as *connétable*, Saint-Pol convinced Louis XI to make use of him (Saint-Pol) to retake Saint-Quentin (this was in December 1470–January 1471).[40] The move led Charles, who up until that point had not interfered with Saint-Pol's split obligations, to confiscate the *connétable*'s Burgundian properties. In December 1473, Saint-Pol raised the ante: he took steps to confirm his own hold on Saint-Quentin.[41] In effect, Saint-Pol used the royally funded military forces he controlled to hold the town hostage from either duke or king.

It is difficult to understand Saint-Pol's effort to claim for himself the most viciously contested piece of real estate in a feud between two deadly opponents from a rational point of view, but this is indeed what Saint-Pol did. From this point forward Saint-Pol's greatest weapon, and ultimately his only defence, consists of alternately taunting Charles with Saint-Quentin and promising to hand the town over to him. Manipulating Charles is the key to manipulating Louis XI. Gradually, Saint-Pol's survival comes to depend on this single card. Frontier geography explains both the danger Saint-Pol courts and his protection from it. "Quelcun pourra demander cy aprés si le Roy ne l'eust sceu faire seul. A quoy je respondz que non, car il estoit assis justement entre le Roy et ledict duc" (Someone in the future could ask if the king could not have done it alone. To which I answer that no, because [Saint-Pol] was seated exactly between the king and the duke [230]). If only one side were to try to punish him, he would simply take himself and his lands to the other. The destruction of Saint-Pol has to come from both sides.[42]

Enrico Pozzi's description of the traitor as someone who, placing himself between A and B, locks them into an impasse whereby he is the arbiter and manager of the balance between them, fits Saint-Pol perfectly. "Redisons-le: la structure de la trahison est irrémédiablement triadique. Elle suppose entre les pôles antagonistes A et B un 'lieu' intermédiaire et irréductible où le traître s'instaure."[43] Saint-Pol constructs just such a "lieu intermédiaire" in the town of Saint-Quentin. Just as Pozzi describes this space as irreducible and the triadic situation it implies as irremediable, so Saint-Pol becomes trapped within the very "lieux" he has hollowed out for himself. On these next pages, I will attempt to demonstrate how the rhetoric Commynes uses to depict the *connétable* enacts this process. We realize, little by little, that Commynes's very turns of phrase sit at the boundaries between figured and more strictly referential speech. This ironic strain has the effect – however paradoxical – of simultaneously imbuing Commynes's narrative with a metaphor-rich density and of producing an impression of bereavement. Commynes's narrative about Saint-Pol reproduces the very thing that it silences: that is, the *connétable*'s suffocation within an irremediably intersticial space. Its narrative resonance comes from the gradually accreting lexical coherence that surrounds the *connétable*'s downfall, described in terms that seethe with associations with annihilation and erasure. The imagery that surrounds Saint-Pol is folded so deeply into Commynes's prose that it almost disappears. What remains is a stifled poetic discourse in which Saint-Pol's geographical and political dilemmas move like a fog through the text. The consequence, and thus the importance, of this texture within Commynes's prose, is to endow Saint-Pol's fate with both eloquence and empathy. These stylistic effects are not, I believe, deliberate ones but rather the opposite, the accidental rhetoric of knowing without knowing.[44] Their traces are slender and sparse. I have evoked the several ways in which Saint-Pol's letters, Cérisay's *greffe* from the deposition, and the circulation of presentation copies of the trial's narrative create an intertextual space through which political subjectivity is produced or coerced. I would now like to consider the ways that Commynes's *Mémoires* in turn filter and renarrate Saint-Pol's reflections on being in-between.

Many factors get in the way of a neat parallel between Saint-Pol and Commynes, but there are enough resemblances between them to make us read Commynes's depiction of Saint-Pol with care. The trial deposition provides Saint-Pol's account of himself as a royal subject. A transcript – especially one that has been rewritten as a book – is not a tape recorder. And yet, however distorted by legal process or the naked alterity of the past, this manuscript of Saint-Pol's deposition allows us to come as close as it is possible to come to hearing the *connétable* talking about his relationships with Charles and Louis XI. The manuscript allows us to eavesdrop (cautiously and self-consciously) on Saint-Pol's confession of what it was like to be caught between the two. Saint-Pol says as little as he can about the textual misdeeds that landed him on trial. When he talks about his state of mind, however, he becomes a different kind of character, expressive and sometimes moving. His words inspire flashes of terror and pity.

The words *défaire* (or *défaçon*) and *détruire* (or *destruction*) run through Commynes's narrative of Saint-Pol, as they do through the *connétable*'s own testimony. At his trial the exhausted, defeated *connétable* explained that he "se doubtoit que le roy voulust faire recouvrer la ville de Saint-Quentin sur lui par force et qu'on le taillast en pieces dedans" (feared that the king wanted to recover the town of Saint-Quentin from him by force and that they would cut him to pieces inside).[45] The same lexicon is present throughout his confession. "Il failloit qu'il en contentast l'un. Interrogué quel contentement il lui pensoit faire, dit sur son ame qu'il ne sceit sinon de le prier et persuader de non plus retourner au traité de sa desfaçon" (He had to make one of them happy. Asked how he planned to make him happy, he says that by his soul he doesn't know except by asking and persuading him not to go back to the agreement about his destruction).[46] The same vocabulary recurs in the *connétable*'s trial and in the *Mémoires*. "Ainsi se commença a praticquer la maniere de deffaire ledict connestable … Et se commencerent a descouvrir toutes parolles et tous traictés menés par luy, tant d'un cousté que d'aultre, et mectre avant sa destruction" (This is how the plan how to destroy the *connétable* began … And all of his words and all of his dealings, on one side and on the other, began to come out, and his destruction began to take shape [230]). The words have powerful connotations. To destroy is to annihilate, to extinguish completely. These are the words used by Jean de Roye or, in their Latin equivalents (*delere, extinguere*), by Thomas Basin, for Louis XI's intentions towards Charles the Bold.[47] Writing about the 1480 trial of Jean de Bourbon – another of those touched by the arrest of Saint-Pol – Olivier Mattéoni observes, "Le verbe a un sens particulièrement fort. On rappellera que 'destruire,' du latin populaire *destrugere*, apparaît en français au milieu du XIe siècle. S'il a d'abord une valeur concrète, il acquiert rapidement (vers 1080) un sens figuré de 'faire disparaître, anéantir' que l'on retrouve ici."[48] Mattéoni suggests that these words are figurative in their political usage, and I agree. *Défaire* and *détruire* are perfect examples of figured language that we risk taking for granted. However, I suggest that we must not forget they are also not figurative, for it is Louis XI's perogative to take his subjects for their direct objects.

Late in the *Mémoires*, the aging Louis XI confides to Commynes that he "passoit temps a faire et a deffaire gens" (passed the time making and unmaking people [474]). Commynes glosses the word himself.

> Il faisoit d'aspres pugnitions, pour estre crainct et de paour de perdre obeissance (car ainsi le me dist il), remuoit offices et cassoit gens d'armes, roignoit pensions, oustoit de tous pointz; et me dist peu de jours avant sa mort qu'il passoit temps a faire et a deffaire gens … que quant on oyoit parler des oeuvres qu'il faisoit, chascun avoit doubte. (474)

> [He exacted harsh punishments, in order to be more dreaded and out of fear of losing obedience (he told me so himself), he moved appointments and fired men at arms, cut pensions, stripped everything away; and he said to me a few days before his death that he spent his time making and unmaking people … so that when someone heard the things he was doing talked about, he worried.]

Commynes uses three different words for fear (*crainte, peur, doute*), each with a different nuance. Idiomatically, *casser quelqu'un* means to demote him, but the transitive verb *casser* literally means "to smash or break an object." The king "breaks" men at arms and "strips everything away." He makes "harsh" punishments. The thing is, when Commynes says this about Louis in his old age, his tone is melancholic and restrained. These are the words that Commynes associates with *défaire* in its least violent expressions![49] These are figurative expressions, except that they also are not. The king truly does make and unmake people: people are his *oeuvres* – his creations, his works – and he can also destroy them. If his will to do so is strong enough, he can even have their bodies ripped apart. Not long after making this confidence to Commynes, Louis stripped everything away from him, too. Louis made and unmade Commynes. The *connétable*'s own annihilation proceeds by degrees. Walls of the towns he holds will be breached, and then their buildings razed. His secrets will be exposed and his body threatened with torture, and then his head chopped off. The reach of royal power breaches fortified walls and even penetrates the interior space of individual bodies.

The town of Saint-Quentin gradually takes on a metonymic role in relation to the *connétable* himself. Addressing a future reader who might not know of Saint-Pol, Commynes explains that the *connétable* "estoit assis justement entre le Roy et ledict duc" (he was seated exactly between the king and the duke [230]). Commynes's language collapses the distance inherent to rhetorical figures. Commynes means to say that the lands Saint-Pol controls sit on the frontier between the two. In the *Mémoires*, the poetic resonance attached to this intermediary space deepens even as its historical and political consequences become more and more pressingly "real." Saint-Pol's pas-de-deux with the town of Saint-Quentin concerns coveted lands – strategic cities – but it is also about being pressured, about not having any space. Both Louis and Charles are trying to take possession of the space Saint-Pol occupies. Both are trying to appropriate his person as an extension of their own dominion. Saint-Pol *is* the space between Louis XI and Charles. The communication between Saint-Pol and his lands flows in both directions. Saint-Pol seeks to create a place for himself where there is none: to hollow out an interstice habitable as both geographic and psychic space. The fortified walls that surround Saint-Quentin take on tremendous metaphorical importance. Defending the city he has more or less stolen comes to serve as the emblem – the *enseigne* – of Saint-Pol's folly, but also of his futile attempt to find a space of refuge from the invasiveness of Louis or Charles's power. The city's fate and his own are inseparable: the integrity of one protects the other; when one is breached, the other will be crushed.

When One's Coin Is Spent: On Being Afraid

Saint-Pol's fate sealed itself in a double sequence of meetings. At the first, at Bouvignes in May 1474, Louis's and Charles's envoys agreed that, "le premier des deux qui luy porroit mettre la main dessus [i.e., seize Saint-Pol], le feroit mourir dedans huyt jours aprés, ou le bailleroit a son compaignon pour en faire a son plaisir" (the first of the two who could get their hands on him, would have him killed within eight days, or would give him to the other to do as he pleased [233]).[50] Saint-Pol has been clinging to Saint-Quentin as his defence against king and duke; now Saint-Quentin becomes the price on Saint-Pol's head (233).[51] Using an expression rich in economic connotations, Commynes writes, "ledict connestable fut adverti que l'on y marchandoit a ses despens" (the *connétable* was warned that they were bargaining at his expense [232]). Commynes has already set up a similar ambiguity using the word *vaillant*, which literally means "having value." Even though Saint-Pol served the king, his possessions – his *vaillant* – were under the duke (171). As a noun, the word *vaillant* here alludes to the *connétable*'s wealth, the objects of value that he possesses. As an adjective, the word *vaillant* has other meanings, ones that describe men's moral character. Commynes's phrase lends itself to being read as either Saint-Pol's worthiness or his net worth. King and duke barter over the price on Saint-Pol's head, and then revel in imagining how they will "cash him in."

In the *Mémoires*, Commynes says that after learning about Charles's and Louis's negotiations at Bouvignes, "oncques puis ne fut seur ledict connestable, mais en souppesson de deux coustés, et par especial en doubte du Roy" (the *connétable* never felt safe again, but he was always suspicious of both sides, and he was especially afraid of the king [256]). Saint-Pol's confession during his trial puts things in more vivid terms. The *connétable*, "avoit de grans craintes et n'ozoit saillir aux champs pour servir de paour qu'on lui meist la main sur la teste" (had terrible fears and didn't dare go outside the city wall on patrol out of fear that someone would grab him).[52] Saint-Pol enunciates this fear over and over again: "chascun jour l'on prenoit ses gens quant ilz alloient par le royaume et que l'on essayoit a gaigner ses gens a Saint Quentin jusques a son barbier et qu'il venoit des gens embrainchéz sur le marché de Saint Quentin qui se pourmenoient" (every day his people were seized when they were about in the kingdom and they tried to buy his people in Saint-Quentin, even his barber, and people came and strolled about the Saint-Quentin market with their faces concealed).[53] The *connétable* is close to out of his mind: "il estoit adverti que Charroloys [Charles] poursuivoit tousjours le traicté de Bouvynes et besongnoit contre lui touchant sa deffaçon, et qu'il ne dormoit pas et y cerchoit tous les remedes qu'il povoit et pareillement le dist a monseigneur de Moy pour le dire au roy" (he was warned that Charles was still pushing for the Bouvignes treaty and was working against him and for his destruction, and he wasn't sleeping and he was looking for every remedy he could and he said as much to monsieur de Moy so that he would tell the king).[54] There is frenzy in Saint-Pol's words. What he describes is a stake-out, the kind you see in the movies, where doomed, crouching men peek out windows from under the hem of heavy curtains. There is, actually, something almost hallucinogenic about Saint-Pol's terror. Men with covered faces loiter on the square. Someone has been whispering to the barber. When people go outside they don't come back. Then again, Saint-Pol is not sleeping: he is hysterical; he may be hallucinating. This is what it looks like to be undone by the king.[55]

A desperate Saint-Pol prevailed on Louis XI to postpone the Bouvignes agreement made with Charles to execute him or hand him over. Instead, he convinced the king to grant him an audience: this is the second of the two meetings that seal the *connétable*'s fate. The two met about twenty-five kilometres south of Saint-Quentin, at Fargniers-sur-Oise, with a barrier between them.[56] The setting, too much like the 1419 bridge at Montereau for Saint-Pol's own good, abounds with dangers anticipated and remembered. Saint-Pol arrives first. Worse still, he comes armed, armed with men whose salaries Louis XI pays. This is a coup d'état that awaits only a gesture. When Saint-Pol realizes how the stage has been set, "sembloit bien a son visaige qu'il en fust estonné et esbaÿ" (it showed on his face that he was surprised and astounded [235]). Afterwards, the rumours that spill from this meeting reach the king's ears, and "il luy sembla follie d'avoir esté parler a son serviteur ... Et si la hayne y avoit esté par avant grande, elle l'estoit encores plus; et du cousté dudict connestable le cueur ne luy estoit point appetissé" (it seemed madness to him to have gone to negotiate with his servitor ... And if their hatred had been great before, it was even more so; and on the *connétable*'s side his heart was not satisfied [234–5]). The phrase "his heart was not satisfied" shifts the register of the whole passage. It redirects Commynes's meditation from a properly political discourse towards the realm of human passions. He was in great danger that day, reflects Commynes ("Il fut ce jour en grand dangier," [235]), and the subject of his sentence appears to be Saint-Pol. However, in the transcript of Saint-Pol's deposition it comes out that Charles's agents had pressed Saint-Pol "de prendre ou tuer le roy a ladicte veue, et par ce moyen toutes les besognes seroient achevées et seroit lui qui parle hors de tous les meschiefz et dangiers ou il estoit et si auroit des biens tant qu'il lui plairoit et tout ce qu'il vouldroit demander" (to seize or kill the king at that meeting, and by that means all the difficult work would be realized and he would be out of all the mischief and danger he was in and he would have all the wealth he wanted and anything he wanted to ask for).[57] These may be the rumours that Louis XI heard, that Saint-Pol was supposed to have killed him that day. Saint-Pol comes to his meeting with Louis XI caught between pressure from Charles's side to assassinate Louis XI, the need to find a haven from that pressure, and terror of what either side would do to him once its fear of losing him to the other had vanished. According to Commynes, Saint-Pol was convinced that Louis XI was afraid of him. The trial leaves one convinced that Saint-Pol was still more afraid of Charles.

"Entre les Deux"

Early in the final act of Saint-Pol's story, Commynes writes that Saint-Pol, "desiroit demeurer en cest estat, navigant entre les deux, car tous deux les craignoit merveilleusement" (desired to remain in that state, navigating between the two, because he was marvellously afraid of both of them [258]). "Naviguer entre les deux," he says, and by "les deux" he means Louis and Charles. Commynes's expression is also caught "entre les deux," however. In the *Dictionnaire du Moyen Français*, the word "naviguer" proves slippery, and quickly leads towards entries for both "nager" and "noer." The word's forms are especially unstable in the idiomatic expressions cited. One can "nager ('naviguer') selon le vent qui court," meaning roughly to "sail as the wind blows," or one can "nager entre deux eaux," which means, "se tenir entre deux partis en ménageant l'un et l'autre."[58] Commynes was the somewhat unhappy owner of a galleass ship called the *Notre-Dame*, and his Talmont lands included the port of Olonne.[59] It is thus not surprising that he turns to nautical imagery. But does Saint-Pol seek to navigate "as they blow" or "between the two"? The image that emerges from his words is a hybrid one of sailing between two winds. But where is the space between two winds? Can one swim between two waters without drowning? Where two winds meet there are storms, but no intermediate spaces.[60] A word or connecting bridge is missing from Commynes's sentence, leaving his expression misshapen. The metaphor ceases to be an idiomatic turn of phrase and becomes the trace of something cosmic and dangerous.

A few pages later, Commynes pauses to consider the letters Saint-Pol is writing in his attempts to manipulate Charles and Louis. "Et qui bien y penseroit, c'est miserable vie que la nostre de tant prendre de travail et de peyne pour s'abreger la vie en disant et escripvant tant de choses presque opposites a leurs pansees" (And if you think about it, ours is a miserable life when one goes to such effort and pain to cut one's life short saying and writing so many things that are almost the opposite of their thoughts [265]). As is sometimes the case, Commynes's pronouns modulate over the course of the sentence. It is as if the line of his thought changed direction repeatedly as he spoke, or as if he were constantly fine-tuning the censor of his own words. Writing things opposite to one's thoughts draws on another kind of interiority. The relation between individual and text gives rise to a mediating, internal psychic space. For Saint-Pol, this fragile internal space offers scarce promise of shelter. "Mais les pensees du connestable ny sa paour qu'il avoit du Roy ne le conduisoient pas encores jusques la; mais luy sembloit encores qu'il useroit de dissimulation, comme il avoit acoustumé, pour les contenter" (But neither the *connétable*'s thoughts nor the fear he had of the king brought him to that point yet; but it still seemed to him that he would use deceit, as he was accustomed, to satisfy them [267]). Saint-Pol's dissimulation entails a psychic function parallel to the geographic one represented by Saint-Quentin. It opens up a protected internal, mediating space in which autonomy can be sought, but which is also, in Commynes's words, miserable. This internal, dissimulated psychic space might be called the space between two winds. When the moment comes, Saint-Pol cannot choose: he is truly paralysed, suffocated in the non-existent space between the two.

Antinomy and the End

The penultimate act in Saint-Pol's tragedy brings us back to letters and the values attached to them. After the fiasco of his meeting with Louis XI at Fargniers-sur-Oise, Saint-Pol turns once more to Charles, even though he knows that Louis and Charles have renewed their agreements about what to do with him. Saint-Pol appeals to the duke for a safe-conduct, and Charles grants the *connétable* the letter he seeks (305). Then, breaking the letter's promise of safe haven, he hands Saint-Pol over to the king. Writes Commynes,

> Ceste delivrance fut bien estrange; et ne le diz pas pour excuser les faultes dudict connestable ne pour donner charge audict duc, car a tous deux tenoit grand tort; mais il n'estoit nul besoing audict duc de Bourgongne, qui estoit si grand prince et de maison si renommee et honnourable, de luy donner une seureté pour le prendre; et fut une grande cruaulté de le bailler ou il estoit certain de la mort, et pour l'avarice. (311)

> [This delivery was very strange; and I'm not saying it to excuse the *connétable*'s mistakes or to put responsibility on the duke, because he [the *connétable*] had done them both great wrong; but there was no need for the

Duke of Burgundy, who was such a great prince of such a renowned and honoured family, to promise him safety in order to seize him; and it was a great cruelty to hand him over to certain death, and for avarice.]

The word "cruelty" carries a heavy weight. Commynes tells his reader repeatedly that Charles's betrayal of his written promise to Saint-Pol caused the duke's death (345). He repeats the accusation twice more (346, 356). The duke's behaviour stands out all the more when contrasted with Louis XI's actions only a short while before. The king had wanted Saint-Pol to come and see him at court, but Saint-Pol had grown wary.

> Ledict connestable estoit bien content de venir, pourveu que le Roy fist serment dessus la croix Sainct Lou a Angiers de ne faire nul mal a sa personne, ne consentir que aultre le feist ... Et a cella luy respondoit le Roy que jamais ne feroit ce serment a homme, mais que tout aultre serment que ledict connestable luy vouldroit demander, qu'il estoit content de le faire. (265)

> [The *connétable* was happy to come, so long as the king made a vow on the cross of Saint Laud in Angers not to do any harm to his person, nor to consent that anyone else do any ... And to this the king answered him that he would never make that vow to anyone, but that any other vow the *connétable* would like to ask from him, he would be happy to make.]

The contrast flatters Louis XI and shows Charles in a poor light, but as a comparison it lacks symmetry. Commynes sets an oral vow made over relics against a written document. Louis XI is willing to make a false promise to the *connétable*, but not a false promise over relics. The juxtaposition highlights the relative value of letters and relics, and written versus oral *fides*. The matter is not one that can be brought to a clean resolution. Maybe Charles would also have refused to swear falsely over relics, or to break a promise once spoken aloud. Louis's words imply that not all vows are equal. Saint-Pol says in his deposition that Charles should be ashamed of having handed him over under "sauf-conduit."[61] Yet, Charles had also promised Louis XI to hand Saint-Pol over within eight days should he be taken, a point the king's men are at pains to make. "Monsr du Bouchaige et aultres ambassadeurs pressoient fort ledict duc de tenir son seellé" (Monsieur de Bouchage and other ambassadors pressured the duke to keep his agreement [308–9]). The duke's two promises are in conflict: his sealed agreement promises to deliver the *connétable* to Louis XI, but his safe conduct letter promises shelter. It becomes difficult to know how to prioritize the competing claims of these distinct vows and promises, their guarantors, or their betrayal.[62]

At the beginning of this chapter I suggested that Commynes's writing about Saint-Pol engages with the tragedy of identity. This engagement is most visible around the question of why Saint-Pol does not flee. Saint-Pol has seen the Bouvignes letters signed and sealed by Charles and Louis arranging for his arrest and trial. He knows that ever since he came armed to Fargniers seeking Louis's forgiveness, both Charles and Louis have pursued him.

During his trial Saint-Pol claimed that, "la plus grant entencion qu'il eust estoit de s'en aller hors du royaume s'il eust peu et qu'il y a grant temps qu'il estoit en ceste voulenté et qu'il n'eust pas actendu lesdiz seelléz s'il eust peu partir" (the main intention that he had was to leave the kingdom if he could, and that he had been of this intention for a long while, and that he would not have waited for the sealed agreements if he could have left).[63] Along with the spilling out of his fear, this ambivalent longing to flee is the sentiment most powerfully articulated by the *connétable*. He repeats it again almost immediately afterwards. "Son entencion estoit tousjours de s'en aller s'il s'en fust peu aller" (His intention was always to leave if he could have gone).[64] Saint-Pol's words also shed light on why he did not flee: "n'eust esté l'estat en quoy feue madame sa femme estoit lors qui estoit grosse preste d'accoucher, il s'en fust des lors parti et allé hors de ce royaume" (if it weren't for the state in which his late wife who was pregnant and close to giving birth was then, he would have left then and gone out of the kingdom).[65] Saint-Pol's words provide harmony to a particularly melancholic passage in the *Mémoires*.

J'ay peu veu de gens en ma vie qui saichent fouyr a temps, ne cy ne ailleurs. Les ungs n'ont point d'{experience} d'avoir veu a l'oeil leurs pays voisins ... Les aultres ont trop d'amours en leurs biens, en leurs femmes et a leurs enffens; et ces raisons ont esté causes de faire periller beaucop de gens de bien. (297–8)

[I've seen few men in my life who know how to flee on time, neither here nor elsewhere. Some have no experience of having seen their neighbouring countries for themselves ... Others have too much love for their

belongings, their wives and their children; and these reasons have been
the cause that many good men have been lost.]

Is Commynes thinking here of Saint-Pol, who preferred to remain by
his wife's side and die rather than to leave her behind, and perhaps live?
His rumination has a grim cast. What does it mean to love one's wife or
children "too much"? Saint-Pol's final action as a free man was to accept
his capture. Having taken only a small escort with him, Saint-Pol goes
to hide out with his friend Antoine Rolin, seigneur de Aimeries. Charles
the Bold orders Aimeries to hold Saint-Pol. Aimeries does not dare to
disobey, "toutesfoiz la garde n'estoit pas estroicte pour ung seul homme, s'il eust eu vouloir de fouyr" (nonetheless the guard wasn't very
strict for just one man, if he had wanted to flee [307]). One might ask
whether, at least as regards Saint-Pol, the tragedy lies in the impossibility of flight or in the acceptance of its impossibility.[66]

Mainte pensee avoit ja eu ce puissant homme ou il prendroit son chemin
pour fouyr, car de tout estoit informé, et avoit veu le double des seellés qui
avoient esté bailléz contre luy a Bouvynes. Unes foiz s'adressoit a aulcuns
serviteurs qu'il avoit, qui estoient Lorrains: avecques ceulx la delibera
fouyr en Almaigne et y porter grand somme d'argent, car le chemin estoit
fort seur, et achapter une place sur le Rin, et se tenir la jusques ad ce qu'il
se fust appoincté de l'un des coustéz. Une aultres foiz delibera tenir son
bon chasteau de Han, qui tant luy avoit cousté: et l'avoit faict pour se
saulver en une telle necessité, et l'avoit pourveu de toutes choses autant
que chasteau qui fust en lieu de nostre congnoissance. Encores ne trouva
il gens a son gré pour demeurer avecques luy, car tous ses serviteurs
estoient néz des seigneuries de l'un prince ou de l'aultre; et par adventure
que sa craincte estoit si grande qu'il ne se ousa suffisamment descouvrir a
eulx, car je croy qu'il en eust trouvé qui ne l'eussent pas habandonné, et
bon nombre. (305–6)

[That powerful man had already had many ideas about what route he
would take to flee, because he knew all about it, and he had seen the copy
of the sealed agreements which had been made against him at Bouvignes.
Once he asked some servitors he had, who were from Lorraine: he decided
to flee with them to Germany and to bring a large sum of money, because
the route was very safe, and buy a place on the Rhine, and stay there until
he had made an agreement with one side. Another time he decided to hold
out in his good castle at Ham, which had cost him so much: and he had

made it to find refuge in case of such a necessity, and he had stocked it with as much of everything as in any castle I know of anywhere. Still he didn't find as many people as he wanted to stay with him, because all of his servitors were born in the lands of one prince or the other; and maybe his fear was so great that he didn't dare fully reveal himself to them, because I think he would have found some, a good number, who wouldn't have abandoned him.]

Commynes creates a sense of cyclical repetition: "Mainte pensee," "unes foiz," "unes aultres foiz," "encores." Running away is the *connétable*'s constant preoccupation. Read slowly the prosody is hypnotic in its lament. With each repetition the word "car" (because) becomes more inexorable, its causal obligation more fatal. Read with greater breath a different kind of phrasing pushes through, one which recalls the way that a person in a pitch of anxiety and excitation will begin, over and over again, to breathily throw out some urgent plan for escape from the panic of their situation, only to realize at the sentence's end its impossibility, to stop short, and then a moment later begin again. Each phrase begins by tracing the path for flight, but then immediately folds back against itself. Saint-Pol could flee to Germany through Lorraine, but once there he would only be holed up, biding his time. The castle at Ham is stocked and provisioned, "tant luy avoit cousté," but since it is practically next door to Saint-Quentin, this possibility is still more futile. The reminder of how much it cost him to outfit this back-yard bunker underscores the sterility of what would inevitably become a doomed standoff against the king's armies assembled at his gate. At the same time, we realize that Saint-Pol had planned and provisioned for just such a show-down. He was expecting this moment. Saint-Pol stands as the figure of resistance and of its futility. His story is properly tragic in that it is brought about by his attempts to free himself from the dangerous consequences inherent in his own identity. Letters were the means by which Saint-Pol struggled against this destiny, and letters were the accusatory pieces that damned him.

There is another layer in this play of silences and intimations. Commynes writes Saint-Pol's story into the *Mémoires*. Although of course he never puts it into precisely such words, the *Mémoires* are Commynes's own narrative about being between Charles and Louis XI. However we imagine Commynes's experience of himself it remains that he, no less than Saint-Pol, lived exactly between the two rulers. Commynes's biography also takes shape as a narrative about lands, erasure, and fear, all in relation to letters. To be *entre les deux* is to be, always, both squeezed and divided. The trope of the two-sided, of duality and dissimulation, of trying to carve out a protected space between the two – something as solid as a walled or fortified city, for example, or as slight as a spoken confidence – comes through again and again in the *Mémoires*. What's more, when Commynes writes about Saint-Pol, he reminds the reader of his own Janus-faced identity. "Murmuroit l'on des deux coustéz contre le conte de Sainct Pol, connestable de France; et l'avoit le Roy prins en grand hayne, et les plus prouchains de lui semblablement. Le duc de Bourgongne le hayoit encores plus, et avoit myeulx cause, *car je suys informé a la verité des raisons des deux coustés*" (Both sides were plotting against the Count of Saint-Pol, *connétable* of France: and the king had conceived a great hatred of him, and of those close to him also. The Duke of Burgundy hated him even more, and had better cause, *because in truth I know both sides' reasons* [229; emphasis mine]). Commynes does repeatedly report on each side's position: this means that he is or was in the middle, too. To see both sides he, like Saint-Pol, has to move between them. Like Saint-Pol, Commynes lived in the narrow pass between conflicting loyalties.

Inspired by his reflections on the *connétable*, Commynes explains, "Et combien que toute personne serche a se mettre hors de subjection et craincte, et aulcunes foiz hait ceulx qui les y tiennent, si n'en y a il nul qui en cest article approuche les princes, car je n'en congneuz oncques nulz qui n'ayt de mortelle hayne a ceulx qui les y ont voulu tenir" (And although every person seeks to put themselves out of subjection and fear, and sometimes hate those who keep them in it, none come close in this matter to princes, because I have never known any who did not have a mortal hatred for those who have wished to possess them [171]). Our hatred of those who want to dominate and frighten us is the only thing greater than our desire to dominate others. These passages are among the most raw and direct in all of the *Mémoires*. The universality within Commynes's words does not make them less applicable to his own, individual experiences. Commynes says, "je conseilleroye a ung mien amy, si je l'avoys, qu'il mist peyne que son maistre l'aymast, mais non point qu'il le craignist" (I would advise a friend of mine, if I had one, that he should take pains that his master love him, but not that he fear him [236]), since a king or a prince, "ayme plus naturellement ceulx qui leur sont tenuz que ne font ceulx a qui ilz sont tenuz" (loves more naturally those who are obligated to them than those to whom they are obligated [237]). What does the word *ami* mean here? And what does it mean that Commynes implies he has none? About Saint-Pol he says, he might not have been so friendless as he imagined, but then he imagines himself that way, too. The phrase "être tenu" is one we recognize from Commynes's portrayal of his own relations with Louis XI. These sentences about Saint-Pol in turn lead to a digression about the balance of obligation and loyalty between king and courtier, one that seems to echo as well with the lessons of Commynes's own experiences. Commynes writes about Saint-Pol, but he describes his own position as a subject *tenu au roi*, for whom there are no *amis*, but only the *amour* that must be sought from *un maître*.

Chapter Seven

The Voice in the Text

Si la psychanalyse apporte une aide précieuse au lecteur d'autobiographie, ce n'est point parce qu'elle explique l'individu à la lumière de son histoire et de son enfance, mais parce qu'elle saisit cette histoire dans son discours et qu'elle fait de l'énonciation le lieu de sa recherche (et de sa thérapeutique).
– Philippe Lejeune, *Le Pacte autobiographique*

Experience is at once always already an interpretation and something that needs to be interpreted. What counts as experience is neither self-evident nor straightforward; it is always contested, and always therefore political.
– Joan Scott, "The Evidence of Experience"

This final, culminating chapter brings an empathic ear to passages from throughout the *Mémoires*, from the first pages of Commynes's narrative to their last. Having examined institutional, intersubjective, and poetic elements in the *Mémoires'* engagement with textuality, we arrive at the ends of this study prepared to confront Commynes's coming to writing. Looking back, we see two "betrayals": in the first instance, Commynes's fury-provoking departure from Charles's court; in the second, Louis XI's deathbed renunciation of his servant, a betrayal of the man who had betrayed everything for him. The two moments counterbalance one another exactly. Legally, the propriety of qualifying either Commynes's departure from Burgundy or Louis's whispered cruelty as a betrayal is dubious. Textually, the silences with which Commynes covers each one are like poles on whose axis the whole of the *Mémoires* turn. Humanely, both demand that we use the word betrayal. In his prologue, Commynes refers to the "pertes et douleurs" he has suffered since Louis's death, and immediately confesses that they have sharpened his memory of the intimacy he once shared with the king. Louis's betrayal is both what has to be told and what it is impossible to tell. The question becomes one of reflection, personal and universal, on what it means to be in the king's service ("être au service du roi"), to live in constant privacy with him ("vivre en continuelle residence"), or to be his subject ("être son sujet"). The form of the *Mémoires* both realizes and seeks to resolve the conflict between desire and the law that so erupts in the Talmont affair.

What Rises against the Current

Midway through the first book of his *Mémoires*, as he recalls the events of the 1465 Guerre du Bien Public, Commynes pauses in his description of Paris besieged and indulges for a moment in a swell of personal reminiscence. His words provide a vivid example of the complex temporalities that define the *Mémoires* and their intertwined elegiac and autobiographical lyricism.

> A tout prendre, c'est la cité que jamais je veisse avyronnée de meilleur pays et plus plantureux, et est chose presque increable que des biens qui y arrivent. Je y ay esté depuis ce temps la avecques le roy Loys demy an sans bouger, logié aux Tournelles, mangeant et couchant avecques luy ordinairement, et, depuis son trespas, vingt moys, malgré moy, tenu prisonnier en son Palais, ou je veoye de mes fenestres arriver ce qui montoit contremont la riviere de Seyne, du costé de Normandie. Du dessus en vient, sans comparaison, plus que n'eusse jamais pensé ne creu ce que j'en ay veu. (53)

> [All things considered, I have never seen a city surrounded by more fertile and verdant country than Paris, and it is almost unbelievable what goods arrive there. I was there with King Louis after that time for half a year without moving, staying at the Tournelles, usually eating and sleeping with him, and after his death twenty months despite myself, held prisoner in his palace, where I saw from my window all that came upriver on the Seine from Normandy. Incomparably more comes than I would ever have thought or believed possible if I had not seen it.]

This brief paragraph, these allusive and elusive words, revivify the gaze of a man who recounts, in a single broad sweep, past and present, youth and the memory of former selves. Each of the three juxtaposed moments encapsulates a distinct period in the narrator's life. The young Commynes who took part in the recalled siege was, at most, twenty years old. The man who returned to Paris years later had shed his naivety to become the private companion of a wily king. The third man is a prisoner, whose friends have abandoned him. This man watched the river flow from his window and remembered the two younger selves who had seen the same waters. The narrator has survived to become an older man still, one whose mind's eye embraces all three younger avatars – eager page, savvy powerbroker, and the uncertain prisoner who waits.

The Seine River binds each of these moments together ("je veoye de mes fenestres arriver ce qui montoit contremont"). Commynes's description contains within it one of literature's most ingrained metaphors for memory, and so becomes a reflection on remembrance itself. By evoking a landscape that endures unchanged before his mind's eye, the narrator pulls our attention towards the erosion time has wrought on the observer. Commynes's words trace the fissures that traverse a self worn by time. Age brings narrowing and confinement: we move from open fields to bedchambers to prison cells. The vision Commynes shares with his reader is made possible by a richly invested vantage point, at once raised high above the landscape and confined to a prison cell. The tension between outside and inside, possibility and limitation, is neatly expressed by the window through which the self-remembered Commynes watched, a window now drawn a second time as the object of recollection. The imprisoned observer resurfaces as the man observed. Each moment is set against the next, until their contradictions assemble into a harmonious chord of fullness and loss, bounty and abandon. These paradoxes of simultaneous presence and absence – Commynes young and old, alone with the king or just alone, of expanse and contraction – give timbre to Commynes's narrative voice. The tension between plenitude and impotence that resonates through this meditation traverses the whole of the *Mémoires*. It is little exaggeration to see in this passage a figural rendering of the abstracted architecture sustaining the whole of Commynes's narrative.

Coming to Writing

Commynes began to write his *Mémoires* while under house arrest, the final stage in his imprisonment for conspiracy against the government of Anne de Beaujeu. Before being allowed to return to the relative freedom of his newly purchased estates at Dreux, Commynes was held at Loches, then in the Conciergerie.[1] At Loches he was shackled and held in an eight-foot cage.[2] House arrest might have been feeling like a narrow escape. Commynes's time at Dreux must have been a time for reflection and taking stock, of weighing possibilities and resignation to those lost. Commynes's rise in the Burgundian court, his timely alignment with Louis XI, his singular role in the king's strategic defeats of Charles the Bold or Edward IV, or the credit he enjoyed in the courts of Northern Italy all showed him to be a canny political survivor, despite the catastrophic failure of his involvement in the Guerre Folle. On the other hand, all Commynes's skill and credit had gone into the sustained campaign needed to dodge the accusation of *lèse-majesté* hanging over his head, to bring him out of prison again, and to hold onto what could be salvaged of his former wealth.

Commynes's relations with Louis XI provided the greatest degree of stability in the author's biography. Orphaned as a young child, an exile from his homeland before he was thirty, dispossessed of his adopted home – over and over Commynes was severed from his past, and thereby from his past self. The king's deathbed words betrayed fifteen years of confidences, and expelled the once-envied courtier into a realm of isolation, public exposure, and humiliation. The Beaujeu-led government of Charles VIII pursued Talmont with a ruthlessness equal to that exercised by Louis XI when he first awarded the properties to Commynes. Disgraced, Commynes had little choice but to engage himself with ever greater desperation in the manoeuverings of the *princes rebelles*, in the hopes that Louis d'Orléans's success might protect him from homelessness and bankruptcy.

At the origins of Louis XI's betrayal of Commynes were two intrigues with letters, that is, written objects, at their centre – the coercive 1472 letters donating Talmont to Commynes, and the letters later found in the La Trémoïlle archives and burned. This distilled vision of the trauma forced upon Commynes in 1483, a trauma whose consequences percolated through the remainder of his lifetime, leads to two observations. First, in so much as the written object formed the engine of both Commynes's union with the king and of their dis-union, Commynes's "coming to writing" is freighted. Second, the memory of Louis XI's repudiation undergirds Commynes's narration of the king and his reign. When Commynes begins to narrate "what he remembers" about Louis it is as one exiled in ways both concrete and metaphorical. From the outset his words are fretted with loss.

The veins of a discrete and fragmented counternarrative run through the *Mémoires*. In shifts of focalization or sudden disturbances to the flow of narrated time, the figure of the author appears, illuminated in *contre-jour*.[3] Commynes's portrait of Louis XI and his telling of the king's reign give voice to an autobiographical meditation on the emergence of the author's own subjectivity, a subjectivity forged by the narrator's relations with the king he commemorates. This authorial subjectivity makes itself felt within the text as an ambivalent tension. The narrator is caught between desire and mourning. There are, in fact, two intertwined traumas: the king's betrayal and his death. From this perspective, the truth which can be sought within the *Mémoires* is a narrative truth in a psychoanalytic sense. We must seek the form of the idea whose structure holds the *Mémoires* under its regime.[4] The *Mémoires* continue a conversation between Commynes and Louis XI, lost interlocutor of his most privileged, most private conversations. The essential vitality which sustains this dialogue-in-absence is so forcefully present that this notion has budded in even the most tenacious of Commynes's critics. "Les *Mémoires* permettent à Commynes de continuer à exister, à imposer toutes les composantes de son être ... Tant et si bien que les *Mémoires*, de support historique, deviennent aussi le lieu privilégié où un personnage nommé Commynes se raconte inlassablement pour exister encore," wrote Jean Dufournet in 1993.[5] Commynes explains in the prologue that he will quite literally follow his words: "je suyvray mon propos."[6] He relinquishes more traditional rhetorical notions of controlling his historical material in favour of a spontaneously emergent narrative guided by associative memory. In this final chapter we seek the simultaneously confessional and resistant discourse that both conceals itself within and drives the visible history of Louis's reign that Commynes avows to recount. The *Mémoires* function as a textual site where the relations between Commynes and his sovereign can be reinscribed.

The spaces that will be uncovered within this narration, like those evoked in remembering the Seine's wealth, are redolent with associations of power and impotence.[7] The words *privé* and *secret* punctuate Commynes's narration and have proximate but not identical meanings. To be *homme fort privé* to another is to form part of an exclusive circle; the word implies favour, confidence, and trust. Things that are *secret* often involve not just discretion but also motivated deception. *Secret* also alludes to events, conversations, or knowledge produced in protected spaces, free from observation. *Secret* can also serve as a near synonym for "alone." It is thus possible to speak of the spaces of intimacy, in keeping with the etymological origins of the word *secret*. The *chambres* and *cabinets* within a chateau are not just private spaces; they are also the spaces of secrets and all that is private. Thus, for example, the drama surrounding the La Trémoïlle letters whose existence and destruction were exposed during the Talmont trial took place in a succession of private or secret spaces, from the *cabinet* at Thouars where censored letters were literally locked up, to the king's *cabinet*, backdrop for unholy vows.

On Memory and Authority: The Prologue

The *Mémoires* open with their author's address to Angelo Cato, archbishop of Vienne and physician to both Charles the Bold and Louis XI. An Italian with a certain reputation as an astrologer, Cato inhabited the margins of French letters and early French humanism.[8] Nearly as soon as Commynes begins to write, however, his prologue ceases to resemble the prologues found in contemporary histories. He makes no mention of great deeds or of glory; he does not cite either mythology or the Virgin Mary; and the only information he provides about himself is that he was closer to Louis XI than anyone else.[9] Commynes introduces his text to Cato as rough notes he has gathered together artlessly, saying, "vous envoy ce dont promptement m'est souvenu" (I send you what came without hesitation to my memory [2]); "la verité que j'ay peu ne sceu avoir souvenance" (the truth as I have been able or known how to remember [1]).[10] Commynes pretends to answer Cato's request for information about Louis XI, expressing hope that Cato intends to write a Latin history of Louis's reign ("esperant que vous le demandés pour le mettre en quelque oeuvre que vous avéz intention de faire en langue latine, dont vous estez bien usité" [2]). Cato, however, never wrote any such work, nor does any record exist beyond Commynes's prologue that he ever intended to do so.[11] Commynes's appeal provides the kind of metanarrative frame we might associate with a legal deposition, just as the doublets with which he first begins ("escripre et mectre par memoire," "sceu et congneu," "j'ay peu et sceu avoir souvenance") recall the conventions of *lettres ouvertes*. What emerges from the prologue, however, is wholly other. Commynes speaks to Cato in a voice that borrows from numerous discursive modes and yet fits comfortably into none of them. The meandering clauses of the *Mémoires'* first folios touch upon a number of themes but make two essential, structuring assertions. The first is that Commynes occupied a unique position in relation to Louis XI and is thus uniquely suited to provide his memories to Cato. The second is that only an autobiographical narrative of Commynes's own movement towards the king can adequately vehiculate the story to be told.

If we were to render the argument Commynes presents in his prologue graphically we would arrive at something vaguely tree shaped.
The "trunk" would contain the primary clause – Commynes's argument
– from which subordinate independent clauses would fork outwards
like branches. These subordinate clauses present notions both universal:
there is both good and evil in kings, "car ilz sont hommes comme nous"
(because they are men like us [1]); and more specific, "mons' de Boschage
et aultres … myeulx vous en sçauroient parler et le coucher en meilleur
langaige que moy" (Monsieur du Bouchage and others … will know
how to speak better and put things more eloquently than I do [3]). To
help us follow the trunk of Commynes's address within the prologue, I
have extracted its core phrases below. To accurately preserve the flow of
the prologue as a whole, some of the subordinate, linking material has
been summarized. The remaining phrases present one unified, hypotac-
tic statement – the performative "trunk."

Mons' l'arcevesque de Vienne, pour satisfaire a la requeste qu'il vous a pleu me faire de vous es-cripre et mectre par memoire ce que j'ay sceu et congneu des faictz du roy Loys unzeiesme, a qui Dieu face pardon, nostre maistre et bienfacteur, et prince digne de tres excellante memoyre, je l'ay faict le plus pres de la verité que j'ay peu ne sceu avoir souvenance.	My lord the Archbishop of Vienne, to satisfy the request that it pleased you to make of me, that I write and put down from memory what I have known and experienced of the deeds of King Louis the elev-enth, may God pardon him, our master and patron, and a prince worthy of most excellent memory, I have done so as close to the truth as I have been able or known how to remember.

I was not present for his youth, but

despuis le temps que je vins en son service jusques a l'heure de son trespas, ou je estoie present, ay faict plus continuelle residance avecques luy que nul aultre	From the time that I came into his service until the hour of his tres-pass, where I was present, I lived in more constant privacy with him than any other

In this portion of his prologue, Commynes reflects on his experiences
with princes and kings, on their foibles, on the virtues of Louis XI, and
on the forthright account that he will give based purely on evidence he
personally knows to be true.

vous envoy ce dont promptement m'est souvenu, esperant que vous le demandés pour le mettre en quelque oeuvre que vous avéz intention de faire en langue latine.

I send you what came without hesitation to my memory, hoping that you ask in order to put it in some work which you intend to write in Latin.

Others like Monsieur de Bouchage might speak more elegantly,

Mais pour obligation d'honneur et grans privaultés et bienfaictz, sans jamais entrerompre jusques a la mort que l'ung ou l'aultre n'y feust, nul n'en devroit avoir meilleure souvenance que moy; et aussi pour les pertes et douleurs que j'ay receues despuis son trespas, qui est bien pour estre revenu a ma memoyre les graces que j'ay receues de luy …

But on account of the obligation that comes from honour and great closeness and kindnesses, without any interruption [thereof] until one or the other person were dead, no one should remember him better than I do; because the losses and suffering I have known since his trespass are also good for bringing back to my memory the graces I received from him …

Et pour vous informer du temps que j'eu congnoissance dudict seigneur, dont faictes demande, m'est force de commancer avant le temps que je vinse en son service; et puis par ordre je [suyvray] mon propos jusques a l'heure que je devins son serviteur, et continueray jusques a son trespas [1–3]

And to inform you about the time when I first knew the lord you are asking me about, I am obliged to begin before the time I entered his service; and then I will follow my story until the hour when I became his servitor, and I will continue [from that point] up to his trespass.

This is a statement at once singular in its purpose and varied in its declarations.

The archives show that others served on Louis's council for more years, or signed more documents.[12] The expression "continuelle residance" denotes a union of sensibilities that offers its own particular guarantee of authority to the forthcoming text. The narrative's "hero" becomes not the "roy Loys unzeiesme, a qui Dieu face pardon" but "je," who "ay faict plus continuelle residance avec luy que nul aultre." Before the first paragraph of the prologue has been brought to a close, the centre of gravity for the whole of the forthcoming narrative has already begun to shift. A second discourse rivals the avowed narrative of Louis XI. Asked to write about historical events, Commynes responds by writing about his own competency to speak about history. The question "what do I know?" becomes "how do I know?" The *Mémoires* enact this epistemological quest; the position they construct for their narrator appropriates a discourse about individual memory as the means to revisit the nature of (historical) authority.

The prologue's insistence on Louis's death and its consequences for Commynes alludes to but does not name the disgrace in which Commynes finds himself when he begins to write. Commynes's narrative originates in the metaphorical distance of a fall from "graces" to "pertes." The promised identity as the king's "serviteur" no longer exists; its disappearance is identical with the "pertes et douleurs" suffered, the same *pertes et douleurs* that have refined the narrator's memory and which now enable him to speak with such authority about the king. The *Mémoires* recount their author's elevation to a unique identity and simultaneously mourn the loss of that identity as well. Commynes's narrative is self-referential in that it proposes to recount its own origins. Louis's death cuts through every sentence; "trespas" chimes as the prologue's very last word ("continueray jusques a son trespas").

The time-defying lyricism of narration begins in the prologue with the play of verbal tenses. At first, Commynes promises, "je l'ay faict le plus pres de la verité que j'ay peu ne sceu avoir souvenance" (1), and now sends this account of "ce dont promptement m'est souvenu" (2). This produces the impression that the address to Cato has been joined to a completed manuscript, and describes a story that the author has already told about events that have already concluded in the past. However, only one folio later, Commynes announces "je continueray." The future tense would seem to refer simultaneously to a narration already completed and to anticipated events yet to be told. This clash in tenses alerts us to a paradox that runs through the whole of the *Mémoires*. The contradiction between past and future opens a narrative space taut with uncertainty. Far from assuring that the king's death will bring the closure seemingly promised, the prologue conjures a dynamic field in which past, present, and future vibrate together. Narrated, textual time offers new possibility to what historical time has ended. *Mectre par memoire* appears at first as an idiomatic synonym for writing, but returns to haunt us as something more. The expression pulses with the rush of viscerally felt emotions. Commynes's voice hovers between anticipation and mourning in a tremor of lyricism that momentarily holds the narrative back from the threshold of its tale. *Mectre par memoire* is to be once again immersed in the currents of the past. The breath of narration resurrects and sustains as it recounts.

Venir et Devenir

The prologue's promise to advance towards the king's death marks a threshold across which the reader passes and through which he enters the spaces of narration. He expects that Commynes's "jusques a" denotes a narrative destination, but the next phrase brings him alongside Commynes on a physical journey – to Lille, on horseback. "Au saillir de mon enfance, et en l'eage de pouvoir monter a cheval, fuz amené a Lisle, devers le duc Charles de Bourgongne, lors appellé conte de Charroloys, lequel me print en son service; et fut l'an mil ccccLxiiij" (When I emerged from childhood, and was of an age to ride a horse, I was brought to Lille, towards the duke Charles of Burgundy, then called Count of Charolais, who took me into his service; and it was the year 1464 [5]).[13] The sentence performs an abrupt shift from the figurative language of a narrative path to a literal referent heavy with metaphoric overtones. Commynes embarks on his narration elevated to the farseeing vantage point of the mounted nobleman. "Au saillir de mon enfance" places the reader face to face with the awakening of an adult sensibility, signalling both an awareness of social status and the opening of new vistas. The older Commynes possessed the avidity for prized hounds and horses typical of his social milieu, so that his horse indexes as well the *affaires du monde* that await.[14] Commynes's younger self is introduced to us as a character subtly possessed of perception and strength, one who enters the world to claim a certain position within it. To be *à cheval* is to bridge a divide and to be divided. We begin the *Mémoires* astride the divide between innocence and experience; fittingly, *à cheval*. Thrown backwards in time to a point of departure, the reader embarks on the journey promised by the *Mémoires*, caught, already and once again, between an irretrievable past and the hunger of ambitions still unformed.

The reader then glimpses a tension between the active "monter a cheval" and the passive "fuz amené a Lisle." The future duke, only a few years older than Commynes himself, "me print en son service" (5). Commynes twice avoids granting himself agency in his dealings with Charles. He does not go to the duke to enter into his service; he is brought to the duke who takes him into service. This passive voice contrasts with Commynes's active description of the narrative and metaphorical journey the *Mémoires* undertake towards Louis XI. The journey we are to accompany will be one which transforms youth into maturity. Commynes is brought to Charles; he goes to Louis; he actively becomes the king's *serviteur*.

Commynes's declaration that he must return deeper within his past in order to explain how he "eu congnoissance dudict seigneur" provides critical insight. When Commynes writes, "m'est force de commancer avant le temps que je vinse en son service; et puis par ordre je continueray mon propos jusques a l'heure que je devins son serviteur, et continueray jusques a son trespas," he points to a beginning ("avant le temps que je vinse a son service"), middle ("l'heure que je devins son serviteur"), and end ("jusques a son trespas"). "Le temps que je vinse en son service" indicates the fulcrum in Commynes's narrative journey. As Carolyn Barros has pointed out, "Autobiography is about change; it narrates a series of transformations ... As a text of a life, autobiography presents the 'before' and 'after' of individuals who have undergone transformations of some kind."[15] Commynes identifies his union with the king as the realization of his becoming (*devenir*). Significantly, Commynes does not actually arrive in the king's service until the end of book three – halfway through the *Mémoires*, and nearly halfway through the twenty years of Louis XI's reign they embrace.[16] Having dismissed the king's youth ("du temps de sa jeunesse ne sçauroys je parler" [1]), Commynes now begins a narrative of his own youth ("le temps de ma jeunesse").

The *Mémoires* initiate a self-descriptive, self-analytic narrative of coming and becoming, *venir* and *devenir*. Commynes's words allude to the sweep of a biographical movement already fixed in the past and a narrative movement hovering in an unwritten future. The path he traces is at once historical and textual, of coming to the king and of becoming his servant ("je vinse en son service"; "je devins son serviteur"). This autobiographical structure determines the whole of Commynes's text. Barros provides the following consideration of the autobiographical.

The change typical of autobiographies is not the product of nature or time ... Change is presented as transformative, a significant mutation in the characteristic qualities and societal relationships of the principal persona. Autobiography offers the various metamorphoses emplotted, bounded, and framed by its language and inscribed in its configurations of words and images. Change is then the operative metaphor in autobiographical discourse.[17]

Commynes announces a narrative arc whose form comes from the convergence of two lives into one, reaching towards a single terminus, a single moment of terminal signification ("sans jamais entrerompre jusques a la mort que l'ung ou l'aultre n'y feust" [3]). The shape of the *Mémoires* is thus dictated by the coincidence of two lives brought together and long joined, then rent apart by death, leaving only the one to tell the story from his own side.[18] In the hagiographic narrative, the cumulative deeds that fill a life sustain narrative momentum, but the key, transformative moment comes in death. The saint's death retrospectively validates the hagiographic narrative that has preceded and invests it with meaning, a meaning made possible only through the final signifying act that is martyrdom. For the *Mémoires* as well, the king's death will retrospectively filter all that has come before.[19]

The *Mémoires* serve as Commynes's confession of himself as a royal subject, presenting that becoming as the defining voyage of his life, and his relationship with the king as unique. Louis XI's death becomes both the narrator's destination and a point of closure, while the quietly spoken "je devins son serviteur" alludes to the transformative event that provides the *Mémoires'* most apparent division between before and after. The movement of *venir* and *devenir* can be understood as a progression through both narrative and narrated space towards the space of a specific, foundational, remembrance. The narrative's destination point – "l'heure de son trespas, ou je estoie present" (1) – anchors the author's narration, effecting a second, traumatic and ambiguous pivotal moment, so that narrative closure is at once promised, enacted, and impossible.

What Remains

In the first lines of Book VI, chapter 5, Commynes inaugurates the final movement of the *Mémoires*. "Je trouvay ung peu le Roy nostre maistre envieilly, et commençoyt a soy dispouser a malladie: toutesfoiz il n'y parut pas si tost, et conduysoit toutes les choses par grant sens" (I found that the king our master had gotten a little older, and was beginning to be prone to illness: nonetheless it didn't show itself right away, and he managed everything with great sense [455]). The observation combines affective confidence and the diplomat's professional estimation. Louis's death, or rather, Commynes's narrative of Louis's death, forms a particularly privileged *lieu de mémoire*. Historian Alain Boureau seized upon Commynes's portrayal of Louis XI's death in his book *Le Simple corps du roi*.

> Parmi ce discours et ces conduites qui manifestent la primauté fragile et angoissée du corps physique de l'homme, sur le mode d'un ressassement circulaire, émerge une parole forte et réflexive qui donne un sens politique à cette conscience obscure et lancinante du corps propre. Les *Mémoires* de Commynes constituent un de ces seuils dont le franchissement permet de penser autrement les rapports du corps propre et de la corporation collective. Quand on parle de Commynes; il ne faut pas songer seulement à un auteur, à un texte particulier, d'ailleurs peu répandu et peu lu, mais plutôt à un type de réflexion qui s'engage ; à la fin du XVe siècle et au début du XVIe siècle, à partir de l'aporie corporelle du pouvoir en la focalisant et l'explicitant et en inventant un genre nouveau, les 'mémoires' politiques.[20]

Although the narrative of Book VI looks outwards to affairs of state, Commynes returns over and over again to the king's decline, building an ever-mounting level of narrative tension as he circles towards the king's final hours. With each successive stage in Louis's illness the narrative slows. Shifts in lexicon, register, and focalization give a rich affective nuance to Commynes's retelling of the king's accelerating demise. Abruptly words seeming to expound upon tax burdens or the post collapse and another voice pierces the surface of the text, insisting on a single image and a single moment. These "moments of being," set apart by changes in focalization, address, and duration, rhythmically punctuate the narrated progress of the king's death.[21]

Louis's fixation on having the Sainte Ampoule brought to his deathbed provides the occasion for one such moment.

> La saincte Ampole, qui est auprés de Rayns, qui jamais n'avoit esté remuee de son lieu, luy fut apportee jusques a sa chambre, au Plessis, et estoit sur son buffet, a l'heure de sa mort, et avoit intencion d'en prendre semblable unction qu'il en avoit pris a son sacre, combien que beaucop de gens cuydoient qu'il s'en voulsist oindre tout le corps, ce que n'est pas vraysemblable, car ladicte saincte Empole est fort petite, et n'y a pas grant

matiere dedans. Je la veiz a l'heure dont je parle, et aussi le jour que le dict
seigneur fut mis en terre a Nostre Dame de Clery. (483–4)

[The Sainte Ampoule, which is at Reims, which had never been moved
from its place, was brought to him in his room, at Plessis, and it was on his
buffet at the hour of his death, and he had the intention of being anointed
from it like he was at his coronation, however much many people thought
that he wanted to smear his whole body with it, which isn't realistic, because the Sainte Ampoule is very small, and there isn't much inside it. I
saw it during the time I'm talking about, and also on the day that his lordship was put in the ground at Notre Dame de Cléry.]

Each clause brings a slight shift. Common knowledge (the Sainte
Ampoule is kept at Reims) is coupled with less-commonly known but
still external facts (the Sainte Ampoule was brought to the king; the king
was at Plessis; the ampoule was there when the king died). Access to the
intentions of the king ("avoit intencion"), and then to the opinion of the
somewhat vague "many people" ("beaucop de gens cuydoient") help
the narrator to present himself as a thoroughly well-informed partici-
pant in events. In yet another evolution in the tone of his phrase,
Commynes then exposes the fruits of his advantaged position. Such
popular belief wasn't rational because, he reveals with an air of authoritative confidence, the vial is very small and contains precious little of its
hallowed substance. The rational detachment ("there's not much in
there") with which Commynes expresses his own reaction to an awe-
some object, one of the most sacred relics in Christianity, epitomizes his
ironic tone. In the final, essential pivot, the narrator reveals the basis for
his authority ("I saw it" – "je la veiz"), and with these words places
himself in the scene observed and narrated.

"L'heure dont je parle" points to when the ampoule was brought to
the sick king, and so signals the first of several superimposed images
layered in these two sentences. The reader is not told how much time
passed between when the Sainte Ampoule was brought to Louis and his
death, nor what provoked rumours that the king desired to be covered
in its ointment. While the total extent of the time narrated remains
vague, three distinct moments, each one identical with an image, anchor
the narrator, and his authority, within remembered time and space.
These moments strain against one another, but cannot be loosened.
"L'heure de sa mort" interrupts the restiveness of a plotting, preoccupied court. For his part, Louis anticipates no such severance from his

earthly kingdom, but intends to be salved against death, anointed again, an eternal king.[22] For Commynes, the hour of the king's death is synonymous with this image of the ampoule resting on the buffet, the object's rarity now become insolent. The "Sainte Ampoule" supreme *enseigne* of the eternal, *très chrétien* Crown of France, grates against the implacable universalism of human death. Above all, the description is telling psychologically. Commynes's memory snags on a small detail (the object's precise location) with all the accidentalness that so often characterizes the images and narration of trauma recollected.[23] Significantly, Commynes does not say "the king's funeral," which would refer to the three days of ceremony transferring the crown of France to Charles VIII, but rather "when he [Louis XI] was put in the ground." He remembers not the grandeur of official ritual but rather, once again, the element common to all human death, the one that most implacably reminds the living who grieve of death's finality. The preterit "je la veiz," the same phrase which grounded the narrator's authority on his presence in the scenes narrated, also inscribes each of these moments into the "now" of spoken narration and into the eternity promised by the written word, in defiance of the ephemerality of human life.

Violence in a Closed Room

Commynes's account of Louis's first stroke offers another pivotal scene often indexed but rarely autopsied.[24] Like several other key episodes in the *Mémoires*, this scene is a kind of set piece belonging to a category that could be labelled, "violence in a closed room."[25] Whereas Commynes's narration of pivotal events, not only in Book VI but throughout the *Mémoires*, tends to perambulate between the narrative fields provided by the distinct actors, causes, or even geographical zones more and less directly implicated in the episode at hand, this first crisis is a model of densely compacted, polysemically charged prose. (I point out that Commynes was not present for the episode he relates.)

> Ja commençoyt a vieillir et devenir malade; et estant aux Forges pres Chinon, a son disner, vint comme en une {percution} et perdit la parolle. Il fut levé de la table et tenu pres du feu, et les fenestres closez; et combien qu'il s'en voulsist approucher, l'on l'en garda (aulcuns cuydoient bien faire). Et fut l'an M CCCC IIII[xx], au moys de mars, que ceste malladie luy print. Il perdit de tous points la parolle et toute congnoissance et memoyre. (461)[26]

[Already he was beginning to grow old and become sickly; and while he was at Forges near Chinon, at his dinner, he had an attack and lost the power of speech. He was lifted from the table and held close to the fire, and the windows were shut; and though he tried to reach them, he was kept from doing so (some thought they were doing the right thing). It was in the year 1480, in the month of March, that this illness took him. He entirely lost his power of speech and all consciousness and memory.]

The scene is ambiguous in all but its violence. Do the king's servants hold him back from the windows or from the fire? Commynes only appears to concede the worthy intentions of those who restrain the king ("aulcuns cuydoient bien faire"). These unnamed, nameless servants seize Louis and hold him in a room made dark and windowless. They imprison him. Notice the three capacities the king loses in this fall – speech, recognition, and memory.

That the dread of losing mastery gives this episode its core is confirmed by Commynes's own analysis. As soon as his recovered strength allows it, Louis inquires who had restrained him during his fit. "Il luy fut dict: incontinent les chassa tous de sa maison" (He was told: immediately he banished them all from his household [462]). To show that being controlled by others is the worst thing that can happen to a king, Commynes even dares to evoke the popular belief that Charles VII would not eat because he feared that Louis was trying to poison him.

Il n'estoit riens dont il [Louis XI] eut si grant craincte que de perdre son obeissance, qu'il avoit bien grande, et qu'on ne luy desobeist en quelque chose que ce fust. D'aultre part, le roy Charles son pere, quant il print la maladie dont il mourut, il entra en ymagination qu'on le vouloit empoisonner a la requeste de son filz, et se mist si avant qu'il ne voulut plus manger: par quoy fut advisé, par le conseil des medicins et de ses plus grans et speciaulx serviteurs, qu'on le feroit manger par force; et ainsi fut faict par grand deliberation et ordre des personnes qui le servoient, et luy fut mis du coulys en la bouche. Poy aprés ceste force, ledict roy Charles mourut. (463)

[There was nothing which he feared so much as losing the obedience he commanded, which was very great, or that he would be disobeyed in something, no matter what it was. Moreover, King Charles his father, when he fell sick with the malady from which he died, began imagining that they were trying to poison him at his son's request, and the idea was so fixed that he didn't want to eat any more: for which reason it was decided, by the counsel of his doctors and his greatest and favourite servitors, that they would force him to eat; and this was done after much deliberation and by the order of the people that served him, and some broth was put into his mouth. Shortly after this force was used, King Charles died.]

Loss of authority is a death that leads directly to the death of the body.[27] Although Louis endures for several years following this first attack, the carapace of his indomitable, shrewd control has been wounded.

While the king still lies subdued on the verge of unconsciousness, Cato arrives. His very presence literally brings light into darkness and restores strength to the fallen king. Recalling these deeds, Commynes reaches outwards in a direct address made both emphatic and poetic by the rare inversion of subject and verb, and in a voice still quivering with emotion.[28]

Sur l'heure y arriva[stes] vous, Monsr, mons[r] de Vienne, qui pour lors estoiéz son medicin, et sur l'heure luy fut baillé ung clistere, et ouvrir les fenestres et bailler l'air. Et incontinent quelque chose de parolle luy revint et du sens, et monta a cheval et retourna aux Forges; car ce mal luy print en une petite parroisse a ung quart de lieue de la, ou il estoit allé ouyr la messe. (461)

[Within the hour you arrived, my lord, monsieur de Vienne, you who were at that time his doctor. Right away he was given a purgative, and you ordered that the windows be opened and that air be given to him. Immediately some words and a little sense came back to him, and he got on horseback and went back to Forges, because this illness came upon him while he was in a small parish a quarter of a league from there, where he had gone to hear Mass.]

Louis XI does not die from this first attack, but the episode marks a clear beginning for the *Mémoires'* final movement. Cato stands here in a double role. He is at once an almost magical adjuvant to the king and the privileged recipient of the story told. Commynes's lyric address to him is so powerful that he actually says Cato's name twice ("Monsr, mons[r] de Vienne"). This address to Cato short-circuits the boundaries between narrative levels. The narrator breaks from telling (diegesis) into an unmediated display of his reaction to events narrated (mimesis). His appeal to the archbishop, both the *Mémoires'* narratee and a character within its story, can be understood symptomatically as reflecting a moment of crisis, a moment in which the intensity of the narrated memory threatens to overwhelm the act of narrating. Commynes turns outwards, to the consecrating listener, breaking the spell. At the same time, this eruption heightens our consciousness of the force this particular diegetic moment contains and of its continued significance to the narrating Commynes.

Although Cato's name appears infrequently in the pages of the *Mémoires*, his role as their narratee is determining, providing far more than a rhetorical flourish or a solicitation for borrowed authority.[29] Commynes entrusts Cato with his narrative. Here and elsewhere, Commynes addresses Cato in the second person and by name, establishing and re-affirming the narrative contract between them and also acknowledging Cato's place as an actor in the narrative. Cato cared for a depressed Charles the Bold during the final stages of the duke's floundering military campaigns. More important still, as the king's physician, Cato shared with Commynes a rare familiarity with the king's illness and death. Commynes enters into his narrative covenant with a man privy to the same inner sanctums, the same royal *chambres* where some of the most important secrets in his story are hidden. Cato's presence provides Commynes with a therapeutic listening ear. It is significant that Cato is a healer. The inversion, the long phrase, and the string of temporal markers ("sur l'heure," "pour lors," "a la mesme heure," "incontinent") in Commynes's lament all translate the urgency of a moment not just remembered but relived in all its anguish. The distance between diegesis and extradiegesis collapses. The cry remains as if fossilized in the text, like an air bubble trapped in amber, within whose air the author's voice still rings, raw with emotion.

Commynes has such feeling for this moment, where he was not present. He writes about being physically mastered and shut up in a dark room, and about the death that comes from the loss of dignity. In between the moment when Louis XI suffers this attack and is physically overwhelmed and shut up in a dark room, and the moment when Commynes comes to the narration of that moment, Commynes has spent many months in prison. I opened this chapter with Commynes's memory of watching boats come upriver, but one of the traces that survives from his time in prison includes a July 1487 order to board over the windows of his room atop the square tower of the Conciergerie.[30] (The order does not appear to have been executed.) How could

Commynes not write of Louis's attack with powerful emotion? He has himself spent months shut against his will in a dark and suffocating room. Commynes's narration of Louis's attack both relives and remembers the fear and anger of imprisonment. The relief that booms through what he says about Louis XI, again able to breathe and promised recovery, applies to himself also. Commynes speaks; he frees himself from suffocation and silence. Cato is present in Commynes's narrative at this singular moment of unparalleled immediacy, and in this moment, Cato plays the role of a liberator. He saves the king from a death both literal and metaphorical. This is also the psychic function that Cato plays for Commynes. He is, in the model discussed in the introduction, the empathic listening other to whom speech is directed and whose presence makes witnessing possible.

The Dream of a Perfect Union

As soon as Louis recovers enough strength to communicate, he summons Commynes.

> Ledict seigneur fut bien pensé, et faisoit des signes de ce qu'il vouloit dire. Entre les aultres choses demanda l'official de Tours pour se confesser, et feist signe que l'on me mandast, car j'estoye allé a Argenton, qui est a quelque dix lieues de la. Quant je arryvay, je le trouvay a table … Il entendoit peu de ce qu'on luy disoit, mais de douleur il n'en sentoit point. Il me fit signe que je couchasse en sa chambre: il ne formoit gueres de motz. Je le servy l'espace de quinze jours a table et a l'entour de sa personne comme vallet de chambre, que je tenoye a grant honneur, et y estoie bien tenu. Au bout de deux ou trois jours, la parolle luy commençoit a revenir et le sens; et luy sembloit que nul ne l'entendoit si bien que moy, par quoy vouloit que tousjours me tinse auprés de luy; et se confessa audict official, moy present, car aultrement ne se fussent entenduz. (461–2)

> [The king was well cared for, and he made signs for what he wanted to say. Among other things he asked for the official of Tours in order to make his confession and made signs that I should be sent for, because I had gone to Argenton which is some ten leagues from there. When I arrived I found him sitting at the table … He understood little of what was said to him, but he didn't feel any pain. He made signs to me that I should sleep in his room; he could barely articulate any words. I served him the space of fifteen days at table and about his person as a chamber valet, which I

esteemed a great honour, and I was duty-bound to do so. After two or three days, his speech started coming back and his clarity; and it seemed to him like no one understood him as well as I did, for which reason he wanted me to stay constantly by his side. He confessed to the Tours official with me there, because otherwise they wouldn't have understood each other.]

This story contains the archaeology of a language. In the first shock of Louis's fall, there is only silence. The king becomes like an infant who cannot yet speak and who strives to communicate the objects of its drives in the language of the body and in inchoate noises. His gestures take shape on the plane of unmediated need, at the fault line between symbol and the impossibility of abstraction. It is from within this state of absolute dependence that Louis desires Commynes's presence, a presence which, reversing every hierarchy, Louis's gestures identify as fulfilling an infant-like need for comfort and protection. Commynes remains by the king's side night and day for two weeks, during which time Commynes tends to Louis's person – to his physical body.

It has long been a commonplace among historians to criticize Commynes's contemporary, Thomas Basin, for his vicious depiction of Louis XI's drooling, uncontrolled body. For Basin and the characters in his history, the stammering, paralytic king who received diplomatic envoys in unlit rooms in order to conceal his deformity was an object for mockery. The cruelty of Basin's account and the disgust it provokes derive from the obvious exhilaration that Basin, and to a lesser degree his characters, experience in giving free expression to a potently sadistic attitude towards the king's de-sacralized body.[31] Commynes shields Louis from posterity's gaze, but the body to which he tends was no less vulnerable. It is within the enclosed, private space of the sick king's *chambre* that Louis becomes slowly able to speak again ("la parolle luy commençoit a revenir et le sens"). Commynes occupies the essential, mediating position in this re-entry into language. The author – and it is vital that we recognize in Commynes the figure of an author – shares with Louis XI a bond so entire, so enclosing, as to be indivisible. No one else understands the king like Commynes does; communication between them does not require coherent words. The narrator is the privileged interpreter of this fragile tongue ("luy sembloit que nul ne l'entendoit si bien que moy"), and then its unique speaker. Commynes acts as an intermediary between the king and his confessor. That is, Commynes situates himself as the necessary term between the king's conscience and God. He becomes the arbiter of Louis XI's soul, an agent through whom the king reaches for grace. Commynes appropriates for himself the most intimate sign of the king's presence, pretending that the two men speak with a single voice. The communication between the king and Commynes is not dialogic. Narration now becomes the doubling of speech not as communication but rather as communion. The narrative of the *Mémoires* renders explicit an intimacy of body and voice to which even Louis XI's priest is an outsider. Commynes becomes the king's alter-ego, the voice of an "other self." Cato serves in turn as Commynes's therapeutic listening Other in the continuation of this most private conversation. If there is a mythology here, it is an erotic mythology of desire perfectly satisfied, the dream of perfect union, or in the phrase Commynes himself murmurs in the prologue, "continuelle residance." Commynes not only speaks from the centre, he speaks that centre, and his voice fills the shadows of guarded rooms where Louis XI once struggled to maintain the illusion of absolute authority. The way that Commynes speaks for Louis XI takes the conceptual metaphors of diplomacy, representation, and epistolarity to a terrible intensity. The authority which inhabits the *Mémoires* is built from the sedimentary accretion of layer after layer of such acts of displacement, delegation, and deferral. Commynes speaks for the king, to Cato, from memory, through a secretary who, recording his words, ratifies the faint echo of the king's voice still audible within Commynes's. For this reason, the voice within the text is always the king's and always Commynes's. It is always the point of fusion and the point of fracture, of an endless now and an irretrievable past.

This fantasy of perfect union transcends – defies – the realities of political subjection. In the scenario scripted by Commynes, Louis needs the narrator in order to have access to his own voice, which is to say, to his own identity, even to his capacity to rule as king.[32] Commynes's schema at first seems to take all the tension out of the strains between subjectivity, political subjectivity, and political subjection. The author's fantasy provides him with an identity born of erasing of the boundaries between himself and the king. But at the moment that Commynes narrates, both his fantasy and the subject position it dramatizes have already been shattered. The image that Commynes holds forth belongs to the same genre of spectrally unified visions of self first glimpsed in his memory of the Seine's cargo driven upriver. The precariousness not just of this identity but even of its fantasy pierces the text in the acknowledgment, "y estoie bien tenu," which allows an entry into consciousness of the obligation inherent to the relations between Commynes and the king, a relationship whose reality was always one of domination and subjugation. The portrait given of the frail king by his *serviteur* is all the more gripping for showing Commynes wrestling in his memory and through his narration with the splitting between reality and fantasy.

Prison

This chapter opened with a close reading of Commynes's remembrance of the Conciergerie prison. It is fitting to end with the consideration of another prison. Prison serves as dominant trope in Commynes's depiction of the king's death and his fear thereof. The trope takes on both associative and spiritual values, expressed through Commynes's recurring comparison of Louis's moral suffering during his final illness to purgatory, imagined as a kind of spiritual prison. First he writes, "je veulx faire comparaison des maulx et douleurs qu'il a faict souffrir a plusieurs et ceulx qu'il a souffert avant mourir, pour ce que j'ay esperance qu'ilz l'auront mené en paradis, et que ce aura esté partie de son purgatoire" (I want to compare the pain and sufferings which he inflicted on others and those which he suffered before dying, because I have the hope that they will have led him to paradise, and that it will have been part of his purgatory [488]). The next mention is equally explicit and more contemplative.

> Fault revenir a dire comme de son temps furent trouvees ces mauvaises et diverses prisons, et comme, avant mourir, il se trouva en semblables et plus grandes, et en aussi grans paours et plus grandes que ceulx qu'il avoit tenuz; laquelle chose je tiens a tres grant grace pour luy et pour partie de son purgatoire. Et le diz ainsi pour monstrer qu'il n'est nul homme, de quelque dignité qu'i soit, qui ne seuffre ou en secret ou en public, et par especial ceulx qui font souffrir les aultres. (494)

> [I have to say again how in his time those evil and various types of prison were invented, and how, before he died, he found himself in similar or even greater ones, and in fear as great or greater than those he had imprisoned. I hold this to be a matter of very great mercy for him and as a part of his [time in] purgatory. And I mention it to show that there is no man, of whatever rank he may be, who does not suffer in secret or in public, and especially those who have made others suffer.]

The narrative draws three congruent prison-like spaces, all of which are related to language, confession, and narration. First there is the river-borne, prismatic vision of self-in-time that emerged from Commynes's memory of a prison cell and the river Seine. Next comes the terror of being physically dominated, and the shuttered windows which followed the stroke that left Louis dumb. Finally, there are the rooms where Commynes tended to the weakened body of a king who hid himself from others' gaze, and where he gave his voice to Louis's ill-formed words. Commynes crosses between remembered prisons and the prison of memory, to the hour anticipated and promised on the first pages of the *Mémoires*, towards the locked chest at their centre.

As the king's strength deteriorates his fear of losing control intensifies.[33] He begins to carry out extravagant acts, just so that people will talk about him and know that he is still alive and in control. He becomes increasingly suspicious of those around him and moves his personnel around constantly. "Le Roy retourna a Tours, et s'enfermoit fort, et tant que peu de gens le veoient. Et entra en merveilleuse suspicion de tout le monde" (The king returned to Tours and so shut himself away that few people ever saw him. He became remarkably suspicious and fearful of everybody [467]). Louis then builds elaborate defensive fortifications around himself.

> Tout a l'environ de la place dudict Plessis, il feit faire ung treylis de gros barreaulx de fer, et planter dedans la muraille dé broches de fer aiant plusieurs poinctz, comme a l'entree par ou on eust entrer aux fousséz. Aussi feist faire quatre moynneaulx, tous de fer bien espoix, en lieu par {ou} on pourroit tirer a son aise; et estoit chose bien triumphante, et cousta plus de vingt mille francs. Et a la fin y mist quarante arbalestriers, qui jour et nuyt estoient en ce foussé, avec commission de tirer a tout homme qui en approucheroit de nuyt, jusques ad ce que la porte seroit ouverte le matin. (469–70)

> [All around Plessis, he had a trellis made from thick bars of iron, and had set into the outside wall iron stakes with several points, at places where one would have entered from the moat. He had four *moineaux* made, all from thick iron, at spots from which one could shoot with ease: and it was quite a triumphant thing, and cost more than twenty thousand francs. And at the end he put forty crossbowmen there, who day and night were in that moat, with the order to shoot at any man who approached at night, before the gate opened in the morning.]

This image so strikes Commynes, both visually and as a metaphor, the
he describes it twice.

> Ledict seigneur, vers la fin de ses jours, feit clore, tout a l'entour de sa mai-
> son du Plessis les Tours, de gros barreaulx de fer en forme de grosses
> grisles; et aux quatre coings de la maison quatre moyneaux de fer, bons et
> grans et espoys. Lesdictes grisles estoient contre le mur, du costé de la
> place. De l'autre part du foussé ... fit mectre plusieurs broches de fer, mas-
> sonnees dedans le mur, qui avoient chascune trois ou quatre poinctes, et
> les feit mectre fort pres l'une de l'autre. (495)

> [The king, at the end of his days, had his castle of Plessis-les-Tours en-
> closed all around with great bars of iron in the form a large railing; and at
> the four corners of the castle [he placed] four iron *moineaux*, solid and large
> and thick. The railings were against the wall, on the defensive side. On the
> other side of the moat ... he had several iron stakes made, set into the wall,
> which each had three or four points, and he had them placed very close to
> one another.]

Ten more crossbowmen remain on each *moineau* around the clock, ready
to shoot at anyone who approaches the castle at night. Louis wants them
to live around the clock at the ready in the moats (495). One might ask
whether this hypervigilance is not meant to guard Louis as much against
death's arrival as against court conspiracies.

The king becomes afraid to roam about even the interior of the palace
freely. Instead of crossing the courtyard he clings to the walls and the
shadowed galleries. Significantly, it is at this point, as Commynes introduces the metaphorical (or poetic, or spiritual, or psychological)
notion of self-imprisonment, that he first evokes the bond between
Louis XI "imprisoned" and those whom he once held in much colder,
less poetic chains.

> Est il donc possible de tenir roy, pour le garder honnestement, en plus
> estroicte prison que luy mesmes se tenoit? Les caiges ou il avoit tenu
> les aultres avoient quelque huyct pieds en quarré; et luy, qui estoit si
> grant Roy, avoit bien une petite court de chasteau a se pourmener; et
> encores n'y venoit la gueres, mais se tenoit en la galerye, sans partir de
> la, sinon que par les chambres alloit a la messe, sans passer par ladicte
> court. (496)

[Is it possible to keep a king, to keep him honestly, in a more narrow prison than he kept himself? The cages where he had held other people were some eight feet square; and he, who was such a great king, had a small courtyard in the castle to walk about; and even then he hardly came there, but stayed in the gallery, without leaving it, except that he passed through the rooms to go to Mass, without crossing through the courtyard.]

What a terrible gaze Commynes levels on his king: rats prefer shadows, and cockroaches cling to edges rather than cross open spaces. Fear has rendered the king completely abject. Louis's self-imprisonment slowly congeals into a thoroughly military standoff, albeit one susceptible to great interpretive depth. Plessis is encrusted with as many defences as "une place de frontiere estroictement gardee" (a tightly guarded frontier post [495]). But this frontier, like the prison in which the king encloses himself, is spiritual, and its boundaries exist only as constructs of Louis's imagination. The narration circles around the now twinned ideas of the literal, physical imprisonment Louis imposed on others and how the king's terror of death was like a prison for him. The king's fears are "aussi grans paours et plus grandes que ceulx qu'il avoit tenuz" (as great fears and greater than those he had imprisoned [494]). Commynes draws Louis's sufferings closer and closer to his own.

> Il est vray qu'il avoit faict de rigoureuses prisons, comme caiges de fer et d'autres de boys, couvertes de platz de fer par le dehors et par le dedans, avecques terribles serrures, de quelques huyt piedz de large et de la haulteur d'ung homme et pied plus ... Plusieurs depuys l'ont mauldit, et moy aussi, qui en ay tasté, soubz le Roy de present, huyt moys. (493)

> [It is true that he had made rigorous prisons, like iron cages and others out of wood, covered with plates of iron on the outside and within, with terrible locks, some eight feet wide and a foot taller than a man's height ... Several people have cursed them since, and I have too, because I was in one, under the present king, for eight months.]

Louis's final sojourn at Plessis takes on the allure of dwelling in a liminal space, from which the dweller gazes back at human existence as through a different lens. To experience the terror of imprisonment, whether in an eight-foot cage or in a palace, is to perceive oneself and all human existence from a position at once tortured and exalted. Louis XI's retreat from the world rhetorically crosses Commynes's confinement in the years following the king's death in a kind of conceptual chiasmus.

The castle at Plessis-les-Tours, fortification		memory (of fear, of waiting)
	PRISON	
anticipation (dread of death)		The prison at Loches, iron cages

The image and the memory of prison become another paratextually constructed site of encounter, and of union, between king and memorialist.

The Hour of His Death

Under the entry for *Désir* ("wish" in English, Freud's *Wunsch*, sometimes *Begierde* or *Lust*) in their *Dictionnaire de la psychanalyse,* Laplanche and Pontalis explain: "Le désir est indissolublement lié à des 'traces mnésiques' et trouve son accomplissment (Erfüllung) dans la reproduction hallucinatoire des perceptions devenues les signes de cette satisfaction."[34] In retelling his own story and the king's, the narrator gives voice to both memory and desire. Narration suspends time and allows Commynes to return, in a sort of hallucination, to a pre-fall state of favour. Having so completely abandoned the apparatus of his Burgundian identity when he left the duke's service, Commynes lived in a state of perpetual exile and of complete dependence upon the king. When Louis's death permanently annuls this contract, Commynes finds himself doubly exiled. A prison cage replaces the king's bedchamber. The engine of the *Mémoires'* most literary qualities is to be found among the layers of this exile, and in the revivifying remembrance of a now-silent voice. In the aftermath of the traumatic loss of the Talmont estates, the lyric textuality of the *Mémoires* serves as a bulwark against the annihilation and self-dispossession implicit in the confiscation of Commynes's Talmont lands. The *Mémoires* bear witness to the language shared by Commynes and his king, the *parole* which both anchored and performed Commynes's privileged relationship with Louis. They also speak in that *parole*, their narration finding its way through silences, repetitions, and dislocations, returning again and again, yet also always pulling back from, the site of the betrayal experienced, a site at once spatial and narrative, at once palace and prison of memory.

It is both evocative and useful to think for a moment about Renaissance theories of linear perspective. It is striking, but by no means necessary, that Commynes would almost certainly have been familiar with these theories, whether from his patronage of artists Jean Pélerin Viator and Jean Fouquet or simply from his extended travels in Italy. What is more important than Commynes's potential knowledge of the mathematics behind the illusions created in these men's work is the way in which the illusion created through linear perspective depends on a vanishing point which "orders" space in the sense of regulating or governing it. In his classic study, *The Birth and Rebirth of Pictorial Space*, John White explained, "In any focused system of perspective, such as that invented in the Renaissance, the vanishing point provides the all-important centre of attention."[35] The painting situates its viewer in consequence of this vanishing point, directing him to engage with pictorial space from a position ideally conceived of to complete the illusion engineered by the artist. From the moment that, in the first sentences of the *Mémoires*, we joined Commynes on his journey to the Burgundian court, we have been within the embrace of the narrative space whose illusion is crafted in the *Mémoires*.

Two edges bound Commynes's narration: the point from which "en l'eage de pouvoir monter a cheval" the narrator enters the world and begins to survey what it contains, and the dark horizon of an aged king "[dont] faillut qu'il passast par la ou les aultres sont passés" (who had to go there where others have gone [484]). This death is the destination point Commynes sets forth in his prologue. The expression "l'heure de son trespas, ou je estoie present" (the hour of his trespass, where I was present [1]) refers both to private, physical spaces and also to metaphysical places. It is in this sense that the notion of a "lieu de l'énonciation" acquires a double meaning, at once the abstracted textual and narrative *lieu* produced by Commynes's narrative and the constantly present, "hidden centre," the place where, at the threshold of death, the king spoke words that Commynes himself is unable to speak. The *Mémoires* map out a "lieu énonciatif" in whose cartographies the bond between Commynes and Louis XI endures in the eternal here and now of narration. The king's death moors narrative spatiality and temporality, and serves as the crucible where text, *hors-texte*, and silence meet. "[L]'heure de son trespas" indicates a vanishing point as well as a "vanished point." Commynes's narration of Louis's illnesses and death constitute at once the *Mémoires'* achievement and their centre. Narrative space becomes a mirror of remembered spaces, the place where words once spoken (and others unspoken) are heard again.

Notes

Introduction

1 "There are two meanings of the word 'subject': subject to someone else by control and dependence; and tied to his own identity by a conscience or self-knowledge. Both meanings suggest a form of power which subjugates and makes subject to" (Foucault, "The Subject and Power," 781).

2 The most recent general biographies of Commynes are Blanchard, *Philippe de Commynes*; Dufournet, *Vie de Philippe de Commynes*; and Liniger, *Philippe de Commynes*. All three make use of a similar body of published archival materials from early modern and nineteenth-century sources, but draw contrasting arguments from them. Blanchard works with unpublished archival sources not used by Dufournet or Liniger, but unfortunately his book contains no scholarly apparatus. Dufournet's is the most partisan of the three, but is also the only one to cite its sources in keeping with scholarly conventions.

   Scholars are divided in situating Commynes's birth in either 1445 or 1447. Dufournet, *Vie de Philippe de Commynes*, 19–20, presents the evidence in favour of 1447; cf. Blanchard's arguments in favour of 1445, *Mémoires* (TLF, 2007), 2:969–70.

3 On the origin of these debts, which were still not acquitted during the first years of Commynes's court service, see Desplanques, "Troubles de la châtellenie de Cassel sous Philippe le Bon." For their October 1469 acquittal, see Stein and Dünnebeil, *Catalogue des actes de Charles le Téméraire*, item 697, page 163.

4 Blanchard, *Mémoires* (TLF, 2007), 1:5. This edition consists of two sequentially paginated volumes, the first of which contains the editor's extensive introduction and bibliography, followed by the whole of Commynes's

narrative; the second is reserved for a substantial critical apparatus. Unless otherwise indicated, all citations from the *Mémoires* have been taken from the first volume of this edition, and will henceforth be cited parenthetically in the main text by page number alone; i.e., for the above example, "5," rather than "1:5." For ease of consultation, references to supporting materials contained in the second volume will continue to be presented in the format volume: page. Additionally, to avoid confusion with other editions of the *Mémoires* cited in the notes, outside the main text, this edition will appear as *Mémoires* (TLF, 2007), followed by page number as appropriate. All translations are my own unless indicated to the contrary. In preparing my translations of the *Mémoires*, I occasionally compared my version to that of Michael Jones (*Memoirs: The Reign of Louis XI, 1461–83*, 1972). I have also occasionally found myself obligated to punctuate translated English text differently from its edited French version.

5 See Duvosquel, "Bourgeoisie ou noblesse?" which includes an assessment of Le Pippre, "La Généalogie des seigneurs de Commines," 251–64; and Leuridan, "Recherches sur les sires de Comines."

6 The English epithet "Spider King" derives from the French "l'universel(le) araigne," which comes from a widely disseminated ballad now usually attributed to the Burgundian *rhétoriqueur* Jean Molinet (but sometimes to his predecessor Georges Chastellain), and which includes the verses, "Ay combattu l'universel araigne / Qui m'a trouvé par ses rébellions / Lyon rampant en crouppe de montaigne."

7 The sentiment has been widespread and often repeated. The phrase appears on the back cover of the 1979 paperback edition prepared by Jean Dufournet for Gallimard's Folio collection.

8 Denis Sauvage claimed to have in his possession a manuscript he called the "vieil Exemplaire," "à la main & copié sur le vray Original de l'Autheur, comme le personnage, auquel il estoit, escrit a la premiere feuille" (*Mémoires*, ed. Sauvage, 1552, unpaginated "Advertissement aux Lecteurs"). Preference between the two best surviving sixteenth-century manuscripts of the *Mémoires*, Polignac and Dobrée (respectively Bibliothèque nationale de France, ms. n.a.f. 20960, and Nantes, Musée Dobrée, ms. 18), has become implicated in the critical debates which have surrounded their reception.

9 Dufournet, "Quand les *Mémoires* de Commynes ont-ils été composés?" tackles the dating of various passages in the *Mémoires*. The notes which accompany Blanchard's 2007 edition of the *Mémoires* bring many detailed clarifications to questions of historical chronology and narrative sequence.

10 A substantial bibliography surrounds the birth of the *Mémoires*. For one survey of potential influences on Commynes, see Blanchard, *Commynes l'Européen*, 337–67; cf. Dufournet, "Commynes et l'invention d'un nouveau genre historique." On royal biography, see Delogu, *Theorizing the Ideal Sovereign*. On historiography and Burgundian court culture, see Devaux, "L'Identité bourguignonne et l'écriture de l'histoire." On Italian *ricordanze*, see, for example, Bec, *Marchands écrivains*. For perspectives on the *Mémoires'* relation to parahistorical genres, see especially Chabaud, "Les 'Mémoires' de Philippe de Commynes: un 'miroir aux princes'?" and Demers, *Commynes, méMORiALISTE*. These two studies propose models that underscore didactic elements within the *Mémoires'* polyphony of discourses and generic traits. In my estimation, however, they share a common limitation, in that they fail to adequately recognize the narrative qualities of the *Mémoires*, that is, to recognize in Commynes's text a temporally rooted account of transformation. The larger question of autobiography's emergence as a genre exceeds the scope of this study; one pertinent point of departure is Bedford, Davis, and Kelly, *Early Modern Autobiography*.

11 For these definitions, see the *Dictionnaire du Moyen Français*, s.v. mémoire. Perhaps most provocatively for this book's reflection on Commynes's coming to writing, memory was also considered one of the three powers of the soul, along with understanding and will. On the broader question of memory in medieval cultures, see below.

12 This limited evidence comes from the poet's apparent knowledge of Commynes's text. We remain ignorant of the conditions in which the narrative could potentially have circulated, or of how many people might have seen it or known of its existence. "Le Séjour de deuil pour la mort de Philippe de Commines," Koninklijke Bibliotheek, The Hague, KB 76 E 13; published in Kervyn de Lettenhove, *Lettres et négociations*, 1:1–35. See Dufournet, "*Le Séjour de deul*: un prosimètre à la gloire de Commynes (1512)."

13 The full title of the work as it appeared with Parisian *libraire* Galliot du Pré in the spring of 1524 was *Cronique et hystoire faicte et composée par feu Messire Phelippe de Commines ... contenant les choses advenues durant le règne du roy Loys XIe, tant en France, Bourgongne, Flandres, Arthois, Angleterre que Espaigne et lieux circonvoisins...* On this first publication, see Armstrong, *Before Copyright*, 107–8 and 262.

It has become a commonplace to point out that the *Mémoires* have never been out of print. Commynes's commercial success contrasts with, for example, the afterlives of Olivier de La Marche or Georges Chastellain.

Chastellain remained unpublished until Buchon's nineteenth-century edition. Each author has been the object of renewed interest since the mid-1990s; see Small, *George Chastelain and the Shaping of Valois Burgundy*; and Emerson, *Olivier de La Marche*. For a first glimpse of the *Mémoires'* early fortunes, see Dufournet, "Premiers lecteurs," which also contains a list of editions and translations of Commynes's *Mémoires* through 1881.

It was Commynes's narration until the year 1483 which Galliot du Pré published in 1524. Sauvage's *vieil exemplaire* also contained only Commynes's account of Louis XI's reign. A further two books, written separately from these first six, describe Charles VIII's 1495 descent into the Italian peninsula. These final two books were first edited by Enguilbert de Marnef in 1528. The first edition to contain both the *Mémoires* of Louis XI and the *Mémoires* of Charles VIII did not appear until 1539 (Dufournet, "Premiers lecteurs," 53 and 92).

14   Commynes, *Les Mémoires de Messire Philippe de Commines*, ed. Sauvage (1552), "Advertissement aux Lecteurs."

15   Sbriccoli, *Crimen laesae maiestatis*, 11.

16   On the specificity of early modern *Mémoires* as a French genre, see Fumaroli, "Mémoires et histoire," 27.

17   In recent years, critical debate about historiography has arguably defined itself by its engagement with the nature and limits of textuality. Discussion has been especially enthusiastic, and especially productive, among scholars working on pre-modern texts. "One of the most important arguments of the New Historicism is that literary texts participate in the construction of the cultural system rather than stand as fixed and frozen products of it" (Zammito, "Are We Being Theoretical Yet?" 795). Commynes might best be understood as pre-modern in the specific sense of coming just before and prefiguring modernity.

18   The "cultures of memory" in medieval Europe have moved to the forefront of scholarship since the 1966 publication of Frances Yates's *The Art of Memory*. The phrase itself belongs to Mary Carruthers. See especially Carruthers, *The Book of Memory*; Carruthers and Ziolkowski, *The Medieval Craft of Memory*; Coleman, *Ancient and Medieval Memories*; and Doležalová, *The Making of Memory in the Middle Ages*. On the German context, especially in the High Middle Ages, see especially the work of Althoff, Fried, and Geary; and on music and memory, that of Anna Maria Busse Berger.

19   Collective memory has become a ubiquitous theme of academic and popular historiography in the aftermath of Pierre Nora's monumental project on the *Lieux de Mémoire*, first launched in 1989. Two salient critiques of the

"memory industry" are Kerwin Lee Klein, "On the Emergence of Memory in Historical Discourse," and Wulf Kansteiner, "Finding Meaning in Memory."

20 Cf. Collard, "Les Découpages périodologiques dans l'historiographie française autour de 1500."

21 Commynes first gestures towards the memory of how Charles VII assassinated John the Fearless (*Mémoires* [TLF, 2007], 76), then alludes to these events outright during his description of the preparations for the Picquigny summit (*Mémoires* [TLF, 2007], 287–8). He makes several other less forthright allusions to civil war.

22 For a critique of this model and its legacy, see Ricoeur, *Memory, History, Forgetting*, 7–15.

23 Scott, "The Evidence of Experience," 779–80.

24 Lanhers, "Deux affaires de trahison." "Ces deux cas, par la différence des situations et grâce à la réflexion très pénétrante des avocats, permettent de saisir l'ambiguïté du concept de trahison pour les hommes qui avait suivi le Dauphin. Vivre après la mort de Charles VI (le 21 octobre 1422), c'està-dire sous le gouvernement anglais, est-ce trahir?" (Lanhers, "Deux affaires de trahison," 323.)

25 For instance, Baudouin de Bourgogne, Jean de Chalon, Philippe de Crevecoeur, or Boffile de Juge.

26 Miller, "Arachnologies," 274; cited by E. Jane Burns, "Raping Men," 130.

27 See above, note 13.

28 There are countless popular and scholarly books dedicated in whole or in part to the topic of betrayal. My own thinking about betrayal was especially enriched by Javeau, *Anatomie de la trahison*; Pozzi, "Paradigme du traître"; Shklar, *Ordinary Vices*, chapter 4, "The Ambiguities of Betrayal"; and Turnaturi, *Betrayals*.

29 Pollock and Maitland, *History of English Law*, 2:503.

30 "For there to be betrayal, the act must be so perceived and so defined by either the person betrayed or the betrayer. Only they can name it as betrayal, acknowledge it, and call it into being," (Turnaturi, *Betrayals*, 17). Enrico Pozzi concurs, "Nous nous heurtons à un noeud structurel de la trahison: c'est la soi-disant victime qui la définit ainsi" (Pozzi, "Paradigme du traître," 3). To some extent, this broadly agreed-upon point forecloses the possibility of a third-party account. It is not possible both to remain neutral and to use the lexicon of betrayal. To describe an action as a "betrayal," without irony, involves an entry into subjective identification, moral judgment, or both.

31 "To speak of betrayal requires previous expectations of loyalty, in both rational and emotive terms, and previously established relations and interactions in which the subjects trusted one another, in part or wholly" (Turnaturi, *Betrayals*, 9).

32 "It is not by chance that in Italian the phrase *a tradimento* can simply mean 'suddenly' or 'unexpectedly'" (Turnaturi, *Betrayals*, 9).

33 This point was made in one form or another by each of these authors: see Javeau, *Anatomie de la trahison*, 10; Pozzi, "Paradigme du traître," 1–2; Shklar, *Ordinary Vices*, 138–41; and Turnaturi, *Betrayals*, 2 and 8.

34 The dyad need not necessarily exist consciously as such in either party's thoughts before the crisis of rupture. The nature of betrayal is such that, where no such consciousness of binary relationality existed before, one is created by the betrayal itself. Just as betrayal can be understood as a fantasy of lost union, so that union – the dyad itself – can be the product of individual fantasy. Cf. Turnaturi, *Betrayals*, 5 and 17.

35 Laplanche and Pontalis, *Vocabulaire de la psychanalyse*, 499; s.v. trauma.

36 Note, however, that in clinical psychology the category of "betrayal trauma" is most often associated with situations of abuse by caregivers.

37 See especially, Caruth, *Trauma: Explorations in Memory*.

38 For the exploration of this relation in literature and cinema, see Caruth, *Unclaimed Experience*; for a critique of the relation between trauma and mimesis with an emphasis on the history of psychoanalysis, see Leys, *Trauma: A Genealogy*.

39 Felman and Laub, *Testimony*, xiv–xv.

40 Ibid., 23.

41 Caruth, *Unclaimed Experience*, 3.

42 Cf. Caruth, *Unclaimed Experience*, 61, on Freud's *Beyond the Pleasure Principle*: "What causes trauma, then, is a shock that appears to work very much like a bodily threat but is in fact a break in the mind's experience of time."

43 Hayden White, "The Historical Text as Literary Artifact," 43.

44 It would not be inappropriate to observe a "religious register" within Commynes's project. However, while the frameworks of confession and conversion do periodically surface in my engagement with the *Mémoires*, I do not believe this religious register defines the text's meaning. Cf. Zimmermann, "Confession and Autobiography in the Early Renaissance."

45 Two of the most glaring omissions concern Commynes's colleague and peer, the Italian *transfuge* (emigré) Boffile de Juge, and Anne de Beaujeu, Louis's favourite daughter, later the de-facto regent during Commynes's futile rebellion.

46 Bois, *Crise du féodalisme*, 299.

47 Krynen, "Droit romain et état monarchique," 18–19. For a complementary perspective, see Contamine, "De la puissance aux privilèges."

48 The role of treason law in both its theory and application has become the subject of significant scholarly debate about state formation, the evolution of the monarchy, and legal (intellectual) history. Consensus exists around the importance of treason, with disagreement anchored largely following the lines of division between national or methodological historical approaches. Cuttler, *Law of Treason and Treason Trials*, provides an obligatory starting point; see especially chapter 10 on Louis XI's reign. Chiffoleau, "Sur le crime de majesté médiéval," and Sbriccoli, *Crimen laesae maiestatis*, examine the theoretical bases within medieval treason law; Blanchard, *Commynes et les procès politiques*, argues that Louis XI's appreciation for treason law derived more from its pragmatic utility than from Christological concerns. On the rhetoric of treason law in the ducal courts, see especially, Michael Jones, "'Bons Bretons et bons francoys,'" and "Trahison et l'idée de lèse-majesté." Less recent but foundational to the debates which followed is Pocquet du Haut-Jussé, "Une Idée politique de Louis XI." Bercé, *Les Procès politiques (XIVᵉ–XVIIᵉ siècle)*, opens up a complementary perspective. Landmark works on the English context include Pollock and Maitland, *History of English Law*, and more recently, Bellamy, *The Law of Treason in England in the Later Middle Ages*.

49 Cuttler, *Law of Treason and Treason Trials*, 242.

50 See the *Trésor de la Langue Française informatisé*, s.v. Lèse.

51 Michael Jones, "Trahison et l'idée de lèse-majesté," 94.

52 Krynen, "Droit romain et état monarchique," 17.

53 "Feudalism is merely a highly general and abstract label of convenience, and it has often been remarked that, like the term Middle Ages, it was only invented after the medieval period had ended and did not exist in anyone's mind at the time itself. Nonetheless, when every qualification has been made as to the many varieties of contractual dependence that were evolved and also as to the ambiguous and variable vocabulary that was used to describe it, fealty and vassalage were important and typical features of many relationships between men of power in this period" (Burns, *The Cambridge History of Medieval Political Thought*, 159–60).

54 Ibid., 160.

55 Cf. the argument made by Major, "'Bastard Feudalism' and the Kiss."

56 These three traits are the virtues demanded of kings from the earliest Greek treatises on the subject. See Burns, *The Cambridge History of Medieval Political Thought*, 26.

57 See Foucault, "The Subject and Power," 780 and 793–5.

58 Pocquet du Haut-Jussé, "Une Idée politique de Louis XI." How sharply can the line between Charles VII and Louis XI be drawn? The divide between the two reigns is acknowledged even by those who warn against oversimplification. Michael Jones, contesting Pocquet du Haut-Jussé's arguments, asserts that the idea that all those living within the limits of the kingdom are the king's subjects was not due to Louis XI. Jones gives credit as far back as Philip the Fair for attempting to use a lexical shift to effect a political one. He then acknowledges that it was during Louis XI's reign that the political intention behind the use of the word "subject" became reality (See Michael Jones, "Trahison et l'idée de lèse-majesté," 105–6).
59 Dubois, "Observations sur la diplomatique des lettres de Louis XI," 342.
60 The last part of the *Grandes Chroniques*, written by Jean Chartier, ends with the reign of Charles VII in 1461.
61 One pertinent study of this broader phenomenon is Daly, "Mixing Business with Leisure."
62 Collard, "Une Oeuvre historiographique du règne de Charles VIII," 85.
63 Cf. Contamine, "De la puissance aux privilèges," 236–7, on the parallel moments of revitalization in historiography which immediately followed the deaths of Philip the Fair and Louis XI.
64 Hayden White, "The Value of Narrativity in the Representation of Reality," 12–13.

1 The Black Box of Péronne, or Commynes and the Canon

1 The events at Péronne and Commynes's role in them have been exhaustively studied. On the event and its broader context, see especially Vaughan, *Charles the Bold*, chapter 1, "The Duke and the Towns: Ghent and Liège," especially 53–8; cf. Cauchies, *Louis XI et Charles le Hardi*, chapter 1, "Le Renard et le loup." For a critical assessment of Commynes's narrative, see especially, Bittmann, "Die Zusammenkunft von Péronne: Das zweite Buch," in *Ludwig XI und Karl der Kühne*, 1:193–367; Dufournet, "L'Entrevue de Péronne," in *La Destruction des mythes dans les* Mémoires *de Philippe de Commynes*, 182–93; Dufournet, "Lire Commynes: l'entrevue de Péronne et l'expédition contre Liège," reprinted as "Comment lire les *Mémoires de Commynes*?" See infra and note 36 below, where I comment on the revision of Dufournet's original study over time, its republication, and its iconic status. Liniger, chapter 4, "La rencontre de Péronne," in *Philippe de Commynes*, 55–66, gives a contrasting, positive, assessment.

2 Until things went awry at Péronne, Louis XI was an eager summiteer, meeting with his homologues relatively free of the angst that Commynes counsels (Contamine, "Rencontres au sommet," especially 283).

3 Passage cited below. Charles III, called "the Simple," was kept prisoner in a castle at Péronne from 923 until his death in 929.

4 Hare, *The Life of Louis XI*, 155.

5 See Berridge, *Diplomatic Classics*, chapter 1, "Commynes: The Memoirs," 18–38.

6 Gachard, *Particularités et documents inédits sur Commines*, 3–4; cited in Dupont, ed. (1840–7), *Mémoires*, 3:11. Charles awarded everything confiscated from Commynes, "passé aujourd'hui même au service de roi de France," to Philippe de Croÿ (Stein and Dünnebeil, *Catalogue des actes de Charles le Téméraire*, item 1409, page 342).

7 Commynes disappeared from Eu, on the Channel coast north of Dieppe; he resurfaced 400 kilometres away, joining the king at Ponts-de-Cé, near Angers in the Loire.

8 Compare, for example, "Commines fut-il gagné à Péronne par l'or de Louis XI ? Y mania-t-il … telle sorte de limon qu'il n'en eut plus jamais les mains nettes ? Nous croyons qu'il y eut des promesses, mais rien de plus" (Kervyn de Lettenhove, *Lettres et négociations*, 1:57–8); "Il est probable en effet que sans l'intervention de Philippe de Commynes à Péronne le destin de Louis XI et par là même celui de la France et de l'Europe auraient suivi un tout autre cours" (Liniger, *Philippe de Commynes*, 56); and, Commynes "s'y révéla très habile, ou du moins il le prétend" (Dufournet, *Vie de Philippe de Commynes*, 25); "Cependant, Commynes continuait à passer pour un bon et loyal serviteur" (Dufournet, *Vie de Philippe de Commynes*, 28). See below for an analysis of these and other judgments.

9 The use of the verb "congnoissoye" stands out here as both rich and awkward. Other manuscripts and early editions flattened Commynes's sentence into "entroye" or "couchoye" [en sa chambre quand je voulais] (*Mémoires* [TLF, 2007], 2:777).

10 "On a fait à ce sujet nombre d'hypothèses, également défavorables au seigneur de Renescure et au maître qu'il abandonnait. L'état d'esprit du duc à ce moment et la rage stupide qui le poussait, le fer et la torche à la main, à ravager la Haute-Normandie laissent supposer qu'entre le prince et son conseiller il a pu se produire quelque éclat; mais Commynes s'est montré à la fois si réservé et si naturel dans les quelque mots qu'il a consacrés à cet épisode capital de sa vie, qu'il est impossible d'en tirer la moindre conclusion" (Mandrot, ed. [1901–3], *Mémoires*, 2:vi).

11 Dupont, *Notice*, xxxv–xxxvi. This separately paginated, biographical study, published in 1847, is generally but not always bound with volume 1 of Dupont's edition of the *Mémoires*.

12 For a quantitative assessment, see Gaussin, "Les Conseillers de Louis XI (1461–1483)." For an examination of Commynes's case, see Blanchard, "Commynes n'a pas 'trahi,'" 339–42; and for one more exceptional still, see Cauchies, "Baudouin de Bourgogne ... Une carrière exemplaire?"

13 Treaty of September 1475. "Et aussi esdictes presentes Tresves & abstinence de guerre en tant qu'il touche lesdits articles de communication, hantise, retour & jouyssance des biens ne seront compris Mr. Baudoin, soy disant bastard de Bourgongne, le seigneur de Renty [Philippe de Croÿ], Messire Jean de Chassa, & Messire Philippe de Comines, ains en seront & demeureront du tout forclos & exceptez" (*Mémoires*, ed. Lenglet Dufresnoy [1747], 3:412–13).

14 Dupont, *Notice*, xxxiv.

15 There are a few traces in the archives from these years, but they resist sure interpretation. Was it during a 1471 mission that the arrangements between Commynes and the king were made for his change of loyalties (Dupont, *Notice*, xxxii –xxxiii)? In what context were 6000 *livres tournois* placed with Jean de Beaune of Tours in Commynes's name? Did some event then lead the king to threaten to confiscate this account while Commynes still remained at the duke's court? Was he, as Dupont speculates, trying to force the hand of a hesitant Commynes? (Dupont, *Notice*, xxxiv–xxxvii.) Commynes kept his secret well. These written traces are not enough to hold onto in our quest for a "real" "truth" of the bonds between them.

16 In January 1850, Sainte-Beuve, reviewing Dupont's just-completed edition of the *Mémoires*, praised Commynes as "en date, le premier écrivain vraiment moderne" (Sainte-Beuve, *Causeries du lundi*, 241). Sainte-Beuve was likely repeating an opinion that had already become conventional wisdom, but his is the slogan that stuck. William Bouwsma called Sainte-Beuve's essay "the most famous of all modern essays on Commynes" and "also perhaps the worst offender in its complete isolation of Commynes from his own historical context. There are elements of modernity in Commynes, but there is much besides" (Bouwsma, "The Politics of Commynes," 316).

17 Frye, *Anatomy of Criticism*, 341. On myth and literary analysis, see also, *The Routledge Encyclopedia of Narrative Theory*, 329–35.

18 Frye, *Anatomy of Criticism*, 341. For the word "allegorization," see Frye's definition of allegory, "an attaching of ideas to the structure of poetic imagery" (89).

19 A wildly successful black legend claimed that Louis XI placed Nemours's children under the scaffolding so that their father's blood would run over them. Commynes's silence about his role in the case contributes to the black legends which surround him, also.

20 Voltaire, *Essai sur les moeurs*, chapter 94, "Du roi de France Louis XI," 119.

21 Dupont, *Notice*, xxxvii.

22 Chabaud, "Les 'Mémoires' de Philippe de Commynes: Un 'miroir aux princes'?" 96.

23 For a pointed synthesis of Commynes's *Mémoires* in early modern political debate, see Bakos, *Images of Kingship in Early Modern France*, 16–19. See also, Bouwsma, "The Politics of Commynes"; Demers, "Montaigne lecteur de Commynes"; Dreyer, "Commynes and Machiavelli"; Dufournet, "Premiers lecteurs" and "Un Interlocuteur privilégié des princes"; Fumaroli, "Mémoires et histoire"; Maissen, "Le 'Commynisme' italien"; Simone, "La prima fortuna di Commynes nella cultura italiana del Rinascimento"; Stegmann, "Commynes et Machiavel"; and Tetel, "Montaigne's Glances at Philippe de Commynes."

24 See Fumaroli, "Mémoires et histoire."

25 Commynes, *De rebus gestis Ludovici, eius nominis Undecimi*, trans. Johann Sleidan, Strasbourg, 1545. On Johann Sleidan, see Kess, *Johann Sleidan and the Protestant Vision of History*; and, Blanchard and Pantin, "Les Débuts de la fortune éditoriale de Commynes." For the question of "pure and true" narration, see Sleidan's dedicatory preface to the 1545 edition. On ideology, Commynes, and the *Mémoire* as a nascent genre, see Fumaroli, "Mémoires et histoire."

26 Sauvage (1552), *Les Mémoires de Messire Philippe de Commines*, unpaginated dedication. Sauvage addressed his edition of the *Mémoires* to King Henri II, calling Commynes "le plus excelent de voz Historiographes François, voire egal aux meilleurs de toutes autres langues" (the most excellent of your French history writers, and truly equal to the best of every other language). Alluding to both Sleidan's 1545 Latin edition and to the *Mémoires'* 1544 translation into Italian under the patronage of Paolo Giovio, Sauvage explained that he could no longer stand to see Commynes, "si longuement tant corrumpu qu'il estoit, au grand deshonneur de nous autres envers les estrangers: qui depuis quelque temps, l'ont mieux eu en Latin et vulgaire Italien, qu'en son propre naturel" (any longer as corrupted as he was, to our great dishonour in regards to other peoples: who, for some time now, have had him better in Latin and in common Italian, than in his own natural). Sauvage undertakes to mend the fragmented body of an author whose textual remains have been unjustly dispersed throughout Europe.

He performs an act of national healing through philological scholarship, and so implicitly places himself, France, and Commynes's vernacular history, shoulder to shoulder with Italian humanists' recovery of their own lost and fragmented "national" histories. Calling himself a "very obedient subject and servant" of the king, Sauvage presents his edition of the *Mémoires* to Henri II as work both necessary and honourable to the health of the nation. His implicit metaphor rallies readers to come together in unity around Commynes's textual body, now become a symbol of the "natural" wholeness of the French body politic.

27 Matthieu, *Histoire de Louys XI*, 181–2.

28 Meyer, *Commentarii sive Annales rerum Flandricarum*, 355v.

29 I base this assertion on the absence of either Meyer or the later Jacques Marchant (1537–1609) from the entries in the *Corpus des notes marginales de Voltaire* (vol. 5, ed. Voronova). Voltaire owned two editions of Commynes's *Mémoires*, but based on his marginal notes (*Corpus des notes marginales*, vol. 2, ed. Voronova and Manevitch), Voltaire read Commynes in the 1747 edition of Lenglet Dufresnoy, who is quite clear about his positive view of Commynes's moral rectitude. "Je ne puis m'empêcher de dire que plus les vrays motifs de la retraite de Philippe de Comines sont restés secrets, plus il y a lieu de les interpréter en sa faveur. Ses ennemis n'auroient pas manqué de les faire connoitre avec éclat" (Lenglet Dufresnoy, ed., *Mémoires*, 1:xcviii).

30 Meyer, *Commentarii sive Annales rerum Flandricarum*, 366. When citing Commynes, Meyer often holds his source at a distance, asserting "teste Cominius" or "inquit Cominius."

31 The cleavage Voltaire attributes to Commynes is political and rhetorical, but the symbolic economy Commynes now enters is best likened to René Girard's sacrificial economy. For the nineteenth and early twentieth centuries, the treacherous, lying, servile, duplicitous Commynes repeatedly occupied the role of an Other who must be purged. One short extract from a 1945 book by Belgian philologist Gustave Charlier will have to suffice here. Charlier's study appeared in a collection titled "Notre Passé." The longer pages from which I have extracted his words teem with raw and passionate feeling. Bizarrely, provocatively, Charlier's full text seethes with barely veiled allegories of anti-Semitism, including terms that harken to a blood libel, something that also recurs in black legends surrounding Louis XI. "Il serait vain," wrote Charlier, "de chercher des excuses à une si éclatante trahison … Sa défection était, sans conteste, un acte criant d'ingratitude, et de la plus noire. Sa mémoire en demeure,

malgré tout, souillée. On regrette qu'une si brillante carrière porte cette tache originelle" (Charlier, *Commynes*, 18).

32   Matthieu, *Histoire de Louys XI*, 181–2.
33   Dufournet, *Destruction des mythes*, 13.
34   Notably Huizinga, for the realism of the Montlhéry battle description, and Pierre Le Gentil, for the newness of Commynes's conception of the political (Dufournet, *Destruction des mythes*, 13.)
35   Dufournet, *Destruction des mythes*, 14.
36   For Dufournet's initial reading of the Péronne episode, see "L'Entrevue de Péronne," in *Destruction des mythes*, 182–93. He returned to the episode fifteen years later in "Lire Commynes, l'entrevue de Péronne et l'expédition contre Liège," first published in the *Mémoires de la Société d'histoire de Comines-Warneton et de la région* (1982), and then reprinted as "Comment lire les *Mémoires* de Commynes? L'entrevue de Péronne et l'expédition contre Liège," in *Philippe de Commynes: un historien à l'aube des temps modernes* (1994), 217–49. This later essay is largely a reassessment in light of Bittmann's work, but its title contains the articulation of a method, albeit one that more justly describes Dufournet's earlier work. See also, Dufournet, "Art et déformation historique," especially in the longer version published in *Etudes sur Philippe de Commynes*.
37   Dufournet, *Etudes sur Philippe de Commynes*, 59.
38   Cf. Bernard de Mandrot, "Ce qui est certain, c'est que Philippe de Commynes n'a pas tenté, et cela lui eût été facile, le moindre essai de justification" ("Autorité historique," 255).
39   Dufournet, *Destruction des mythes*, 35.
40   Bittmann, *Ludwig XI und Karl der Kühne*, 3 vols.
41   Chabaud, "Les 'Mémoires' de Philippe de Commynes: un 'miroir aux princes'?" 96, note 4.
42   This is, at least, what Chabaud boldly insinuates in "Les 'Mémoires' de Philippe de Commynes: un 'miroir aux princes'?" It is certain that Bittmann's death put an abrupt end to the project.
43   Vaughan, review of Bittmann, *Ludwig XI und Karl der Kühne*, 1529.
44   On structuralism and historiography, see Clark, *History, Theory, Text*, chapter 3, "Language and Structures," 42–62.
45   Dufournet was born in 1933. He passed away in May 2012.
46   Blanchard, *Commynes l'Européen*, 29.
47   On nostalgia and the Revolution, see Fritzsche, "Specters of History"; on Louis XI and the nineteenth-century historical imagination, see Durand-Le Guern, "Louis XI entre mythe et histoire."

48 See also Michelet, *Histoire de France*, 6:492.
49 Frye, *Anatomy of Criticism*, 136.

2 *Enseignes*: What History Writes on the Body

1 Soutet and Thomasset, "Des Marques de la subjectivité," 28. On the narrative "I" in medieval historiography, see Marnette, *Narrateur et points de vue
   dans la littérature française médiévale*, and "The Experiencing Self and the
   Narrating Self in Medieval French Chronicles."
2 In order to maintain a separation between my own interventions and the
   editor's corrections, especially in view of cases where both appear in a
   cited passage, I have replaced brackets in the published text with "{ }."
3 Vouge: subst. masc. ou fém. "Arme d'hast à hampe courte et à lame marge,
   tranchante d'un côté" (extracted from the *Dictionnaire du Moyen Français*).
      Halberd, Halbert: "A military weapon, especially in use during the 15th
   and 16th centuries; a kind of combination of spear and battle-axe, consist-
   ing of a sharp-edged blade ending in a point, and a spear-head, mounted
   on a handle five to seven feet long" (*Oxford English Dictionary*).
4 Guidon: subst. masc. "Enseigne servant en temps de guerre à rallier les
   hommes d'armes"; "étendard"; "étendard d'une compagnie de grosse
   cavalerie" (extracted from the *Dictionnaire du Moyen Français*).
5 Folio 8r of the Polignac manuscript, as per the indications in the published
   text of the *Mémoires* (TLF, 2007), 28–9.
6 Soutet and Thomasset, "Des Marques de la subjectivité," 28. Emphasis in
   original.
7 I cite the information that the duke's face had been partially eaten on the
   authority of Vaughan, *Charles the Bold*, 432. See also the list of contemporary
   sources for the battle Vaughan gives on page 427, note 1. Cf. Thomas Basin,
   who explains that the duke's face had adhered to the frozen ground, ripping
   the flesh and leaving him unrecognizable (*Histoire de Louis XI*, 2:344).
8 Cf. Joinville's account of Louis IX's death in *Vie de Saint Louis*.
9 In the passage which follows I have removed a chapter break (first)
   artificially imposed by Denis Sauvage in order to demarcate Commynes's
   reflections from the surrounding sequence of narrated events. One consequence of this separation is to triage the distinct strands of the *Mémoires*.
   My point is precisely to underscore the continuity and coherence within
   Commynes's speech by making visible the stream of consciousness. This
   is what the passage about Charles's defeat and death looks like when we
   let Commynes's voice flow without interruption.

10 Commynes omits the identification of this signet as the emblem of the Order of the Golden Fleece.

11 For Charles's single-minded adherence to his increasingly doomed ambitions of conquering an empire for himself, see Vaughan, *Charles the Bold*.

12 Charles's favoured heroes included Alexander, Caesar, and Jason. Olivier de La Marche wrote that Charles never went to sleep without first being read to for two hours, often by the Lord of Humbercourt, who appears several times on these pages (La Marche, *Mémoires*, 2:334). In her study of La Marche, Catherine Emerson shares an apocryphal tale about manuscripts found in Charles's baggage after Nancy which further supports the idea that Charles's contemporaries made an association between the duke's folly and his reading habits (Emerson, *Olivier de La Marche*, 136). See also, Chrystèle Blondeau, *Un conquérant pour quatre ducs*. For an overview of the manuscripts Commynes is known to have owned, see Jones (1972), ed. and trans. *Mémoires*, 28–30. Special consideration should be given to the volumes of Valerius Maximus in Commynes's library, and to the copy he owned of Froissart's fourth book.

13 Cf. Emerson, *Olivier de La Marche*, 136. The idea that Charles's excessive fondness for epic tales played a part in his downfall was current at the time. Legend has it that the duke's prized copy of Vasque de Lucène's *Traitté des faiz et haultes prouesses de Cyrus* was among the baggage lost and looted at Nancy. See Gallet-Guerne, *Vasque de Lucène*, 40, cited by Emerson, 136.

14 The standard biographical essay on Campobasso is Croce, "Cola di Monforte, conte di Campobasso."

15 In Commynes's version of events, Campobasso offers to deliver Charles to Louis XI, but Louis XI wants nothing to do with Campobasso, and even tries to warn Charles (*Mémoires* [TLF, 2007], 314 and 347), but the archives say otherwise. Cf. Vaesen and Charavay, *Lettres de Louis XI*, 5:103–5 and especially 6:62–3.

16 Cf. Thomas Basin, *Histoire de Louis XI*, 2:255–60; La Marche, *Mémoires*, 3:239; and Molinet, *Chroniques*, 1:162–7.

17 Croce, "Cola di Monforte, conte di Campobasso," 141–59.

18 The most recent and probably definitive examination is in Walsh, *Charles the Bold and Italy*, 367–79 and 398–403 (notes 107–51). In addition to Croce, see also Calmette, "Campobasso et Commynes," and Schneider, "Campobasso en Lorraine."

19 Marchal, ed., *Chronique de Lorraine*, The author of the *Chronique de Lorraine* was close enough to René II to identify himself as a witness to or actor in the events narrated, but he does not give his name.

20 *Chronique de Lorraine*, 261. There is something folkloric and endearing about the *Chronique de Lorraine*'s effusive patriotic gusto. For instance, news that help is on the way makes the beseiged Nancy burghers "si joyeux [que] plus rien ne craindoient." Brackets in original.

21 On the strategic role of the garrisons in villages surrounding Nancy, see Vaughan, *Charles the Bold*, 420.

22 *Chronique de Lorraine*, 260.

23 Ibid., 261.

24 Ibid., 262. My translation smooths out the syntax of this passage, which recalls the halting, paratactic movement of the *Chanson de Roland* and emphasizes that Charles's glove was metal (mail).

25 *Chronique de Lorraine*, 267. Capital letters in published text.

26 Ibid., 303. Cf. Haidu, *The Subject of Violence*, 18 and 26–30, on Roland's arrangement of his body into a legible sign.

27 Croce reports that Charles answered one reproach of cruelty with a would-be adage, "dead men don't make war" (gli uomini morti no fanno guerra) (Croce, "Cola di Monforte, conte di Campobasso," 137, note 2).

28 See Vaughan, *Charles the Bold*, 167.

29 *Chronique de Lorraine*, 285.

30 Dupont, *Notice*, xxiii, note 2, citing Le Pippre, "La Généalogie des seigneurs de Commines," 263. Although this is not the version generally cited as the first one published, it is the version which later scholars have generally preferred.

31 This connection between the "tête bottée" story and Commynes's defection has been suggested repeatedly over the centuries by historians sympathetic to Commynes.

32 Marchant, *Flandria commentariorium lib. IIII descripta*, 166–7. Notably reprinted by the Godefroys in their "Eloges de Philippe de Comines" (many editions; with and separately from the text of the *Mémoires*); and in the proofs of Lenglet Dufresnoy, ed. *Mémoires* (1747), vol. 4, part 2, 163–4. [Note the existence of a printer's error in the pagination of at least one copy digitized by Google.]

33 Dupont, *Notice*, xxiv, note continued from previous page, citing Le Pippre, "La Généalogie des seigneurs de Commines," 263.

34 Dufournet, *Destruction des mythes*, "Commynes et Campobasso," 54–64.

35 Ibid., 64.

36 Ibid.

37 Ibid.

38 I think it worthwhile to consider the presence of additional social and historical factors as well. It is true that Commynes and Campobasso share

precisely the traits or experiences that often forge deep, intuitive identification between individuals, but that also frequently conspire to make that identification conflicted. Each man was a *transfuge* and in exile. More than once, Commynes remembers the political causes of Campobasso's exile, and reminds the reader of them also (309, 342). Campobasso "estoit sans terre, car a cause des guerres … il en estoit banny et avoit perdu sa terre" (was without lands, since because of these wars … he was banished and had lost his land [313]). When the traitor bargains over Charles's life, he wants cash and, especially, vast lands ("une bonne conté," 342). However, other possible factors also deserve consideration. Social class and political factionalism offer two complementary (potential) explanations for Commynes's execration of Campobasso. First, Commynes likely looked down on the condottiere Campobasso with the class prejudice native to his adopted Italian diplomatic and mercantile milieu. Garrett Mattingly explains, "Business men were delighted by the skills of the diplomat, the nimble anticipation of the next move on the chess board, the subtle gambit which could trip a stronger opponent, the conversion of an enemy into a partner against some common rival, the snatching of victory from defeat by bluff and persuasion and mental dexterity. These qualities were surely more admirable than the brute valour of the condottiere. Diplomacy was for rulers; war for hired men" (Mattingly, *Renaissance Diplomacy*, 62). Campobasso was just such a hired man. Political context complicates the matter, also. It is not clear how treacherous it would be for the Angevine Campobasso to conspire with René II de Lorraine, who was, after all, René d'Anjou's grandson. "Le rappel que Campobasso était originellement un sujet des Angevins et non du Bourguignon n'est pas anodin à cet endroit. Peut-on toujours parler de trahison pour qualifier sa défection du camp du Téméraire?" (*Mémoires* [TLF, 2007], 2:1100). Is it possible that Commynes's animosity towards René II d'Anjou, Duke of Lorraine, influenced the genesis of this narrative? Commynes repeatedly mentions Campobasso's Angevine alliances, while Commynes's *destinataire* Angelo Cato was Neapolitan. We may question whether either factor suffices to justify the viciousness in Commynes's contempt for Campobasso; both help contextualize it.

39 Vaughan, *Charles the Bold*, 166.
40 Walsh, *Charles the Bold and Italy*, 401, note 138.
41 I do not claim that Commynes knew the *Chronique de Lorraine*. I find it, however, extremely likely that he and the Lorraine chronicler based their stories on a single episode, reported separately to each by one of the scene's witnesses.

42 de But, *Chronique*, 1:514. De But was a monk at the Ten Duinen Abbey at Koksijde, Belgium; his chronicle covers the years 1431–88.

43 Walsh, *Charles the Bold and Italy*, 400, note 116.

44 I thank Pär Larson of the *Opera del Vocabolario Italiano* for his answers to my queries about this word (personal communication of 23 February 2011).

45 Vaughan, *Charles the Bold*, 159.

46 On this episode, see Vaughan, *Charles the Bold*, 238–9. It is Vaughan who describes de Chassa as an "insignificant nobleman." Cf. Blanchard, "Commynes n'a pas 'trahi,'" 335–8. De Chassa's statement is quoted in the 1747 preface to Lenglet Dufresnoy, ed., *Mémoires*, 1:xcii–xcv; cited passage on xciv. Moreover, de Chassa is one of the three men who, along with Commynes, were excluded from the Treaty of Soleuvre. Commynes alludes to this incident, but does not name de Chassa, only his companion, Baudouin de Bourgogne (*Mémoires* [TLF, 2007], 167–8).

47 Commynes is mentioned as "écuyer échanson" in letters of October 1467, and then as "*chevalier*, conseiller et chambellan" in an act dated 19 January 1468 (Dupont, *Notice*, xxii, note 2).

48 Lenglet Dufresnoy, ed., *Mémoires* (1747), 1:xcvii.

49 Walsh, *Charles the Bold and Italy*, 400, note 116.

50 Commynes vividly portrays the moment by moment wait for information, the king's delight at Charles's defeat, and the anxiety this news provoked in his servitors (*Mémoires* [TLF, 2007], 360–3). On 9 January Louis penned an exuberant letter to Georges de La Trémoïlle, seigneur de Craon, giving instructions and thanking him for "les bonnes nouvelles que m'avez fait savoir" (Vaesen and Charavay, *Lettres de Louis XI*, 6:111–12). The same day, he warned the city of Dijon, "se ainsi estoit, que sa personne [i.e. Charles] feust prinse ou mort, que Dieu ne vueille, vous savés que vous estes de la coronne et du royaulme" (6:113). On 12 January he ordered the town of Poitiers to hold solemn processions in honour of "les bonnes et agréables nouvelles que premièrement nous ont aportées noz chevaucheurs de nostre escuyrie" (Vaesen and Charavay, *Lettres de Louis XI*, 6:114). To appreciate the efficacy of Louis's postal relays, see Armstrong, "Some Examples of the Distribution and Speed of News."

51 For the persistent rumours that Charles had escaped and was alive, see Basin, *Histoire de Louis XI*, 2:342 and 2:346.

52 Cf. Basin who says that Charles's identity was confirmed by those who had served him in his most intimate life ("in camera et secretioribus ministrarant") and recognized him from the most secret particularities of his body ("ex quibusdam corporis sui secretioribus notis") (*Histoire de Louis*

XI, 2:344). Molinet also lists both the signs on the duke's body and the wounds that killed him (*Chroniques*, 1:168). As if to soften his report of this "chose pitoyable à regarder et de grant admiration," however, Molinet improbably places the body's washing before its identification (*Chroniques*, 1:167).

53 *Chronique de Lorraine*, 306.
54 de Roye, *Chronique scandaleuse*, 2:40–1.
55 For Molinet, see note 52; for a list of further sources, see Basin, *Histoire de Louis XI*, 2:344, note 1; cf. the sources regarding the battle itself indicated by Vaughan, in note 7 of this chapter.

3 *Enseignes*: Crosses and Coins, Bridges and Fences

1 Cf. Brigitte Bedos-Rezak's far-ranging study of sigillography and medieval sign theory, *When Ego Was Imago*.
2 The *Mémoires* provide an important eyewitness account of this episode in English history. Angelo Cato, to whom Commynes addresses his *Mémoires*, commissioned a Latin history of Richard III (see Armstrong, *The Usurpation of Richard the Third*). Commynes alludes to Cato's thorough knowledge of English affaires; e.g., "De ses secretz, habilitiés ou tromperies, qui se sont faictes en noz contrees de deça, n'entendréz vous plus veritablement de nulle autre personne, au moins de celles qui sont advenues plus de vingt ans" (*Mémoires* [TLF, 2007], 188; see also 180); cf. Armstrong, *The Usurpation of Richard the Third*, 53–4. Commynes himself is exceptionally well informed; in one instance he asserts that Edward IV "luy propre m'a compté" (*Mémoires* [TLF, 2007], 190); in another he claims the Duke of Hastings as his source (*Mémoires* [TLF, 2007], 191).
3 Pollard, *The Wars of the Roses*, 28.
4 The version of events that follows is the version presented by Commynes.
5 Wenlock later avoids mentioning Commynes's gaffe (*Mémoires* [TLF, 2007], 198), a sign either that he considers Commynes too young to have known better or that the supremely shrewd Wenlock likes his counterpart.
6 Cf. Calmette and Durville, eds, *Mémoires* (1924–5), 1:196 and *Mémoires* (TLF, 2007) 2:1041.
7 The landmark work remains Rice, *The Renaissance Idea of Wisdom*. See also, Archambault, "Commynes's *Saigesse* and the Renaissance Idea of Wisdom."
8 On this topos, see Hampton, *Fictions of Embassy*, chapter 2, "The Useful and the Honorable: The Ethics of Mediation in the Late Renaissance."

Consider also the saying later attributed to Louis XI, "qui nescit dissimulare, nescit regnare"; see Bakos, *Images of Kingship in Early Modern France*, chapter 5, on Louis XI and *raison d'état*. For a different approach to the matter of ethical discourse, exemplarity, and the problem of lying, cf. Denery, "Christine de Pizan against the Theologians."

9 Commynes calls Warwick a count, when his proper title was earl.

10 Gold coins called "Rose-Nobles," for instance, depicted Edward holding sword and shield aboard a ship on one side, and on the other, a rose. Silver groats and pennies showed his head on one side and a long cross on the other.

11 What saves Edward IV in the end is that his brother, the Duke of Clarence, who had once betrayed him for Warwick, then betrayed Warwick for Edward IV (*Mémoires* [TLF, 2007], 202).

12 Only the Dobrée manuscript at Nantes gives the logical and correct "noué"; all the other witnesses read "noir." Cf. Calmette and Durville, eds, *Mémoires* (1924–5), 1:209.

13 Although our arguments about subjectivity are not uniformly compatible, Susan Crane's discussion of the varieties and uses of signage on clothing to represent identity and alliance is extremely relevant to this chapter's analyses. Notes Crane: "Badges value alliances and communications. They situate identity in visible signs and audible mottos." Unlike coats of arms, badges "can be distributed … Badges perpetuate heraldry's bright symbolization, its compact and esoteric communication of identity. Badges then push heraldic communicativeness beyond its bounds: they take signs of a self-chosen, distinctive identity to be negotiable and transferable" (all passages in this note from Crane, *Performance of Self*, chapter 1, "Talking Garments," 20).

14 The white crosses index royal France. See Le Roux de Lincy, *Chants historiques et populaires*, 151–75. One item included by Le Roux de Lincy, and which could well have formed part of the graffiti on Commynes's door, includes the call, "Vous qui estes dedens Calaix, / Pilliés castiaux, villes, pallaix, / Pilliés tout jusqu'au feurre; / … / Vengiés maintenant la traïson / Qui en France fut faite, / Destruiziés l'ordene à la toison / Que jà ne soit refaite" (*Chants historiques et populaires*, 157–8).

15 See Cazelles, *Lettres closes*, 7–10, for a description of this category of letter.

16 The town of Picquigny lies on the left bank of the Somme River approximately ten kilometres from Amiens. The meeting between Edward and Louis took place during the final days of August 1475.

17 This is the second time in the *Mémoires* that Commynes explicitly mentions Montereau. During the negotiations between Charles and Louis XI leading

up to the Traité de Conflans (after the Guerre du Bien Public), the two men find themselves deep in conversation and unwittingly ride away from their men and into a secluded garden alley. Charles's men are furious, "et alleguoient le {grand} inconveniant advenu a son grand pere a Montereau Fault Ionne, present le roy Charles VIIme" (*Mémoires* [TLF, 2007], 76). Afterwards, the normally haughty Charles remains sombre when one of his men dares to give him a tongue-lashing. "{Plus} luy dist ledict mareschal en sa presence qu'il n'avoit faict en son abscence. Ledict seigneur baissa la teste sans riens respondre et s'en revint dedans son ost, ou tous estoient joyeulx de le revoir; et louoit chascun la foy du Roy. Toutesfois ne retourna oncques depuis ledict conte en sa puissance" (*Mémoires* [TLF, 2007], 77).

18 Is my account of Montereau perhaps too influenced by Burgundian sources, or might Commynes's be so? I am thankful to an anonymous reader for this press for the observation that since "what different individuals know/ remember about Montereau can be radically different," this murder/ vengeance can be "at once known, misknown, differently known. Montereau marks the subjectivity and the ambiguity of memory." For a bipartisan assessment, see Guenée, *Un Meurtre, une société*, 265–89.

19 See also, Oschema, "Amis, favoris, sosies." Note also that the purpose of the king's gesture can be variously interpreted. Dressing Commynes in clothing to match the king is a gesture of intimacy but not necessarily of confidence. Louis's broad protective measure has the specific effect of preventing Commynes from participating in any conspiracy such as the one which awaited John the Fearless at Montereau. Commynes cannot plot against the king for the simple reason that the king's vulnerability has become his own as well. Commynes serves as the king's decoy, to be stabbed or slain in his place. Louis offers up his double in place of himself. The king's choice of Commynes to wear gowns matching his own could thus be perceived as a gesture of ambivalence. The text leaves us uncertain, and interpretation remains tentative.

20 On signage, mimesis, and desire, cf. Crane, *Perfomance of Self*, chapter 1, "Talking Garments," 23–4. In another, more enigmatic, instance of this mimetic desire, Commynes would appear to have modelled his own funeral monument on the one Louis XI designed and had made for himself at Notre-Dame de Cléry (near Orléans). The original statue, carried out under the direction of Jean Bourré, was destroyed during the Wars of Religion, but showed the king as a young man dressed in hunting garb with a hound by his side. Most importantly, there was no *gisant* (see Favier, *Louis XI*, 903–4). Commynes's monument, of similar design minus the

hunting garb, survives in the collections of the Louvre museum. See
Beaulieu, "Note sur la chapelle funéraire de Philippe de Commines."
21 *Oxford English Dictionary*, s.v. identity, definition 1a.
22 *Oxford English Dictionary*, s.v. identity, definition 2a.
23 Cf. Blanchard, *Commynes l'Européen*, 346–7, and 353.
24 The contrasting work of Howard Bloch, Gabrielle Spiegel, Zrinka Stahuljak,
and others, has sharpened contemporary medievalists' discussion of
genealogy as a conceptual structure. Cf. Bloch, *Etymologies and Genealogies*;
Spiegel, *The Past as Text*; or Stahuljak, *Bloodless Genealogies of the French
Middle Ages*.

4 The Prince of Talmont

1 Francesco da Pietrasanta to the Duke of Milan, 20 July 1476. First published, in French, in Kervyn de Lettenhove, *Lettres et négociations*, 3:3. Joël
Blanchard identifies Kervyn de Lettenhove's source as *Archivio di stato di
Milano, Carteggio generale visconteo-sforzesco, Potenze Estere, Francia*, 542, but
again publishes the well-known French translation (Blanchard, *Commynes
l'Européen*, 128).
2 Kervyn de Lettenhove, *Lettres et négociations*, 1:111–12.
3 Dupont, ed. (1840–7), *Mémoires*, 3:7–10. All subsequent citations of Dupont,
ed., are to the 1840–7 edition. Louis XI threatened to take back these monies, a move which would potentially have exposed the account's existence
– and thus Commynes's duplicity – to Charles.
4 For the letters of 28 October 1472, granting this pension, see Dupont,
ed., *Mémoires*, 3:20–6. For a complete list of the gifts Louis XI paid to
Commynes see 3:182–8; and for letters documenting these gifts, see 3:20–
74. Some of the documents published by Dupont were later included by
Kervyn de Lettenhove in his *Lettres et négociations*. A great many of the
documentary "proofs" surrounding Commynes have been published
and republished from one century to the next. Only the principle location consulted will be cited.
5 Argenton is situated in the modern-day department of Lot-et-Garonne.
Significant land and legal interests undergirded this marriage for the
family of Hélène de Chambes as well. For the 27 January 1473 marriage
contract, see Dupont, ed., *Mémoires*, 3:38–53, and Fillon, "Documents
inédits sur Ph. de Commynes." On the occasion of his marriage, Commynes commissioned a pair of *livres d'heures* from the workshop of Jean
Fouquet (now Bibliothèque nationale de France, ms. lat. 1417, and British
Library, Harley 2863).

6 Dupont, ed., *Mémoires*, 3:14. The chateau de Talmont is located in the modern-day department of the Vendée. "Les terres de Bran et Brandois" were also attached to this gift (Dupont, ed., *Mémoires*, 3:29–33). For the sake of brevity, I refer collectively to the ensemble as Talmont except where one or more of the smaller properties is specifically concerned. In fact, the Talmont principality included some 1700 fiefs and *arrière-fiefs* (Liniger, *Philippe de Commynes*, 268). These substantial holdings included a commercial sea-port, at modern-day Sables d'Olonne. Commynes also received important tax exemptions towards the fortification of the town and the expansion of its commercial capacities, further augmenting their value (Dupont, ed., *Mémoires*, 3:33–8, 3:59–60).

7 On these debts, see especially Desplanque, "Troubles de la châtellenie de Cassel sous Philippe le Bon." Renescure lies halfway between Lille and Calais; the chateau was mostly destroyed during the Revolution.

8 Dupont, *Notice*, xxxiv.

9 On the characteristic descriptive traits of *lettres patentes* from the Valois and Bourbon chancelleries, see Giry, *Manuel de diplomatique*, 764–80. Throughout this chapter usage of all diplomatic vocabulary in French follows Giry, with equivalents based on the *Oxford English Dictionary* provided as possible.

10 Dupont, ed., *Mémoires*, 3:12.

11 Ibid.

12 Ibid., 3:12–13.

13 While I have made every effort to accurately render the original tone of these diplomatic and legal documents, in the interest of clarity, I have on occasion found it necessary to repeat proper nouns, invert the sequence of proper names and pronouns, and reorder clauses within a given sentence.

14 Dupont, ed., *Mémoires*, 3:12.

15 On physical proximity and power in courtly life, see Oschema, *Freundschaft und Nähe*.

16 See my discussion of violence in Charles's relations to his courtiers in chapter 2. Charles's reputation for moderate or excessive violence as a military leader generally deteriorated as he aged.

17 Dupont, ed., *Mémoires*, 3:13–14.

18 For recent studies of the tensions between regional identities and national consciousness, see Daly, "'Centre,' 'Power' and 'Periphery' in Late Medieval French Historiography," 124–8.

19 "Par la loy générale de nostre royaume, toutes fois que aucun estranger et non natif de iceluy nostre royaume va de vie à trespassement sans lettres de naturalité et habilitation et puissance de nous de tester tous les biens

qu'il a en nostre dict royaume à l'heure de son dict trespas nous competent et appartiennent par droit d'aubenage" (By the general law of our kingdom, whenever a foreigner and non-native of this our kingdom goes from life to death without letters of naturalization and habilitation and the right granted by us to leave a testament all the goods which he has in our kingdom at the hour of his death depend on and belong to us by the right of aubaine) [cited in Billot, "L'Assimilation des étrangers," 273–4] (my translation). The passage Billot cites dates from the year 1475. The habitual phrasing concerning foreign immigrants and property ownership was, "Tenir et posséder en cestuy nostre royaulme pays, terres et seigneryes de nostre obéissance" (Billot, "L'Assimilation des étrangers," 285).

20 Dupont, ed., *Mémoires*, 3:15.

21 It is striking that, in a reversal of the schema presented in so many *chansons de geste*, Louis seems to be calling on his subjects to rebel against their feudal lords, that is, to betray in the name of France. Cf. Dessau, "L'Idée de la trahison au Moyen Age."

22 Dupont, ed., *Mémoires*, 3:16.

23 "Dans les actes d'autorité, l'obéissance était commandée nonobstant toutes ordonnances ou décisions qui pourraient être contraires à l'ordre exprimé; un jugement était déclaré exécutoire nonobstant opposition ou appel; l'auteur d'un testament le déclare valable nonobstant toutes autres dispositions antérieures. C'est l'objet des clauses dérogatives" (Giry, *Manuel de diplomatique*, 557). "La clause dérogative prescrit d'obéir nonobstant toute ordonnance, loi, coutume, us ou style à ce contraire ... *elle affirme la pleine souveraineté législative du roi*" (Olivier-Martin, *Les Lois du roi*, 247; emphasis mine).

24 "Warranty had other, more precise connotations in customary law. The *guarant* (Latin warantus) is best regarded as a surety, one who has personally bound himself to another, with the assurance that he will attest to the truth of their relationship or the central facts on which it rests. Normally, he would warrant his own grant of land to a vassal. Only when the underlying relationship or grant was challenged would the warrantor be required to carry out his promise. Since the natural outcome, in the absence of compromise, was trial by battle, the warrantor had much in common with an advocate or champion, although his commitment originated elsewhere, most usually in a lord's reception of homage. Warranty was, in effect, the mystical homage bond represented in terms of the lord's obligation to his man" (Hyams, "Henry II and Ganelon," 34).

25 Dupont, ed., *Mémoires*, 3:17–18.

26 Ibid., 3:18.

27 Ibid., 3:14.

28 Ibid., 3:15.

29 This summary extracts only those elements strictly necessary to Commynes's fortunes. Talmont changed hands repeatedly during the long-running feud between d'Amboise and La Trémoïlle. See Peyronnet, "Les Complots de Louis d'Amboise contre Charles VII (1428–1431)."

30 Jacques de Beaumont, the seigneur de Bressuire, was the king's principle agent in this seizure. See Bouineau, "Jacques de Beaumont ... du seigneur local à l'agent du roi."

31 The purchase price agreed to by Louis d'Amboise was 100,000 écus, a sum that eloquently conveys the scale of the domains in question.

32 The Chambre's role as guardian of the kingdom had been institutionalized since the fourteenth century, although their objections to the king's actions were not uniformly heeded. On the procedural aspects of royal confiscations and donations, see Jassemin, *Chambre des comptes*, 179–216. For a more theoretically oriented history of *alienation du domaine,* see Leyte, *Domaine et domanialité publique dans la France médiévale (XIIᵉ–XVᵉ siècles).* My arguments in this chapter must necessarily approach this core topic in legal history from the limited perspective imposed by our interest in Commynes.

33 "Sur certain points, la doctrine est hésistante: le don des confiscations constitue-t-il ou non une aliénation du fonds du domaine? Il semble qu'en général les confiscations récentes et portant sur des biens qui n'avaient jamais appartenu au roi aient été assimilées à des aubaines, et que leur don ait été vérifié par les gens des comptes seulement. Mais l'aliénation des confiscations anciennes, ou portant sur des biens ayant autrefois fait partie du domaine, devait être enregistrée d'abord au Parlement" (Jassemin, *Chambre des comptes*, 182); "La jurisdiction domaniale de la Chambre était beaucoup plus étendue que celle du Parlement, puisque aucune mesure aliénant le domaine n'était valable, même avec le consentement du Parlement, que si elle avait passé à la Chambre, mais qu'un grand nombre d'aliénations pouvaient se faire sans autre intervention que celle des gens des comptes" (Jassemin, *Chambre des comptes*, 183).

34 Dupont, ed., *Mémoires*, 3:15–16.

35 Ibid., 3:19.

36 For a synthetic view of Louis XI's manipulations of Parlement, see Gaussin, *Louis XI: un roi entre deux mondes*, "Les Parlements," 160–5. See also, Stocker, "Office and Justice." For a broader study of Parlement itself, the

classic source remains Félix Aubert's two-volume *Histoire du Parlement de Paris*; a more recent study is Shennan's *The Parlement of Paris*. In the *Mémoires*, Commynes remarks, "Ainsi [Louis XI] desiroit de tout son cueur de pouvoir mectre une grant police en ce royaulme, principallement sur la longueur des procés et, en ce passaige, bien brider cest court de Parlement; non point dyminuer leur nombre ne leur auctorité, mais il avoit contre cueur plusieurs choses dont ilz usoient" (*Mémoires* [TLF, 2007], 458). More pointedly still, the king's manoeuvering at Péronne leads Commynes to explain, "il desiroit aller a Paris faire publier leur appoinctmeent en la court de Parlement, pour ce que c'est la coutume de France de publier tous acords, ou aultrement ne seroient de nulle valeur; *toutesfoiz les Roys y peuvent tousjours beaucop*" (*Mémoires* [TLF, 2007], 155; my emphasis).

37 See Krynen, "Droit romain et état monarchique."

38 La Trémoïlle's letter gives no indication of year; its editor has placed it sequentially during 1473. However, a date of 1472 makes more sense to me given the sequence of letters from the king which follow. Weary, "La Maison de La Trémoïlle pendant la Renaissance," sheds light on the Talmont affair from a contrasting perspective. See below on the family's arrangements with Anne de Beaujeu.

39 La Trémoïlle, *Les La Trémoïlle pendant cinq siècles*, 2:23–4. For a study of grass-roots alliances and their impact on royal administration, see Lewis, "Reflections on the Role of Royal Clienteles."

40 See Contamine, "Pouvoir et vie de cour dans la France du XVᵉ siècle," and Oschema, *Freundschaft und Nähe*, 365–80.

41 Letters commanding obedience; especially, letters from the French king ordering Parlement to register an ordinance. "Mandement par lequel le roi, sur le refus d'une cour d'enregistrer quelque ordonnance, édit, déclaration, ou autres lettres patentes, lui enjoint d'avoir à y procéder" (Giry, *Manuel de diplomatique*, 778).

42 Vaesen and Charavay, *Lettres de Louis XI*, 5:111.

43 Ibid.

44 Ibid., 5:238–9. It is curious that the king refers here to Commynes as the "sire d'Argenton" and not as the "prince de Talmont." In fact, the marriage contract between Commynes and Hélène de Chambes in January 1473 remains the only document to call the memorialist by that title (Dupont, *Notice*, xlvi, note 1). Commynes, however, appears to have used the title with more regularity, as indicated in a recently published letter from 1485 in which he refers to himself as, "Phelippes de Commines, chevalier, seigneur d'Argenton et de Thalemont, conseiller chambellain du Roy

nostre seigneur et senneschal de Po[ictou]" (Blanchard, "Commynes et les princes rebelles," 212; brackets in published text).

45 Dupont, ed., *Mémoires*, 3:19.

46 Ibid., 3:19–20.

47 "Le parlement, après une honorable résistance, avait enfin cédé; mais, le lendemain même de son acte de soumission aux ordres du roi, il consignait sur ses registres sa protestation première et déclarait que son adhésion ayant été forcée ne pouvait aucunement porter préjudice aux droits des La Trémoille, en faveur desquels il renouvelait ses réserves" (Dupont, *Notice*, lviii–lix). On the practices of opposition to the king's *lettres patentes*, see Olivier-Martin, *Les Lois du roi*, 325–36.

48 Dupont, ed., *Mémoires*, 3:76; my emphasis.

49 The king's *lettres de jussion* date from May 1480. Parlement registered them on the last day of July; the Chambre des comptes did so in August of the same year (Dupont, ed., *Mémoires*, 3:78–9).

50 This inquest opened at the chateau d'Amboise, the same site where, in 1472, Louis XI had first bestowed Talmont on Commynes (Kervyn de Lettenhove, *Lettres et négociations*, 2:13).

51 The phrase serves as a chapter title. See Dufournet, *Vie de Philippe de Commynes*, 141.

52 This description of the conspirator's crimes belongs to his 24 March 1489 sentencing to "house arrest," i.e., confinement to one of his or his wife's estates (see Godefroy, *Histoire de Charles VIII*, 576–7). Ambassadorial letters provide the most direct testimony to the news of Commynes's arrest. In 2000, Blanchard, citing the letterbook of Venetian ambassador Girolamo Zorzi, placed Commynes's arrest in early February rather than late January (Blanchard, "Commynes et les princes rebelles," 220, note 35), but in his 2006 biography of Commynes returns to the date of 14 January 1487, without, however, identifying his source.

53 "Depuis la condamnation à mort de Louis d'Amboise par Charles VII jusqu'au versement d'une forte indemnité à Commynes par Charles VIII toute l'affaire de Talmont fait ressortir combien la justice, à cette époque, dépendait du pouvoir" (Liniger, *Philippe de Commynes*, 272).

54 Commynes's direct statements in the *Mémoires* about the years of his disgrace are extremely rare. He is, in fact, noticeably silent about many of those who opposed him.

55 The events that marked the military and political struggles now collectively referred to by the etiquette "la Guerre Folle," the Mad War, fall outside the scope of this study. Although now used to refer to an escalating series

of intrigues and confrontations between 1484 and 1488, the phrase "insana militia" was originally penned by Paolo Emilio (1460–1529) in his *De rebus gestis Francorum* to describe the second revolt in this series, cut short in September 1485 before the two armies could enter into battle. Louis II de La Trémoïlle served at the head of the Beaujeu regency's army at Bourges and again at the battle of Saint-Aubin-du-Cormier, where on 28 July 1488, Louis d'Orléans was captured and the Guerre Folle effectively quashed.

56 Historians are unanimous in their agreement on Commynes's key role in the intrigues surrounding Louis d'Orléans. On the night of Louis XI's death, Pierre de Rohan was already writing to Alain d'Albret, urging, "Il est besoing que vous envoyés devers monseigneur de Comynes, afin que par votre moyen il se range avec vous et avec vos amys" (You need to write to monseigneur de Commynes, so that by your intervention he will align himself with you and your friends [Kervyn de Lettenhove, *Lettres et négociations*, 3:88]). Commynes is also widely believed to have been the strategic force behind Louis d'Orléans's push to convene the 1484 Etats Généraux. Further agreement regarding precise dates, Commynes's whereabouts, or the nature of his involvement in pivotal events tends to be less forthcoming. "Il faut dire que les indices sont tenus et les documents rares" (Blanchard, "Commynes et les princes rebelles," 208). Liniger (*Philippe de Commynes*, 233–62) provides a useful account, although his idealized view of Commynes's motives may be regarded with some scepticism.

57 "Pareillement audit mois de Ianvier mille quatre cent·quatre-vingt & six [*nouveau style* 1487], le Roy fut adverty que les Evesques de Perigueux, surnommé de Pompadour, & de Montauban, surnommé de Chaumont, & les Seigneurs d'Argenton & de Bucy frere dudit Evesque de Montauban, avoient intelligence avec Monseigneur d'Orleans & Monseigneur de Dunois, & d'autres qui s'estoient retirez en Bretagne, & qu'ils leur faisoient sçavoir toutes nouvelles de Cour; mesme fut trouvé un homme allant d'Amboise (ou ils estoient avec le Roy) en Bretagne, portant des lettres d'eux, & crois bien que le porteur desdites lettres fit sous main sçavoir son message afin d'estre trouvé chargé d'icelles lettres: Pour ce sujet le Roy les fit un matin constituer prisonniers, & à chacun d'eux bailla des gardes, & les fit mettre en lieu seur" (Jaligny, in Godefroy, *Histoire de Charles VIII*, 14–15). For an evaluation of Jean II de Bourbon's reconciliation with Beaujeu and Commynes's subsequent arrest, see Jaligny, in Godefroy, ed., *Histoire de Charles VIII*, 6–15. See also Pélicier, *Essai sur le gouvernement de la Dame de Beaujeu*, 117–21; and Maulde-La-Clavière, *Histoire de Louis XII*, 2:168–9. Only one of the ciphered letters which helped to condemn

Commynes survives (Commynes, *Lettres*, ed. Blanchard, 126–30); see chapter 5.

58 Commynes was reconfirmed in this post on 2 October 1483. Charles VIII first sought to strip him of the position in September 1485, but Commynes mounted a sustained legal challenge.

59 Commynes was one of three members added to the twelve-member *conseil* during the fall of 1483.

60 This ordinance was first given at Amboise on 22 September 1483 (Pastoret, *Ordonnances des rois de France*, 19:140–2). "Les exemples abondent des domaines conservés aux officiers de Louis XI malgré les édits de restitution" (Pélicier, *Essai sur le gouvernement de la Dame de Beaujeu*, 91, note 3). In the *Mémoires*, Commynes concludes a list of Louis XI's most extravagant gifts to the church during the time of his illness saying, "Des terres donna il grant quantité aux esglises; mais ce don de terre n'a point tenu: aussi il en y avoit trop" (*Mémoires* [TLF, 2007], 472).

61 Anne de Beaujeu chose not to oppose the La Trémoïlle revindication and instead, on 17 December 1483, agreed to relinquish her claim to the title *vicomtesse de Thouars* in exchange for 17,000 écus. A quittance dated 10 May 1484 confirms her receipt of 10,000 écus and a diamond ring (*Archives de Thouars*, cited by Kervyn de Lettenhove, *Lettres et négociations*, 2:14–15).

62 Joël Blanchard contemplates, but does not develop, a similar hierarchy; see "Commynes et les princes rebelles," 210.

63 See the *Dictionnaire du Moyen Français*, s.v. trespasser.

64 The younger Duke of Gueldres is punished, "comme se Dieu n'eust pas encore esté saol de venger cest oultraige qu'il avoit faict a son pere" (*Mémoires* [TLF, 2007], 241); Edward IV reprimands the *connétable* Saint-Pol that "si luy eust tenu ce qu'il luy avoit promis, qu'il n'eust point faict cest appoinctement. Lors fut de tous points nostre connestable desesperé" (*Mémoires* [TLF, 2007], 284); the events at Montereau would not have occurred, "si n'y eust point eu de huys a ceste veue dont je parle, on n'eust point eu occasion de semondre ledict duc de passer, et ce grand inconveniant n'y feust poinct advenu" (*Mémoires* [TLF, 2007], 288), to cite only a few examples.

65 On Etienne de Vesc and his place in the court circles of Louis XI, Charles VIII, and Louis XII, see Boislisle, *Notice ... sur Etienne de Vesc.*

66 Dupont, ed., *Mémoires*, 3:81.

67 Ibid., 3:81–2.

68 Ibid., 3:76.

69 The interpretation of the word "estranger" in this context has occasionally resulted in debate. It is impossible to know whether the king actually used

this phrase, or whether the words come from de Jarrye. Regardless of this word or another, Commynes himself has confessed that what de Jarrye recounts actually happened. Ultimately, it matters relatively little whether this label originates in the king's speech or in the collective act of testimony made at his trial. What matters is the purging and Othering the label carries.

70 Dupont, *Notice*, lix, note 1, which continues onto page lxx; emphasis and ellipsis both in Dupont.

71 "On peut chiffrer les prises du roi dans le vivier politique princier: 27 conseillers sont venus de chez le duc de Bourgogne" (Gaussin, "Les Conseillers de Louis XI (1461–1483)," 131).

72 The Argenton fiefs formed the object of a multigenerational family dispute between the branches of Hélène de Chambes's family. The Argenton lands did not form a *dot* per se, but rather the object of a sale between Jean de Chambes, his daughter, and her new husband. Louis XI provided the majority of the monies tendered, while a significant portion of the remainder was put forward by such members of the royal entourage as Pierre Doriole and Jean Bourré. Louis XI's arrangement of the marriage between Commynes and Hélène de Chambes included overturning a previous legal ruling and restoring the Argenton estates to the de Chambes branch of the family. By selling the Argenton lands, and his daughter, to the king's new favourite, Jean de Chambes nimbly protected and expanded his own interests in that dispute against his Chabot cousins. However, these estates would eventually cause Commynes, Hélène de Chambes, and their descendants, significant additional legal troubles. For a history of this dispute see Liniger, *Philippe de Commynes*, 273–5, which condenses the unwieldy Michaud, *Au Pays argentonnais*. For details of the marriage contract, see above, note 5. During the Talmont trial, when Commynes resisted obeying orders to surrender the properties pursued by La Trémoïlle, attempts were made to seize the Argenton lands (see Kervyn de Lettenhove, *Lettres et négociations*, 2:65–6).

73 Dreux is in the department of Eure-et-Loir. On the complicated financial transactions between Commynes and Alain d'Albret which led Commynes to retire to these lands on his release from prison, see Blanchard, *Philippe de Commynes*, especially 209–10 and 359–62; and Rahlenbeck, "Philippe de Commines dans ses rapports avec la maison d'Albret."

74 Dupont, ed., *Mémoires*, 3:18.

75 Ibid., 3:82. De Jarrye's testimony evokes the iconography of the "good death" portrayed by the *Ars Moriendi*. In this picture-book imagery, devils frolic at the foot of the dying man's bed, while beside him angels pray for

his soul to repent and be allowed into heaven. In de Jarrye's descriptions, Vesc and others, each zealous of the king's preparation for heaven, take the place of guiding angels. Consider the king's payment of 24 *livres* to "Jehan Bourdichon, paintre et enlumineur ... pour avoir escript et paint d'azur cinquante grans rouleaulx que le dit seigneur a fait mettre en plusieurs lieux dedans le Plessis-du-Parc, esquels est escript *Misericordias Domini in aeternum cantabo*, et pour avoir paint et pourtraict d'or, d'azur et autres couleurs, trois anges de trois pieds de haulteur ou environ, qu'ils tiennent chacun un des dits roulleaux en leur main, et est escrit le dit *misericordia*" (Cimber, *Archives curieuses*, 108). These painted angels sing orations for the king's soul and should be directly associated with the angels who guard the dying man's bedside in the *Ars Moriendi*. Cf. Seidel, "The Value of Verisimilitude in the Art of Jan van Eyck," 33–4.

76 The situation of the Thouars chateau in the years following Louis d'Amboise's death remains ambiguous. Anne de France received the title corresponding to the property; the seigneur de Bressuire appears to have acted as its administrator, enjoying its usage without possessing it per se. Kervyn de Lettenhove asserts that Bressuire "n'avait agi qu'au nom du roi, et Commines paraît avoir seul étendu son autorité à Thouars" (*Lettres et négociations*, 2:14, note 1), commenting that the revindications against Commynes include Thouars. Pélicier maintains the opposite, "Cette donation [de l'héritage de Louis d'Amboise à Commynes] ne comprenait pas la terre de Thouars, cédée par le roi à sa fille aînée en mai 1470" (Pélicier, *Essai sur le gouvernement de la Dame de Beaujeu*, 56, note 3). I have discovered no evidence that the La Trémoïlle family challenged Anne's right to the title *vicomtesse de Thouars* prior to their 1483 repurchase of the title from her.

77 Because Louis XI had paid only the first 10,000 écus of the 100,000 écu price agreed to by Louis d'Amboise, the La Trémoïlle heirs insisted that the sale was not only invalid but also incomplete. This point, however valid, remained ultimately tangential to the post-1483 dispute.

78 Dupont's sentiment typifies reactions to this hunting party. "Pour soutenir les droits de son domaine contre les revendications obstinées de La Trémoïlle, et pour conserver un faux-semblant de justice tout en se livrant à la plus révoltante iniquité, le roi nomma une commission d'enquête chargée de rechercher dans les archives de Thouars s'il ne s'y trouvait point quelques lettres qui pussent lui servir dans son procès" (Dupont, *Notice*, lxi–lxii).

79 "Au moyen et par vertu desquelles lettres de nostre commission, Jehan Maillart, huissier du conseil, et Leonnet Moutart, sergent en la seneschaussee de Lyon, nous certifierent avoir adjourné ledict procureur du

Roy et aussi ledict seigneur d'Argenton ... noble et puissant seigneur messire Jacques de Beaumont, chevalier, seigneur de Bressuyre, maistre Richart Estivalle, procureur du Roy en la viconté de Thouars, maistre André Martineau, chastelain dudict lieu de Thouars, Jehan Richart, clerc, maistre Loys Tindo, president de Bordeaux, maistre Jehan Chambon, conseiller et maistre des requestes à l'hostel du roy, maistre Raoul Pichon, conseiller dudict seigneur de Gyé, mareschal de France, pour ... porter tesmoignage de verité ... Tous et chascuns lesquels tesmoings nous avons fait jurer sollempnellement aux saintes evangiles de Dieu ..." (Dupont, ed., *Mémoires*, 3:96; all ellipses hers). For a timeline of each side's legal manoeuvrings, see Dupont, *Notice*, lxxxix et sqq.

80 For a useful consideration of witnessing as an act which may be collective or individual, intersubjective or personal, performative or descriptive, see Frisch, *Invention of the Eyewitness*, 11–40.

81 Dupont, ed., *Mémoires*, 3:107–8.

82 Ibid., 3:116. This is the king's formula as recalled by Richard d'Estivalle, responsible for the archives at Thouars, and a witness to each of the affair's episodes.

83 On the juridical status of written and oral proofs (*lettres passent temoins* versus *temoins passent lettres*), see Gilissen, "Individualisme et sécurité juridique."

84 Dupont, ed., *Mémoires*, 3:123.

85 Ibid.; testimony of 19 July 1484.

86 Other witnesses, especially the clerks who had once copied them, gave very precise descriptions of the letters held at Thouars.

87 Gilissen, "Individualisme et sécurité juridique," 34.

88 Cf. Frisch's discussion of how compurgative testimony was evaluated "first and foremost in terms of the witnesses' imbrication in an ethical community" (*Invention of the Eyewitness*, 24). Both the intersubjective ethical aspect of witnessing analysed by Frisch and the property-and-the-individual aspect of proofs analysed by Gilissen are in play in Commynes's trial, where a community of oral witnesses unite around an ethical refusal of Louis XI and Commynes's behaviour in regards to a written document. Practical considerations render it impossible to examine in full the intersubjective dimension of the accusations brought against Commynes.

89 Cf. Foucault, "The Subject and Power," 789.

90 Dupont, ed., *Mémoires*, 3:120–1.

91 Ibid., 3:127.

92 The phrase is ambiguous, both in the meaning of "moins de plus grant somme" and in the direction of the obligation between "il" and "lui."

Although it is clear that the obligation is between Commynes and Louis, interpretations in either direction seem plausible given the difficult meaning of the phrase "tenu envers," translatable as "obligated."

93 Dupont, ed., *Mémoires*, 3:127–8.

5 Paper and Parchment

1 This motto appears on Commynes's funerary chapel sculpture, the surviving portions of which are now at the Louvre. It paraphrases the concluding sentence of 2 Thessalonians 3:8–10, frequently adapted during the Middle Ages, notably by Bernard of Clairvaux. On Commynes's funerary sculpture, see Beaulieu, "Note sur la chapelle funéraire de Philippe de Commines."

2 This motto appeared in the form of a rebus elsewhere in situ at the chapel's original location (Kervyn de Lettenhove, *Lettres et négociations*, 2:281, note 3). The *Dictionnaire du Moyen Français* quickly strips away any illusion that the word "abus" ought to be taken in a Christian sense to refer to the vanity of earthly existence. Its definitions include, "mauvais usages [des textes]"; "exercice excessif d'un pouvoir"; "abus de justice"; "exaction"; "faire erreur que de"; and "pensée confuse (ici à la suite d'une trahison)"; s.v. abus.

3 Tessier, *Diplomatique royale française*, unpaginated frontispiece. The document in question is a *lettre patente*, dated July 1364 (Archives nationales J 154, n°5: Musée, AE II 383).

4 See Kantorowicz, *The King's Two Bodies*, section IV, "Law-Centered Kingship," 87–192.

5 This is also the tradition out of which the documents alleged by the La Trémoïlle family come to us, albeit not unsmudged. The standard edition of Louis XI's letters is that of Vaesen and Charavay, *Lettres de Louis XI*. Henri Dubois, ed., *Louis XI, Lettres choisies*, contains a very useful introduction and critical apparatus. See also Dubois, "Observations sur la diplomatique des lettres de Louis XI."

6 The *Mémoires* use the word letters to describe a variety of documents. The modern English word letter belies the range of documents, textual practices, and traditions the word embraces when applied to the Middle Ages. Some of these resemble what we still use the word letters to mean. Commynes could also use the word letters to describe things that we today would call charters, or patents, or instructions, but these are not our focus in this chapter. See Dubois, *Louis XI, Lettres choisies*, 5–8, and cf. Cazelles, *Lettres closes*. For a broader approach to the epistolary

and to diplomacy during the Middle Ages, see Constable, *Letters and Letter-Collections*; Giry, *Manuel de diplomatique*; and Guyotjeannin et al., *Diplomatique médiévale*.

7 "There was a Milanese resident ambassador to France from 1463–1475, the first embassy of the kind at the French court from any Italian state, and during most of the 1460s, the only resident embassy established beyond the Alps" (Mattingly, *Renaissance Diplomacy*, 97).

8 On the Pazzi conspiracy, see Martines, *April Blood*. On the reaction to and depiction of this event in France and Burgundy, see Jodogne, "La Conjuration des Pazzi."

9 See, notably, Anderson, *The Rise of Modern Diplomacy 1450–1919*, chapter 1; Mattingly, *Renaissance Diplomacy*; and Queller, *The Office of Ambassador*. For a critique of Mattingly's influence and a discussion of more recent scholarship, see Watkins, "Toward a New Diplomatic History of Medieval and Early Modern Europe."

10 Joël Blanchard has written extensively about this period of diplomatic maturity in Commynes's life as an apprenticeship to the ethos defined by the principles of *bilanza, credita, and pratica*, whose concomitant modes of behaviour guided Italian affairs. See especially Blanchard, *Commynes l'Européen* and *Philippe de Commynes*.

11 Commynes makes a point of admiring Angelo Cato or Saint François de Paule's mastery of Latin. He praises Cato in his prologue for writing "en langue latine, dont vous estez bien usité" (*Mémoires* [TLF, 2007], 2). Commynes describes himself as "non lettré" (*Mémoires* [TLF, 2007], 403), and then implicitly defines *lettré* as "knowing Latin" when he talks about Saint François de Paule (*Mémoires* [TLF, 2007], 473). What remains less clear is the extent to which Commynes perceived this lacuna as a source of embarrassment. At moments his attitude towards Latin reflects condescension towards clerical pedantry. It is likewise possible that, thinking of the erudite Cato, Commynes emphasizes his own humility.

12 Ian Arthurson credits Commynes with "the classic pronouncement that messenger, spy and diplomat amount to the same thing" (Arthurson, "Espionage and Intelligence," 134).

13 Watkins, "Toward a New Diplomatic History of Medieval and Early Modern Europe."

14 Hampton, *Fictions of Embassy*, 16; emphasis in original. See also, Ilardi, "Diplomatic History as 'Total' History?" 118; Mattingly, *Renaissance Diplomacy*, chapter 11, "The Duties of a Resident Ambassador"; and Queller, *The Office of Ambassador*, chapter 5, "Letters and Reports," especially 226.

15 I wish to acknowledge the significant influence of Hampton's *Fictions of Embassy* on the development of this chapter.

16 "Diplomacy is thus a political practice that is also a writing practice. It is deeply invested in the dynamics of writing, in the structuring of narrative, and in the development of scriptural authority" (Hampton, *Fictions of Embassy*, 7). Cf. Blanchard, "Political and Cultural Implications of Secret Diplomacy," 246–7; and Commynes, *Lettres*, ed. Blanchard, 17.

17 Commynes, *Mémoires*, ed. Calmette and Durville (1924–5), 2:340. In the Polignac manuscript a scribe has glossed the word literature, writing instead, "Mais a parler naturellement, comme homme qui n'a grant sens naturel ne acquis, mais quelque peu d'esperiance" (*Mémoires* [TLF, 2007], 511).

18 The narrator's allusions to his text as an object merit similar consideration; for example: "comme j'ay dict ailleurs plus au long en cest *Memoire*" (*Mémoires* [TLF, 2007], 127; cf. 154; 344; 352, etc.).

19 Commynes, *Lettres*, ed. Blanchard.

20 See ibid., 7–20.

21 Ibid., 29.

22 One can readily imagine that Louis XI chose to send Commynes to Italy precisely because of the skill he had shown against Burgundy.

23 That is, eighteen fully autograph letters (Commynes, *Lettres*, ed. Blanchard, 11; cf. the further precisions regarding autograph *souscriptions* and letters in Italian, page 12).

24 "Even as diplomatic scribes were producing mountains of new knowledge about the states of Europe and various non-European neighbours, they struggled constantly with the question of what it was that they were writing, what they were writing about, and what the scope and authority of that writing might be" (Hampton, *Fictions of Embassy*, 25).

25 Commynes, *Lettres*, ed. Blanchard, 109.

26 Ibid., 29.

27 Ibid., 36–7.

28 Ibid., 46. The Ferdinand in question is Ferdinand II of Aragon, better known as Ferdinand the Catholic.

29 Ibid., 114. Letter of [1478–82]; brackets indicate the attributed date is uncertain. Emphasis mine. The man Commynes calls by the code name "Jacques" has never been identified. Sixteen of Commynes's surviving letters are addressed to Gaddi, Florence's ambassador at the French court. For a detailed study of these letters, see Sozzi, "Lettere inedite di Commynes a Francesco Gaddi." Like Angelo Cato, Gaddi is a fascinating and well-known figure among Italian humanists of the period. He was an important collector of

manuscripts, the author of his own *ricordanze*, and a predecessor of Machiavelli at the Florentine chancellery. There are unfortunately no traces of conversations about humanism or history which Commynes and Gaddi may have had together.

30 Paravicini, "Peur, pratiques, intelligences," 194.

31 See Arthurson, "Espionnage and Intelligence."

32 Commynes boasts of missions to persuade Burgundian townsmen to come around to the king's side. The hatred directed at Commynes by fifteenth- and sixteenth-century Burgundian authors justifies the memorialist's view of his own importance. The passionate venom in Jacques Meyer's *Commentarii sive Annales rerum Flandricarum* is well known; see also Adrien de But, *Chronique*, 1:573 and 669.

33 This is because it does not pertain to the relations between polities.

34 Commynes, *Lettres*, ed. Blanchard, 126–7.

35 Ibid., 127, note 137. Cf. Blanchard, "Commynes et les princes rebelles."

36 Ibid., 298. The year 1505 is uncertain.

37 Ibid., 96. Letter of [December 1480]. The "ly" in question is Giuliano della Rovere, the future Pope Julius II (Commynes, *Lettres*, ed. Blanchard, 98, note 105).

38 Cf. These instructions to burn letters in the context of secret diplomacy and the romantic exaltation are analysed in Haroche-Bouzinac, "Les Lettres qu'on ne brûle pas."

39 On letters of credence, see Queller, *The Office of Ambassador*, 111–14.

40 Bought and captured letters show up in several episodes of the *Mémoires* and figure in the correspondence, as well. See for example, in the *Mémoires*, Commynes's discussion of letters in Monsieur d'Urfé's hand bought from an English secretary for sixty silver marks (*Mémoires* [TLF, 2007], 247). In a letter Commynes wrote to Cicco Simonetta in November [1478], he speaks of forwarding a duplicate of letters which had been seized from a courier in Roussillon. "J'ay baillé à Jennet Ballarin des doubles de lettres, lesquelles vous seront monstreez en passant a Millan, que les gens du Roy qui sont en Rouxillon ont prins sur ung courrier. Le Roy les a leues tout au long" (Commynes, *Lettres*, ed. Blanchard, 54).

41 Cf. Ilardi, "Diplomatic History as 'Total' History?" 130, note 30, on the "use of secret signs and symbols to authenticate Renaissance correspondence"; this note expands on Ilardi's earlier study, "Crosses and Carets: Renaissance Patronage and Coded Letters of Recommendation." See also Queller, *The Office of Ambassador*, 140–1.

42 Vaesen and Charavay, *Lettres de Louis XI*, 7:60–1. Letters dated 12 May 1478, from Arras. Also published in Desjardins, *Négociations diplomatiques*

de la France avec la Toscane, 1:171–2; and in French translation in Kervyn de
Lettenhove, *Lettres et négociations*, 1:171–2.

43 Commynes, *Lettres*, ed. Blanchard, 90. Letter written at Angers, 26 June
1480.

44 Queller, *The Office of Ambassador*, 112. In the first instance (note 13), Queller
refers to Ganshof, *Le Moyen Age*, 275; in the second (note 14) to Kern, *Acta
Imperii, Angliae et Franciae*, 9, note 16.

45 Commynes, *Lettres*, ed. Blanchard, 93. Letter written at Plessis-du-Parc
(Tours), possibly in [1480?].

46 Cf. Hampton, *Fictions of Embassy*, especially chapters 2 and 5.

47 *Mémoires* (TLF, 2007), 1:cxviii–cxix; cxix, note 137.

48 On Rouville's role in this delicate moment, see de Roye, *Chronique scandaleuse*, 1:61, note 1. On the uses and abuses of blanks, see Queller, *The Office of
Ambassador*, 130–7.

49 Thomas Basin gives extensive development to this metaphor in his *Apologie,
ou Plaidoyer pour moi-même*, including descriptions of this precise surveillance. "Vias eciam omnes atque itinera, quibus ad terram ducis Burgundie
ex Normannia patere potuisset accessus, tam exacta vigilancia observari
fecit, ut vix ex una terra in alteram vel lepus transire potuisset" (He had all
the roads and paths which gave access from Normandy to the duke of
Burgundy's domains watched with such exact vigilance that a hare could
scarcely have passed from one to the other [65]). The treasonous Saint-Pol
compares the king to a birder setting netted snares; see chapter 6.

50 This episode opens the door to direct negotiations between Edward IV and
Louis XI, resulting in Edward's eventual abandonment of his commit-
ments towards Charles and in the Treaty of Soleuvre. See chapter 3.

51 See Paravicini, "Des Animaux pour un roi mourant."

52 Cf. Commynes's dismissal of one embassy not taken seriously: "Leur
audience fut courte et en publicque, et ne demeurerent que ung jour"
(*Mémoires* [TLF, 2007], 94).

53 Charles de Valois, also known as Charles de France and, successively,
Duke of Berry, Normandy, and Guyenne. Louis XI was in fact suspected of
poisoning him.

54 Dubois, "Observations sur la diplomatique des lettres de Louis XI," 341.

55 Kervyn de Lettenhove, *Lettres et négociations*, 1:330 claims that Madame de
Thouars – i.e., Hélène de Chambes – was made Marguerite's *gouvernante*;
other sources, for example, Dupont, ed., *Mémoires*, 3:345–52, name Madame
de Segré as responsible for the three-year-old princess.

56 The events behind Commynes's narration have received significant attention from historians. See especially Boone, "Justice en spectacle"; Gachard,

"Note sur le jugement et la condamnation de Guillaume Hugonet";
Haemers, *For The Common Good*; and Paravicini, *Guy de Brimeu*, 450–92.
Dufournet characteristically attacks the accuracy of Commynes's scene
(Dufournet, *Etudes sur Philippe de Commynes*, 145–7). See also, Allemand,
"La Réversion du duché de Bourgogne au Royaume de France"; Devaux,
"Le Rôle politique de Marie de Bourgogne au lendemain de Nancy"; and
Saenger, "Burgundy and the Inalienability of Appanages in the Reign of
LXI."

57 See Mattingly, *Renaissance Diplomacy*, 41; and Hamilton and Langhorne,
The Practice of Diplomacy, 49–50.
58 Cf. Hampton, *Fictions of Embassy*, chapter 7, "The Tragedy of Delegation."
59 This execution took place on 3 April 1477.
60 Gachard, "Note sur le jugement et la condamnation de Guillaume
Hugonet," 329; see also, Vanderjagt, "Guillaume Hugonet's Farewell
Letter to His Wife on April 3, 1477."
61 As per Commynes's narrative, Adolf of Egmond, Duke of Guelders, imprisoned his father in 1465, as part of an attempt to lay precocious claim to
his inheritance. He was later caught trying to flee and imprisoned. After
Charles's death, the townsmen of Ghent freed him. He was killed at the
Battle of Tournai in June 1477, "meschamment et mal acompaigné, comme
se Dieu n'eust pas encore esté saol de venger cest oultraige qu'il avoit faict
a son pere" (*Mémoires* [TLF, 2007], 241).
62 This view has been validated by recent scholarship. See Boone, "Justice en
spectacle," 53, note 35, which further refers the reader to Favier, *Louis XI*,
735; and to Sablon du Corail, "Croix fourchues contre croix droitez."
63 Cf. Hampton, *Fictions of Embassy*, 34–5, on the scene of diplomatic failure
as an opening to generic innovation.
64 The sexual subtext of Burgundy's dilemma surfaces explicitly more than
once. Debate over whether Mary should marry the dauphin is cut short by
one counsellor's bold allusion to their sexual incompatibility: the idea of
marrying Mary to the eight-year-old Charles VIII is all well and good, but
the princess needs an heir, not a child. "Se tint quelque conseil sur ceste matiere, ou se trouva madame de Hallewin, premiere dame de ladicte damoiselle, laquelle dist, comme me fut rapporté, qu'il avoient besoing d'ung
homme et non point d'ung enffant, disant que sa maistresse estoit femme
pour porter enffant, et que de cela le pays avoit besoing. A ceste oppinion se
tindrent tous" (*Mémoires* [TLF, 2007], 437). Madame de Hallewin is Jeanne
de La Clite, Lady of Comines, and the memorialist Philippe's cousin.
65 See also, Nancy Jones's political reading of Chrétien de Troyes's *Philomena*
("The Daughter's Text," 168).

66 For Louis XI as Mary of Burgundy's godfather, see Vaesen and Charavay, *Lettres de Louis XI*, 6:113, note 2; for his desire to marry her to the dauphin, see 6:112.

67 See Bullough and Brundage, *Sexual Practices and the Medieval Church*, chapter 13, "Rape and Seduction in the Medieval Canon Law"; and Wolfthal, "'A Hue and a Cry.'"

6 The Treasonous Saint-Pol

1 de Roye, *Chronique scandaleuse*, 1:361. Molinet says 100,000 (*Chroniques*, 1:134).

2 The *connétable*'s letters themselves have not survived, but we will approach them through his testimony. For the text of that trial, see Blanchard, *Commynes et les procès politiques de Louis XI*, "Le Procès de Saint-Pol," 63–156 (henceforth abbreviated "Procès de Saint-Pol"), which provides a critical edition of Bibliothèque nationale de France ms. fr. 3869. A nineteenth-century *Ecole des chartes* thesis devoted to the *connétable* has not survived, and there is still no book-length biography of him. The best study of the stages of Saint-Pol's treason remains Paravicini's "Peur, pratiques, intelligences," on which I have relied for my own understanding and presentation of the *connétable*'s career. See also, Dufournet, "Au Coeur des *Mémoires* de Commynes."

3 "... que l'oyseleur parloit bien doulcement pour prendre les oyseaulx et qu'il ne se fyast en chose que le roy lui promeist" ("Procès de Saint-Pol," 146). The *greffe* transposes all speech into reported speech.

4 The expression is especially pretty on account of Louis XI's passion for hunting, a pleasure that he enjoyed more than any other, and which formed a substantial topos in criticism of his tyranny. Louis was reputed to exterminate every animal to be found on the lands where he hunted, and banned others from hunting at all. See Michelet, *Histoire de France*, 6:79–80, for a digest of contemporary sources; note that the best known of these, Thomas Basin, appears under the name "Amelgard."

5 "En tout cas, ces scellés étaient des documents extrêment dangereux qu'il fallait mettre en lieu sûr et faire disparaître au bon moment. Ce n'est pas par hasard si ceux dont je parle ici ne sont apparemment pas conservés. Le comte du Maine brûla le contre-scellé du duc de Bretagne avant de se rendre au roi. La duchesse de Nemours brûla des archives avant la capitulation de la forteresse de Carlat. Saint-Pol, lui, avait son dépôt en dehors du royaume, à Cambrai" (Paravicini, "Peur, pratiques, intelligences," 195).

6 Chiffoleau, "Sur le crime de majesté médiéval," 184.

7 Cf. Paul Archambault's discussion of tragedy in, "History as Entropy in Commynes' *Mémoires*," and "Thucydides in France."

8 On the primacy of theoretical or pragmatic approaches to treason law and treason trials under Louis XI's reign, and in regards to Saint-Pol's case in particular, cf. Blanchard, "Procès de Saint-Pol," 8, 61; and Cuttler, *Law of Treason and Treason Trials*, 15.

9 "Procès de Saint-Pol," 156. See Cuttler, *Law of Treason and Treason Trials*, 2.

10 "Toute sa vie politique qui commence tôt, vers 1438, a été déterminée par cette situation ambiguë qu'il tente de mettre à profit en faisant monter les enchères en vrai virtuose de la négociation secrète" (Paravicini, "Peur, pratiques, intelligences," 185). Saint-Pol's participation at Philip the Good's 1454 Feast of the Pheasant provides a telling presage of later quarrels: alone among those whose vows are recorded, Saint-Pol resists formulating his allegiance in the terms demanded by the duke.

11 Gaussin, *Louis XI: un roi entre deux mondes*, 124. For the scale of these figures, see Gaussin, "Les Conseillers de Louis XI (1461–1483)," especially 128–9.

12 Saint-Pol's second wife was Marie de Savoie, sister of Louis XI's second wife Charlotte de Savoie. See Paravicini, "Peur, pratiques, intelligences," 185, for an analysis of the economic and political stakes of this marriage, arranged by Louis XI.

13 On the *connétable*'s family tree, see Paravicini, "Peur, pratiques, intelligences," 189–91; see also Harsgor, "Fidélités et infidélités au sommet du pouvoir."

14 "Dit que, en parlant de mesdicts seigneurs ses petiz enfans dont l'un est filleul du roy, il lui est souvenu que mondict seigneur de Bourgoigne, estant a Malines en venant devers le roy d'Angleterre, sceut que feue madame femme de il qui parle [Saint-Pol] estoit lors grosse preste d'acoucher, [et] en parlant a ung de ses gens … [le duc] s'offrit fort d'estre son compere" ("Procès de Saint-Pol," 129; and 129, note 143, on the use of "compere" for "parrain").

15 "Procès de Saint-Pol," 76.

16 Saint-Pol's behaviour is distinct from that of individuals who passed back and forth between the two courts. Saint-Pol is simultaneously feigning loyalty to each side.

17 All told, Saint-Pol's trial lasted less than one month. He was delivered to the king on 24 November 1475; his trial began on 27 November and concluded just three weeks later. Molinet reports that Louis XI first wanted the trial dispatched within eight days. Molinet, *Chroniques*, 132.

18 As a further act of mercy in consideration of being the king's own brother-in-law, Saint-Pol was buried, head and body together, in "terre sainte." See Molinet, *Chroniques*, 134, 137.

19 Paravicini, "Peur, pratiques, intelligences," 194. See also, the rich lexicon spread out for the reader in Blanchard, "Sémiologie du complot," based on the Nemours trial.

20 *Trésor de la Langue Française informatisé*, s.v. recommandation. See also, as cited there, Olivier-Martin, *Histoire du droit français des origines à la Révolution*, 82.

21 Cf. Paravicini, "Peur, pratiques, intelligences," 193: "donner des nouvelles, c'est déjà favoriser et servir."

22 "Procès de Saint-Pol," 154.

23 Lenglet Dufresnoy, ed., *Mémoires* (1747), 3:458–9. For an overview of several such poems, including the one here cited, see Tyson, "A Newly Discovered Poem on the Death of Louis de Luxembourg (1475)."

24 "Selon les droits et toute raison, la seule science en crime de leze-majesté, quand elle n'est revelée, soit digne de pareille punition que l'effect et execution du crime," Pastoret, *Ordonnances des rois de France*, 18:315–17; passage cited on page 316.

25 Analysed by Paravicini, "Peur, pratiques, intelligences," 191; recounted in de Roye, *Chronique scandaleuse*, 1:352–3. On de la Driesche, see Dumolyn, "Jan van den Driessche."

26 "Procès de Saint-Pol," 110.

27 See Vaesen and Charavay, *Lettres de Louis XI*, 6:32–3. There are no published letters between 8 November and 26 December 1475.

28 Vaesen and Charavay, *Lettres de Louis XI*, 6:88–91. Jean Blosset, seigneur de Saint-Pierre, held offices including seneschal of Normandy, bailiff of Rouen, and captain of Talmont and the *archers de la garde*. "Chargé particulièrement de missions policières, judiciaires et militaires," he held a singular authority under Louis XI (Dubois, *Louis XI, Lettres choisies*, 549).

29 "Gardez bien qu'il ne bouge plus de sa cage, et que l'on voyse besongner là avecques luy, et que l'on ne le mecte jamais dehors, si ce n'est pour le gehenier, et que l'on le gehenie en sa chambre" (Vaesen and Charavay, *Lettres de Louis XI*, 6:90).

30 Ibid., 6:89.

31 Ibid., 6:91. I base the translation "fulfil your obligations to me" on the nature of "service"; the tone of Louis's request is much more threatening than if he had used the equally possible words "content" or "plaisir."

32 Jacques d'Armagnac, Duke of Nemours, was arrested in February 1476 but not executed until August of 1477. His trial occupied approximately nine

months of that time (September 1476–June 1477). See Blanchard, "Sémiologie du complot"; Cuttler, *Law of Treason and Treason Trials*. A team of French
researchers is presently at work on an edition of Nemours's treason trial,
Paris, B.S.G. ms. 2000.

33 Paravicini, "Peur, pratiques, intelligences," 185. We possess a striking
    number of copies of Saint-Pol's trial. Blanchard identifies eleven at the
    Bibliothèque nationale de France alone, and at least one more at the
    Vatican ("Procès de Saint-Pol," 63, note 1). On political trials and manu-
    script collections, see Chiffoleau, "Le crime de majesté, la politique et
    l'extraordinaire."

34 Cf. *Mémoires* (TLF, 2007), 1:cxviii–cxix, and cxix, note 137.

35 Iser, "Indeterminacy and the Reader's Response in Prose Fiction," 4.

36 Cf. Blanchard, "Sémiologie du complot," especially 79–8. Louis XI appears
    to have kept the "book" composed from the manuscript *procès verbal* of
    Jacques d'Armagnac's trial near him in a chest at Amboise ("Sémiologie du
    complot," 84, note 80), and, in Blanchard's view, studied it. "C'est pour le
    roi l'occasion d'avoir la 'mémoire' du procès, dans lequel il pourra puiser
    les arguments, les moyens d'anticiper une autre menace" ("Sémiologie du
    complot," 84). Blanchard amputates his own interpretation at this point. I
    would suggest that there is much more in Louis's behaviour than a concern
    for utility. There is also evidence of Louis XI as the deliberate and conscious
    architect of his own and others' reading experiences, with all that that en-
    tails for what Iser calls the "negotiation of meaning." On the particularities
    and composition of this "book of Nemours" (my phrase) executed for the
    king's reading pleasure, see "Sémiologie du complot," 79–80 and 85.

37 In alphabetical order, these Somme River towns are Abbeville, Amiens,
    Corbie, Doullens, Mondidier, Péronne, Roye, Saint-Quentin, and Saint-
    Riquier. "Quatre d'entre elles ne sont pas baignées par le fleuve mais elles
    n'en sont éloignées que de 12 à 30 kilomètres. Elle forment une ligne conti-
    nue de points fortifiés face au domaine royal" (Cauchies, *Louis XI et
    Charles le Hardi*, 38; Arabic numerals in original).

38 These negotiations culminated in the Treaty of Conflans (5 October 1465).
    Its terms promised the return of the Somme River towns to Charles; the
    marriage of Louis XI's daughter Anne (then age 4) to the recently re-wid-
    owed Charles the Bold; and the appointment of Louis de Luxembourg as
    connétable de France.

39 According to Pierre-Roger Gaussin, Saint-Pol, "ne jouit jamais, contraire-
    ment à Charles du Maine et à Jacques d'Armagnac, de la faveur du roi qui
    voulut seulement essayer de le gagner pour ce qu'il représentait" (Gaus-
    sin, *Louis XI: un roi entre deux mondes*, 123).

40 de Roye, *Chronique scandaleuse*, 1:250–1, gives a date of December 1470; Blanchard (*Mémoires* [TLF, 2007], 2:1032) prefers January 1471.

41 *Mémoires* (TLF, 2007), 177; cf. de Roye, *Chronique scandaleuse*, 1:307, 312–13.

42 As presented above, this in-between situation explains the efficacy behind Saint-Pol's strategy of nurturing discord between the two: catching him requires that they cooperate.

43 Pozzi, "Paradigme du traître," 11.

44 My purpose in highlighting this "knowing without knowing" is to emphasize the continuity between Commynes's narration and contemporary theoretical approaches to the trauma of historical witness. Commynes's portrayal of Saint-Pol is disjunctive, symptomatic, and unknowing. The "work" of transformation in Commynes's retelling dramatizes the anxieties within Commynes's own subject position.

45 "Procès de Saint-Pol," 119. He was right: see Molinet, *Chroniques*, 1:131.

46 "Procès de Saint-Pol," 72–3.

47 The observation is made by Mattéoni, "Couronne en forme sphérique ne se peut diviser sans perdre sa figure," 158.

48 Ibid., 158, note 3. See the *Dictionnaire du Moyen Français*, s.v., défaire and détruire.

49 Caught and made to testify against the Duke of Nemours, Jean Richier, "l'instrument du double jeu de Saint-Pol," testified that he had pleaded with his master, "Monseigneur, vous m'avez fait jurer de vous loyaument servir, je le feray et si congnois bien que pour vous, moy, ma femme et enffans serons *destruictz*" ("Procès de Saint-Pol," 80, note 49).

50 The town in question is Bouvignes-sur-Meuse, in Belgium, not to be confused with the French Bouvines, where Philippe Auguste fought his famous battle of 1214. The terms agreed to at Bouvignes appear in the Treaty of Soleuvre. See Lenglet Dufresnoy, ed., *Mémoires* (1747), 3:422–6. On the unofficial networks between negotiators on both sides of this agreement, cf. *Mémoires* [TLF, 2007], 233, and "Procès de Saint-Pol," 165.

51 The detail is not exactly right; Louis XI seized Saint-Quentin for himself, although he ceded other lands belonging to Saint-Pol to Charles. As "inaccuracies" go, this particular slippage or condensation is an interesting one. Cuttler points out Commynes's mistake (*Law of Treason and Treason Trials*, 225).

52 "Procès de Saint-Pol," 76.

53 Ibid., 108.

54 Ibid., 104.

55 Cf. the reaction of Werner Paravicini, "Peur, pratiques, intelligences," 186.

56 Fargniers is now part of the commune of Tergnier, on the right bank of the Oise River, in the Aisne department. This meeting follows close after the king's negotiations at Bouvignes.

57 "Procès de Saint-Pol," 127. It is not entirely clear how involved Charles himself was in this plan.

58 *Dictionnaire du Moyen Français*, s.v. nager, cf. s.v. naviguer. A search of "locutions" using the term "entre deux" produces the best results. The entry for "naviguer" does not include any of the expressions cited. The slippage from nager to noer [noyer] is aural, based on their crossed historical phonologies; the words are not strictly homonyms; see the *Dictionnaire du Moyen Français*, s.v. noyer^2.

59 See Fierville, *La Ferme du sel aux Ponts-de-Cé et la galéasse Notre-Dame*; La Fontenelle de Vaudoré, *Philippe de Comyne en Poitou*; Rigaud, "'Une galeasse qui estoit myenne'"; and Spont, *La marine française sous le règne de Charles VIII, 1483–1493*, 57–8 and 66.

60 See Roques, "Le Vent dans les locutions et expressions médiévales françaises," 187, note 7, and 191–3.

61 "Procès de Saint-Pol," 124–5.

62 Louis XI succeeds in laying his hands on Saint-Pol because he destroys Saint-Quentin (September 1475), thus undercutting either Edward IV or Charles's motivation for protecting the *connétable*.

63 "Procès de Saint-Pol," 115.

64 Ibid., 116.

65 Ibid., 105. See also Paravicini, "Peurs, pratiques, intelligences," 188–9, on the logistics of escaping Louis XI's kingdom, and on the parallel measures taken by Saint-Pol's co-conspirators. Saint-Pol's wife died in childbirth "au plus fort de la crise" (Paravicini, "Peurs, pratiques, intelligences," 188, note 5).

66 Sainte-Beuve, thinking of Commynes's "escape" from the increasingly violent Charles, answered that "Commynes était de ce petit nombre qui savent saisir l'heure et le moment" (Sainte-Beuve, *Causeries du lundi*, 252). This was not entirely true: Commynes thought about fleeing to Italy during the debacle of his conflicts with the Beaujeu regency, but after inquiries with Lorenzo de Medici, was not able to face a second exile.

7 The Voice in the Text

1 Commynes's possession of Dreux (now in the department of Eure-et-Loir) was the result of a web of complex financial transactions with Alain d'Albret. See Blanchard, *Philippe de Commynes*, especially 209–10 and

359–62; Rahlenbeck, "Philippe de Commines dans ses rapports avec la maison d'Albret."

2 Dupont, ed., *Mémoires*, 3:141–3.

3 "Commynes has two conceptions of time. There are moments in his chronicle (as in any) when time is a unit of measure … But linear time is but an analogous, imperfect reflection of real time … Commynian time, in this second sense, is consciousness of self-duration and self-identity through the continuity of past experience … Time, then, is not a juxtaposition but a fusion of interior states" (Archambault, "Commynes, History as Lost Innocence," 105).

4 Cf. "My effort has been, in each case, to reach that level of analysis at which a persistent textual organization is revealed, whose coherence throws into jeopardy the apparent intentions of the author and expropriates him in an intertextual circuit of relations" (Mehlman, *A Structural Study of Autobiography*, 14).

5 Dufournet, "Philippe de Commynes et l'écriture du juste milieu," 128. Increasingly oriented towards legal history, Joël Blanchard's most recent work has nonetheless paid greater heed to affective and performative facets of Commynes's relation to Louis XI. See Blanchard, "De l'oralité à l'écriture chez Commynes."

6 Nantes, Musée Dobrée, ms. 18. This is the manuscript used by Calmette and Durville, eds., *Mémoires* (1924–5).

7 For a consideration of public and private "spaces," see Melville and von Moos, *Das Öffentliche und Private in der Vormoderne*. Hermann Kamp's study of Commynes in that collection refers primarily to performance and secrecy in the realm of diplomacy ("Philippe de Commynes und der Umgang mit der Öffentlichkeit in der Politik seiner Zeit," 687–716); editor Peter von Moos's "Vorbemerkungen" pertinently outlines the difficulties posed by these concepts for studies of the fifteenth century.

8 The archbishopric of Vienne has its see in the modern-day Isère department; it is now part of the archdiocese of Lyon. On Angelo Cato, see especially Armstrong, introduction to *The Usurpation of Richard the Third*; Croce, "Il personaggio italiano che esortò il Commynes a scrivere i 'Mémoires'"; and Dufournet, "Angelo Cato et les *Mémoires* de Commynes."

9 For an introduction to the prologue in late medieval historiography, see Marchello-Nizia, "L'Historien et son prologue." Dufournet, *Destruction des mythes*, 14–20, usefully surveys the rhetorical tropes invoked by Commynes's closest contemporaries.

10 Cf. The lesson "et," in lieu of "ne," is more common.

11 Cato passed away in March 1496. His death did not, however, put an end to Commynes's writing. For a glimpse at Cato's sense of the public literary

space created by the printing press, see E. Armstrong, *Before Copyright*, 55. On Cato as patron, see C.A.J. Armstrong, *The Usurpation of Richard the Third*.

12 See Gaussin, "Les conseillers de Louis XI (1461–1483)."

13 "Immédiatement, nous voyons que la chronologie historique est dépendante de la chronologie personnelle de Commynes" (Florentin, "Le Temps dans les *Mémoires* de Philippe de Commynes," 32).

14 Froissart, whose chronicle featured in Commynes's library, used the scenario of riding alongside his sources, royal or otherwise, as a fictionalized set-piece through which to portray himself as investigative reporter turned royal confidant. Throughout the *Mémoires* Commynes describes horses with a keen descriptive eye. Horses, like dogs and falcons, were frequent gifts in the circulation of favours between courts. See Commynes, *Lettres*, ed. Blanchard, 100–1.

15 Barros, *Autobiography: Narrative of Transformation*, 1.

16 This identification of a "half-way point" is based on the view of Books I–VI as a coherent and complete unit. Commynes's laconic, "envyron ce temps, je vins au service du Roy (et fut l'an mil cccclxxii)" (226) comes in the eleventh chapter of Book III.

17 Barros, *Autobiography: Narrative of Transformation*, 2.

18 Could Commynes have known Cicero's *De amicitia*? Would he have allowed himself to think consciously of Louis XI as his friend?

19 Joinville writes of Saint Louis's life as the cumulative product of his deeds and words (his 'faits et dits'). In contrast, the descriptive title "mémoires" grasps all that is inalienably subjective, personal, and interior to the speaking subject. Moreover, while Joinville's subject sought saintliness in his own and others' eyes, Commynes begins by saying that kings are men like others, prone to at least as many flaws as non-kings ("En luy [Louis XI] et tous aultres princes que j'ay congneuz ou servis, ay congneu du bien et du mal, car ilz sont hommes comme nous: a Dieu seul appartient la perfection [1]). Cf. my discussion of genre and Commynes's literary models in the Introduction to this book.

20 Boureau, *Le Simple corps du roi*, 60. The most comprehensive historical study of Louis XI's death is Paravicini, "Sterben und Tod Ludwigs XI." Paravicini examines Commynes's account of this death in comparison with available archival evidence; he also includes an exhaustive bibliography of particular use for evidence of Louis XI's diplomatic, patronage, and collecting activities during the final years of his life. For a more literary consideration of death as a theme in fifteenth- and sixteenth-century historiography, see Tenenti, "Il significato della morte nella storia fra

Commynes e Guicciardini." Compare, more broadly, Kantorowicz, *The King's Two Bodies*, and Giesey, *The Royal Funeral Ceremony in Renaissance France*.

21 Although the expression is associated with Virginia Woolf, I use the phrase in a distinct sense. I do not intend any reference to a fusion between the self and other human beings or the natural universe, but rather use the expression to describe moments of intense consciousness, whether of self, of the material world, or of the relations between the self and others, marked in the text by abruptly heightened narrative density.

22 The Sainte Ampoule, of course, symbolizes the eternity of the French Crown – not the man who wears it! A lust for immortality would be very problematic from the perspective of Christian doctrine, but the impression given by the *Mémoires* is precisely that Louis XI wants to forestall death indefinitely. See also Paravicini, "[D]er König nicht oder kaum für das Seelenheil nach dem Tode stiftete, sondern für das Überleben in dieser Welt" ("Sterben und Tod Ludwigs XI," 96).

23 See also Laplanche, *Vie et mort en psychanalyse*, 60, on the "circonstance contingente de l'événement traumatique … qui … est demeurée dans la mémoire à titre de symptôme ou de 'symbole' de la scène première."

24 Historians have produced a substantial bouquet of medical diagnoses for the ailments that afflicted Louis XI during the last years of his life. Thomas Basin accuses the king of being stricken with leprosy! See Brachet, *Pathologie mentale des rois de France*; Dufournet, *Destruction des mythes*, 252–6; Paravicini, "Sterben und Tod Ludwigs XI," 109.

25 Other scenes that fall into this category include the close-up of Charles the Bold pacing from pent-up rage at Péronne (134; see my chapter 1) or Mary of Burgundy's humiliation at court during the negotiations that followed her father's death (391–7, especially 392; see my chapter 5).

26 A word is missing from the Polignac manuscript. The Dobrée manuscript reads, "luy vint comme une perclusion"; Bibliothèque nationale de France, ms. fr. 3879 and the lost manuscript "M" both read "percucion." There has been some debate over the probable date of this first attack. See Kendall, *The Universal Spider*, appendix III (unpaginated), and *Mémoires* (TLF, 2007), 2:1155.

27 In contrast, the *Mémoires* place the king's second attack after a military inspection at Pont l'Arche. Commynes and the others present immediately commend the king to Saint Claude, and immediately the king can again speak and rise. "Et s'en retourna a Tours, auquel lieu luy reprint sa maladie, et de rechief perdit la parolle, et fut quelque deux heures qu'on

cuydoit qu'il fust mort; et estoit en une gallerye couché sur une paillasse, et plusieurs avecques luy. Monsr du Bouchaige et moy le vouasmes a monseigneur sainct Claude; et tous les aultres qui estoient presens luy vouerent aussi. Incontinent la parole luy revint, et sur l'heure alla par la maison, tres foible: et fut ceste seconde maladie l'an mil cccc iiii^xx et ung" (*Mémoires* [TLF, 2007], 465). After this attack, "alloyt par pays comme devant, et alla chez moy, a Argenton, ou il fut ung moys, et y fut fort malade" (*Mémoires* [TLF, 2007], 465).

28 "Chez Commynes, l'emploi du sujet inverti, devenu facultatif dès le début du XIVe siècle, peut être considéré surtout comme un trait de style. Chez lui, le tour inverti s'emploie pour des raisons esthétiques, pour garder l'équilibre dans la phrase. Quoique la prépondérence de l'ordre S-V soit évidente dans nos matériaux tirés des *Mémoires*, c'est justement l'emploi de l'ordre V-S qui enrichit le récit d'une manière effective" (Piiparinen and Suvanto, "Aspects de l'ordre des mots en moyen français," 78). This "effective" enrichment is most often "affective."

29 Barros underscores the importance of the narratee to the three-pointed narrative contract that transforms speech into autobiography: "Autobiography involves telling someone else about something that happened to me" (Barros, *Autobiography: Narrative of Transformation*, 6). Addresses to Cato appear on ten occasions in the *Mémoires*. In each instance Commynes uses the second person, although rhetorically the remarks directed to Cato are quite diverse. Three offer metacommentaries on the narration intended for Cato and three relate to Cato's familiarity with events or his observations concerning them. A further four refer to Cato's participatory role in the subjects of Commynes's account.

30 Dupont, ed., *Mémoires*, 3:142–3.

31 See Basin, *Histoire de Louis XI*, 3:308. Such "allégations venimeuses" are "parfaitement déplaisants, quand par exemple on voit tourner en ridicule certains gestes mal assurés que la maladie imposait au vieillard malade: aberration que la haine elle-même n'excuse pas et qui ne fait pas honneur à la charité chrétienne d'un prélat," wrote Basin's own translator in his introduction to the work (Charles Samaran, introduction to Basin, *Histoire de Louis XI*, 1:xxi).

32 Consider Commynes's description, first seen in chapter 5, of how he read the king's letters to him: "Et vouloit veoir les lectres closes qui estoient arriveez et qui arrivoient chascune heure. L'on luy monstroit les principalles et je les luy lisois. Il faisoit semblent de les entendre, et les prenoit en sa main et faisoit semblant de les lire, combien qu'il n'eust nulle congnoissance" (He wanted to see the closed letters which had arrived and which

were arriving by the hour. They showed him the most important ones and I read them to him; he pretended to understand them, and he took them in his hand and pretended to read, even though he had no capacity to do so [*Mémoires* (TLF, 2007), 464]).

33 Cf. Blanchard, "Au moment de sa mort le roi est <maistrié>, sans recours, et la peur est la marque d'un pouvoir qui lui échappe" ("Commynes et la nouvelle histoire," 295).

34 Laplanche and Pontalis, *Vocabulaire de la psychanalyse*, 121; s.v. *désir / wish / Wunsch*, sometimes *Begierde* or *Lust*.

35 White, *The Birth and Rebirth of Pictorial Space*, 35.

Selected Bibliography

Manuscripts

The Hague
Koninklijke Bibliotheek, KB 76 E 13. "Le Séjour de deuil pour la mort de Philippe de Commines."

London
British Library, Harley 2863. Book of Hours commissioned by Commynes from workshop of Fouquet.
British Library, Harley 4374 and 4375. Valerius Maximus from Commynes's library.
British Library, Harley 4379 and 4380. Book IV of Froissart's *Chroniques* from Commynes's library.

Nantes
Musée Dobrée, ms. 18. "Dobrée" manuscript of the *Mémoires*.

Paris
Bibliothèque nationale de France, ms. fr. 3869. Treason trial of Louis de Luxembourg, copy having belonged to Chancellor Doriole.
Bibliothèque nationale de France, ms. fr. 5727. Letter-writing protocol book from the reign of Louis XI.
Bibliothèque nationale de France, ms. lat. 1417. Book of Hours commissioned by Commynes from the workshop of Fouquet.
Bibliothèque nationale de France, ms. n.a.f. 20960. "Polignac" manuscript of the *Mémoires*.

Bibliothèque Sainte-Geneviève, ms. 2000. Treason trial of Jacques d'Armagnac, Duke of Nemours.

Major Editions of Commynes's *Mémoires*

Commynes, Philippe de. *Cronique & hystoire ... par feu Messire Phelippe de Co[m] mines chevalier, seigneur Dargenton.* Paris: Galliot du Pré, 1524.
– *Croniques du roy Charles huytiesme de ce nom ...* Paris: Enguilbert de Marnef, 1528.
– *Chronicque et histoire ... contenant les choses advenues durant le règne du roy Loys unziesme ... Chronicques du roy Charles huytiesme ...* Paris: A. Langellier, 1539.
– *La Historia famosa de monsignor di Argenton delle guerre & costumi di Ludovico undecimo re di Francia: con la battaglia et morte del gran duca di Borgogna.* Translated by Nicolas Raince. Venice: Michel Tramezino, 1544.
– *De rebus gestis Ludovici, eius nominis Undecimi.* Translated by Johann Sleidan. Strasbourg: Cratonem Mylium, 1545.
– *De Carolo Octavo Galliae rege, & bello Neapolitano, commentarii.* Translated by Johann Sleidan. Strasbourg: Iosias Rihelius, 1548.
– *Les Mémoires de Messire Philippe de Commines, chevalier ...* Edited by Denis Sauvage. Paris: Galliot du Pré, 1552.
– *Les Mémoires de Messire Philippe de Commines, seigneur d'Argenton ...* Edited by Denys Godefroy. Paris: Imprimerie nationale, 1649.
– *Mémoires de messire Philippe de Comines, seigneur d'Argenton.* Edited by Nicolas Lenglet Dufresnoy. 4 vols. Paris, 1747.
– *Mémoires de Philippe de Commynes.* Edited by L.M. Emille Dupont. 3 vols. Paris: J. Renouard for the Société de l'Histoire de France [SHF], 1840–7.
– *Mémoires de Philippe de Commynes.* Edited by Bernard de Mandrot. 2 vols. Paris: Alphonse Picard et fils, 1901–3.
– *Mémoires.* Edited by Joseph Calmette and Georges Durville. 3 vols. Paris: Classiques de l'Histoire de France au Moyen Age [CHFMA], 1924–5.
– *The Memoirs of Philippe de Commynes.* Translated by Isabelle Cazeaux. Edited by Samuel Kinser. 2 vols. Columbia, SC: University of South Carolina Press, 1969–73.
– *Memoirs: The Reign of Louis XI, 1461–83.* Translated by Michael Jones. Harmondsworth: Penguin Books, 1972.
– *Mémoires sur Louis XI: 1464–1483.* Edited by Jean Dufournet. Paris: Gallimard, 1979.
– *Mémoires.* Edited by Joël Blanchard. 2 vols. Textes Littéraires Français [TLF]. Geneva: Droz, 2007.

Published Archival Sources by and about Commynes

Barbaud, Gabriel. "Notice sur Philippe de Commines et la Principauté de Talmont." *Bulletin du Comité des Travaux Historiques* 1–2 (1900): 49–65.

Benoist, Edmond. *Les Lettres de Philippe de Commynes aux archives de Florence.* Lyon: Léon Perrin, 1863. Reprint, Geneva: Slatkine, 1972.

Blanchard, Joël. *Commynes et les italiens: lettres inédites du mémorialiste.* Paris: Klincksieck, 1993.

Commynes, Philippe de. *Lettres.* Edited by Joël Blanchard. Geneva: Droz, 2001.

Dupont, L.M. Emille. *Notice sur Philippe de Commynes.* Paris: SHF, 1847. Most often bound with volume 1 of Dupont's edition of the *Mémoires.*

Fierville, Charles. "Documents inédits." *Recueil des publications de la Société havraise d'études diverses* 29 (1878): 417–41.

– *Documents inédits sur Philippe de Commynes.* Paris, 1881. 2nd ed. Le Havre, 1890. Reprint, Geneva, 1972.

– *La Ferme du sel aux Ponts-de-Cé et la galéasse Notre-Dame.* Offprint, in 8°. Le Havre, 1879.

Fillon, Benjamin. "Documents inédits sur Ph. de Commynes." *Revue des provinces de l'Ouest (Nantes)* 4 (1856): 160–9.

La Fontenelle de Vaudoré, Armand-Désiré de. *Philippe de Comyne en Poitou: notice lue à la 3e session du congrès scientifique de France, tenue à Douai en septembre 1835.* Paris: Lance, 1836.

Gachard, Louis Prosper. *Particularités et documents inédits sur Commines, Charles le Téméraire et Charles-Quint.* Brussels: Wouters, 1842.

Kervyn de Lettenhove, Joseph Marie Bruno Constantin. *Lettres et négociations de Philippe de Commines.* 3 vols. Brussels: Victor Devaux et Cie., 1867–74. Reprint, Geneva: Slatkine, 1972.

Sozzi, Lionello. "Lettere inedite di Commynes a Francesco Gaddi." *Studi di bibliografia e di storia in onore di Tammaro de Marinis,* 4:205–62. Verona: Stamperia Valdonega, 1964.

Further Primary Sources

Armstrong, C.A.J., ed. and trans. *The Usurpation of Richard the Third: Dominicus Mancinus ad Angelum Catonem, De occupatione regni Anglie per Ricardum Tercium libellus.* 2nd ed. Oxford: Clarendon Press, 1969.

Basin, Thomas. *Apologie, ou Plaidoyer pour moi-même.* Edited and translated by Charles Samaran and Georgette de Groër. CHFMA. Paris: Les Belles Lettres, 1974.

– *Histoire de Louis XI.* Edited and translated by Charles Samaran and M.-C. Garand. 3 vols. CHFMA. Paris: Les Belles Lettres, 1963–72.

Bernier, A., ed. *Procès-verbaux des séances du Conseil de régence du roi Charles VIII pendant les mois d'août 1484 à janvier 1485.* Paris: Imprimerie Royale, 1836.

Berridge, Geoff R., ed. *Diplomatic Classics: Selected Texts from Commynes to Vattel.* Studies in Diplomacy and International Relations. Houndmills, UK, and New York: Palgrave Macmillan, 2004.

Bodin, Jean. *Method for the Easy Comprehension of History.* Translated by Beatrice Reynolds. New York: Columbia University Press, 1945.

– *Methodus ad facilem historiarum cognitionem.* Paris: Martinum Iuvenum, 1566.

– *On Sovereignty: Four Chapters from the Six Books of the Commonwealth.* Edited and translated by Julian H. Franklin. Cambridge: Cambridge University Press, 1992.

– *Les six livres de la République.* Paris: Iacques du Puys, 1576.

Brion-Guerry, Liliane. *Jean Pélerin Viator: sa place dans l'histoire de la perspective.* Paris: Les Belles Lettres, 1962.

Buchon, J.A.C., ed. *Choix de chroniques et mémoires sur l'histoire de France, avec notices biographiques.* Paris: A. Desrez, 1836.

Carruthers, Mary J., and Jan M. Ziolkowski, eds. *The Medieval Craft of Memory: An Anthology of Texts and Pictures.* Philadelphia: University of Pennsylvania Press, 2002.

Cazelles, Raymond, ed. *Lettres closes: lettres "de par le roy" de Philippe de Valois.* Paris: SHF, 1958.

Chastellain, Georges. *Oeuvres de Georges Chastellain.* Edited by Joseph Marie Bruno Constantin Kervyn de Lettenhove. 8 vols. Brussels: F. Heussner, 1863–6.

Cimber, Louis Lefaist, ed. *Archives curieuses de l'histoire de France depuis Louis XI jusqu'à Louis XVIII.* Vol. 1. First series. Paris, 1834.

De But, Adrien. *Chronique.* In *Chroniques relatives à l'histoire de la Belgique sous la domination des ducs de Bourgogne,* also called *Livre des trahisons,* edited by Joseph Marie Bruno Constantin Kervyn de Lettenhove, 1:211–717. Brussels: F. Hayez, Imprimeur de l'Académie Royale de Belgique, 1870.

De Roye, Jean. *Chronique, connu sous le nom de Chronique scandaleuse (1460–1483).* Edited by Bernard de Mandrot. 2 vols. SHF. Paris: Librairie Renouard, 1894 and 1896.

Desjardins, Abel, ed. *Négociations diplomatiques de la France avec la Toscane.* 6 vols. Vols 1, 2. Paris: Imprimerie Nationale, 1859, 1861.

Dubois, Henri, ed. *Louis XI, Lettres choisies.* Lettres Gothiques. Paris: Librairie Générale Française, 1996.

Emilio, Paolo. *De rebus gestis Francorum.* Paris, c. 1516–39.

Gentillet, Innocent. *Anti-Machiavel, Edition de 1576*. Edited by C.E. Rathé. Geneva: Droz, 1968.

– *Discours sur les moyens de bien gouverner ... contre Nicolas Machiavel*. n.p., 1576.

Godefroy, Théodore, ed. *Histoire de Charles VIII, roy de France, par Guillaume de Jaligny, André de la Vigne, et autres historiens de ce temps-là*. Paris: Imprimerie Royale, 1684.

Joinville, Jean de. *Vie de Saint Louis*. Edited by J. Monfrin. Paris: Classiques Garnier, 1995. Reprint, Lettres Gothiques. Paris: Librairie Générale Française, 2002.

Kendall, Paul Murray, and Vincent Ilardi, eds. *Dispatches with Related Documents of Milanese Ambassadors in France and Burgundy, 1450–83*. 3 vols. Vols 1–2, Athens, OH: Ohio State University Press, 1970–1; Vol. 3, Dekalb, IL: Northern Illinois University Press, 1981.

Kervyn de Lettenhove, Joseph Marie Bruno Constantin, ed. *Chroniques relatives à l'histoire de la Belgique sous la domination des ducs de Bourgogne*, also called *Livre des trahisons*. 3 vols. Brussels: F. Hayez, Imprimeur de l'Académie Royale de Belgique, 1870–6.

La Marche, Olivier de. *Mémoires*. Edited by Henri Beaune and Jules d'Arbaumont. 4 vols. SHF. Paris: Librairie Renouard, 1883–8.

La Trémoïlle, Louis de. *Archives d'un serviteur de Louis XI: Documents et lettres, 1451–1481, publiés d'après les originaux par Louis de La Trémoïlle*. Nantes: Emile Grimaud, 1888. Reprint, Geneva: Mégariotis, 1978.

– *Correspondance de Charles VIII et de ses conseillers avec Louis II de La Trémoïlle pendant la guerre de Bretagne (1488)*. Paris, 1875. Reprint, Geneva: Mégariotis, 1978.

– ed. *Les La Trémoïlle pendant cinq siècles*. 5 vols. Vol. 2. Nantes: Emile Grimaud, 1892.

Le Roux de Lincy, Antoine Jean Victor. *Chants historiques et populaires du temps de Charles VII et de Louis XI*. Paris: Aug. Aubry Libraire, 1857.

Mandrot, Bernard de, and Charles Samaran, eds. *Dépêches des ambassadeurs milanais en France sous Louis XI et François Sforza*. 4 vols. SHF. Paris: Librairie Renouard, 1916–23.

Marchal, Laurent, ed. *La Chronique de Lorraine*. Recueil de documents sur l'histoire de Lorraine. Nancy: Wiener, aîné et fils, libraires, 1859 [1860].

Marchant, Jacques. *Flandria commentariorum lib. IIII descripta*. Antwerp: Ex officina Plantiniana, 1596.

Masselin, Jehan. *Journal des États-Généraux de France tenus à Tours en 1484 sous le règne de Charles VIII*. Edited and translated from the Latin by A. Bernier. Paris: Imprimerie Royale, 1835.

Matthieu, Pierre. *Histoire de Louys XI roy de France et des choses memorables adve-nuës en l'Europe durant vingt & deux années de son regne.* Paris: Matthieu Guil-lemot, 1628. (First edition Paris: P. Mettayer, 1610.)

Meyer, Jacques. *Commentarii sive Annales rerum Flandricarum.* Antwerp: Ioannis Steelsii, 1561.

Molinet, Jean. *Chroniques.* Edited by George Doutrepont and Omer Jodogne. 3 vols. Brussels: Palais des Académies, 1935–7.

Naudé, Gabriel. *Addition à l'histoire de Louis XI.* Paris: Fayard, 1999.

– *Considérations politiques sur les coups d'état.* Paris: Les Editions de Paris, 1989.

Pastoret, Claude Emmanuel J.P. de, ed. *Ordonnances des rois de France de la troisième race, recueillies par ordre chronologique.* Vols 18–20. Paris: Imprimerie Royale, 1828–40.

Périnelle, Georges. "Un Texte officiel sur l'exécution du connétable de Saint-Pol." *Mélanges d'archéologie et d'histoire de l'Ecole française de Rome* 23 (1903): 427–32.

Poncelet, Edouard. "L'Exécution de Louis de Luxembourg, comte de Saint-Pol, en 1475." *Bulletin de la Commission royale d'histoire* 91 (1927): 181–98.

Saint-Gelais, Jean. *Histoire de Louys XII, roy de France ...* Edited by Theodore Godefroy. Paris: A. Pacard, 1622.

Samaran, Charles. *Archives de la maison de La Trémoïlle (chartriers de Thouars et de Serrant, papiers Duchâtel).* Paris: Champion, 1928.

Samaran, Charles, and Lucie Favier. "Louis XI and Jacques d'Armagnac, duc de Nemours: Les Instructions secrètes du roi au chancelier Pierre Doriole pour la conduite du procès." *Journal des Savants* (1966): 65–77.

Stein, Henri, and Sonja Dünnebeil, eds. *Catalogue des actes de Charles le Témé-raire (1467–1477).* Sigmaringen, Germany: Jan Thorebecke, 1999.

Störmer-Caysa, Uta, ed. *Über das Gewissen: Texte zur Begründung der neuzeitli-chen Subjektivität.* Weinheim, Germany: Beltz Athenäum, 1995.

Tyson, D.B. "A Newly Discovered Poem on the Death of Louis de Luxem-bourg (1475)." *Nottingham Medieval Studies* 49 (2005): 125–41.

Vaesen, Joseph, Etienne Charavay, and Bernard de Mandrot, eds. *Lettres de Louis XI, roi de France.* 11 vols. SHF. Paris: Librairie Renouard, 1883–1909.

Secondary and Critical Works

Allemand, Marie-Thérèse. "La Réversion du duché de Bourgogne au royaume de France, vue à travers des mémoires contemporains." In *Cinq-centième an-niversaire de la Bataille de Nancy (1477)*, 207–35.

Allmand, Christopher, ed. *Power, Culture, and Religion in France c. 1350–c. 1550.* Woodbridge, UK: Boydell, 1989.

– *War, Government and Power in Late Medieval France*. Liverpool: Liverpool University Press, 2000.

Althoff, Gerd, Johannes Fried, and Patrick J. Geary, eds. *Medieval Concepts of the Past: Ritual, Memory, Historiography*. Cambridge and New York: Cambridge University Press, 2002.

Anderson, Matthew Smith. *The Rise of Modern Diplomacy 1450–1919*. London and New York: Longman, 1993.

Archambault, Paul. "The Analogy of the 'Body' in Renaissance Political Literature." *Bibliothèque d'Humanisme et de la Renaissance* 29 (1967): 21–53.

– "Commynes: History as Lost Innocence." In *Witnesses to History: Seven French Chroniclers*, 101–15. Syracuse, NY: Syracuse University Press, 1974.

– "Commynes's *Saigesse* and the Renaissance Idea of Wisdom." *Bibliothèque d'Humanisme et de la Renaissance* 29 (1967): 613–32.

– "History as Entropy in Commynes' *Mémoires*." *Symposium* 27 (1973): 5–18.

– "The *Mémoires* of Commynes as a Manual of Political Philosophy." PhD thesis, Yale University, 1964.

– "Thucydides in France: The Notion of Justice in the *Mémoires* of Philippe de Commynes." *Journal of the History of Ideas* 28, no. 1 (1967): 89–98.

Archibald, Elizabeth. *Incest and the Medieval Imagination*. Oxford: Oxford University Press, 2001.

Armstrong, C.A.J. "Some Examples of the Distribution and Speed of News in England at the Time of the Wars of the Roses." In *England, France and Burgundy in the Fifteenth Century*, 97–122. London: Hambledon Press, 1983.

Armstrong, Elizabeth. *Before Copyright: The French Book-Privilege System 1498–1526*. Cambridge: Cambridge University Press, 1990.

Arthurson, Ian. "Espionage and Intelligence from the Wars of the Roses to the Reformation." *Nottingham Medieval Studies* 35 (1991): 134–54.

Aubert, Félix. *Histoire du Parlement de Paris de l'origine à François Ier 1250–1515*. 2 vols. Paris: A. Picard et fils, 1894.

Austin, J.L. *How To Do Things with Words*. Cambridge, MA: Harvard University Press, 1962.

Autrand, Françoise, Claude Gauvard, and Jean-Marie Moeglin, eds. *Saint-Denis et la Royauté: études offertes à Bernard Guenée*. Paris: Publications de la Sorbonne, 1999.

Baer, Leo, and Georg Swarzenski. "Philippe de Comynes and the Painter Jean Foucquet." *The Burlington Magazine for Connoisseurs* 25, no. 133 (April 1914): 40–59.

Bakos, Adrianna. *Images of Kingship in Early Modern France: Louis XI in Political Thought 1560–1789*. London and New York: Routledge, 1997.

Barros, Carolyn A. *Autobiography: Narrative of Transformation*. Ann Arbor: University of Michigan Press, 1998.

Baumann, Heidrun. *Der Geschichtsschreiber Philippe de Commynes und die Wirkung seiner politischen Vorstellungen in Frankreich um die Mitte des 16. Jahrhunderts*. Munich: Minerva, 1981.

Bayer, Hans. "Zur Soziologie des mittelalterlichen Individualisierungsprozesses." *Archiv für Kulturgeschichte* 58 (1976): 115–53.

Beaulieu, Michèle. "Note sur la chapelle funéraire de Philippe de Commines au couvent des Grands Augustins de Paris." *Revue du Louvre* 16, no. 2 (1966): 65–76.

Bec, Christian. *Les Marchands écrivains: affaires et humanisme à Florence (1375–1434)*. Paris, La Haye: Mouton, 1967.

Bedford, Ronald, Lloyd Davis, and Philippa Kelly, eds. *Early Modern Autobiography: Theories, Genres, Practices*. Ann Arbor: University of Michigan Press, 2006.

Bedos-Rezak, Brigitte Miriam. *When Ego Was Imago: Signs of Identity in the Middle Ages*. Leiden and Boston: Brill, c. 2011.

Bellamy, J.G. *Bastard Feudalism and the Law*. London: Routledge, 1989.

– *The Law of Treason in England in the Later Middle Ages*. Cambridge: Cambridge University Press, 1970.

Bercé, Yves-Marie, ed. *Les Procès politiques (XIVe–XVIIe siècle)*. Rome: Ecole française de Rome, 2007.

Beugnot, Bernard. "De l'invention épistolaire: à la manière de soi." In *L'Epistolarité à travers les siècles: Geste de communication et/ou d'écriture*, ed. Bossis, 27–38.

Billoré, Maïté, and Myriam Soria, eds. *La Trahison au Moyen Age: de la monstruosité au crime politique (V^e–XVe siècle)*. Rennes: Presses universitaires de Rennes, 2009.

Billot, Claudine. "L'Assimilation des étrangers dans le royaume de France aux XIVe et XVe siècles." *Revue historique* 270, no. 2 [548] (1983): 273–96.

Bittmann, Karl. *Ludwig XI und Karl der Kühne: die Memoiren des Philippe de Commynes als historische Quelle*. 3 vols. Göttingen: Vandenhoeck & Ruprecht, 1964–70.

Blanchard, Joël. "Argenton haut lieu de la diplomatie commynienne: une lettre inédite de Commynes." *Bulletin de la Société historique et scientifique des Deux-Sèvres*, 3rd series, 6 (1998): 391–401.

– "Commynes et la nouvelle histoire." *Poétique* 79 (1989): 286–98.

– "Commynes et les princes rebelles (1484–1487): documents inédits." *Bulletin de la Société historique et scientifique des Deux-Sèvres*, 3rd series, 8 (2000 [published 2003]): 208–21.

– *Commynes et les procès politiques de Louis XI: du nouveau sur la lèse-majesté.* Paris: Picard, 2008.
– "Commynes le diplomate: 'archéologie' d'une formation intellectuelle." In *Miscellanea Mediaevalia, mélanges offerts à Philippe Ménard*, ed. J. Claude Faucon, Alain Labbé, and Danielle Quéruel, 1:147–59. Paris: Champion, 1998.
– *Commynes l'Européen: l'invention du politique.* Geneva: Droz, 1996.
– "Commynes n'a pas 'trahi': pour en finir avec une obsession critique." *Revue du Nord* 91, no. 380 (2009): 327–60.
– "Commynes on Kingship." In *War, Government and Power in Late Medieval France*, ed. Allmand, 106–23.
– "Le corps du roi: mélancolie et 'recreation': implications médicales et culturelles du loisir des princes à la fin du Moyen Age." In *Représentation, pouvoir et royauté à la fin du Moyen Age*, ed. Blanchard, 199–214.
– "De l'oralité à l'écriture chez Commynes: nouvelles émotions et nouvelle communication?" In *Norm und Krise von Kommunikation. Inszenierungen literarischer und sozialer Interaktion im Mittelalter*, ed. Alois Hahn, Gert Melville, and Werner Röcke, 173–91. Münster: Lit, 2006.
– "The Dispersal of Power – New Relays, New Models." In *The Propagation of Power in the Medieval West*, ed. Martin Gosman, Arjo Vanderjagt, and Jan Veenstra, 383–403. Groningen: Egbert Forsten, 1997.
– "L'Histoire commynienne: pragmatique et mémoire dans l'ordre politique." *Annales. Histoire, Sciences Sociales* 46, no. 5 (1991): 1071–105.
– "Nouvelle histoire, nouveaux publics: les *mémoires* à la fin du Moyen Age." In *L'Histoire et les nouveaux publics dans l'Europe médiévale (XIIIe–XVe siècle)*, ed. Jean-Philippe Genet, 41–54. Paris: Publications de la Sorbonne, 1997.
– *Philippe de Commynes.* Paris: Fayard, 2006.
– ed. *Philippe de Commynes (1511–2011): droit, écriture, deux bâtisseurs de la souveraineté.* Geneva: Droz, c. 2011.
– "Political and Cultural Implications of Secret Diplomacy: Commynes and Ferrara in the Light of Unpublished Documents." In *The French Descent into Renaissance Italy 1494–95, Antecedents and Effects*, ed. David Abulafia, 231–47. Aldershot, UK: Variorum, 1995.
– ed. *Représentation, pouvoir et royauté à la fin du Moyen Age.* Paris: Picard, 1995.
– "Sémiologie du complot sous Louis XI: le procès de Jacques d'Armagnac, duc de Nemours." In *Le Crime de l'ombre: complots, conspirations et conjurations au Moyen Age*, ed. Corinne Leveleux-Texeira and Bernard Ribémont, 63–85: Paris: Klincksieck, 2010.
Blanchard, Joël, and Isabelle Pantin. "Les Débuts de la fortune éditoriale de Commynes: l'exemplaire annoté par Sleidan – les premières éditions des *Mémoires*." *Le Bulletin du bibliophile* 1 (1998): 37–60.

Bloch, R. Howard. *Etymologies and Genealogies: A Literary Anthropology of the French Middle Ages.* Chicago: University of Chicago Press, 1983.

Blockmans, Wim. "La Position du comté de Flandre dans le royaume à la fin du XVe siècle." In *La France de la fin du XVe siècle: renouveau et apogée,* ed. Chevalier and Contamine, 71–89.

Blondeau, Chrystèle. *Un conquérant pour quatre ducs: Alexandre le Grand à la cour de Bourgogne.* Paris: Comité des travaux historiques et scientifiques [CTHS] and Institut National d'histoire de l'Art, 2009.

Bois, Guy. *Crise du féodalisme: économie rurale et démographie en Normandie orientale du début du 14e siècle au milieu du 16e siècle.* Paris: Presses de la Fondation nationale des sciences politiques, 1976.

Boislisle, Arthur-Michel de. *Notice biographique et historique sur Etienne de Vesc, sénéchal de Beaucaire.* Nogent-le-Rotrou: Imprimerie de Daupeley-Gouverneur, 1884. Extracted from the *Annuaire-Bulletin de la Société de l'histoire de France.*

Boone, Marc. "Destroying and Reconstructing the City: The Inculcation and Arrogation of Princely Power in the Burgundian-Habsburg Netherlands (14th–16th centuries)." In *The Propagation of Power in the Medieval West,* ed. Martin Gosman, Arjo Vanderjagt, and Jan Veenstra, 1–33. Groningen: Egbert Forstein, 1997.

– "La Justice en spectacle: la Justice urbaine en Flandre et la crise du pouvoir 'bourguignon' (1477–1488)." *Revue historique* 305, no. 1 [625] (2003): 43–65.

– "Urban Space and Political Conflict in Late Medieval Flanders." *Journal of Interdisciplinary History* 32, no. 4 (2002): 621–40.

Bossis, Mireille, ed. *L'Epistolarité à travers les siècles: Geste de communication et/ou d'écriture.* Stuttgart: Franz Steiner, 1990.

Boudet, Jean-Patrice. "Faveur, pouvoir et solidarités sous le règne de Louis XI: Olivier le Daim et son entourage." *Journal des Savants* 4, no. 1 (1986): 219–57.

Bouineau, Jacques. "Jacques de Beaumont (vers 1426–1492), seigneur de Bressuire: du seigneur local à l'agent du roi." *Bulletin de la Société des antiquaires de l'Ouest,* 5th series, 1 (1987): 189–99.

Boureau, Alain. *Le Simple corps du roi: l'impossible sacralité des souverains français, XVe-XVIIIe siècle.* Paris: Les éditions de Paris, 1988.

– *De Vagues individus: la condition humaine dans la pensée scolastique.* Paris: Les Belles Lettres, 2008.

Bourrilly, V.L. "Les Idées politiques de Commynes." *Revue d'histoire moderne et contemporaine* 1 (1899): 93–123.

Bousmanne, Bernard, Tania van Hemelryck, and Céline van Hoorebeeck, eds. *La Librairie des ducs de Bourgogne: Manuscrits conservés à la bibliothèque royale de Belgique.* Turnhout: Brepols, 2000–c. 2009.

Bouwsma, William J. "The Politics of Commynes." *Journal of Modern History* 23, no. 4 (1951): 315–28.

Brachet, Auguste. *Pathologie mentale des rois de France: Louis XI et ses ascendants ...* Paris: Librairie Hachette, 1903.

Bratu, Mihai Cristian. "L'Emergence de l'auteur dans l'historiographie en prose en langue française." PhD dissertation, New York University, 2007.

Bridge, John S.C. *A History of France from the Death of Louis XI.* Vol. 1, *Reign of Charles VIII, Regency of Anne de Beaujeu, 1483–1493.* Oxford: Clarendon Press, 1921.

Bullough, Vern L., and James Brundage, eds. *Sexual Practices and the Medieval Church.* Buffalo, NY: Prometheus Books, 1982.

Bulst, Neithard. "Louis XI et les Etats Généraux de 1468." In *La France de la fin du XVe siècle: renouveau et apogée*, ed. Chevalier and Contamine, 91–104.

Bulst, Neithard, Robert Descimon, and Alain Guerreau, eds. *L'Etat ou le roi: les fondations de la modernité monarchique en France (XIVe–XVIIe siècles).* Paris: Maison des Sciences de l'Homme, 1996.

Burckhardt, Jacob. *The Civilization of the Renaissance in Italy.* Translated by S.C.G. Middlemore. Harmondsworth: Penguin, 1990.

Buridant, Claude. "L'Expression de la causalité chez Commynes." *Verbum* 9, no. 2 (1986): 141–212.

Burns, E. Jane "Raping Men: What's Motherhood Got to Do with It." In *Representing Rape in Medieval and Early Modern Literature*, ed. Elizabeth Robertson and Christine M. Rose, 127–60. New York: Palgrave, 2001.

Burns, J.H., ed. *The Cambridge History of Medieval Political Thought c. 350–c. 1450.* Cambridge: Cambridge University Press, 1988.

Burns, J.H., with Mark Goldie, eds. *The Cambridge History of Political Thought 1450–1700.* Cambridge and New York: Cambridge University Press, 1991.

Buser, B. *Die Beziehungen der Mediceer zu Frankreich während der Jahre 1434–1494.* Leipzig: von Duncker and Humblot, 1879.

Busse Berger, Anna Maria. *Medieval Music and the Art of Memory.* Berkeley: University of California Press, 2005.

Cagé, Carlos. "Louis de Luxembourg, comte de Saint-Pol, connétable de France (1418–1475)." *Positions des thèses de l'Ecole des Chartes* (1885): 29–41.

Calmette, Joseph. "Campobasso et Commynes." *Annales de Bourgogne* 7, no. 2 (1935): 172–6.

Carbonnières, Louis de. *La Procédure devant la Chambre criminelle du Parlement de Paris au XIVe siècle.* Paris: Champion, 2004.

Carruthers, Mary J. *The Book of Memory: A Study of Memory in Medieval Culture*. Cambridge and New York: Cambridge University Press, 2008.

Caruth, Cathy, ed. *Trauma: Explorations in Memory*. Baltimore and London: Johns Hopkins University Press, 1995.

– *Unclaimed Experience: Trauma, Narrative, and History*. Baltimore and London: Johns Hopkins University Press, 1996.

Cauchies, Jean-Marie "Baudouin de Bourgogne (v. 1446–1508), bâtard, militaire et diplomate: une carrière exemplaire ?" *Revue du Nord* 77, no. 310 (1995): 257–81.

– *Louis XI et Charles le Hardi. De Péronne à Nancy (1468–1477): Le Conflit*. Brussels: DeBoeck Université, 1996.

Cavaillé, Jean-Pierre, ed. *Dis/simulations … Religion, morale et politique au XVIIᵉ siècle*. Paris: Champion, 2002.

Certeau, Michel de. *Histoire et psychanalyse entre science et fiction*. Paris: Gallimard, 1987.

Chabaud, Frédérique. "Les 'Mémoires' de Philippe de Commynes: un 'miroir aux princes'?" *Francia: Forschungen zur westeuropäischen Geschichte* 19, no. 1: *Mittelalter – Moyen Age* (1992): 95–114.

Chambers, Ross. *Room for Maneuver: Reading (the) Oppositional (in) Narrative*. Chicago and London: University of Chicago Press, 1991.

Charlier, Gustave. *Commynes*. Collection Notre Passé. Brussels: La Renaissance du Livre, 1945.

Chevalier, Bernard, and Philippe Contamine, eds. *La France de la fin du XVᵉ siècle: renouveau et apogée*. Paris: Editions du CNRS, 1985.

Chiffoleau, Jacques. "Le Crime de majesté, la politique et l'extraordinaire: note sur les collections érudites de procès de lèse-majesté du XVIIᵉ siècle français et sur leurs exemples médiévaux." In *Les Procès politiques (XIVᵉ–XVIIᵉ siècle)*, ed. Bercé, 577–662.

– "Sur le crime de majesté médiéval." In *Genèse de l'État moderne en Méditerranée*, 183–213. Rome: Ecole française de Rome, 1993.

Cinq-centième anniversaire de la Bataille de Nancy (1477): Actes du colloque organisé par l'Institut de recherche régionale … de l'Université de Nancy II (Nancy, 22–24 septembre 1977). Annales de l'Est 62 (1979). Special issue.

Clark, Elizabeth A. *History, Theory, Text*. Cambridge, MA: Harvard University Press, 2004.

Cohen, Ralph. "History and Genre." *New Literary History* 17, no. 2, (1986): 203–18.

Coleman, Janet. *Ancient and Medieval Memories: Studies in the Reconstruction of the Past*. Cambridge and New York: Cambridge University Press, 1992.

– "The Individual and the Medieval State." In *The Individual in Political Theory and Practice*, ed. Janet Coleman, 1–34. New York: Oxford University Press, 1996.

Collard, Franck. "Les Découpages périodologiques dans l'historiographie française autour de 1500." In *Périodes: La Construction du temps historique. Actes du Ve colloque d'histoire au présent*, ed. Olivier Dumoulin and Raphaël Valéry, 81–9. Paris: Editions de l'Ecole des hautes études en sciences sociales, 1991.

– "Une oeuvre historiographique du règne de Charles VIII et sa réception: le *Compendium de origine et gestis Francorum* de Robert Gaguin." *Nouvelle Revue du Seizième siècle* 13, no. 1 (1995): 71–86.

Constable, Giles. *Letters and Letter-Collections*. Typologie des sources du Moyen Age Occidental 17. Turnhout: Brepols, 1976.

Contamine, Philippe. "Un Aspect de la 'tyrannie' de Louis XI: variations sur le thème du 'roi marieur.'" In *La Femme au Moyen Age*, ed. Michel Rouche and Jean Heuclin, 431–42. Publication de la Ville de Maubeuge: Diffusion Jean Touzot, 1990.

– "De la puissance aux privilèges: doléances de la noblesse française envers la monarchie aux XIVe et XVe siècles." In *La Noblesse au Moyen Age*, ed. Philippe Contamine, 235–57. Paris: Presses universitaires de France, 1976.

– "'Inobédience,' rébellion, trahison, lèse-majesté: observations sur les procès politiques à la fin du Moyen Age." In *Les Procès politiques (XIVe–XVIIe siècle)*, ed. Bercé, 63–82.

– "Pouvoir et vie de cour dans la France du XVe siècle: les mignons." *Comptes-rendus des séances de l'Académie des Inscriptions et Belles-Lettres* 138, no. 2 (1994) 541–54.

– "Les Rencontres au sommet dans la France du XVe siècle." In *Im Spannungsfeld von Recht und Ritual: soziale Kommunikation in Mittelalter und Früher Neuzeit*, ed. Gert Melville and Heinz Durchhardt, 273–90. Cologne, Weimar, and Vienna: Böhlau, 1997.

Crane, Susan. *The Performance of Self: Ritual, Clothing, and Identity during the Hundred Years War*. Philadelphia: University of Pennsylvania Press, 2002.

Croce, Benedetto. "Cola di Monforte, conte di Campobasso." In *Vite di avventure di fede e di passione*, 59–173. Milan: Adelphi Edizione, 1989. First edition Bari, 1936; previously serialized as "Un condottiero italiano del quattrocento, Cola di Monforte conte di Campobasso, e la fede storica del Commynes." *La Critica* 31 (1933): 401–30; and 32 (1934): 16–36 and 88–121.

– "Il personaggio italiano che esortò il Commynes a scrivere i 'Mémoires.'" In *Vite di avventure di fede e di passione*, 174–95. Milan: Adelphi Edizione, 1989. First edition Bari, 1936. Originally published in *La Critica* 31 (1933): 53–64.

Cuttler, Simon H. *The Law of Treason and Treason Trials in Later Medieval France.* Cambridge: Cambridge University Press, 1981.

Daly, Kathleen. "'Centre,' 'Power' and 'Periphery' in Late Medieval French Historiography: Some Reflections." In *War, Government and Power in Late Medieval France*, ed. Allmand, 124–44.

– "Mixing Business with Leisure: Some French Royal Notaries and Secretaries and their Histories of France, c. 1459–1509." In *Power, Culture, and Religion in France c. 1350–c. 1550*, ed. Allmand, 99–115.

Delogu, Daisy. *Theorizing the Ideal Sovereign: The Rise of the French Vernacular Royal Biography.* Toronto: University of Toronto Press, 2008.

Demers, Jeanne. "À l'origine d'une forme: Les *Mémoires* de Commynes." *Cahiers de l'Association internationale des études françaises* 40 (1988): 7–21.

– *Commynes, méMORiALISTE.* Montreal: Presses de l'Université de Montréal, 1975.

– "Montaigne lecteur de Commynes." In *Seconda miscellanea di studi e ricerche sul Quattrocento francese*, ed. Franco Simone, Jonathan Beck, and Gianni Mombello, 203–16. Chambéry-Turin: Centre d'études franco-italien, 1981.

Denery, Dallas G. "Christine de Pizan against the Theologians: The Virtue of Lies in *The Book of the Three Virtues.*" *Viator* 39, no. 1 (2008): 229–47.

Desplanque, A. "Troubles de la châtellenie de Cassel sous Philippe le Bon (1427–1431)." *Annales du Comité flamand de France* 8 (1864–5): 218–81.

Dessau, Adalbert. "L'Idée de la trahison au Moyen Age et son rôle dans la motivation de quelques chansons de geste." *Cahiers de civilisation médiévale* 3, no. 1 (1960): 23–6.

Devaux, Jean. "La Fin du Téméraire, ou la mémoire d'un prince ternie par un des siens." *Le Moyen Age* 95, no. 1 (1989): 105–28.

– "L'Identité bourguignonne et l'écriture de l'histoire." *Le Moyen Age* 112, no. 3–4 (2006): 467–76.

– *Jean Molinet, indiciaire bourguignon.* Paris: Champion, 1996.

– "Le Rôle politique de Marie de Bourgogne au lendemain de Nancy: Vérité ou légende?" *Le Moyen Age* 97, no. 3 (1991): 389–405.

DeVries, Kelly, and Robert Douglas Smith. *The Artillery of the Dukes of Burgundy, 1363–1477.* Woodbridge, UK: Boydell, 2005.

Doležalová, Lucie, ed. *The Making of Memory in the Middle Ages.* Leiden and Boston: Brill, 2010.

Dreyer, K. "Commynes and Machiavelli: A Study in Parallelism." *Symposium* 5, no. 1 (1951): 38–61.

Dubois, Henri. "Observations sur la diplomatique des lettres de Louis XI." *Bulletin de la Société nationale des antiquaires de France* (1996): 332–42.

Dubruck, Edelgard, and Barbara Gusick, eds. *Death and Dying in the Middle Ages*. New York: Peter Lang, 1999.

Dufournet, Jean. "Angelo Cato et les *Mémoires* de Commynes." In *Mélanges offerts à Pierre le Gentil*, 213–22. Paris: Société d'édition d'enseignement supérieur [SEDES], 1973.

– "Art et déformation historique dans les *Mémoires* de Commynes." *Romania* 90 (1969): 145–73.

– "Au Coeur des *Mémoires* de Commynes: l'affaire Saint-Pol, un cas exemplaire." *Le Moyen Age* 112, no. 3–4 (2006): 477–94.

– "Charles le Téméraire vu par les historiens bourguignons." In *Cinq-Centième anniversaire de la Bataille de Nancy (1477)*, 65–81.

– "Cinq lecteurs de Commynes de 1822 à 1832." *Mémoires de la Société d'histoire de Comines-Warneton et de la région* 19 (1989): 73–98.

– *Commynes en ses Mémoires*. Paris: Champion, 2011.

– "Commynes et l'ambiguïté du monde." *L'Information littéraire* 33, no. 5 (1981): 190–7.

– "Commynes et l'invention d'un nouveau genre historique: les *Mémoires*." *Mémoires de la Société d'histoire de Comines-Warneton et de la région* 18 (1988): 57–72.

– "Commynes ou la nostalgie de la patrie perdue." *Mémoires de la Société d'histoire de Comines-Warneton et de la région* 10 (1980): 77–94.

– *La Destruction des mythes dans les* Mémoires *de Philippe de Commynes*. Geneva: Droz, 1966.

– *Etudes sur Philippe de Commynes*. Paris: Champion, 1975.

– "Un Interlocuteur privilégié des princes: Commynes, de Fénelon à Vauvenargues." *Cahiers de Recherches Médiévales (XIIIᵉ–XVᵉ s.)* 2 (1996): 109–17.

– "Lire Commynes: l'entrevue de Péronne et l'expédition contre Liège." *Mémoires de la Société d'histoire de Comines-Warneton et de la région* 12 (1982): 25–54.

– "Philippe de Commynes et l'écriture du juste milieu." *Revue des langues romanes* 97 (1993): 127–32.

– *Philippe de Commynes: un historien à l'aube des temps modernes*. Brussels: DeBoeck Université, 1994.

– "Les Premiers lecteurs de Commynes ou les *Mémoires* au XVIᵉ siècle." *Mémoires de la Société d'histoire de Comines-Warneton et de la région* 14 (1984): 51–94.

– "Quand les *Mémoires* de Commynes ont-ils été composés?" In *Mélanges de langue et de littérature du Moyen Age et de la Renaissance offerts à Jean Frappier*, 2:267–82. Geneva: Droz, 1970.

- "*Le Séjour de deul*: un prosimètre à la gloire de Commynes (1512)." In *"Chançon legiere a chanter": Essays on Old French Literature in Honor of Samuel N. Rosenberg*, ed. Karen Fresco and Wendy Pfeffer, 49–66. Birmingham, AL: Summa Publications, 2007.
- *Sur Philippe de Commynes: quatre études*. Paris: SEDES, 1982.
- *La Vie de Philippe de Commynes*. Paris: SEDES, 1969.

Dumolyn, Jan. "Jan van den Driessche / Jehan de la Driesche, un fonctionnaire flamand au service de Louis XI." *Revue historique* 309, no. 1 [641] (2007): 71–90.

Durand-Le Guern, Isabelle. "Louis XI entre mythe et histoire." *Cahiers de Recherches Médiévales (XIIIᵉ–XVᵉ s.)* 11 (2004): 31–45.

Durville, Georges. "Notice sur le manuscrit de Philippe de Commynes du Musée Dobrée." In *Catalogue de la Bibliothèque du Musée Thomas Dobrée*, vol. 1, *Manuscrits*, 455–583, 649–58. Nantes: Musée Dobrée, 1903.

Duvosquel, Jean-Marie. "Bourgeoisie ou noblesse? à propos des origines familiales de Philippe de Commynes: perspectives de recherche." In *Et c'est la fin pour quoy sommes ensemble: hommage à Jean Dufournet*, ed. Jean-Claude Aubailly, 2:535–48. Paris: Champion, 1993.
- "L'Emploi des langues à Comines et Warneton du Moyen Age à nos jours." *Mémoires de la Société d'histoire de Comines et de la région* 3 (1973): 9–62.

Emerson, Catherine. *Olivier de La Marche and the Rhetoric of Fifteenth-Century Historiography*. Woodbridge, UK: Boydell, 2004.

Favier, Jean. *Louis XI*. Paris: Fayard, 2001.

Fédou, René. "Fidélité lyonnaise et propagande bourguignonne au temps de Louis XI." In *Mélanges d'histoire André Fugier*, 71–80. Clermont, Lyon, and Grenoble: Editions des Cahiers d'Histoire, 1968.

Felman, Shoshana, and Dori Laub. *Testimony: Crises of Witnessing in Literature, Psychoanalysis, and History*. New York and London: Routledge, 1992.

Florentin, Danick. "Le Temps dans les *Mémoires* de Philippe de Commynes." *Revue des langues romanes* 97 (1993): 31–41.

Foucault, Michel. "Nietzsche, la généalogie, l'histoire." In *Dits et écrits II: 1970–1975*, ed. Daniel Defert, 136–56. Paris: Gallimard, 1994.
- "The Subject and Power." *Critical Inquiry* 8, no. 4 (1982): 777–95.

Freud, Sigmund. *The Interpretation of Dreams*. Translated by James Strachey. Harmondsworth: Penguin, 1976.

Frisch, Andrea. *The Invention of the Eyewitness: Witnessing and Testimony in Early Modern France*. Chapel Hill, NC: University of North Carolina Department of Romance Languages, 2004.

Fritzsche, Peter. "Specters of History: On Nostalgia, Exile, and Modernity." *American Historical Review* 106, no. 5 (2001): 1587–618.

Frye, Northrop. *Anatomy of Criticism.* Princeton, NJ: Princeton University Press, 1957. Reprint, New York: Penguin Books, 1990.

Fumaroli, Marc. "Mémoires et histoire: le dilemme de l'historiographie humaniste au XVIe siècle." In *Les Valeurs chez les mémorialistes français du XVIIe siècle avant la Fronde,* ed. Noémi Hepp and Jacques Hennequin, 21–45. Paris: Klincksieck, 1979.

Gachard, Louis Prosper. "Note sur le jugement et la condamnation de Guillaume Hugonet, chancelier de Bourgogne, et de Guy de Brimeu, comte de Meghem, seigneur d'Humbercourt, décapités à Gand le 3 avril 1477." Extracted from the *Bulletins de l'Académie royale des sciences et belles-lettres de Bruxelles* 6 (1839): 296–361.

Gallet-Guerne, Danielle. *Vasque de Lucène et La Cyropédie à la cour de Bourgogne (1470).* Geneva: Droz, 1974.

Gaussin, Pierre Roger. "Les Conseillers de Louis XI (1461–1483)." In *La France de la fin du XVe siècle: renouveau et apogée,* ed. Chevalier and Contamine, 105–34.

– *Louis XI, roi méconnu: un roi entre deux mondes.* Paris: Nizet, 1976.

Gauvard, Claude. *"De Grace especial": crime, etat et société en France à la fin du Moyen Age.* 2 vols. Paris: Publications de la Sorbonne, 1991.

Geary, Patrick J. *Phantoms of Remembrance: Memory and Oblivion at the End of the First Millennium.* Princeton, NJ: Princeton University Press, 1994.

Giesey, Ralph E. *The Royal Funeral Ceremony in Renaissance France.* Geneva: Droz, 1960.

Gilissen, John. "Individualisme et sécurité juridique: la prépondérance de la loi et de l'acte écrit aux XVIe siècle dans l'ancien droit belge." In *Individu et société à la Renaissance,* 32–58. Brussels: Presses Universitaires de Bruxelles, 1967.

Girard, René. *La Violence et le sacré.* Paris: Hachette, 1998. First edition Paris: B. Grasset, 1972.

Giry, A. *Manuel de diplomatique.* Paris: Hachette, 1894. Reprint, Hildesheim: Georg Olms, 1972.

Green, Richard Firth. *A Crisis of Truth: Literature and Law in Ricardian England.* Philadelphia: University of Pennsylvania Press, 1999.

Guenée, Bernard. "Histoire, annales, chroniques: Essai sur les genres historiques au Moyen Age." *Annales. Histoire, Sciences Sociales* 28, no. 4 (1973): 997–1016.

– *Histoire et culture historique dans l'Occident médiéval.* Paris: Aubier Montaigne, 1980.

– *Un Meurtre, une société: l'assassinat du duc d'Orléans 23 Novembre 1407.* Paris: Gallimard, 1992.

– *Politique et histoire au Moyen Age: recueil d'articles sur l'histoire politique et l'historiographie médiévale (1956–1981).* Paris: Publications de la Sorbonne, 1981.

Guyotjeannin, Olivier, Jacques Pycke, and Benoît-Michel Tock. *Diplomatique médiévale*. 3rd edition. L'Atelier du médiéviste. Turnhout: Brepols, 2006.

Haemers, Jelle. *For the Common Good: State Power and Urban Revolts in the Reign of Mary of Burgundy (1477–1482)*. Turnhout: Brepols, 2009.

Haidu, Peter. *The Subject Medieval/Modern: Text and Governance in the Middle Ages*. Stanford, CA: Stanford University Press, 2004.

– *The Subject of Violence: The Song of Roland and the Birth of the State*. Bloomington: Indiana University Press, 1993.

Hamilton, Keith, and Richard Langhorne. *The Practice of Diplomacy: Its Evolution, Theory and Administration*. London and New York: Routledge, 1995.

Hampton, Timothy. *Fictions of Embassy: Literature and Diplomacy in Early Modern Europe*. Ithaca, NY: Cornell University Press, 2009.

Harding, Alan. *Medieval Law and the Foundations of the State*. Oxford: Oxford University Press, 2002.

Hare, Christopher. *The Life of Louis XI: The Rebel Dauphin and the Statesman King*. New York: Charles Scribner's Sons, 1907.

Haroche-Bouzinac, Geneviève. "Les Lettres qu'on ne brûle pas." *Revue d'histoire littéraire de la France* 103, no. 2 (2003): 301–8.

Harsgor, Mikhaël [Michel]. "Fidélités et infidélités au sommet du pouvoir." In *Hommage à R. Mousnier, clientèles et fidélités en Europe à l'époque moderne*, ed. Yves Durand, 259–77. Paris: Presses Universitaires de France, 1981.

Herman, Arthur L., Jr. "The Language of Fidelity in Early Modern France." *Journal of Modern History* 67, no. 1 (1995): 1–24.

Huppert, George. *The Idea of Perfect History: Historical Erudition and Historical Philosophy in Renaissance France*. Urbana, Chicago, and London: University of Illinois Press, 1970.

Hyams, Paul R. "Henry II and Ganelon." *The Syracuse Scholar* 4 (1983): 23–35.

Ianziti, Gary. *Humanistic Historiography under the Sforzas: Politics and Propaganda in Fifteenth-Century Milan*. Oxford: Clarendon Press, 1988.

Iggers, Georg G., and James M. Powell, eds. *Leopold von Ranke and the Shaping of the Historical Discipline*. Syracuse, NY: Syracuse University Press, 1990.

Ilardi, Vincent. "Crosses and Carets: Renaissance Patronage and Coded Letters of Recommendation." *American Historical Review* 92, no. 5 (1987): 1127–49.

– "Diplomatic History as 'Total' History? A Fifteenth-Century Perspective." *Fifteenth Century Studies* 16 (1990): 111–30.

– *Studies in Italian Renaissance Diplomatic History*. London: Variorum Reprints, 1986.

Iser, Wolfgang. "Indeterminacy and the Reader's Response in Prose Fiction." In *Aspects of Narrative: Selected Papers from the English Institute*, ed. J. Hillis Miller, 1–45. New York: Columbia University Press, 1971.

Jameson, Fredric. *A Singular Modernity: Essay on the Ontology of the Present*. London and New York: Verso, 2002.

Jassemin, Henri. *La Chambre des comptes de Paris au XVᵉ siècle*. Paris: Picard, 1933.

Javeau, Claude. *Anatomie de la trahison*. Belval: Editions Circé, 2007.

Jodogne, Pierre. "La Conjuration des Pazzi racontée par les chroniqueurs français et bourguignons du XVᵉ siècle: Commynes, A. de But, Th. Basin, J. Molinet." In *Culture et politique en France à l'époque de l'Humanisme et de la Renaissance*, ed. Franco Simone, 169–212. Turin: Accademia delle Scienze, 1974.

– "La Rhétorique dans l'historiographie bourguignonne." In *Culture et pouvoir au temps de l'Humanisme et de la Renaissance*, ed. Louis Terreaux, 51–69. Paris: Champion, 1978.

Jones, Michael. "'Bons Bretons et bons françoys': The Language and Meaning of Treason in Later Medieval France." *Transactions of the Royal Historical Society*, 5th series, 32 (1982): 91–112.

– "Trahison et l'idée de lèse-majesté dans la Bretagne du XVᵉ siècle." In *La Faute, la répression et le pardon*, 91–106. Paris: Comité des Travaux Historiques et Scientifiques, 1984.

Jones, Nancy A. "The Daughter's Text and the Thread of Lineage in the Old French *Philomena*." In *Representing Rape in Medieval and Early Modern Literature*, ed. Elizabeth Robertson and Christine M. Rose, 161–88. New York: Palgrave, 2001.

Kamp, Hermann. "Philippe de Commynes und der Umgang mit der Öffentlichkeit in der Politik seiner Zeit." In *Das Öffentliche und Private in der Vormoderne*, ed. Melville and von Moos, 687–716.

Kansteiner, Wulf. "Finding Meaning in Memory: A Methodological Critique of Collective Memory Studies." *History and Theory* 41, no. 2 (2002): 179–97.

Kantorowicz, Ernst H. *The King's Two Bodies: A Study in Medieval Political Theology*. With a new preface by William Chester Jordan. Princeton: Princeton University Press, 1997.

Kendall, Paul Murray. *Louis XI, the Universal Spider*. New York: W.W. Norton, c. 1971.

Kess, Alexandra. *Johann Sleidan and the Protestant Vision of History*. Aldershot, UK, and Burlington, VT: Ashgate, 2008.

Kinser, Samuel. Review of *La Destruction des mythes dans les Mémoires de Ph. de Commynes*, by Jean Dufournet. *Renaissance Quarterly* 21, no. 4 (1968): 464–9.

Klein, Kerwin Lee. "On the Emergence of Memory in Historical Discourse." *Representations* 69 (2000): 127–50.

Kong, Katherine. *Lettering the Self in Medieval and Early Modern France*. Cambridge: D.S. Brewer, 2010.

Krieger, Leonard. *Ranke: The Meaning of History*. Chicago: University of Chicago Press, 1977.

Krynen, Jacques. "Droit romain et état monarchique, à propos du cas français." In *Représentation, pouvoir et royauté à la fin du Moyen Age*, ed. Blanchard, 13–23.

– *L'Empire du roi: idées et croyances politiques en France, XIIIe–XVe siècles*. Paris: Gallimard, 1993.

– *Idéal du prince et pouvoir royal en France à la fin du Moyen Age (1380–1440): étude de la littérature politique du temps*. Paris: Picard, 1981.

– "Réflexion sur les idées politiques aux Etats Généraux de Tours en 1484." *Revue historique de droit français et étranger* 62, no. 2 (1984): 183–204.

Kuperty, Nadine. "Les *Mémoires* de Commynes, un discours de la culpabilité?" *Travaux de littérature* 8 (1995): 43–55.

Kuperty-Tsur, Nadine. *Se Dire à la Renaissance: les* Mémoires *au XVIe siècle*. Paris: Vrin, 1997.

Labande-Mailfert, Yvonne. *Charles VIII et son milieu (1470–1498): la jeunesse au pouvoir*. Paris: Klincksieck, 1975.

Labbie, Erin Felicia. *Lacan's Medievalism*. Minneapolis: University of Minnesota Press, 2006.

Laborde, Alexandre de. *Les Manuscrits à peintures de la Cité de Dieu de Saint Augustin*. 3 vols. Paris: Société de Bibliophiles François, 1909.

Lanhers, Yvonne. "Deux affaires de trahison défendues par Jean Jouvenel des Ursins (1423–27)." *Recueil de mémoires et travaux publié par la Société d'histoire du droit et des institutions des anciens pays de droit écrit* 7 (1970): 317–28.

Laplanche, Jean. *Vie et mort en psychanalyse*. Paris: Presses Universitaires Françaises, 2008. First edition Paris: Flammarion, 1970.

Laplanche, Jean, and Jean-Bertrand Pontalis. *Vocabulaire de psychanalyse*. Edited by Daniel Lagache. 11th ed. Paris: Presses Universitaires Françaises, 1992.

Lefèvre, Sylvie, ed. *La Lettre dans la littérature romane du Moyen Age*. Orléans: Editions Paradigme, 2008.

Le Guay, Laetitia. *Les Princes de Bourgogne lecteurs de Froissart: les rapports entre le texte et l'image dans les manuscrits enluminés du Livre IV des "Chroniques."* Paris: Editions du CNRS; Turnhout: Brepols, 1998.

Lejeune, Philippe. *Le Pacte autobiographique*. Paris: Seuil, 1st ed. 1975, rev. ed. 1996.

Le Pippre, Antoine. "La Généalogie des seigneurs de Commines et de Messire Philippe de Commines." In *Intentions morales, civiles et militaires*, 251–64. Antwerp: Pierre and Jean Bellere, 1625.

Leroquais, Victor. *Les Livres d'heures manuscrits de la Bibliothèque Nationale*. 3 vols. Paris and Mâcon: Protat frères, 1927.

Leuridan, Th. "Recherches sur les sires de Comines." *Bulletin de la Commission historique du département du Nord* 15 (1899): 161–255.

Lewis, Peter S. "Decayed and Non-Feudalism in Later Medieval France." In *Essays in Later Medieval French History*, 41–68. London: Hambledon Press, 1985.

– "Les Pensionnaires de Louis XI." In *La France de la fin du XVe siècle: renouveau et apogée*, ed. Chevalier and Contamine, 167–81.

– ed. *The Recovery of France in the Fifteenth Century*. Translated by G.F. Martin. London: Macmillan, 1971.

– "Reflections on the Role of Royal Clienteles in the Construction of the French Monarchy (mid-XIVth/end-XVth centuries)." In *L'Etat ou le roi: les fondations de la modernité monarchique en France (XIVe–XVIIe siècles)*, ed. Bulst, Descimon, and Guerreau, 51–67.

Leys, Ruth. *Trauma: A Genealogy*. Chicago: University of Chicago Press, 2000.

Leyte, Guillaume. *Domaine et domanialité publique dans la France médiévale (XIIe–XVe siècles)*. Strasbourg: Presses Universitaires de Strasbourg, 1996.

Libera, Alain de. *Archéologie du sujet*. Paris: Vrin, 2007.

Liniger, Jean. *Philippe de Commynes, un "Machiavel en douceur."* Paris: Librairie Académique Perrin, 1978.

Lojkine, Stéphane. "La Manipulation des sources dans *L'Essai sur les moeurs* de Voltaire." In *Sens du devenir et pensée de l'histoire au temps des Lumières*, ed. Betrand Binoche and Franck Tinland, 85–96. Seyssel, France: Champ Vallon, 2000.

Maissen, Thomas. "Le 'Commynisme' italien: Louis XI, héros de la Contre-Réforme." *Bibliothèque d'Humanisme et de la Renaissance* 58, no. 2 (1996): 313–49.

– *Von der Legende zum Modell: das Interesse an Frankreichs Vergangenheit während der italienischen Renaissance*. Basel and Frankfurt: Helbing und Lichtenhahn, 1994.

Major, J. Russell. "'Bastard Feudalism' and the Kiss: Changing Social Mores in Late Medieval and Early Modern France." *Journal of Interdisciplinary History* 17, no. 3 (1987): 509–35.

Mandrot, Bernard de. "L'Autorité historique de Philippe de Commynes." *Revue historique* 73, no. 2 (1900): 241–57; and 74, no. 1 (1900): and 1–38.

– "Jacques d'Armagnac, duc de Nemours, 1433–1477." *Revue historique* 43, no. 2 (1890): 274–316; and 44, no. 2 (1890): 241–312.

Marchello-Nizia, Christiane. "L'Historien et son prologue: forme littéraire et stratégies discursives." In *La Chronique et l'histoire au Moyen Age*, ed. Poirion, 13–25.

Marnette, Sophie. "The Experiencing Self and the Narrating Self in Medieval French Chronicles." In *The Medieval Author in Medieval French Literature*, ed. Virginie Greene, 117–36. New York: Palgrave Macmillan, 2006.

– *Narrateur et points de vue dans la littérature française médiévale: une approche linguistique*. Bern, New York: Peter Lang, 1998.

Martines, Lauro. *April Blood: Florence and the Plot against the Medici*. Oxford and New York: Oxford University Press, 2003.

Mattéoni, Olivier. "'Couronne en forme sphérique ne se peut diviser sans perdre sa figure': une leçon sur la souveraineté monarchique." In *Les Procès politiques (XIVᵉ–XVIIᵉ siècle)*, ed. Bercé, 157–81.

Mattingly, Garrett. *Renaissance Diplomacy*. Boston: Houghton Mifflin, 1955. Reprint, New York: Dover, 1988.

Maulde-La-Clavière, René de. *Histoire de Louis XII*. 6 vols. Vol. 2. Paris: E. Leroux, 1890.

Mehlman, Jeffrey. *A Structural Study of Autobiography: Proust, Leiris, Sartre, Lévi-Strauss*. Ithaca, NY: Cornell University Press, 1974.

Melville, Gert, and Peter von Moos, eds. *Das Öffentliche und Private in der Vormoderne*. Cologne, Weimar, and Vienna: Böhlau, 1998.

Mesnard, Pierre. "Le Commerce épistolaire, comme expression sociale de l'individualisme humaniste." In *Individu et société à la Renaissance*, 15–31. Brussels: Presses Universitaires de Bruxelles, 1967.

Meyer, Wolfgang J. *Erlebte Geschichte: Möglichkeiten ihrer Darstellung am Beispiel der Memoiren von Philippe de Commynes*. Munich: Wilhelm Fink, 1977.

Michaud, Gustave. *Au Pays argentonnais, glanes d'histoire régionale: Argenton Château*. Angers: J. Fromageau, 1931.

Michelet, Jules. *Histoire de France*. Vol. 6, *Louis XI et Charles le Téméraire*. Paris: Hachette, 1844.

Miller, Nancy K. "Arachnologies: The Woman, the Text and the Critic." In *The Poetics of Gender*, ed. Nancy K. Miller, 270–95. New York: Columbia University Press, 1986.

Monfrin, Jacques. "La Connaissance de l'antiquité et le problème de l'humanisme en langue vulgaire dans la France du XVᵉ siècle." In *The Late Middle Ages and the Dawn of Humanism outside Italy*, ed. Gérard Verbeke and Josef IJsewijn, 131–70. Leuven: Leuven University Press, 1972.

Moos, Peter von, ed. *Der Fehltritt: Vergehen und Versehen in der Vormoderne*. Cologne, Weimar, and Vienna: Böhlau, 2001.

Mousnier, Roland. "Les Concepts d'"ordres,' d'"états,' de 'fidélité' et de 'monar-chie absolue' en France de la fin du XVe siècle à la fin du XVIIe." *Revue historique* 247, no. 2 [502] (1972): 289–312.

Nabert, Nathalie. *Les Réseaux d'alliance en diplomatie aux XIVe et XVe siècles: étude de sémantique.* Paris: Champion, 1999.

Naïs, Hélène. "Héros et prince: Charles le Téméraire?" In *Cinq-centième anni-versaire de la Bataille de Nancy (1477)*, 127–34.

Nora, Pierre. "Between Memory and History: *Les Lieux de Mémoire.*" Translat-ed by Marc Roudebush. *Representations* 26 (1989): 7–24.

Olivier-Martin, François. *Histoire du droit français des origines à la Révolution.* Paris: Domat Montchrestien, 1948.

– *Les Lois du roi.* Paris: Editions Loysel, 1988.

Ornato, Monique, and Nicole Pons, eds. *Pratiques de la culture écrite en France au XVe siècle.* Louvain-la-Neuve: Féderation International des Instituts d'Études Médiévales; Turnhout: Brepols, 1995.

Oschema, Klaus. "Amis, favoris, sosies: Le vêtement comme miroir des rela-tions personnelles." In *Mode und Kleidung im Europa des späten Mittelalters / Fashion and Clothing in Late Medieval Europe*, ed. Klaus Oschema, Regula Schorta, and Rainer C. Schwinges, 181–92. Basel: Schwabe, c. 2010.

– *Freundschaft und Nähe im spätmittelalterlichen Burgund: Studien zum Span-nungsfeld von Emotion und Institution.* Cologne, Weimar, and Vienna: Böhlau, 2006.

Paravicini, Werner. "Des Animaux pour un roi mourant: Louis XI et les Hansé-ates de 1479 à 1483." In *Commerces, finances et société (XIe–XVIe siècles)*, ed. Philippe Contamine, Thierry Dutour, and Bertrand Schnerb, 101–21. Paris: Presses de l'Université de Paris-Sorbonne, 1993.

– *Guy de Brimeu, der burgundische Staat und seine adlige Führungsschicht unter Karl dem Kühnen.* Bonn: Ludwig Röhrscheid, 1975.

– "Peur, pratiques, intelligences: formes de l'opposition aristocratique à Louis XI d'après les interrogatoires du connétable de Saint-Pol." In *La France de la fin du XVe siècle: renouveau et apogée*, ed. Chevalier and Con-tamine, 183–96.

– "Sterben und Tod Ludwigs XI." In *Tod im Mittelalter*, ed. Arno Borst, Gerhart von Graevenitz, Alexander Patschovsky, and Karlheinz Stierle, 77–168. Constance: Universitätsverlag Konstanz, 1993.

Pélicier, Paul. *Essai sur le gouvernement de la Dame de Beaujeu, 1483–1491.* Chartres: E. Garnier, 1882. Reprint, Marseille: Lafitte Reprints, 1983.

Perret, Paul M. "Boffile de Juge, comte de Castres, et la République de Venise." *Annales du Midi* 3 (1891): 159–231.

Peyronnet, Georges. "Les Complots de Louis d'Amboise contre Charles VII (1428–1431): un aspect des rivalités entre lignages féodaux en France au temps de Jeanne d'Arc." *Bibliothèque de l'Ecole des chartes* 142, no. 1 (1984): 115–35.

Philippe-Lemaître, Delphine. *Histoire de la ville et du château de Dreux.* Dreux: Lemenestrel et Huchot, 1850. Reprint, Marseille: Lafitte Reprints, 1977.

Phillips, Mark. *The Memoir of Marco Parenti: A Life in Medici Florence.* Princeton, NJ: Princeton University Press, 1987.

Piiparinen, Kaisa, and Sari Suvanto. "Aspects de l'ordre des mots en moyen français: l'ordre des éléments S-V dans la phrase principale déclarative chez Philippe de Commynes." In *Approches du Moyen Français II*, ed. Ellen Sakari and Helena Häyrynen, 71–81. Jyväskylä, Finland: University of Jyväskylä, 1992.

Pocock, J.G.A. "The Reconstruction of Discourse: Towards the Historiography of Political Thought." *Modern Language Notes* 96, no. 5 (1981): 959–80.

Pocquet du Haut-Jussé, Barthélemy-Amadée. "Une Idée politique de Louis XI: la sujétion éclipse la vassalité." *Revue historique* 226, no. 2 (1961): 383–98.

Poirion, Daniel, ed. *La Chronique et l'histoire au Moyen Age.* Paris: Presses de l'Université Paris-Sorbonne, 1984.

Pollard, A.J. *The Wars of the Roses.* 2nd ed. Houndmills, UK: Palgrave, 2001.

Pollock, Frederick, and Frederic William Maitland. *The History of English Law before the Time of Edward I.* 2nd ed. 2 vols. Cambridge: Cambridge University Press; Boston: Little, Brown, & Co., 1905.

Pozzi, Enrico. "Le Paradigme du traître." In *De la trahison*, ed. Dominique Scarfone, 1–33. Paris: Presses Universitaires Françaises, 1999.

Prucher, Auda. *I 'Mémoires' di Philippe de Commynes e l'Italia del Quattrocento.* Vol. 6. *Biblioteca dell'archivo storico italiano.* Florence: L.S. Olschki, 1957.

Queller, Donald E. *The Office of Ambassador in the Middle Ages.* Princeton, NJ: Princeton University Press, 1967.

Rahlenbeck, Charles. "Philippe de Commines dans ses rapports avec la maison d'Albret." In *Messager des Sciences Historiques, ou Archives des Arts et de la Bibliographie de Belgique* (1867): 210–45. Reprinted in booklet form as *Philippe de Commynes et la maison d'Albret*, n.p., n.d.

Ranke, Leopold von. *The Secret of World History: Selected Writings on the Art and Science of History.* Translated and edited by Roger Wines. New York: Fordham University Press, 1981.

Rey, Alain, ed. *Dictionnaire historique de la langue française.* 3 vols. Paris: Dictionnaires Le Robert, 1998.

Rice, Eugene F. *The Renaissance Idea of Wisdom.* Cambridge, MA: Harvard University Press, 1958.

Ricoeur, Paul. *Memory, History, Forgetting*. Translated by Kathleen Blamey and David Pellauer. Chicago: University of Chicago Press, 2004. First published in French as, *La Mémoire, l'histoire, l'oubli*. Paris: Editions du Seuil, 2000.

Rigaud, Philippe. "'Une galeasse qui estoit myenne': La *Nostre Dame Saincte Marie* de Philippe de Commynes." In *Philippe de Commynes (1511–2011)*, ed. Blanchard, 355–68.

Roguet, Yves. "Le Portrait dans les *Mémoires* de Commynes." In *Le Portrait littéraire*, ed. K. Kupisz, G.-A. Pérouse, and J.-Y. Debreuille, 33–8. Lyon: Presses Universitaires de Lyon, 1988.

Roover, Raymond de. *The Rise and Decline of the Medici Bank, 1397–1494*. Cambridge, MA: Harvard University Press, 1963.

Roques, Gilles. "Le Vent dans les locutions et expressions médiévales françaises." *Travaux de linguistique et de littérature* 25, no. 1 (1987): 181–206.

Routledge Encyclopedia of Narrative Theory. Edited by David Herman, Manfred Jahn, and Marie-Laure Ryan. London and New York: Routledge, 2005.

Russell, Joycelyne Gledhill. *The Congress of Arras, 1435: A Study in Medieval Diplomacy*. Oxford: Clarendon Press, 1955. Reprint New York: Biblo and Tannen, 1972.

Sablon du Corail, Amable. "Croix fourchues contre croix droitez: Aspects militaires de la guerre pour la succession de Charles le Téméraire de Nancy jusqu'au Traité d'Arras (5 janvier 1477–23 décembre 1482)." Unpublished thesis, Ecole nationale des chartes, 2001.

Saenger, Paul. "Burgundy and the Inalienability of Appanages in the Reign of Louis XI." *French Historical Studies* 10, no. 1 (1977): 1–26.

– "The Earliest French Resistance Theories: The Role of the Burgundian Court." *Journal of Modern History* 51, no. 4, On Demand Supplement (1979): D1225–49.

Sainte-Beuve, Charles Augustin. *Causeries du lundi*. 3rd ed. Vol. 1, 241–59. Paris: Garnier Frères, 1857. Article of 7 January 1850.

Sbriccoli, Mario. *Crimen laesae maiestatis: il problema del reato politico alle soglie della scienza penalistica moderna*. Milan: Giuffrè, 1974.

Schmidt-Chazan, Mireille. "Les Traductions de la 'Guerre des Gaules' et le sentiment national au Moyen Age." *Annales de Bretagne et des Pays de l'Ouest [Actes du Congrès de la Société des Historiens médiévistes de l'enseignement supérieur, Tours, 10–12 juin 1977]* 87, no. 2 (1980): 387–407.

Schneider, Jean. "Campobasso en Lorraine." *Le Pays Lorrain* 63, no. 1 (1982): 5–24.

– "Charles le Hardi, duc de Bourgogne et de Lorraine (1475–1477)." *Le Pays Lorrain* 58, no. 1 (1977): 19–40.

Scott, Joan. "The Evidence of Experience." *Critical Inquiry* 17, no. 4 (1991): 773–97.

Scott, Walter. *Quentin Durward*. Edited by John H. Alexander and G.A.M. Wood. Edinburgh: Edinburgh University Press, 2001.

Searle, John R. *Speech Acts: An Essay in the Philosophy of Language*. London: Cambridge University Press, 1969.

Seidel, Linda. "The Value of Verisimilitude in the Art of Jan van Eyck." *Yale French Studies* 80 (1991): 25–43.

Shennan, J.H. *The Parlement of Paris*. Ithaca, NY: Cornell University Press, 1968.

Sheridan, Geraldine. *Nicolas Lenglet Dufresnoy and the Literary Underworld of the Ancien Régime*. Studies on Voltaire and the Eighteenth Century. Oxford: Voltaire Foundation at the Taylor Institution, 1989.

Shklar, Judith N. *Ordinary Vices*. Cambridge, MA: Belknap Press of Harvard University Press, 1984.

Simone, Franco. "La prima fortuna di Commynes nella cultura italiana del Rinascimento." In *Studi in onore di Carlo Pellegrini*, 109–18. Turin: Società Editrice Internazionale, 1963.

Skinner, Quentin. "Motives, Intentions, and the Interpretation of Texts." *New Literary History* 3, no. 2 (1972): 393–408. Reprinted in *Meaning and Context: Quentin Skinner and His Critics*, ed. James Tully, 68–78. Princeton, NJ: Princeton University Press, 1988.

Slattery, Maureen. "King Louis XI – Chivalry's Villain or Anti-Hero: The Contrasting Historiography of Chastellain and Commynes." *Fifteenth Century Studies* 23 (1997): 49–73.

Slattery Durley, Maureen. "The Sociological Dimensions of the Theme of Fear in Commynes' Mémoires." *Revue de l'Université d'Ottawa* 53, no. 2 (1983): 155–67.

Small, Graeme. *George Chastelain and the Shaping of Valois Burgundy: Political and Historical Culture at Court in the Fifteenth Century*. Woodbridge, UK: Boydell, 1997.

Soumillion, Daniel. "Le Procès de Louis de Luxembourg (1475): l'image d'un grand vassal de Louis XI et de Charles le Téméraire." *Publications du Centre Européen d'Etudes Bourguignonnes* 37 (1997): 205–29.

Soutet, Olivier, and Claude Thomasset. "Des Marques de la subjectivité dans l'écriture des *Mémoires* de Commynes." In *La Chronique et l'histoire au Moyen Age*, ed. Poirion, 27–44.

Spearing, A.C. *Textual Subjectivity: The Encoding of Subjectivity in Medieval Narratives and Lyrics*. Oxford and New York: Oxford University Press, 2005.

Spencer, Mark. *Thomas Basin (1412–1490): The History of Charles VII and Louis XI*. Nieuwkoop: De Graaf, 1997.

Spiegel, Gabrielle M. *The Past as Text: The Theory and Practice of Medieval Historiography*. Baltimore: Johns Hopkins University Press, 1997.

Spont, Alfred. *La Marine française sous le règne de Charles VIII, 1483–1493*. Paris: Bureaux de la Revue, 1894.

Stahuljak, Zrinka. *Bloodless Genealogies of the French Middle Ages: Translatio, Kinship, and Metaphor*. Gainesville: University Press of Florida, 2005.

Stegmann, André. "Commynes et Machiavel." In *Studies on Machiavelli*, ed. Myron Gilmore, 265–84. Florence: Sansoni, 1972.

Stein, Henri. *Charles de France, frère de Louis XI*. Paris: Picard, 1919.

Stocker, Christopher W. "Office and Justice: Louis XI and the Parlement of Paris (1465–1467)." *Mediaeval Studies* 37 (1975): 360–86.

Strayer, Joseph R. *On the Medieval Origins of the Modern State*. With new forewards by Charles Tilly and William Chester Jordan. Princeton, NJ: Princeton University Press, 2005.

Taranto, Domenico. *Studi sulla protostoria del concetto di interesse, da Commynes a Nicole (1524–1675)*. Naples: Liguori, 1992.

Tarbé, Prosper. *Louis XI et la Sainte Ampoule*. Reims: Jacquet, 1842.

Tenenti, Alberto. "Il significato della morte nella storia fra Commynes e Guicciardini." *Intersezioni: Rivista di storia delle idee* 7, no. 2 (1987): 215–34.

Tessier, Georges. *Diplomatique royale française*. Paris: Picard, 1962.

Tetel, Marcel. "Montaigne's Glances at Philippe de Commynes." *Bibliothèque d'Humanisme et de la Renaissance* 60, no. 1 (1998): 25–39.

Timbal, Pierre-Clément. "La Confiscation dans le droit français des XIIIe et XIVe siècles." *Revue historique de droit français et étranger*, 4th series, 22 (1943): 44–79, and 23 (1944): 35–60.

Turnaturi, Gabriella. *Betrayals: The Unpredictability of Human Relations*. Translated by Lydia G. Cochrane. Chicago: University of Chicago Press, 2007. First published in Italian as, *Tradimenti, l'imprevedibilità nelle relazioni umane*. Milan: Feltrinelli, 2000.

Ullmann, Walter. "The Development of the Medieval Idea of Sovereignty." *English Historical Review* 64, no. 250 (1949): 1–33.

Vanderjagt, Arjo. "Guillaume Hugonet's Farewell Letter to His Wife on April 3, 1477: 'My Fortune Is Such That I Expect to Die Today and to Depart This World.'" *Fifteenth Century Studies* 32 (2007): 176–90.

van der Vekene, Emile. *Johann Sleidan (Johann Philippson): Bibliographie seiner gedruckten Werke und der von ihm übersetzten Schriften von Philippe de Comines …* Stuttgart: Hiersemann, 1996.

Vaughan, Richard. *Charles the Bold: Last Valois Duke of Burgundy*. Rev. ed. Woodbridge, UK: Boydell, 2002.

- "Quelques observations sur la Bataille de Nancy." In *Cinq-centième anniversaire de la Bataille de Nancy (1477)*, 23–32.
- Review of *Ludwig XI und Karl der Kühne* [Bittmann] and *The Universal Spider* [Kendall]. *American Historical Review* 76, no. 5 (1971): 1529–30.
Viala, Alain. "La Genèse des formes épistolaires en français et leurs sources latines et européennes: Essai de chronologie distinctive." *Revue de littérature comparée* 55, no. 2 [218] (1981): 168–83.
Visser-Fuchs, Livia. "'Il n'a plus lion ne lieppart, qui voeulle tenir de sa part': Edward IV in exile, October 1470 to March 1471." *Publications du Centre Européen d'Etudes Bourguignonnes* 35 (1995): 91–106.
Viti, Paolo. "Tre schede su Francesco Gaddi." In *Forme letterarie umanistiche: studi e ricerche*, 263–5. Lecce: Conte, 1999.
Vitz, Evelyn Birge. *Medieval Narrative and Modern Narratology: Subjects and Objects of Desire*. New York: New York University Press, 1989.
Voltaire. *Essai sur les moeurs et l'esprit des nations*, vol. 2. In *Oeuvres complètes*. Vol. 12. Paris: Garnier Frères, 1878.
Voronova, T., and S. Manevitch, eds. *Corpus des notes marginales de Voltaire*. Vols 2 and 5. Berlin: Akademie-Verlag, 1983, 1994.
Voss, Jürgen. *Das Mittelalter im historischen Denken Frankreichs*. Munich: Wilhelm Fink, 1972.
- "Philippe de Commynes und sein Memoirenwerk in der Forschung seit 1945." *Deutsches Archiv für Erforschung des Mittelalters* 29 (1973): 224–35.
- "Le problème du Moyen Age dans la pensée historique en France (XVIe–XIXe siècle)." *Revue d'histoire moderne et contemporaine* 24, no. 3 (1977): 321–40.
Walsh, Richard J. *Charles the Bold and Italy (1467–1477): Politics and Personnel*. Liverpool: Liverpool University Press, 2005.
Warner, George Frederic. *Valerius Maximus: Miniatures of the School of Jean Fouquet, Illustrating the French Version by Simon de Hesdin and Nicholas de Gonesse, Contained in a Ms. Written about A.D. 1475 for Philippe de Comines*. London: B. Quaritch, 1907.
Watkins, John. "Toward a New Diplomatic History of Medieval and Early Modern Europe." *Journal of Medieval and Early Modern Studies* 38, no. 1 (2008): 1–14.
Weary, William A. "The House of La Trémoïlle, Fifteenth through Eighteenth Centuries: Change and Adaptation in a French Noble Family." *Journal of Modern History* 49, no. 1, On Demand Supplement (1977): D1001–38.
- "La Maison de La Trémoïlle pendant la Renaissance: une seigneurie agrandie." In *La France de la fin du XVe siècle: renouveau et apogée*, ed. Chevalier and Contamine, 197–212.

White, Hayden. "The Historical Text as Literary Artifact." In *The Writing of History: Literary Form and Historical Understanding*, ed. Robert H. Canary and Henry Kozicki, 41–62. Madison: University of Wisconsin Press, 1978.

– "The Value of Narrativity in the Representation of Reality." In *The Content of the Form: Narrative Discourse and Historical Representation*, 1–25. Baltimore: Johns Hopkins University Press, 1990. First published in *Critical Inquiry* 7, no.1 (1980).

White, John. *The Birth and Rebirth of Pictorial Space*. London: Faber and Faber, 1957.

Win, Paul de. "The Lesser Nobility of the Burgundian Netherlands." In *Gentry and Lesser Nobility in Late Medieval Europe*, ed. Michael Jones, 95–118. New York: Saint Martin's Press, 1986.

Wolff, Hélène. "Traîtres et trahison, d'après quelques oeuvres historiques de la fin du Moyen Age." In *Exclus et systèmes d'exclusion dans la littérature et la civilisation médiévales*, 41–55. Sénéfiance, no. 5. Aix-en-Provence: CUERMA, 1978.

Wolfthal, Diane. "'A Hue and a Cry': Medieval Rape Imagery and Its Transformation." *Art Bulletin* 75, no. 1 (1993): 39–64.

Yates, Frances. *The Art of Memory*. Chicago: University of Chicago Press, 1966.

Zammito, John. "Are We Being Theoretical Yet? The New Historicism, the New Philosophy of History, and 'Practicing Historians.'" *Journal of Modern History* 65, no. 4 (1993): 783–814.

Zimmermann, T.C. Price. "Confession and Autobiography in the Early Renaissance." In *Renaissance Studies in Honor of Hans Baron*, ed. Anthony Molho and John A. Tedeschi, 119–40. Florence: Sansoni, 1971; and Dekalb, IL: Northern Illinois University Press, 1971.

Online Reference Materials

Académie royale de langue et de littérature françaises de Belgique. http://www.arllfb.be/composition/.

Arlima: Archives de littérature du Moyen Age. www.arlima.net.

Dictionnaire du Moyen Français. ATILF – Nancy Université & CNRS. http://www.atilf.fr/dmf.

Oxford English Dictionary. http://www.oed.com/.

Trésor de la Langue Française informatisé. CNRS. http://atilf.atilf.fr/tlf.htm.

Index